POWER AND THE STATE

EXPLORATIONS IN SOCIOLOGY

*A series under the auspices of the
British Sociological Association*

Published by Tavistock
   1 Race and Racialism
      edited by Sami Zubaida

   2 Knowledge, Education, and Cultural Change
      edited by Richard Brown

   3 Deviance and Social Control
      edited by Paul Rock and Mary McIntosh

  .4 Sociology and Development
      edited by Emanuel de Kadt and Gavin Williams

   5 The Social Analysis of Class Structure
      edited by Frank Parkin

   6 Sexual Divisions and Society: Process and Change
      edited by Diana Leonard Barker and Sheila Allen

Published by Longman
   7 Dependence and Exploitation: Work and Marriage
      edited by Diana Leonard Barker and Sheila Allen

Published by George Allen & Unwin
   8 Industrial Society: Class, Cleavage and Control
      edited by Richard Scase

Published by Croom Helm
   9 Health Care and Health Knowledge
      *edited by Robert Dingwall, Christian Heath,
      Margaret Reid and Margaret Stacey*

  10 Health and the Division of Labour
      *edited by Margaret Stacey, Margaret Reid,
      Christian Heath and Robert Dingwall*

  11 Power and the State
      *edited by Gary Littlejohn, Barry Smart,
      John Wakeford and Nira Yuval-Davis*

POWER AND THE STATE

Edited by
Gary Littlejohn, Barry Smart
John Wakeford and Nira Yuval-Davis

CROOM HELM LONDON

© 1978 British Sociological Association
Croom Helm Ltd, 2-10 St John's Road, London SW11
ISBN 0-85664-663-6 (HB)
ISBN 0-85664-664-4 (PB)

British Library Cataloguing in Publication Data

Power and the state.
    1. Political sociology – Congresses 2. State,
    The – Congresses
    I. Littlejohn, Gary II. British Sociological
    Association. Annual Conference, 1977.
    301.5'92   JA76

    ISBN 0-85664-663-6
    ISBN 0-85664-664-4 Pbk

Printed and bound in Great Britain by
Billing & Sons Limited, Guildford, London and Worcester

CONTENTS

Introduction   9

1. Capitalism and Democracy: The Best Possible
   Political Shell? *Bob Jessop*   10

2. Theories of Nationalism *Sami Zubaida*   52

3. Classes and Politics in Marxist Theory *Barry Hindess*   72

4. On the Shape and Scope of Counter-Insurgency Thought
   Philip Schlesinger   98

5. Business and the State: Management Education and
   Business Elites in France and Great Britain
   Jane Marceau, Alan B. Thomas and Richard Whitley   128

6. The Family-Education Couple: Towards an Analysis of
   the William Tyndale Dispute *Miriam E. David*   158

7. The Police and the State: Arrest, Legality and the Law
   Doreen J. McBarnet   196

8. Violence and the Social Control of Women
   Jalna Hanmer   217

9. The Regulation of Marriage: Repressive Benevolence
   Diana Leonard Barker   239

10. Sociologists Not At Work — Institutionalised Inability:
    A Case of Research Funding *Robert Moore*   267

Notes on Contributors   303

Index   307

INTRODUCTION

The scope, pervasiveness and significance of the state has been much neglected in modern sociology. The relationship of sociologists themselves to the state through their employment as teachers and researchers is essentially ambiguous and often delicate; few have paid much attention to the basic understandings which underpin their own employment and allocation of research funds. Sociologists are frequently responding to choices presented to them — of relevance, of theory, perspective and methodology, even of possible remedies for social problems — so that the very nature of the sociological enterprise has excluded questions of the state and its influence.

Clearly we need to move beyond the assumption of the state as a neutral arbiter of social affairs, and at the 1977 Annual Conference of the British Sociological Association many of the contributors recognised the value of alternative disciplines and paradigms. In this volume we have collected ten papers that are representative and focus on the impact of the state on various components of the social structure through legitimation, regulation, modification and the creation of institutions and processes. However they have been deliberately selected with an emphasis on concrete and empirical studies of the mechanisms that produce particular effects in capitalist society rather than on theoretical analysis and abstraction.

At a time when the teaching of sociology and sociological investigations are increasingly under attack for their lack of relevance for and commitment to state and industrial policies an examination of the state and facets of its influence are particularly apposite for all who are involved in the sociological enterprise.

1 CAPITALISM AND DEMOCRACY: THE BEST POSSIBLE POLITICAL SHELL?

Bob Jessop

The aim of this paper is to consider the relation between capitalism and democracy. This is obviously a large question and no attempt is made to examine all possible aspects of the relation nor to consider any single aspect in all its detail. The discussion will be organised around four principal concerns: (a) the degree of association between capitalism and democracy, (b) the major determinants or causes of that association, (c) the effects of democratic forms on political class struggle, and (d) future developments in the capitalist state. In each case I shall present some relevant views advanced by other theorists and comment on them. The paper will conclude with some more general reflections on the nature of state power in capitalist societies.

Epistemological and Theoretical Considerations

It is common for a certain kind of academic Marxism to preface any analysis of concrete issues with general epistemological considerations and abstract theoretical determinations. I can see no reason for breaking with precedent. For a brief discussion of the nature of capitalism and democracy will reveal the criteria with which one can assess previous commentaries on the relations, if any, between these two phenomena. It will also prepare the ground for my own arguments as to the nature, causes, and effects of capitalist democracy.

Capitalism is a system of commodity production characterised by the private ownership and control of the means of production and by formally free labour power. The direct labourers neither own nor control the means of production and must therefore sell their labour-power in order to live. Production is controlled by non-labourers (capitalists) who purchase and combine the factors of production (including labour-power) and sell the material goods and services that result. Although surplus-value is *created* during the process of production, it is *realised* only through the exchange of commodities on the market. The basic dynamic of the CMP is the expanded reproduction of capitalist relations of production through the capitalisation of the surplus-value realised on the market. The process of capital accumulation involves class struggle between capital and wage-labour to secure (or transform) the subordination and exploitation of the latter within definite relations of production. For, without such exploitation and subordination, it would be impossible for capital to appropriate surplus-value)

Now, although it is possible to construct the concepts of different modes of production such as primitive communism, feudalism, or capitalism, at an abstract and simple level of analysis, no such modes exist in pure form in the real world. For, not only are there variant forms forms of each mode of production and different stages in their development, a given mode of production is also always inserted into a social formation in which its conditions of existence are more or less successfully realised and in which it co-exists with other modes of production and/or other forms of social and private labour. This means that the analysis of a pure mode of production must be concretised and complexified if it is to prove adequate to the analysis of specific social formations. Thus, in the case of any discussion of the relations between capitalism and democracy, it is essential that any analysis allow for variation in the form of capitalism and its articulation with other modes of production and forms of labour. The implications of this criterion will become apparent as we proceed.

The same point can be made in a different way. For democracy is a determination of the state (or state power) and must therefore be analysed on the conceptual terrain of the social formation rather than the pure mode of production. The state is the principal institutional locus of political power in *capitalist societies* and cannot be derived from an abstract consideration of the *pure capitalist mode of production.* Indeed, it is one of the principal difficulties in the capital logic school of analysis of the capitalist state, that it neglects the more concrete problem of *state power in a given social formation* in favour of the *ideal collective capitalist in the CMP.* This makes it impossible for the school to grasp the nature of the capitalist state.

It is important to recognise the nature of the state in this respect. Three points merit special emphasis. These are (a) the state is a structural ensemble rather than a subject, (b) the state is a system of political domination rather than a neutral instrument, and (c) state power is a complex social relation that reflects the changing balance of social forces in a determinate conjuncture. Let us consider these points in turn.

First, the state is a set of institutions and apparatuses of political representation and intervention that cannot, *qua* set of structures, exercise power. In this context it is acceptable to define the institutional boundaries of the state in terms of the legal distinction between 'public' and 'private' provided one neither sees it as an originating subject endowed with an essential unity nor neglects the role of private institutions and bodies in securing political domination. This is especially important in the analysis of capitalist democracies. For to treat the state as a real (as opposed to legal) subject is to exclude from consideration political struggles within and between state apparatuses as well as the effects of its institutional structure on political struggles in general. Likewise, to endow the state with an essential unity or inevitable bourgeois character is to engage in crude reductionism and to suggest that the only valid form of political struggle is one concerned to smash the existing state apparatuses. Moreover, if one adopts such an essentialist position or simply argues that all institutions of class domination or social cohesion should be included in one's definition of the state, then it becomes impossible to differentiate between democratic and non-democratic forms of domination and to discuss the effects of changes in the institutional boundaries of the state.

Second, even though the state has been defined in institutional terms rather than as a subject capable of exercising power, this should not be interpreted as an argument that the state is a *neutral instrument* that can be used with *equal facility and equal effectiveness* by all classes and social forces regardless of their location in the social formation or their political goals. For the institutional structure of the state has unequal and asymmetrical effects on the ability of different social forces to realise their interests through political struggle. This argument against a crude instrumentalist view of the state is reinforced through consideration of the various ways in which political forces themselves are constituted in part through the constraints associated with different forms of state. This means that classes should not be seen as already-constituted political forces which exist outside and independently of the state and which are capable of manipulating it as an instrument. For, although classes are defined at the level of relations of production, their political weight depends on the forms of organisation and means of intervention through which economic interests are expressed. These considerations also apply to other political forces besides wage-labour and capital. Thus the state should be viewed as a system of political domination whose structure has a definite influence on class struggle through its impact on the balance of social forces and the forms of political practice.

Third, although the state is not a real subject that exercises power, state power certainly exists and, indeed, constitutes the principal focus of political class struggle. State power is a complex social relation that reflects the changing balance of social forces in a determinate conjuncture insofar as they are concerned to control, reorganise, and restrict state apparatuses and state intervention. It is always contingent upon the circumstances in which the political struggle between such forces occurs as well as the correlation of forces — circumstances which are influenced in part by the institutional structure of the state itself. This view involves a firm rejection of any attempt to differentiate between 'state power' and 'class power' either as descriptive concepts or principles of explanation. This distinction can be sustained only be treating the state itself as a subject and/or ignoring the continuing class struggle within the state as well as that outside it. One should treat state power as a complex social relation whose changing nature depends on various interrelated factors.

It is within this context that we must locate the second term in the relation between capitalism and democracy. This can be seen as a determination of the state and/or state power. Thus democracy can be treated as an aspect of the institutional structure of representation and intervention and/or as a system of effective self-administration by the people. Indeed, if radical democratic theories focus on self-administration or popular control of government, liberal democratic theories emphasise the role of institutional mechanisms that enable the people at best to choose passively between political elites and government policies. Likewise, if Marx advocated genuine democracy based on government from below, he also criticised the formalism of bourgeois democracy and stressed its contribution to the continued rule of capital. The implications of formal democratic institutions in a capitalist society will therefore differ from those of substantive self-government in a classless society and it is correspondingly necessary to maintain the distinction between institutional forms and effective state power or political control.

What does democracy entail? In the institutional context of the capitalist state it refers to the legal entitlement of 'citizens' to participate in the determination of the policies to be executed by the state in its capacity as sovereign legal subject; and, in addition, to the legal conditions of existence of such participation. Citizenship involves the institution of an individual juridical subject endowed with specific political rights as well as obligations and the extension of this legal status to all adult members of the society without reference to their class position or other attributes. In this sense the institutionalisation of citizenship can vary across social formations in terms of the scope and specification of the political rights of participation and in terms of the inclusiveness of the citizenry in relation to the total adult population. Democracy also has other legal preconditions. These focus on the institutionalisation of certain political freedoms (e.g. freedom of association, freedom of speech, free elections) and of parliamentary (or equivalent) control over the executive and administration. They are the necessary juridical supports to the formal exercise of the citizen's rights of political participation. The popular-democratic struggle in capitalist societies takes the form of struggles to extend the scope of citizens' rights of participation, to include more of the 'people' within the category of citizens, and to institute the legal conditions appropriate to democracy. Moreover, because formal democratic institutions do not guarantee real control by the 'people', popular-democratic struggle also encompasses struggle to establish and maintain the social conditions in which such control can be realised. In this connection the 'people' is not a formal juridical subject (as in People v. Dunleavy) but a real political force constituted during the struggle to democratise the relations of political and ideological domination in a given social formation. To the extent that its struggle is successful, state power itself becomes more democratic.

We are now in a position to restate our initial problem. The focus of this paper is on the relation between democratic forms of political representation and generalised commodity production. More precisely, it is concerned with the relation between the operation of democratic institutions and the expanded reproduction of capital in social formations dominated by the capitalist mode of production. And, since capital accumulation is contingent on class struggle, the effects of democratic forms of state on the struggle between capital and wage-labour are particularly significant. But we must first consider the extent to which democratic forms of state are associated with societies dominated by the capitalist mode of production.

The Correlation between Capitalism and Democracy

Several attempts have been made to correlate capitalism and democracy and to decuce the one from the other. Such efforts can be found among radical and Marxist writers as well as among conservative and liberal theorists. Indeed, given the contrasting political and ideological positions of such authors, it is surprising to discover a series of parallels in their analyses. This can be illustrated with reference to the work of social market economists and of various leftwing theorists.

Milton Friedman has argued on both historical and logical grounds

that economic freedom is correlated with political freedom. He argues
that the typical state of mankind is tyranny, servitude, and misery and
that the nineteenth and early twentieth century in the Western world
are remarkable exceptions to this general trend. This suggests that the
free market and the development of capitalist institutions are a
necessary condition of political freedom. Moreover, even though the
dominance of private enterprise has been associated with authoritarian
regimes such as Italian Fascism, Bismarckism and Tsarist autocracy, the
degree of freedom available to citizens in such cases was much greater
than is true of totalitarian states like communist Russia or Nazi
Germany. And, with the introduction of collective economic planning
since the end of World War II, there has been a corresponding reduction
in political freedom for the individual. But, since historical evidence by
itself can never be convincing, Friedman also tries to establish certain
logical links between capitalism and political freedom. He argues that

> the kind of economic organisation that provides economic freedom
> directly, namely, competitive capitalism, also promotes political
> freedom because it separates economic power from political power
> and in this way enables the one to offset the other. (1962, p.9)

This is possible because the market removes the organisation of economic activity from the control of political authority and so reduces,
rather than reinforces, the concentration of power. Almost identical
arguments are offered in a recent pamphlet on the social market
economy produced by the Conservative party's Centre for Policy
Studies and introduced by Sir Keith Joseph. This argues that economic
freedom is a necessary (but not a sufficient) condition of political
freedom and that private ownership acts as a check on the accumulation
of power by government and thus safeguards personal liberties. Likewise, in a book entitled *The Case for Capitalism* and produced under the
auspices of Aims of Industry, Laurence Clark draws on the work of
C.B. MacPherson to show the close association between capitalism and
liberal democracy and to establish thereby a political case for the 'other
democracy' of the free market.

None of these writers is an anarchist. They do advocate a degree of
government intervention in the economy as well as a central role for the
state in maintaining social order. Thus Friedman argues that

> [a] government which maintained law and order, defined property
> rights, served as a means whereby we could modify property rights

and other rules of the economic game, adjudicated disputes about the interpretation of the rules, enforced contracts, promoted competition, provided a monetary framework, engaged in activities to counter technical monopolies and to overcome neighbourhood effects widely regarded as sufficiently important to justify government intervention, and which supplemented private charity and the private family in protecting the irresponsible, whether madman or child — such a government would clearly have important functions to perform. (1962, p. 34)

But it would also be a government with limited functions and, in association with the franchise and a system of personal liberties, it would be a liberal democratic government.

The Centre for Policy Studies takes an essentially similar line but goes a little further. It recognises the shortcomings as well as the advantages of the market — in particular it admits that the market

does not in itself ensure that the occasional divergence of private and social costs/benefits is reflected in prices; it often fails to provide for those who, through misfortune, cannot provide for themselves; it may bring about a distribution of income, wealth and economic power which many people find unacceptable. (1975, p. 9)

It follows that there is a

clear need to complement the market system with various 'social' policies — especially to help the old, the ill, the handicapped, the disabled and the unemployed, and to ease the transition in industries in which rapid structural changes are taking place. (ibid)

But the government should still rely as far as possible on the market mechanism in support of its social policies as well as in economic organisation and the promotion of economic growth.

These arguments are interesting, not just as expressions of bourgeois and petit bourgeois ideology, but also as reflections on the nature of the capitalist state. Several points are worth emphasis. First, these theorists stress that there is

an intimate connection between economics and politics . . . (and there is) no justification for thinking that individual liberty is a political issue whereas material welfare is an economic issue and that any

permutation of economic and political systems is practicable.
(Centre, 1975, pp. 13-14)

Second, they argue that capitalism requires a specific separation of
economic and political power so that economic power can be used to
prevent the abuse of political power and political power can be employed to counteract the shortcomings of the market. Third, they admit
the state must nonetheless intervene to maintain the conditions in
which competitive capitalism can operate — especially in relation to the
appropriate legal and monetary framework and the provision of certain
goods and services. Fourth, provided these general conditions are realised through the actions of the liberal democratic state, competitive
capitalism will expand in a crisis-free manner owing to the smooth operation of the market mechanism. It is when the government intervenes
through attempts to manage economic demand through monetary and
fiscal techniques and/or to impose central planning that crises develop.
Finally, although there is an intimate connection between competitive
capitalism and liberal democratic government, the danger is ever-present
that political power be employed to undermine individual economic and
political freedom if the wrong people employ the power of the state for
the wrong purposes. It is in this connection that a widespread diffusion
of economic power is a significant check on totalitarian political rule.

The arguments of the 'capital logic' school are similar in certain
respects to those of the 'social market economy' theorists. The former
derives the nature of the capitalist state from the nature of the capital
relation. It argues that, although competition between capitals secures
some of the conditions necessary to capital accumulation (especially in
terms of realising the law of value[1]), it is also essential that there be an
institutional complex that is not directly subordinate to the law of value
to accomplish the conditions that competition does not secure. These
include the provision of an appropriate legal framework for generalised
commodity production, the creation of the general material conditions
of production (infrastructure), the regulation of the conflict between
wage-labour and capital, and the protection and expansion of the total
national capital on the world market (cf. Altvater, 1973). Thus, despite
the appearance of institutional separation and political autonomy, the
state is actually an ideal collective capitalist and a necessary political
moment in the social accomplishment of capital. This view is not dissimilar from that of Friedman. But, whereas he is committed to the
view that capitalist production is non-exploitative and essentially crisis-
free, Marxist writers argue that capitalism is exploitative and that the

most fundamental barrier to continued accumulation is not misguided state intervention but capital itself. This implies, contrary to the view of the social market theorists, that the liberal democratic state is not the co-guarantor (together with competitive capitalism) of individual freedom. Indeed, as MacPherson has argued,

> the more nearly the society approximates Friedman's ideal of a competitive capitalist market society, where the state establishes and enforces the individual right of appropriation and the rules of the market but does not interfere in the operation of the market, the more completely is political power being used to reinforce economic power. (1973, pp. 148-149)

Thus, far from the separation of political from economic power underwriting individual freedom, it is a ruse of capital whose effect is to secure the conditions in which the working class can be subjected to the exploitation of capital. This is the basis for Moore's generalisation that, '[where] exploitation takes the form of exchange, dictatorship tends to take the form of democracy' (1957, p. 85).

Moreover, although the point is nowhere stated explicitly in the work of the capital logic school, it also follows that the liberal democratic state not only reinforces and underwrites economic exploitation but is in turn restricted and confined in its activities by the need to maintain business confidence. For, so long as the state does not itself engage in production but remains dependent on revenues generated within the private sector, it remains indirectly subordinate to the law of value and open to pressures from capital. This is the material basis of the social market economists' arguments concerning the implications of diffuse economic power for the restriction and limitation of totalitarian (or socialist) political rule. In those situations when a radical popular or socialist party is elected into political office, it can be circumscribed by a 'strike of capital' as well as by more direct political interventions and struggles.

Arguments similar to those of the capital logic school can also be developed to derive the nature and limits of individual liberty and the liberal democratic state from the nature of the capitalist mode of production. This is clear in the analysis of bourgeois law offered by Eugen Pashukanis in an early Soviet text often cited by capital logicians. He notes that generalised commodity production is the historical precondition for the full development of modern law. Modern law is characterised by the constitution of juridical subjects endowed with justiciable and, in certain cases, alienable rights. This reflects the individuation and competition of the owners of commodities (including labour-power) and the manner of their confrontation as equals in the market place. Moreover, precisely because of their formal equality, it is necessary to constitute a public power to regulate the exchanges between these juridical subjects and to provide the necessary legal framework within which they act. Thus, not only does generalised commodity production presuppose the formal equality of wage-labour and capital, it also requires an institutional separation and co-ordination of the market and the political level. The juridical system thus constituted may then be extended to include formal equality in the political sphere proper, i.e. the institution of legal subjects (citizens) with equal rights of participation. And, indeed, it is precisely because exploitation takes the form of equal exchange and wage-slavery therefore receives no legal expression, that it is unnecessary for the exercise of political power to be restricted formally to the dominant economic class. Moreover, to the extent that there is no formal legal monopoly of power, the political domination of the bourgeoisie is effectively masked behind the appearance of political liberty and equality. In this sense, then, there is a definite affinity between capitalism and democracy (1968, pp. 183-7).

There is a fundamental difficulty with these analyses of the right and the left alike. This is the obstinate fact that capitalism is not universally associated with formal political democracy. This is recognised by social market economists in their admission that competitive capitalism is a necessary, but not a sufficient, condition of democracy. And it is also recognised by Marxists in at least two ways: for they distinguish between 'normal' and 'exceptional' forms of the capitalist state and they argue that the increasing importance of the tendency of the rate of profit to fall (TRPF[2]) leads to increasing state intervention and the demise of the liberal state. Now, if there is no one-to-one correlation between capitalism and democracy in specific societies, it is clear that the relation between them must be contingent rather than a relationship of logical entailment. Moreover, if the latter were indeed the case, history would be reduced to an effect of the self-realisation of a concept (Capitalism) in true Hegelian fashion. This means that the question must be posed as follows: given that democracy is a possible form of state in societies dominated by the capitalist mode of production, what determines the extent to which this possibility is realised? It is to this problem that we now turn.

Capital Accumulation and Forms of Capitalist State

Democracy has been found in the most dissimilar social formations: in primitive communist groups, in the slave states of antiquity, and in mediaeval communes. And similarly absolutism and constitutional monarchy are to be found under the most varied economic orders. When capitalism began, as the first production of commodities, it resorted to a democratic constitution in the municipal communes of the Middle Ages. Later, when it developed to manufacturing, capitalism found its corresponding political form in the absolute monarchy. Finally, as a developed industrial economy, it brought into being in France the democratic republic of 1793, the absolute monarchy of Napoleon I, the nobles' monarchy of the Restoration Period (1815-1830), the bourgeois constitutional monarchy of Louis Phillippe, then again the democratic republic, and again the monarchy of Napoleon III, and finally, for the third time, the republic . . No absolute and general relation can be constructed between capitalist development and democracy. The political form of a given country is always the result of the composite of all the existing political factors, domestic as well as foreign. It admits within its limits all variations of the scale from absolute monarchy to the democratic republic. (R. Luxemburg, 1970, pp. 72-4)

In this passage from *Reform or Revolution*, Rosa Luxemburg notes that democratic institutions are found in pre-capitalist societies and need not be found in capitalist societies. But she also notes that the relation is not random but contingent on the general political conjuncture. This is certainly correct but, before we consider the specifically political factors, it is worthwhile considering whether specific forms of capitalism are more or less conducive to democratic forms of government. This is implied in Luxemburg's own analysis — where simple commodity production and industrial production are associated with the democratic form and manufacturing is associated with absolutism. In short, given that capitalism does not exist in its pure form, is there nonetheless an association between specific variant forms or stages of capitalism and the forms of state with which they are associated?

One of the most interesting answers to this question has been suggested by Holloway and Picciotto in a series of papers. They attempt to establish the nature of the capitalist state in terms of the development of capital accumulation. For example, since capitalism is a historically specific form of production there is necessarily a transition period during which its preconditions are established. This requires state intervention and compulsion – for it is only once these conditions are secured that capital accumulation can proceed on the basis of exchange between 'equals'. In transitional conjunctures, therefore, an absolutist state pursuing mercantilist policies is the appropriate form of capitalist state. However, once the conditions of existence of capital accumulation have been assured, the appropriate form of state is a liberal state which gives the fullest possible freedom to individual capitals compatible with securing the general conditions for capital accumulation. This implies a combination of general *laissez-faire* with specific interventions to redress the effects of unfettered competition (e.g. factory legislation). The liberal state, it should be noted, need not be a liberal *democratic* state. But it is common for the liberal state to be associated with parliamentarism. However, the further development of capital accumulation is associated with the increasing importance of the TRPF and the need for state intervention to restructure capital in a way that facilitates the renewal of capitalist exploitation. The liberal state is replaced by the interventionist state (Holloway and Picciotto, 1977).

This analysis suggests that the liberal state is not the ideal norm for the capitalist mode of production as a whole, whether or not that state is democratic, but is merely the ideal counterpart of a certain stage of accumulation which has now passed. The same point is made even more explicit by Ernest Mandel in his seminal work on *Late Capitalism*. He argues that, not only is monopoly capitalism and the TRPF associated with increased economic intervention by the state (and hence the decline of the liberal state), it is also associated with growing political influence on the part of the working class movement. This is a contradictory process. For, although the extension of the franchise to workers encourages their incorporation into bourgeois society through the illusion of formal equality as citizen (reinforcing the illusion of formal equality as seller of a commodity), it also means the mass entry of social-democratic and communist deputies into parliament and deprives it of its role as arbiter of the interests of competing capitals. In short, if the property-based bourgeois parliament provides a forum for the formulation and implementation of policies in the interests of capital in general, it tends to lack legitimacy in terms of the liberal and egalitarian values of the dominant bourgeois ideology. But, if the liberal democratic state provides means to integrate the working class and legitimate the power of the capitalist state, it also weakens and restricts its ability to intervene effectively on behalf of capital. Thus, if the contradictions associated with the tendency of the rate of profit to fall demand an increasingly *interventionist rather than liberal* state, the contradictions involved in capitalist democracy demand an increasingly *authoritarian rather than democratic* state. Thus late capitalism leads to the development of a strong state with weak parliament and limited opportunities for popular participation in government. Thus Mandel concludes that the state in late capitalism, far from being liberal and democratic, tends towards growing hypertrophy and autonomy as well as growing interventionism (1975, pp. 482-6).

This analysis can be extended backwards in time to consider the process of capital accumulation in the early stages of imperialism and its implications for the form of the state. For it is incorrect to treat the development of capitalism in each social formation in isolation and to assume that there is a necessary unilinear sequence of stages through which each capitalist economy and each capitalist state must proceed. This is particularly clear in the case of competitive capitalism and the liberal state. For it is only in those metropolitan nations that industrialised in the first wave that we find an extended period of competitive capitalism. Thus it is in countries such as England, Holland, Belgium and the United States that we find competitive capitalism, a strong bourgeoisie, and a liberal state. In those countries which industrialised in the second wave, the role of banks and the state was much greater and the stage of competitive capitalism was correspondingly weaker and more truncated. In these countries the phase of mercantilism (with or without absolutism) and the phase of interventionism tend to merge and the liberal state was absent or ineffective. This can be seen in Bonapartism and Bismarckism in Europe and in the Tsarist autocracy. The post-colonial state in Africa and Asia and the state in many Latin American countries display different features again. In short, if we are to establish any relation between capitalism and forms of government, it must be in terms that allow for variant forms and stages of capitalism and for the insertion of given societies into the world market and imperialist chain.

The Hypothesis of the Dual Movement of the Capitalist State

So far we have treated the relation between capitalism and democracy in a rather mechanical fashion. The emphasis has been on the derivation of democratic forms of government from the pure capitalist mode of production and, given the inadequacies of that approach, the derivation of such forms from an analysis of the stages of capital accumulation. The difficulties with such attempts were signalled in the quotation from Rosa Luxemburg, namely, the association of even a single stage of accumulation with various forms of state. This suggests the need to examine the political conjuncture as well as economic determinations. It is in this connection that an analysis of the capitalist state written by Tom Wengraf is particularly interesting.

Wengraf argues that an examination of the work of Marx and Engels on the capitalist state reveals two related hypotheses about its development. The first hypothesis refers to the constant accentuation of the repressive character of the state and the constant improvement of its machinery. This is the essence of the development of the capitalist state, whatever its forms may be. The second hypothesis refers to a short-term cycle superimposed upon the long-term trend. It suggests that the 'executive' and the 'parliamentary' forms of state are invariant forms which alternate according to the changing forms and effects of the political class struggle. Thus, as class struggle intensifies and threatens the process of capital accumulation, the bourgeoisie adopts an 'executive' form of class rule. Conversely, once the class emergency has been dealt with through repression, the 'parliamentary' form becomes advantageous and possible. The interaction of the long-term trend and the short-term cycle leads, in a general way, to a secular decline in 'constitutional democracy' both as a bourgeois ideology and as capitalist practice. More and more regions of world capitalist society have longer and longer periods of 'executive rule', shorter and more restricted periods of a decreasingly meaningful 'capitalist parliamentary democracy' (1970, passim).

Several questions could be raised concerning the presentation of Wengraf's analysis but it is valuable because it focuses on the effects of class conflict on the viability and adequacy of different forms of capitalist state. Thus, although he follows the class-theoretical approach of the political writings of Marx and Engels rather than the capital-theoretical approach of *Das Kapital* and the capital-logicians, Wengraf does establish the critical role of the class struggle over capital accumulation in determining the form of the state. Moreover, although the dichotomy between the invariant 'executive' and 'parliamentary' forms is inadequate and there is a large measure of voluntarism in the analysis of their alternation, the hypothesis of dual movement is more adequate to the concrete variation of the capitalist state than the one-sided accounts of the capital-logicians. But this thesis still needs to be reworked and elaborated to produce a set of determinations that can account for this variation without resort to 'essentialism' or 'speculative empiricism'. We consider this problem below.

Class Struggle, Classes in Struggle, and the Capitalist State

At this stage of the discussion no mention has yet been made of the presence of classes other than wage-labour and capital on the political scene. But, as was pointed out in the introductory section, the state is situated on the terrain of the social formation rather than a pure mode of production. This means that other classes and social forces may be pertinent to the analysis. There are two aspects of this problem that are relevant to our discussion — firstly, the implications of the articulation of different modes of production and/or forms of labour for the form of government and, secondly, the implications of classes outside the capitalist mode of production for the form of state power. In neither case can consideration of the CMP in isolation furnish an adequate understanding of these problems.

For all its faults, Barrington Moore's work on *The Social Origins of Dictatorship and Democracy* is important and relevant to both issues. For, despite a certain reputation to the contrary, it is not written from a crude economic determinist position. The principal variables specified by Moore are the relation between the landed upper classes, if any, and the peasantry and, secondly, the form of alliance, if any, between the landed upper classes and the urban bourgeoisie. Thus, to the extent that capitalist agriculture does not develop and labour-repressive modes of agricultural production are dominant, a repressive state apparatus is required to maintain the subordination of an exploited agricultural labouring class. If there is a class alliance, it is dominated by the non-capitalist landed class. Conversely, where capitalist agriculture develops (either in the form of the English three-class agricultural system or in the form of American peasant agriculture without a capitalist landlord class) and the landed upper class allies with the urban bourgeoisie under the political hegemony of the latter, democracy is likely. The case of nineteenth century France is intermediate between the Prussian and the English patterns. For, although there was a bourgeois revolution, it did not resolve the peasant problem nor create the conditions favourable to a strong urban bourgeoisie. Thus, although democratic forms of government were instituted in nineteenth-century France, they proved unstable and ineffective (1966, passim).

Similar arguments are deployed by Marx, Engels and Lenin. In particular, we may note that, in his review of Guizot's book on the English revolution, Marx attributes the differential effects of the English and French revolutions to the alliance between the English bourgeoisie and the big capitalist landlords (premised on their common interests in capital accumulation) and the impossibility of such an alliance in France owing to the abolition of big landownership through the parcellation of land to small-holding peasant farmers. It is this latter class (together with the lumpenproletariat) that is identified as the principal political support of the pseudo-parliamentary Bonapartist regime of the French Second Empire. Indeed, Bonapartism reveals the possibilities of universal suffrage to underpin a strong state and the domination of finance capital. Conversely, in the case of Bismarckism, we find a three-class suffrage system instituted to underpin an alliance of Junker landlords and bourgeoisie under the political dominance of the former. The political implications of this are identified by Engels in terms of Bismarck's failure to introduce a bourgeois democratic republic favourable to the political domination of the bourgeoisie rather than a declining feudal class (1968, p. 95). Likewise, in his review of the agrarian programme of social democracy in Russia, Lenin draws a sharp distinction between the Prussian and the American routes to capitalist agriculture. The Prussian route is characterised by the utmost preservation of bondage and serfdom (remodelled on bourgeois lines) and implies the greatest oppression and exploitation of peasantry and proletariat alike. The American route presupposes the absence or dissolution of the landlord economy and the transformation of the patriarchal peasant into a capitalist farmer. Thus, given that Russian agriculture is embarking on the path of bourgeois agrarian revolution, Lenin supports the development of capitalist farming on the grounds that it is most conducive to the democratic dictatorship of the proletariat and peasantry. This follows from the preconditions of instituting and guaranteeing American-style agrarian development, namely, the radical transformation of the central as well as the local state apparatuses in a democratic direction and the total nationalisation of land. In this way Lenin takes account of the existence of various classes and formulates his revolutionary strategy in terms of an alliance between the proletariat and the peasantry against the big landlords, usury capital, the industrial bourgeoisie, and the Tsarist autocracy (1907, passim).

It is not my intention to pronounce on the adequacy of these analyses to the explanation of the specific historical events with which they are concerned. They are cited only to highlight the importance of examining the political conjuncture at the level of the social formation in an analysis of forms of state and state power. For, although this is influenced by the articulation of the dominant mode of production and subordinate modes and/or social and private forms of labour, it cannot be deduced automatically from that articulation considered in isolation. Different forms of articulation have quite different implications for forms of government. Thus, whereas the use of coercion to conserve homeland agriculture, underwrite African labour-power, and subordinate the black majority to capitalist exploitation precludes the grant of democratic rights to native labour in the South African state, these rights can be extended to black labour in the USA because it is a minority subject to exploitation through equal exchange rather than compulsion. But the same form of articulation can be combined with different political conjunctures to give different prospects for formal democratic institutions and real democratic control. For it is the balance of political forces involved in the struggle for the appropriation and exercise of state power and the reconstitution of state apparatuses that is the immediate determinant of these factors. This places the popular-democratic struggle at the heart of any analysis of democratic institutions. And it is in this context that we should investigate the adequacy of different forms of government to securing the economic, political, and ideological conditions necessary to the expanded reproduction of capital. And, since democracy is a determination of state apparatuses, its effects can only be assessed in relation to the political conjuncture as a whole and not in terms of abstract speculation concerning the general effects of democratic forms of representation.

The Effects of Democratic Representation

If one accepts the view that the state is neither an originating subject nor a neutral instrument but a system of apparatuses and institutions that have determinate effects on the political struggle, it is essential to consider the effects of democratic representation on the class struggle between wage-labour and capital in capitalist societies. In this respect it should be noted immediately that 'representation' is not an expressive relationship in which representer and represented are related in a manner that guarantees the accurate representation of the views or interests of the represented. For the means of representation have their own effects on the process of representation in exactly the same way that the means of scientific enquiry affect the representation of the real world in the production of scientific knowledge. Nor can one side-step this problem through a resort to reductionist or essentialist arguments that determine the interests of a given class without reference to the means of representation in a determinate political situation and then assess the extent to which a given form of representation distorts these interests. For the means of representation are themselves part of the conjuncture that determines class interests (cf. Hirst, 1976 and Hindess, 1978). Indeed, it is precisely this problem that is at the heart of the long-standing debate in the socialist movement concerning the correct strategies and tactics of revolutionary struggle in bourgeois democratic republics. Let us now consider the effectivity of the means of representation.

Lenin stated his belief in *The State and Revolution* that

[a] democratic republic is the best possible political shell for capitalism, and therefore capital, once in possession . . . of this very best shell, establishes its power so securely, so firmly, that *no* change of persons, of institutions, or of parties in the bourgeois democratic republic can shake it. (1963, p. 296)

This view was anticipated by Engels, who referred to the bourgeois democratic republic as 'the logical form of bourgeois rule' (Engels to Bernstein in Zurich, 24 March 1884); and it is shared by many other Marxists past and present. Thus, in a recent issue of *New Left Review*, Perry Anderson argued that 'the general form of the representative state − bourgeois democracy − is itself the principal ideological lynchpin of Western capitalism' (1977, p. 28). Now, although it is certainly true that the democratic republic is a *possible* form of capitalist state, it is less certain that it is the *best* or most adequate form of capitalist state. What reasons have been offered in support of this claim?

One argument that has been adduced for this claim rests on an alleged parallel between commodity fetishism and the fetishism of political relations in the bourgeois democratic republic. This parallelism is particularly clear in the work of Pashukanis but also appears in the work of Ollman on political alienation and of Holloway and Picciotto on the capitalist state. There is some disagreement as to the source of political fetishism. Thus, whereas Ollman bases his analysis on the 1844 manuscripts and draws a series of analogies with Marx's early philosophical writings on alienation, Pashukanis is concerned to develop the theory of commodity fetishism in *Capital*. He notes that commodity fetishism in the economy is reflected on the juridical level in the couplet of 'persons' and 'things'. Indeed, as Pashukanis, Poulantzas and Anderson have pointed out, the juridical concepts of bourgeois law constitute the kernel of bourgeois ideology in general. Thus Pashukanis argues that, although bourgeois law is rooted in capitalist relations of production, it denies the existence of exploitation and establishes a juridical system of formally equal juridical subjects under the authority of an impartial and independent *Rechtsstaat*. Moreover, although the *Rechtsstaat* is a mirage, it is a mirage extremely convenient to the bourgeoisie. For it replaces religious ideology and obscures from the masses the fact of bourgeois domination. But it is a mirage grounded in the real world. For, insofar as a society is dominated by generalised commodity production, an authority standing outside and above society is needed to regulate the market in the 'general interest' (1968, pp. 188ff). Likewise, Poulantzas claims that 'juridico-political ideology holds a dominant place in the dominant ideology of this [i.e. capitalist] mode of production, taking a place analogous to religious ideology in the dominant ideology of the feudal mode of production' (1973, p. 128). And, in the words of Perry Anderson, '[t]he existence of the parliamentary State thus constitutes the formal framework of all other ideological mechanisms of the ruling class. It provides the general code in which every specific message elsewhere is transmitted' (1977, p. 28). In short, these theorists argue that the effect of bourgeois law in general and parliamentarism in particular is to misrepresent and mystify the nature of bourgeois political domination as well as of bourgeois economic exploitation.

   The problem with this analysis is identical to that with commodity fetishism. For, insofar as commodity fetishism is seen to be an automatic effect of the system of generalised commodity production, the fact of capitalist production automatically produces one of its (ideological) conditions of existence. If the successful constitution of a bourgeois democratic republic automatically generates political fetishism, then yet another of these conditions of existence is automatically generated. In such circumstances, how could capitalism ever disappear — except through some in-built teleological drive towards self-destruction? But, if it is accepted that commodity fetishism and political fetishism are not automatic effects of a specific structure, how are they generated and reproduced? It is here that Balibar's comments on commodity fetishism are particularly germane. He writes that,

   [a]s we are now beginning to understand, an ideological effect
   (i.e., an effect of allusion-illusion, of recognition-misrecognition
   objectively produced through and in social practice) can only be
   explained through a *positive* cause, through the existence and
   functioning of genuine *ideological social relations* (juridical,
   moral, religious, aesthetic, political, etc.) that are constituted historically in the process of class struggle. (1973, p. 31)

   In short, far from seeing political fetishism as an automatic effect of the parliamentary republic with its constitution of formally equal citizens and a sovereign state representing the national interest, it is vital to examine the ideological social relations and ideological class struggles that are involved in the reproduction (and transformation) of this phenomenon. This requires the analysis of political parties, trade unions, and pressure groups as well as the more obviously ideological apparatuses.

But even to talk about political parties, trade unions, and pressure groups is to presuppose an important material basis of political fetishism, namely, the institutional separation in capitalist societies between the economic and political instances of the social formation. This is a generic feature of such societies but nonetheless has specific effects in liberal democratic regimes. For the latter involve a clear demarcation between private and public spheres and thereby separate economic and political class struggle to the advantage of capital and the detriment of labour. The growth of economic intervention by the state weakens this separation and threatens to unify the two forms of struggle. From the viewpoint of capital the ideal position is one in which economic class struggle is confined within the limits of the market relation and political class struggle is confined within the limits of bourgeois parliamentarism. There would be a clear division between trade union struggles concerned with wages and conditions and political struggles to promote social reforms through parliamentary majorities and the mobilisation of public opinion. To the extent that these struggles are unified, it would be through a social democratic movement. But even this would involve a division of labour between the industrial and political wings of the movement: industrial power would be confined to industrial disputes rather than be employed to reinforce parliamentary action, state power would be confined to the 'public' sphere and not employed to interfere in private disputes. For, given such an institutional separation and its corresponding forms of class struggle, the prospects for the economic and political domination of capital would be much enhanced. It was the recognition of this that motivated the ruling class strategy aimed at 'constitutionalising' the labour movement in Britain and vindicated in the outcome of the General Strike (cf. J. Foster, 1976, passim).

The contribution of such separation and renunciation to the political domination of capital can be understood through a consideration of a recent essay by Offe and Ronge. They note that the institutional separation between the economic and political implies a specific relation between the capitalist state and the economy, viz.: (a) political power is prohibited from organising production according to its own criteria —

property is *private* (this includes labour-power as well as capital); (b) political power rests indirectly on the rate and volume of private accumulation since the state depends on revenue from taxation; (c) since the state depends on a process of accumulation which it is unable to control and organise, every occupant of state power acquires a fundamental interest in promoting those conditions most favourable to accumulation; and (d) in democratic political regimes, political groups or parties can appropriate state power only through winning sufficient electoral support. Thus, although the exercise of state power is actually conditioned by the demands of capital accumulation, in democratic regimes it appears to be determined by the preferences of the electorate and is thereby legitimated (1975, pp. 137-8). Now, although Offe and Ronge replace the problem of the specificity of the capitalist state as a system of political domination with an instrumentalist theory of the state (with the twist that it is in the self-interest of officials and politicians to use state power to promote the interests of capital), this account contains a number of ideas that merit further attention. In particular, since exploitation in the CMP is based on equal exchange, the bourgeoisie do not need to control the state itself provided state power is employed to maintain the juridical and monetary framework in which capital accumulation occurs. Conversely, since the executive depends on accumulation for revenue, it shares a common interest with capital in the exploitation of the proletariat (cf. Fernbach, 1973, pp. 16-17). This analysis is particularly relevant to exceptional forms of the capitalist state (such as military dictatorship or Bonapartism) but, *pace* Offe and Ronge, it is less clear how it applies to democratic regimes. For electoral politics are not irrelevant to the exercise of state power nor are they necessarily overridden by the demands of capital accumulation. The relation between them is problematic and cannot simply be ignored.

One possible solution to this problem has been suggested with great clarity by Andrew Gamble in his study of *The Conservative Nation*. In a discussion of electoral politics, he distinguishes between the 'politics of support' and the 'politics of power'. The former refers to the constraints entailed in a democratic electoral system characterised by the institutionalisation of 'one-man-one-vote-one-value' and, within the specific limits imposed by particular electoral systems, it implies that electoral success is contingent on securing the support of a majority or at least a significant plurality of votes. But it is also necessary for electoral programmes to be realistic in terms of the politics of power. The latter refers to the constraints on the exercise of state power where power is not parcelled out in equivalent lots to each and every citizen but is contingent on the changing economic, political, and ideological conjuncture as a whole. Thus the politics of support must be practised within the constraints imposed by the politics of power. For politicians and parties that go beyond these constraints will either be electorally unpopular (because their programmes seem sectional, extreme, or unrealistic) or will be forced to undertake U-turns and/or to embrace the prevailing orthodoxies if elected. Thus, far from electoral competition being irrelevant to the activities of the capitalist state, it has a crucial role to play in the determination of its policies. And, given the implications of a universal franchise in conjunction with uneven development of political consciousness and the existence of non-proletarian classes, parliamentary democracy works to reinforce the political domination of capital at the expense of revolutionary socialist movements. For, unless these are prepared to accept the rules of the electoral game and the realities of political power, they will be confined to electoral impotence and thus, in the terms of parliamentary politics, illegitimacy. And, whether or not one attributes these constraints to 'self-interest' (with its voluntarist implications) or to the effects of universal suffrage in a situation of bourgeois political and ideological domination, it is apparent that electoral systems have determinate effects on political class struggle (1974, pp. 3-11).

If the parliamentary republic has specific effects on working class political and economic struggle, it also has specific effects on the practices of the bourgeoisie. This has been emphasised particularly by Poulantzas in his most recent work on the *Crisis of the Dictatorships.* His arguments can be summarised quite briefly as follows. The capitalist state must be adequate to the twofold task of organising the unity of the power bloc and effecting the disorganisation of the dominated classes. This task is necessary since the competition among capitals poses the problem of their political unity at the same time as class struggle unifies the working class politically. This means that the state must be relatively autonomous from all classes in order to be able to intervene in the political class struggle on behalf of capital. This excludes the possibility that the state is a mere instrument manipulated at will by an already unified bourgeoisie. Nor can this autonomy be based on the final and absolute political authority of an independent subject such as the Crown-in-Parliament — even if its power is relativised through the constraints entailed in the law of value. For the state cannot, *qua* structure, exercise power. Rather, since the state is a social relation, its ability to intervene in the political class struggle must be an effect of its stucture. But what sort of institutional arrangement can guarantee the relative autonomy of the state required by capital?

Poulantzas suggests that the coupling of individual citizenship as a legal institution with the nation-state as a juridical subject is particularly effective in this respect. For, not only does the constitution of all members of society as political subjects endowed with equal rights, regardless of their class belonging, complement their formal equality as economic subjects, it also encourages their atomisation and individuation and disguises the substantive inequalities in political rule. In this sense the commodity fetishism engendered by exchange relations is mirrored in liberal political and legal institutions. Conversely, not only does the emergence of a nation-state correspond to the need for an 'ideal collective capitalist', it also implies the existence of a national or popular interest that reflects the common interests of all its citizens. But, since citizenship is not based on class membership, these common interests must cut across class antagonisms. It is this that underpins the petit bourgeois belief in a neutral state which is able to reconcile class conflicts. It also sustains liberal democratic politics by harming the electoral prospects of any parties that emphasise the necessity of class struggle and the revolutionary transformation of society. Moreover, given the dominance of the CMP at the economic level and the integration of the state into the circuit of finance capital, it is likely that the national interest will be defined in such a way as to favour capital.

Poulantzas also suggests that, within the context of individual citizenship and a nation-state, free elections and parliamentary government are particularly favourable to the political domination of capital. For, not only does parliament provide a forum for different interests to hammer out a common policy in conditions where failure to do so will immobilise effective government in the interests of capital, it also permits modifications in the balance of power without serious threat to the stability of the state apparatuses. The imperatives of electoral competition also require that the power bloc articulate and aggregate the interests of the dominated classes as well as its own interests. It is here, indeed, that the articulation of popular-democratic struggle with class struggle is particularly significant. And, if we accept the force of Gamble's arguments concerning the articulation of the politics of support with the politics of powe it follows that a party that is able to project a programme that is realistic on behalf of capital and popular with the electorate will become the natural governing party and so contribute both to the legitimacy and effectiveness of the capitalist state. In turn, since surplus-labour is appropriated through the the economic mechanism of the market rather than through extra-economic compulsion, it is possible for capital to offer political concessions (such as welfare state benefits) without threatening the continued accumulation of capital. There are determinate limits to this latter policy, of course, signified in the developing fiscal crisis of the state and its repercussions on legitimacy. But, in normal conditions, it will prove effective. Thus, whereas the so-called 'exceptional' forms of the capitalist state, such as military dictatorship and fascism, *appear* strong because they are dictatorial or totalitarian in form, they are actually brittle and cannot respond very effectively to the struggles, contradictions, and crises inherent in capitalist social formations. In contrast, since universal suffrage, competing parties, the separation of powers, and parliamentary government ensure a degree of flexibility, the power bloc in a democracy is able to maintain social cohesion and thereby ensure the social conditions necessary to capital accumulation. In short, for Poulantzas, the importance of the bourgeois democratic republic consists not only in the effects of the system of represen-tation on working class politics but also in the opportunities it gives to the different fractions of the dominant class to bargain, compromise, and adjust their interests in a way that realises the long-term interests of capital.

This analysis can be taken further through a more detailed consider-ation of the flexibility permitted by democratic forms of representation to working class struggle as well as to the power bloc. For it is arguable that working class struggle is itself a mechanism of capital accumulation insofar as it forces capital to secure the reproduction of wage-labour as well as other conditions necessary to the self-expansion of value. With-out such struggle, competition between capitals might prevent adequate provision for reproduction. This is apparent from Marx's analysis of factory legislation. Now, if factory legislation was essential to secure the long-term survival of labour power, the struggle for its introduction was not confined to parliament. In addition to parliamentary pressure within the bourgeois parties, there was pressure from organised public opinion and working class movements such as trade unions and Chartism. However, although working-class struggle was instrumental in securing the interests of capital in general, it was necessarily confined to extra-parliamentary and potentially dangerous channels. The problems posed by Chartism are relevant here. Thus, if working class struggles are to be effective moments in the reproduction of capital, it is essential that they be institutionalised. This can be secured through the recog-nition (and regulation) of trade unions and the extension of the fran-chise to workers. In this way, provided the separation of industrial and

political struggles is maintained and the working class movement is
attached to political parties subject to the 'dull compulsion of
bourgeois-political relations' (Holloway and Picciotto, 1976, p. 22), the
democratic republic can function in the interests of capital in general
precisely because it offers opportunities for working class reformism. In
short, not only do 'normal' forms of capitalist state provide opportunities for the continual adjustment of interests within the power bloc,
they also provide continual opportunities for subordinate classes to
struggle on behalf of their own interests in a way that favours the continued domination of capital. This is particularly significant where a
'natural governing party' emerges that is able to articulate the reformist
and popular-democratic demands of the subordinate classes with the
interests of the dominant class. For, to the extent that this occurs, the
most important condition for the effective functioning of parliamentary
democracy will have been secured (see below).

    The discussion so far has focused on the effects on the system of
representation in the democratic republic. But there is another side to
the state. This is state intervention. For, although a system of self-
government would entail a fusion between representation and intervention, it is an essential characteristic of the liberal democratic state (and,
indeed, other forms of capitalist state) that representation is separate
from administration. This is not to deny that the class struggle is
reproduced within the administrative apparatuses of the state itself but
simply to assert that capitalist democracy is characterised by a formal
separation of representative and administrative institutions and the
presupposition of official neutrality in contrast to the partisanship of
the elected representatives in charge of the state. This has been noted
forcibly by Max Weber in his analyses of bureaucracy. For, if we ignore
his twin tendencies to treat bureaucracy as a technically efficient,
neutral instrument and bureaucrats as an originating collective subject
interested in the usurpation of political power, Weber provides an
incisive account of the nature and effects of bureaucracy. He argues
that the most significant feature of the modern state is bureaucratic
domination and that the most significant check to the domination of
bureaucrats is the consolidation of a strong parliament based on universal suffrage. A system of plebiscitary democracy (sic) would provide the
means to eliminate usurpation and abuse and to control the bureaucracy
in the interests of the nation as a whole. It does no disservice to Weber
to point out that he equated the German national interest with that of
the national bourgeoisie. It is, in any case, more important to note the
effects of bureaucratic domination on political class struggle.

The fundamental importance of bureaucracy in this respect is the separation of the masses from the means of administration — the separation of bureaucrats themselves from possession of such means being secondary. This applies as much to the means of economic intervention and welfare administration as it does to the means of coercion and repression. The growth of bureaucracy in general and the growing concentration and centralisation of state power in particular therefore reinforce the political subordination of the people as a whole. For it separates them from the exercise of state power and leads to their individuation and isolation as clients or consumers of the administration and its services. This is reinforced by the monopoly of official secrets and state control over information. Moreover, to the extent that parliamentary control is weak, the bureaucracy tends to represent the interests of big capital — since it is big capital that is best organised to influence and to negotiate with the bureaucrats (Weber, 1968, pp 283-4). This effect is, of course, strengthened by the development of tripartite forms of intervention. Here the representation of monopoly capital is institutionalised at the expense of small and medium capital and the trade union movement is confined to an economic-corporate role (see concluding section). Moreover, in both the liberal democratic and the interventionist states, popular control over government is further limited by the proliferation of administrative apparatuses. For this fragments the targets of political struggle and transforms the people into a series of clientele groups in competition with each other for resources. The separation of powers produces the same effect on a more general level — particularly where the juridical and repressive apparatuses are not subject to popular control through formal mechanisms of representation (cf. Bunyan, 1976, p. 298; Hirst, 1976, p. 119; Wright, 1974-5, passim). It is in this context that the growth of claimants' unions, groups such as DIG, and so on, are significant because they represent a collective response of a popular-democratic kind to the process of bureaucratic domination. But even these remain at the level of economistic struggles and compete with each other for resources.

Finally, we may note that several writers have argued that the bourgeois democratic republic is conducive to the rule of capital because it permits an extensive system of corruption or indirect influence over the government. In *State and Revolution*, for example, Lenin cites direct and indirect bribery of officials and politicians by capitalists as well as the general alliance between the government and the stock exchange (1963, p. 295). Others point to the embourgeoisement of working class representatives as a form of political corruption and betrayal of those

they represent (e.g. Kline, 1974, p.8). To the extent that these phenomena occur, however, they can hardly be said to be unique to democratic regimes. The fundamental problem remains to determine the
specificity of the bourgeois democratic republic and its effects on
political class struggle. This can be understood better if we also consider
the disadvantages of democracy for capital accumulation.

The Contradictions of Capitalist Democracy

The preceding discussion suggests that the mechanism of democratic
representation through parliaments combined with bureaucratic
administration is optimal for capital accumulation. But several qualifications are necessary. For, contrary to the implications of the theory of
political fetishism, bourgeois democratic republics are not automatic
guarantors of consent and stability. This should be apparent from the
formal character of democratic institutions. These do not exist in a
political vacuum but receive substance from the conjuncture of which
they form part. This implies that the adequacy of the bourgeois democratic republic is contingent on the overall political, economic and
ideological situation. It is therefore imperative to determine the conditions under which democracy is (or is not) adequate to securing the
rule of capital.

    There is a growing body of bourgeois opinion opposed to the present
democratic system in Britain. This is evident in the work of journalists
such as Peter Jay, politicians such as Lord Hailsham and academics such
as Sam Finer. The principal arguments are directed against the effects
of the adversary system of parliamentary electoral politics on the
management of the economy and against the opportunities the present
system offers to socialist and popular-democratic movements inimical
to the continued domination of capital. In turn the principal solutions
offered fall broadly into two groups. First, claims to reform the electoral
system to ensure greater 'representativeness', i.e. to ditch the chances of
radical, popular-democratic or socialist governments in favour of centre-
right governments and, in the short run, calls for coalition government,
governments of national unity, etc; and, secondly, proposals to limit
the powers of parliament and the elected political executive through a
Bill of Rights, the return to *laissez-faire* , or the institution of quasi-non-
governmental organisations that would assume certain powers of the
state and exercise them without parliamentary or popular influence.
In addition there is a more general movement towards increased
repression through the courts and the reorganisation of repressive state
apparatuses such as the police and armed forces.

The flavour of these arguments can be appreciated from the
following typical cases. Jay argues that full employment, free collective
bargaining, stable prices and democracy are irreconcilable in the long-
term and, indeed, predicts the collapse of democracy in Britain by 1980
unless the government introduces tough deflationary measures (1974).
More recently he has advocated the establishment of a Currency Commission whose function would be to control the rate of increase in the
money supply so that, taking one year with another, it does not exceed
the rate of increase in output by more than 2 per cent. This new institution would be accountable to parliament but independent in its overall
activities (1976). Another liberal monetarist, Sam Brittan, suggests a more
comprehensive series of reforms to include proportional representation,
fixed-term parliaments, a Bill of Rights, currency stabilisation, control of
union monopoly power, and industrial reorganisation (1975, pp. 110-16).
Their arguments are extended in the volume edited by Finer. In his introduction to *Electoral Reform and Adversary Politics,* Sam Finer asserts
that the system of adversary politics is incompatible with the requirements of sound economic management because (a) it encourages economic intervention in the interests of electoral success rather than capital
accumulation, (b) it gives power to the extremists in the governing party
as a condition of its political unity and cohesion and thus of its ability
to continue in office, (c) this means that the centre of gravity in each
party is different from that in the electorate as a whole — thereby exag-
gerating oscillations in policy as parties alternate in office, and (d) it encourages governments to avoid confronting crises and critical issues if
the appropriate solution is electorally unpopular. Finer therefore recom-
mends electoral reform coupled with increased parliamentary control
over government. Similar views were presented in the Report of the
Hansard Society Commission on Electoral Reform (1976, pp. 21-3 and
passim). Lord Hailsham, in last year's Dimbleby Lecture, expressed
more concern that the powers of the British parliament are absolute and
unlimited so that the government is virtually an 'elective dictatorship'.
His solution is a written constitution incorporating a Bill of Rights and
restricting the power of parliament to amend or suspend that constitution (1976). The concern in Hailsham's case is not so much with the
effects of the adversary system as such but with the opportunities it
offers to political forces of which he disapproves to gain control of parliament. For, in the context of an alleged 'elective dictatorship', this
enables radical parties to introduce legislation that threatens the rule of
law and/or the rule of capital.

These criticisms and proposed solutions represent a response to an
economic and political crisis in Britain. But the principal aspect of this

crisis is economic rather than political and the solutions are to be implemented by parliamentary means rather than an exceptional form of
state. Elsewhere, of course, parliaments themselves have been dissolved.
Examination of the conditions leading to the successful institution of
'exceptional' capitalist states helps to establish the conditions under
which the bourgeois democratic republic is an adequate political shell
for capital. Perhaps the most important point to note immediately is
that it is not economic crisis as such that threatens the stability of
parliamentary government. For it is precisely through the mechanism of
crisis that capital reproduces and accumulates. It is a measure of the
strength of the bourgeoisie how well it takes advantage of economic
crises to restructure capital and restore the conditions for continued
capital accumulation. This depends in turn on the extent to which the
bourgeoisie is politically and ideologically dominant as well as economically dominant.

In the context of parliamentary democracy two aspects of bourgeois domination are especially important. These are the attachment
of the working class and other subordinate classes to parliamentary
forms of representation and the articulation of working class and
popular-democratic demands into political programmes and ideologies
conducive to the ideological domination of a power bloc organised
under the hegemony of the bourgeoisie or one of its fractions. In the
absence of these conditions we find a 'representational crisis' and a
crisis of hegemony.

A *representational crisis* has been defined by Poulantzas as a 'split
between the political parties and the classes and class fractions they
represented' (1974, p. 102). It is characterised by the development of
extra-parliamentary forms of organisation and political action and the
transformation of parties into parliamentary coteries. In the rise of
fascism and Nazism, for example, we find the proliferation of
'corporate-economic' organisations that directly confront the executive
as well as paramilitary organisations that engage in open violence and
political intimidation. The origins of such crises clearly vary from case
to case. But their content is typically a crisis of hegemony (cf. Gramsci,
1971, p. 210). This is reflected in the questioning of the dominant
ideology and the detachment of popular-democratic movements from
subordination to the dominant forms of ideological discourse and
practice. For, as Laclau has argued in a paper on 'Fascism and Ideology',
a fundamental condition of ideological hegemony is the ability to
integrate popular-democratic values and demands into an ideology and
programme that secures the representation of bourgeois interests (1977).

Much the same point is made by Gamble in relation to the articulation of the 'politics of support' and the 'politics of power' (see above). Thus, in the rise of both fascism and Nazism, we find that the petit bourgeoisie detaches itself from the dominant ideology in a general ideological crisis and regroups around the Fascist and Nazi parties which articulate an ideology and programme that *appeals* more directly to petit bourgeois sentiments (although it does not necessarily realise their interests in its policies once in power). Likewise, in the case of military dictatorships in Latin America, a major factor leading to *coups d'état* has proved to be an organic crisis of the ruling class and the failure of the bourgeoisie to consolidate its own hegemony in parliamentary regimes (cf. Nun, 1967, pp 77-109, and Murphy, 1976, passim). In the case of both fascist and military regimes, the crisis of representation is ended through the simple expedient of dissolving political parties and resorting to repression. But this does not solve the problem of representation as such and it is necessary to develop new forms of representation that do not threaten the rule of capital. This problem is particularly clear in military regimes in relation to the return to 'civilian' rule (cf. Huntington, 1968, pp. 241-63). It appears in different guise in fascist regimes — particularly in relation to the role of economic-corporate groups such as the Italian corporations and the German Labour Front and middle class guilds. In the case of fascist parties, it is important to reject the mythology of totalitarian rule and examine the forms assumed by class and popular-democratic struggles within the party itself. For, regardless of the form of regime in capitalist states, some mechanism of representation is necessary to ensure the flexibility and cohesion of the social formation in the face of crises.

We are now in a position to define the conditions under which democracy is the best possible political shell for capital. These are dependent on the political conjuncture within which democratic institutions are situated and not on the innate qualities or effects of such institutions. They are tied to the class practices of the various classes in the social formation and their articulation to popular-democratic and other political and ideological practices. In short, the bourgeois democratic republic is the best possible political shell for capital to the extent that the bourgeoisie is politically and ideologically dominant. This view is not, of course, original. It has also been expressed quite explicitly by José Nun in an essay on the middle-class military coup. He writes that

the validity of the classical Marxist proposition according to which representative democracy is the form of government which most closely corresponds to the interests of the bourgeoisie depends on the previous consolidation by the latter of its hegemonic supremacy, its development of a metaphysical justification of its leading role, and its demonstration of its efficacy as a ruling class. (Nun, 1968, p.99)

However, where the bourgeoisie is not politically dominant in political struggle (i.e. at the level of political forces rather than political institutions) and ideologically dominant in ideological struggle (i.e. in terms of the articulation of ideologies rather than the system of ideological apparatuses), the democratic republic poses serious threats to the rule of capital in relation to the appropriation and exercise of state power. Whether or not capital can consolidate its rule through the institution of an exceptional form of state or the working class can institute a socialist republic is then contingent on the balance of forces in the particular conjuncture then obtaining.

Corporatism and the Democratic Republic

So far we have tended to identify the bourgeois democratic republic with the parliamentary democratic republic. This is also implied in the traditional distinction drawn by Marxists between 'normal' and 'exceptional' forms of the capitalist state. However, if the preceding argument is correct, any form of capitalist state in which there are institutionalised mechanisms for popular control of government *and* the bourgeoisie is politically and ideologically dominant could be defined as 'normal'; whereas 'exceptional' states would be those where the continued rule of capital is secured through force and the suppression of popular representation. One should also note the existence of 'crises' in which democratic institutions occur in the absence of bourgeois hegemony. In such situations it is the balance of social forces that determines how the crisis will be resolved, if at all, and thus whether normality is restored, an exceptional form of state consolidated, or a revolutionary form of rule is established. And, in this connection, one should not exclude the possibility of alternative forms of 'normal' bourgeois rule. Accordingly, in this section, I shall consider the nature of 'corporatism'.

For, given the development of the interventionist state in place of the liberal state in capitalist societies, are there corresponding changes emerging in the system of representation? If parliamentarism is adequate to state intervention through general legislation under the rule of law and through macro-intervention using fiscal and monetary techniques, is it still appropriate to a period of administrative discretion on an *ad hoc* basis in which the state intervenes directly in the labour process, the reorganisation of capital, and the operation of the market? If the adversary system involved in parliamentary politics is inimical to capital accumulation, would a system of permanent representation of affected interests reduce or eliminate harmful oscillations in state policy? If parliamentary representation on the basis of residence no longer adequately reflects the problems of economic management in a worldwide capitalist system, would a system of functional representation be more suited to securing the conditions for accumulation on a world scale? If parliamentarism encourages irresponsible opposition (sic), would an alternative system that demands greater responsibility be more adequate? In short, is corporatism replacing parliamentarism as the most appropriate form of democratic representation in late capitalist societies?

The answer to this question must be formulated carefully. Firstly, it should be noted that we are treating corporatism only as a form of representation and not as a new mode of production different from capitalism and communism. Secondly, although corporatism has been associated with fascist regimes (although never strongly institutionalised or effective), we are treating corporatism in the context of 'democratic' representation rather than 'exceptional', repressive regimes. Thirdly, despite a deep-seated tendency to glorify parliamentary democracy (especially in the land of the Mother of Parliaments), we are asking only whether corporatism is replacing parliamentarism as the most adequate form of democratic representation in capitalist social formations. The issue of whether democracy can be anything more than formal (whether in parliamentary or corporatist guise) is a separate one. Finally, although it is phrased in terms of democratic representation, we are also leaving open the issue of whether non-democratic forms of rule may be still more appropriate to the complex conditions of existence of late capitalism.

This said, the following case can be made for the adequacy of corporatism to the needs of late capitalism. Corporatism is a system of representation in which capital and wage-labour are entitled to participate in the formulation and implementation of state intervention in the economy and in other matters relevant to capital accumulation. Such participation is conditional on the 'corporations' concerned accepting the legitimacy of the overall system within which they operate, i.e. confining themselves to an 'economic-corporate' role. This means that such participation involves accepting the imperatives of capital accumulation and subordinating all policies to those imperatives. At the same time corporatism does provide a mechanism for the representation of specific interests at an economic-corporate level and their consideration in the formulation of a general programme of state intervention. The effect of these two factors should be to encourage the development of a consistent, workable economic strategy. This process is reinforced to the extent that 'corporations' acquire greater control over their members. For, not only is late capitalism associated with the growing tendency of the rate of profit to fall and the need to mobilise its counter tendencies, it also shifts the balance of short-term economic strike power in favour of labour (owing to the socialisation of production, technological changes, the capital-intensity of production, etc.) and thus increases the need to control labour-power. Thus, insofar as participation in a corporatist system depends on accepting an economic-corporate role and the renunciation of economic strike power in favour of political representation, corporatism should weaken working-class organisation at the point of production through the transfer of bargaining from shop stewards and rank-and-file movements to national trade union leaders and from the firm or industry to the national political arena. In short, to the extent that it acquires rights of corporate political representation, organised labour also foregoes the use of industrial action. Likewise, while small and medium capital may gain some measure of political influence in a corporatist regime, they still remain subject to the constraints of the law of value in their competition with other capitals. Conversely, to the extent that corporatist forms of representation and intervention prove adequate to realising the various conditions of capital accumulation in late capitalism, it is monopoly capital in general that will be their principal beneficiary. For these conditions include the continued concentration and centralisation of capital and the consolidation of the circuit of finance capital at the expense of specific fractions or subordinate circuits. This asymmetry in the position of organised labour, small and medium capital, and monopoly capital in corporatism is masked by the fact that the interests of 'capital in general' are by no means identical to the interests of any particular capital and thus involve sacrifice as well as benefit. The restructuring of capital consequent upon economic crises and state intervention will typically involve the devalorisation or elimination of some capitals as well as increased opportunities for accumulation by others. It is therefore in the interests of individual unions and individual capitals alike to engage in bargaining over the incidence of gains and losses within the framework of securing the conditions necessary to capital accumulation. And, given this framework, a system of permanent bargaining and representation that can reflect the changing balance of forces in the course of capital accumulation is desirable.

So far our discussion of the case for the adequacy of corporatism (arguments against will be considered below) has ignored the so-called 'third party' in the tripartite system, namely, the executive apparatus itself. This includes the bureaucracy and the elected government. Within the framework of corporatism, the role of the bureaucracy is to provide administrative support and to secure the representation of the national interest (the interest of capital in general) on a permanent basis. The role of the elected government is to secure the legitimation of the resulting intervention and pilot any necessary legislation through parliament. In both cases, of course, the performance of these roles is over-determined by other factors. Thus, while the bureaucracy has a certain responsibility for ensuring the co-ordination and cohesion of policies (a responsibility reflected in the centralisation of decision-making and the development of new agencies of co-ordination), it is also riven by struggles between different interests concerning the most appropriate economic strategy. And, although the elected executive has a certain legitimating role, it is also confronted with constraints rooted in the problems of party management and the demands of electioneering. These constraints are complicated by the extension of government responsibilities and political struggles beyond the 'economic-corporate' and the need to articulate different types of demand into a coherent political programme.

It is in these latter respects that corporatism in isolation would prove inadequate to the problems of representation in the capitalist state. For, in the absence of an elected government to control the activities of the corporations, the legitimacy of the system would be questioned and the flexibility introduced through electoral politics would be lost. Moreover, even if greater democracy were introduced into the 'corporations' themselves through organisational reforms and increased membership participation, it would still be necessary to combine parliamentary and corporate forms of representation. Given the strength of the parliamentary tradition in Britain, the most that can be expected is the displacement of the dominant position within the hierarchy of state apparatuses of representation from parliament to tripartite institutions. Parliament would retain a subordinate role within this hierarchy. Moreover, as corporatism is a system of representation appropriate to economic intervention (as it is based on function within the economy rather than other interests), it is inappropriate as a total system of representation. In particular corporatism remains inadequate

to the representation of popular-democratic struggle over the reorganisation of the relations of political and ideological domination. The
development of nationalist parties in the Celtic fringes, the emergence
of race as a major political issue in Britain, and the struggle over civil
liberties, for example, are issues that would be difficult to resolve
through corporatist forms of representation. It is in the articulation of
these issues with the imperatives of capital accumulation that the role of
political parties and parliaments would continue to be significant.
Indeed, in this sense, a measure of electoral reform to secure more
adequate representation of minorities coupled with the development of
stronger corporatist institutions might be appropriate. For, whereas the
electoral reforms might encourage the fragmentation of political party
representation and thus create the conditions for permanent rule by the
centre (rather than oscillation between right and left), the institution of
corporate representation might provide the means to secure the consent
of both capital and wage-labour to measures of industrial reorganisation
and regeneration in Britain.

The short answer to the question posed above is that corporatist
institutions are *displacing* parliamentary institutions as the dominant
state apparatus in Britain and that these constitute a *contradictory
unity*. Both corporatist and parliamentary representation are necessary
to the reproduction of capital in the present situation. The relations
between these two bases of representation constitute the focus of class
and popular-democratic struggles; and there are interrelated struggles
taking place within each form of representation and over their transformation and reorganisation. These struggles pose problems of cohesion and unity for the capitalist state that are best resolved through
the dominance of social democratic parties. Let us elaborate these
arguments.

Corporatism is necessary to capital accumulation because it is a
mechanism of representation appropriate to the interventionist state in
the post-Keynesian period of the mixed economy and welfare state.
For, once intervention goes beyond monetary and fiscal contra-cyclical
measures coupled with full employment and welfare benefits, it is
necessary to secure the active and continuous involvement of labour as
well as capital (the former having been much longer involved) in economic intervention. Parliamentarism is necessary to provide a forum for
popular-democratic struggles beyond the ambit of economic intervention and to secure the legitimacy and popular accountability of state
intervention. But corporatism is associated with the centralisation and
concentration of state power and with the consolidation of the domina-

tion of monopoly capital. Parliamentary government, on the other hand, is associated with local representation and favours small and medium capital as well as regionalised or localised minority interests. Thus monopoly capital has stronger interests in promoting corporatism, small and medium capital have stronger interests in promoting parliamentarism. Likewise, if there is much scope for the democratisation of the 'corporations', there is also a strong interest on the part of popular-democratic movements with concerns outside the relations of production to defend parliamentarism against the encroachments of corporatism. But one should also note here that corporatist forms of representation are emerging at local and regional level; this is linked with the centralisation of local power and its insulation from popular control through the reorganisation of the local state.

Social democracy is the appropriate form of ruling party (natural governing party) in this context because it fuses several important political roles in one organisation. It has close links with the labour movement whose participation in corporatist institutions is essential to their success; it has a relatively strong electoral base even now in the working class and lower middle class; it manages to integrate popular-democratic and economic corporate claims into a programme that favours state intervention in the interests of accumulation. In short it provides adequate means to fuse parliamentary and corporatist forms of representation and adapt them to changing conditions. And, at the same time, its political and ideological presence is such as to weaken independent forms of working class action that will unify economic and political struggles against the rule of capital. This is not to argue that such struggles are therefore impossible — only that they are difficult to organise and make effective. Even independent economic struggles can make the efficient operation of corporate institutions impossible as we have seen in the grass roots trade union opposition to continued incomes restraint in a period of inflation and historically high postwar unemployment. But, despite the effective veto imposed by organised labour on the proposed Phase 3 policy, it has not yet proved possible to raise the struggle beyond a defensive and economic-corporate level to that of a unified mass political movement. And in this connection the role of social democracy within the labour movement cannot be ignored even if it is sometimes overrated.

Thus, far from corporatism being 'fascism with a human face' (to quote Pahl and Winkler[3]), it is more appropriately described as 'the highest form of social democracy'. Corporatism in Britain is not assimilable to fascism as it lacks a mass base in the petit bourgeoisie and does not arise in response to an acute national crisis requiring the liquidation of normal forms of representation. Indeed, to the extent that there is opposition to corporatism in Britain it comes from the traditional petit bourgeoisie and upper ranks of the new middle class as much as from revolutionary socialist movements. Likewise, in contrast to the destruction of independent trade unions and the creation of organic, mixed corporations or compulsory, state-controlled labour corporations that occurred under Fascism and Nazism, corporatism in Britain involves strengthening the existing labour and employer organisations as vehicles of political representation. And it has developed out of the post-war Keynesian political economy rather than from the pre-war depression. If the Keynesian mixed economy and welfare state represent the first stage of social democracy as a form of state, corporatism represents its second and highest stage. Moreover, whereas Keynesian policies simply involve the accommodation of organised labour and its representation through parliament, corporatism involves the integration of organised labour into the administration so that it becomes a quasi-non-governmental organisational complex. Likewise, whereas the success of the Keynesian political economy depended on material concessions to labour and thus on continued capital accumulation, corporatism requires the hegemonisation of organised labour and its mobilisation in support of accumulation. The current economic crisis and continued strength of rank-and-file movements make this requirement hard to accomplish. It is in this context that one should interpret the renewed emphasis on monetarist policies within the political executive. For, in addition to their role in the restructuring of capital, control over the money supply and state expenditure is also being used to create the conditions required for reorganising the labour movement itself and integrating it more effectively into the state apparatus. Thus the monetarist policies of the Labour government should be seen as complementary to its corporatist strategy rather than as a viable long-term alternative.

Although social democratic regimes need not be characterised by the rule of social democratic parties, particularly during their first, Keynesian stage, such parties tend to be(come) the natural governing party and provide the model for any party that aspires to that status. For one of the fundamental preconditions of filling that position in a party system is that the party's programme is both electorally popular and realistic. It is the inability to formulate an appropriate programme in this respect that has undermined the traditional political hegemony of the Conservative Party. For, while it was able to maintain this position in the era of Keynesianism, it has encountered increasing difficulties with the development of corporate forms of representation and intervention. Thus, despite its apparent electoral popularity and possible success in the next general election, its programme is dominated by liberal, monetarist and petit bourgeois interests and values. It is unable to reach a satisfactory accommodation with monopoly capital as well as with organised labour. And, if returned to office in its current programme, it would almost certainly repeat the history of the Heath government in 1970-74.

Lest it be felt that the preceding account is unduly determinist in its forecasts about the 'coming corporatism' and unduly voluntarist in its emphasis on political programmes, two qualifications should be stated. Our analysis of corporatism has concentrated on its adequacy as a form of state power in late capitalist metropolitan societies and has assumed that there are no serious crises of representation or hegemony. Thus it is most relevant to societies in north-west Europe, north America, Australasia and Japan. But, even in this limited context, there is still no generic form of capitalist state. The precise forms of state and the changing nature of state power are determined by an immense range of factors and variables. The preceding analysis attempts to specify some of the most important of these determinations. Nor does this analysis seek to suggest that the success of capital accumulation depends on the ability of specific political parties to prepare and implement a certain type of political programme. The fundamental barrier to capital accumulation is not incompetent government but capital itself. This means that the exercise of state power is necessarily limited and constrained by the contradictions inherent in capital accumulation and thus by the forms of class struggle which accumulation entails. It is these that finally determine the adequacy of forms of state and shape state power.

Conclusions)

This paper has been characterised by a movement from the abstract to the indeterminate. For, while it started out with some abstract definitions of capitalism, the state and democracy, it has ended with speculations about the future development of the British state. It is hoped that this movement has thrown some light on the relations between capitalism and democracy. To that end, it seems appropriate to conclude with a *précis* of the main arguments.

1. Democracy refers to the legal entitlement of 'citizens' to participate

in the determination of policies to be executed by the state in its capacity as sovereign legal subject; and, in addition, to the legal conditions of existence of such participation.

2. Parliamentary democracy refers to a democratic system in which 'citizens' participate through the exercise of voting rights in relation to a parliament from which the political executive is then recruited from representatives who command a majority in parliament; for the purposes of this paper the term has been extended to include presidential systems of the American kind where citizens elect the political executive separately from the legislature. The key factor in both cases is the participation of citizens as individual electors.

3. Corporate democracy refers to a democratic system in which 'citizens' participate through the exercise of voting rights in relation to a corporation which represents their interests in the formulation of state policy; the unit of representation is the corporation rather than the constituency organised on a territorial basis and citizens participate in their capacity as economic agents.

4. Contemporary capitalist democracies are characterised in varying degrees by the contradictory unity of parliamentary and corporatist forms of democratic representation; there has been a gradual displacement of representation from parliamentary to corporatist forms in parallel with the growing centralisation and concentration of state power.

5. The fundamental precondition of continued bourgeois domination in democracy is the political and ideological domination of the bourgeoisie: in the case of parliamentarism, this takes the form of the attachment of the electorate to political parties that are committed to the rules of parliamentary politics and whose programmes are articulated with the dominant ideology; in the case of corporatism, this takes the form of an 'economic-corporate' orientation, i.e. representation of the interests of the corporation or those of a class (represented by several corporations) on a purely economic level — this involves the problem of state power 'but only in terms of winning politico-juridical equality with the ruling groups: the right is claimed to participate in legislation and administration, even to reform these — but within the existing fundamental structures' (Gramsci, 1971, p. 181). In both cases the domination of the bourgeoisie is secured through acceptance of the existing fundamental structures and the articulation of popular-democratic claims with pursuit of the interests of the bourgeoisie in capital accumulation on an expanded scale.

6. In the absence of bourgeois political and ideological domination,

democratic forms of representation cannot secure the conditions required for expanded reproduction. This is indicated by representational and ideological crises: the detachment of the masses from bourgeois political parties (social democratic parties included) and from trade unions or 'corporations' and/or the collapse of ideological hegemony on the part of bourgeois intellectuals, ideological apparatuses, and so on. Crises do not engender their own solutions. How they are resolved, if at all, depends on the balance of forces in each case. The manner of their resolution determines the forms of appearance of subsequent crises.

7. Liberal democratic representation based on parliamentarism is appropriate only to certain stages of capital accumulation at certain points in the total world economy; thereafter corporate democratic representation may prove more adequate to securing the conditions necessary for capital accumulation. And, in other social formations outside the metropolitan centres, 'exceptional' forms of state may be typical. The transition from parliamentarism to corporatism is not automatic but has specific origins in the continuing play of political forces in each society. The current situation in Britain is characterised by the contradictory unity of parliamentarism and corporatism under the dominance of the former mediated through the Cabinet.

8. Since democracy is a form of representation that acquires substance only in specific conjunctures, it is necessary for socialist and popular-democratic forces to struggle for the realisation of those legal and social conditions necessary to popular control of government. But this is a struggle that must be articulated with the struggle against inequality in the sphere of production if the end-result is not to be a more perfect bourgeois democratic shell for capital accumulation. In this context corporatism represents a critical area of political struggle. For the exact nature and significance of corporatism and the extent of its democratisation are still open issues.

Notes

1. The law of value is the most important principle regulating the process of commodity production and is itself an effect of commodity production. It determines the pattern of investment, i.e. the circuit of capital between different branches of production, according to the deviation of their specific rate of profit from the average rate of profit. The average rate of profit is the effect of competitition between capitals which ensures that each capital appropriates a part of the total surplus-value proportionate to the fraction of total social capital which it represents. The need for each capital to make at least the average rate of profit to ensure its long-term reproduction ensures the subordination of the labour-process to the valor-

isation (or surplus-value production) process within each enterprise.

2.   The tendency of the rate of profit to fall is a fundamental tendency of capital accumulation analysed in terms of value theory. It refers to the effect of an increasing organic composition of capital on the value rate of profit considered in isolation from changes in the rate of exploitation, the value of wage-labour and the technical composition of capital. For, given these restricted conditions and the assumption that labour-power is the sole source of added value, it necessarily follows that the average rate of profit expressed in value terms must fall as the value of constant capital (means of production, raw materials, etc.) increases in relation to the value of variable capital (labour-power). It is important to realise, however, that this effect is tendential. It is possible to avoid or offset this tendency insofar as the rate of exploitation can be increased, the value of labour-power decreased, etc. It is the mobilisation of these counter-tendencies that constitutes the crux of state intervention in late capitalism.

3.   Winkler has since regretted using the phrase 'fascism with a human face' and it does not appear in his later writings (personal communication to the author).

References

Aims of Industry, *The Case for Capitalism* (London, 1967).

Altvater, E., 'Notes on Some Problems of State Interventionism', *Kapitalistate*, 1 and 2 (1973).

Anderson, P., 'The Antinomies of Antonio Gramsci', *New Left Review*, 100, 1977.

Balibar, E., 'Sur La Dialectique Historique', *La Pensee*, 1973.

Brittan, S., 'A "Manifesto" for 1975', in *Crisis '75?* (Institute of Economic Affairs London, 1975).

Bunyan, T., *The Political Police in Britain* (Freemann, London, 1976).

Centre for Policy Studies, *Why Britain Needs a Social Market Economy* (Centre for Policy Studies, London, 1975).

Engels, F., *The Role of Force in History* (International Publishers, New York, 1968).

Fernbach, D., 'Introduction', in K. Marx, *Surveys from Exile* (Harmondsworth, Penguin, 1973).

Finer, S.E., *Electoral Reform and Adversary Politics* (Antony Wigram, London, 1976.

Foster, J., 'The State and Ruling Class During the General Strike', *Marxism Today*, May 1976.

Friedman, M., *Capitalism and Freedom* (University of Chicago Press, London, 1962).

Gamble, A. *The Conservative Nation* (Routledge and Kegan Paul, London, 1974).

Gramsci, A., *Prison Notebooks* (Lawrence and Wishart, London, 1971).

Hailsham, Lord, 'Elective Dictatorship', Richard Dimbleby Lecture, 14 October 1976.

Hansard Society, *The Report of the Hansard Society Commission on Electoral Reform* (Hansard Society, London, 1976)

Hindess, B., 'Classes, Politics, and the State in Contemporary Marxist Theory', this volume.

Hirst, P.Q., *Social Evolution and Sociological Categories* (Allen and Unwin, London, 1976).

—— 'Althusser and the Theory of Ideology', *Economy and Society*, 5 (1976).

Holloway, J. and S. Picciotto, 'Capital, the State, and European Integration' (mimeo, 1976).

——'Capital, Crisis and the State', *Capital and Class* 2 (1977).

Huntington, S.P., *Political Order in Changing Societies* (Yale University Press, London, 1968)

Kline, R., *Can Socialism Come Through Parliament?* (I.S. Pamphlet, London, 1973)

Laclau, E., *Ideology and Politics in Marxist Theory* (New Left Books, London, 1977)

Lenin, V.I., *The Agrarian Programme of Social Democracy* (1907)
    The State and Revolution (1917) in *Selected Works*, Vol. 1. (Moscow, 1963)

Luxemburg, R., *Rosa Luxemburg Speaks* (Pathfinder Press, New York, 1970).

McPherson, C.B., *Democratic Theory* (Oxford University Press, London, 1973)

Mandel, E., *Late Capitalism* (New Left Books, London, 1975)

Marx, K., 'A Review of Guizot's Book, Why Has the English Revolution Been Successful?' in Marx and Engels, F., *On Britain* (Moscow 1962).

—— *The Eighteenth Brumaire of Louis Bonaparte.*

—— and F. Engels, *Selected Correspondence* (Lawrence & Wishart, London, 1975).

Moore, B., Jr., *The Social Origins of Dictatorship and Democracy* (Allen Lane, London, 1968).

Moore, S.W., *The Critique of Capitalist Democracy* (Paine-Whitman, New York, 1957).

Murphy, S.D. 'Argentina: The Impact of Monopoly Capitalism on the Political Structure' (MA Dissertation, University of Essex, 1976).

Nun, J., 'The Middle Class Military Coup', in C. Veliz (ed.), *The Politics of Conformity in Latin America* (Oxford University Press, London, 1967).

Offe, C. and V. Ronge, 'Theses on the Theory of the State', *New German Critique*, 6 (Fall 1975).

Ollman, B., *Alienation* (Cambridge University Press, London, 1971).

Pahl, R. and J. Winkler, 'The Coming Corporatism', *New Society*, 10 October 1974.

Pashukanis, E.B., 'The Marxist Theory of Law and the State', in H. Babb (ed.), *Soviet Legal Philosophy* (Harvard University Press, Cambridge, Mass., 1968 reprint).

Poulantzas, N., *Political Power and Social Classes* (New Left Books, London, 1972).

—— *The Crisis of the Dictatorships* (New Left Books, London, 1976).

Weber, M., *Economy and Society* (Bedminster Press, New York, 1968).

Wengraf, T., 'Notes on Marx and Engels Theories of the Development of the Capitalist State' (mimeo, 1970).

Wright, E.O., 'To Control or to Smash Bureaucracy: Weber and Lenin on Politics, the State, and Bureaucracy', *Berkeley Journal of Sociology*, xix (1974-5).

2 THEORIES OF NATIONALISM

Sami Zubaida

Nationalist ideologies and movements, taken from various parts of the world from the beginning of the nineteenth century till the present day, represent a formidable array of diversity both in terms of the nature of the ideologies and the sociologies of movements. It will be argued in this paper that the ideologies however diverse, can be seen to share a common ideological field but that the writing of a unitary sociology of 'nationalism' presents insurmountable theoretical problems, however many sub-types of nationalism such a sociology might postulate.

Nationalist ideologies share the common problem of the definition and the conception of 'a nation'. 'Nations' or nation-designates in the modern world almost invariably have a problem of boundary definition in time and space, the problems of the unit of nationality. Why is it, for instance, India and not say the Punjab which constitutes a national unit? Or is the 'right' national unit the whole of the Arab world, as claimed by the pan-Arab nationalists or the particular Arab country, say Syria, as claimed by the regional nationalists. This problem of the designation of the national unit and its boundaries arises in terms of a number of dimensions: territory, ethnicity, culture and language.

On territory, the problem arises in relation to discrepancies between the boundaries of the actual habitat of the national unit and those of its claimed habitat, usually worked out on the basis of the supposed historical habitat of the presumed ancestors of the unit. It also arises when two or more postulated national entities inhabit a shared but disputed territory (e.g. the Kurds in relation to Arabs, Persians and Turks). The Turks, for instance, acquired their present territory, 'Turkey', as waves of conquering Turkoman tribesmen (often fighting between themselves) culminating in the victory and overall suzerainty of the Osmanli dynasty. The territory of the Turkomans still extends far into Iran, the Soviet Union and China. The Greeks still call Istanbul 'Polis', and some of their nationalists would still claim it as a Greek city. Here is the historical raw material for the great flourishes of territorial aspirations and historical constructions to justify them which were engaged in by the contending factions of Turkish and Greek nationalists.

The problems of language and ethnicity/culture in relation to nationality are too well known to need elaboration here. Diverse ethnicities and language groups co-exist within the boundaries of nation states, sometimes harmoniously and sometimes uneasily with demands for autonomy or independence for ethnic/regional/language groups. Even when nationality is defined exclusively in terms of one culture or ethnicity, there is still the problem of drawing the boundaries of a culture or an 'ethnic group'. For culture and ethnicity, too, are shifting and overlapping identities, easily sub-divided into smaller or enclosed within wider specifications.

In the foregoing paragraphs, references to national units are qualified with 'supposed', 'presumed' or 'designated'. This does not reflect a wish by the author to question the validity of designation of national units. It is just to indicate that from the point of view of the sociologist or any social theorist, there cannot be any systematic way of designating a 'nation'. Any attempt to do so can only be a purely arbitrary definition. Through a combination of historical conjunctures, national boundaries have been and continue to be drawn. The old colonial entity of India is divided into three main nation states, one division on the basis of religion, the other on ethnicity. But each one of them, especially the largest, India, still contains a multiplicity of ethnic, linguistic and religious entities. Why does India constitute a 'nation' while the old Ottoman Empire, arguably with greater homogeneity than modern India, did not? The answer is clearly in terms of historical conjunctures. There is no systematic way in which any social theoretical discourse can justify the state of nationhood in the one case and deny it in the other. If social scientific discourse was to try systematically to define what a nation *should be* rather than justify criteria of nationhood for existing nations, it would have to have equal recourse to arbitrary definitional criteria.

For ideologies of nationalism on the other hand, the designation of the national entity is the central concern. This is the common ideological enterprise of nationalism. In drawing the boundaries of the national entity, it has to justify its inhabited or claimed territory, to highlight ethnic/cultural/linguistic community of the nation, and if no such homogeneity is evident, to explain why heterogeneity is no obstacle to unity, or how some other overriding factor, such as religion, is of more fundamental importance in generating national unity. It has to draw distinctions from and maintain boundaries against other nationalities in terms of ethnicity/territory/culture, etc.

In short, nationalist ideologies have to specify a national 'essence', which underlies and guarantees the unity and temporal continuity of the nation. For the 'nation' to have a plausible existence and boundaries in the present, its 'essence' has to be demonstrated in its history. The writing of a history in which the national unit is shown to have temporal depth of ancestry, of common experience, consciousness and destiny is an essential part of nationalist enterprise. Extensive examples of this practice are given by Elie Kedourie (Introduction, 1970), who has emphasised the importance of historical constructions in nationalist ideologies. But Kedourie seems to think that 'history', like 'nation' and 'nationalism', is an import from Europe.[1] While the influence of European political thought throughout the modern world cannot be denied, the adaptation, and sometimes transformation of such thought in relation to particular ideological/political contexts should not be overlooked. Witness the diverse adaptations of Marxism! 'History' as a temporal legitimation and as a repository of examples of 'national' manifestations is clearly an important aid in the solution of the ideo- logical problem of the national entity. Even if it was not available in European thought, it could easily have been invented.

But in the realm of history there is a problem which nationalist ideologies seldom face. It is that the concept of 'nation' and the forms of political units now called 'nation states' are both historically recent. In many of the historical states and empires, the state was constituted by court/bureaucracy/military organisations which ruled over diverse populations. The state personnel may or may not have been ethnically homogeneous, and may or may not have shared this common ethnicity with one or other section of the subject population. What is more, shared ethnicity between ruler and ruled did not always constitute grounds for favour or mutual support. The state and military apparatus of the Ottoman Empire was by no means exclusively Turkish (not always exclusively Muslim for that matter). It included the various Caucasian ethnicities. Albanians (as in the case of Muhammad Ali and his dynasty in Egypt and Syria) and Kurds. What is more Turkish speaking populations were not systematically favoured over others (although clearly, knowledge of the Turkish tongue was important for high ranking bureaucratic and military service). In short, rulers and ruled, soldier and peasant, landlord and peasant were not divided along ethnic or 'national' lines (as some nationalist writers have sought to establish in modern times). Within this form of political organisation, the units of identity and solidarity were by no means always those of ethnicity, common language, culture, etc., but varied and overlapped in different times and places (as they still do). Village, lineage, sect, ethnic minority, military fealty were among the many criteria of community and solidarity. The contending sides in conflicts and wars were not

always homogeneous in terms of any of the modern criteria of nationality; one Kurdish group would be included in the forces of one Arab or
Turkish lord fighting another Kurdish group in the service of another
lord. But modern nationalist ideologies in seeking to establish the
historical continuity and ancestry of the designated national entiy,
evade these obstacles, or explain them away as manifestations of past
national oppressions and dispersions. The 'national essence' lies dor-
mant through these historical episodes only to be activated and
expressed in other moments of glory. The present seeks to transform
the future into a repeat of these glorious precedents.

We have tried in the foregoing paragraphs to draw a sketch of what
has been advanced as the common elements of nationalist doctrines. For
the purposes of the present paper there is no need to elaborate this
sketch or illustrate it with examples and references. The main task of
the paper is to consider critically some sociological and Marxist
writings on nationalism. The purpose of this sketch is to define and
delineate nationalism as an ideology and to show that some of its
central themes in working the concept of 'nation' cannot be justified in
a systematic socoiological/social scientific discourse. There is no reason,
of course, why nationalists should conform to what can be justified in
sociological or other systematic social scientific discourse. The problem
is that sometimes, the themes and assumptions of nationalist doctrines,
and the questions these give rise to are shared by historians and sociologists writing on nationalism, like the assumption of the possibility of
defining and delineating a nation. We shall consider an example of this
practice in what follows.

It should be noted that to argue that all nationalisms share the
problem of national definition is not to imply any further uniformities
or agreement in nationalist ideologies. A cursory glance at modern
nationalist ideologies will show that they vary from the democratic
constitutionalist to the crypto-Fascist; from the populist to the elitist/
statist, from the 'narodnik'/romantic to the sternly modernist, from free
enterprise advocates (admittedly rare) to socialist.

Sociological Theories of Nationalism

'Nationalism' has featured prominetly in a number of contexts of
sociological work, but perhaps chiefly in the field of the 'sociology of
development'. Nationalist ideologies and movements are clearly
important features in the politics of 'under-developed', 'developing',
'third world', 'modernising' countries (whichever happens to be the
appropriate designation in the particular conceptual or terminological

practice used). In studies of particular situations, clearly account has to
be taken of the 'nationalist' parties and movements which are involved
as political forces. But apart from these particular studies, some general
theories of 'nationalism' in various countries and contexts have been
advanced. A theory of 'nationalism' would have to postulate 'nationalism' as a unitary general phenomenon, perhaps with particular
variants and sub-types. It has been argued here that the various
'nationalisms' can be seen to be operating within a common ideological
field, from a common problem to do with establishing a national
'essence'. A sociological theory of nationalism, however, cannot stop at
the ideological homogeneity of nationalisms, but would also entail a
sociological homogeneity, i.e. that there are common social structures
and processes which underlie the ideological/political phenomena. This
is precisely what theories of nationalism do assume and set out to
demonstrate. And it is this assumption or thesis which is being
challenged in this paper.

It is also our contention here that in spite of the widely varying
theoretical positions of the authors and in spite of the varying conceptual and terminological usages, there is still a basic account common to
many theories of nationalism. To illustrate this basic structure, let us
take Ernest Gellner's formulation, perhaps the clearest and also the
most influential. Gellner (1964) is clearly aware of the 'arbitrariness of
the nationalist idea' (p. 174) which has been emphasised in the earlier
section of this paper. But he clearly thinks that wherever nationalism
arises in its 'modern' form (as distinct from disguised traditional or
dynastic units), it does so in a common socio-historical context and is
carried by common socio-political forces, namely the intelligentsia and
the proletariat (p. 168). The common socio-historical context is that of
modernisation and industrialisation:

> . . . as the wave of industrialisation and modernisation moves out-
> wards, it disrupts the previous political units. These are generally
> either small and intimate (village, tribe, feudal unit), or large but
> loose and ill-centralised (traditional empires, which of course
> contain the small intimate groupings as parts). It disrupts them both
> directly and by undermining the faiths and practices which sus-
> tained them. This by itself would already lead to the formation of
> political units. But, more specifically, the wave creates acute
> cleavages of interest between sets of people hit by it at differing
> times — in other words the more and the less advanced. This cleavage
> and hostility can express itself with particular sharpness if the more

and the less advanced populations can easily distinguish each other, by genetic or rigid cultural traits. (Gellner, 1964, p. 171)

Here are the main common elements of the story: a world historical process (modernisation/industrialisation, and for other authors 'development' and/or spread of capitalism); traditional societies which this process hits like a wave, but at a differential pace leading to differences in the degree of 'advance' or 'backwardness', which results in the breakdown of traditional ties of village, kin, religious fraternity, etc.; particular social groups (intelligentsia and proletariat for Gellner, but could be intelligentsia and someone else, like peasants or 'traditional elites' for other authors) taking up the double fight: against tradition (not always explicit – the 'narodnik' syndrome) and against external enemies, whether colonialists, imperialists or querulous neighbours, these are the nationalists. The process ends up with the establishment of national states (jobs for the intelligentsia, but what about the workers?). There follows the struggle to generate national loyalty among the population at large in place of the traditional loyalties. This, for Gellner, is generated by universal literacy in particular, and in general an educational system which produces citizens with qualifications which they need to obtain jobs only obtainable within the orbit of that particular educational system, i.e. the national state (what, a nation of intelligentsia?!)

It is a common feature in modern sociological and other social scientific work to postulate a world historical process sweeping across the various parts of the world with transformative or revolutionary consequences. The terms in which such a process is conceptualised vary widely across the lines of theoretical and ideological divisions in these fields. To American-style 'functionalists', it is 'modernisation', the transition from 'tradition' to 'modernity' (Rostow, Lerner, Eisenstadt, etc.). To radicals and some neo-Marxists, the world-historical context is capitalist-led colonialism/imperialism and its aftermath of 'third-world' quest for independence and then 'development'. 'Industrialisation' can be a component of the process in either of these terms. As we have seen in the case of Gellner's formulation, this process, however conceived hits the varying societies at an uneven pace leading to differential degrees of 'advance'. It is in the transformations resulting from this process (however designated) that conflicts are generated within these societies between 'tradition' and 'modernity' or between various classes and modes of economic organisation. The vanguards in these struggles are particular social groups variously designated. These almost always include the 'intelligentsia' and the other classes or groups, depending on the nature of the theories and contexts of their elaboration: the 'middle classes' are favourites, but it could be urban groups, 'modernising elites', proletariats or even peasants. It is these vanguard classes who are the carriers of nationalism.

It is our contention here that the construction of 'nationalism' as a unitary object of sociological investigation is not a viable enterprise. This will be argued in terms of the problems of postulating a world-historical process, however designated and the heterogeneity of the phenomena grouped under its general ambit. It will also be argued that the sociological designation and explanations of nationalist movements are in terms of processes and groups which are not comparable or generalisable between the various social contexts.

Let us first consider the historical process designated as 'modernisation'. The limitations of this concept and the theories which use it are by now well known. The 'blanket' notions of 'tradition' and 'modernity', the teleology of development to an idealised image of Western democracy and the generality of 'transition' without clearly specifiable beginning or end. What should, perhaps, be emphasised here is that some of the elements usually included under 'modernisation', like education and mass communication, are not as homogeneous across societal boundaries as the unitary designation would indicate. Educational systems, even when modelled on common colonial examples, still have widely differing forms, locations and consequences in relation to the different societies. Gellner's educational system producing general literacy and educating citizens for jobs in the national occupational structure, is for most countries in the world today a fiction (sometimes an official fiction). Levels of literacy and relationships between education and occupational structures are highly variable. So, I suspect would be the ideological consequences of education. It would seem that 'modernisation' is a general and vacuous concept and the elements included under its ambit very heterogeneous.

'Industrialisation' has a much clearer reference. It can be defined with apparent precision in terms of the increase of the proportion of the work force engaged in industry as against the other sectors. However, when considered in particular socio-economic contexts, this precision becomes illusory. 'Industry' covers a range of forms of production, in scale from small workshops employing a few workers to nuclear power stations. Not only in scale, but also in terms of the social location and consequences of industrial development in particular economies there is great variation: capital intensivity, the stratification or segmentation of labour markets (urban/rural, ethnic/social, exclusive labour monopolies, etc.), the source, nature and duration of capital investment, the relationship of industry to the agricultural and extractive sectors, all these are dimensions of variation (seldom linear) which in cominbations, result in very different socio-economic configuration. The apparent precision and unity of 'industrialisation' do not stand up to examination: the concept refers to a range of specificities which have not been successfully formed into sub-types of a unitary designation.

There are no systematically specifiable relationships between the introduction of scientific and technological applications to the instruments of production and distribution and transformations of social relations. To assume otherwise is to fall into the easiest traps of technologism. The context, the nature and the consequences of technological applications have to be examined in the particular case.

'Capitalism' and its expansion on a world scale, in so far as the concept is used in the Marxist sense, can perhaps have the strongest claim to precision in that it is specified in a body of systematic theory. But while 'capitalism' can be thus specified and its world wide spread and expansion established, its consequences for particular countries must be examined in the specificity of the particular conjuncture. The incorporation of various countries and regions within the sphere of world capitalism does not necessarily lead to the prevalence of capitalist relations of production, not even necessarily the dominance of the commodity form. Particular economic sectors in a country can be producing for a capitalist world market and at the same time be organised on the basis of non-capitalist relations of production. Many parts of Eastern Europe, for instance, were producing grain with serf labour, but for a capitalist market. Particular sectors of an economy can be organised along capitalist lines and integrated in one way or another into a world capitalist market, but at the same time co-exist with other sectors which are not capitalist. The capitalist and non-capitalist sectors are related together in various forms of articulation which have to be determined in every particular case. Harold Wolpe's (1972) studies of South Africa, for instance, provide a good example of such an articulation between a dominant capitalist economy and a subordinated non-capitalist African village economy. Ernesto Laclau (1971), in criticising Gunder Frank's general conception of an all-enveloping capitalist market, also points out the necessity of specifying the connections between capitalism and pre-capitalist economic sectors in Latin America.

'Capitalism' and its world expansion do not entail uniform sets of development in the various countries and regions into which it had

penetrated. Like 'modernisation' and 'industrialisation', it does not
specify a universally homogeneous context for the development of
social and political forces which carry 'nationalism'. If we were to
substitute for 'capitalist expansion', 'colonial' or 'imperial' expansion,
or the 'impact of the West', we would just be substituting less precise
terms and would end up with similar problems in trying to establish
the homogeneity of the process or its effects. Except of course that the
colonial/imperial designation carries with it the implication of foreign
domination, and the 'impact of the West' designation implies diffusion
of the 'nationalist idea' from the West. It is clearly the case that the
national idea and the model of the nation-state, originting in Europe,
did play some part in the formulation of nationalist ideologies. This
probably contributed to the uniformity of some of the theories in the
common ideological problematic outlined earlier in the paper. But this
ideological diffusion cannot by itself account for its adoption, nor for
the variety of contexts in which it was adopted, nor the variety of
social and political forces which 'carried' the ideologies. Colonial
domination, too, is clearly involved in setting up the context of
nationalist movements in many countries, but equally clearly it cannot
by itself be advanced as an explanation of these movements. While
some form of oppositional response to colonial domination is probable
(though not necessary), there is nothing to justify the supposition that
this response must be nationalist (unless all responses to foreign domination are defined as 'nationalist'). Indeed, many of the early responses
to colonial expansion were clearly not 'nationalist', for example,
religious revivalist movements like the Mahdiyya in the Sudan, and the
various tribal, lineage, or age-set based revolts in parts of Africa.[2] There
is one respect, however, in which colonial rule contributed to the
emergence of nationalism and nation-states. When, for a variety of
reasons, colonial powers were preparing for the eventuality of independence, the nation-state model is clearly the only one that was available
for post-independence statehood. What possible alternative model could
an independence movement or the colonial power concerned have for
the independent state? Even when the government at independence
consisted of traditional chieftains/aristocrats/religious lineages and
where the existence of a national entity, however defined, within
arbitrarily drawn boundaries, was no more than an official fiction (for
example Nigeria or the Gulf States), even then the nation-state organisational model and rhetoric had to prevail. In these respects, the end of
colonialism (not always through local opposition) had to bring with it
'nationhood'. Equally, opposition to colonialism in the modern world

could only be in nationalist terms. This is a point which one would have thought is obvious, but does not seem to be sufficiently realised or emphasised. And it need not necessarily have the implication of questioning the *bona fide* or sincerity of nationalist movement in general — many of them were clearly nationalist regardless of this conceptual/political constraint.

So far, we have attempted to dismantle one of the main props common to theories of nationalism — a variously designated world historical process and its impact on countries and regions. Let us now turn to the 'internal' sociology of nationalism. We shall examine one central element of such a sociology: the social composition of nationalist movements.

A cursory examination of the range of nationalist movements would reveal that the social composition of these movements is highly variable in different countries, and in different phases of the nationalist movements within the one country. This has been recognised by some writers in the field (Smith, 1971). Others, like Gellner have emphasised the role of particular classes like the proletariat and the intelligentsia (the intelligentsia are always a favourite). Yet other approaches, like that of Peter Worsley (1964), have outlined phases of nationalist movements, with different strata assuming prominence during each phase. Anthony Smith (1971), in a work based on a wide ranging study of nationalisms sums up the variety of social compositions of nationalist movements in the following passage:

> The social composition of nationalist movements is highly variegated — both over time, and space. It is impossible to tie nationalism to the aspirations of any social group *in a consistent manner* — be it workers or petty bourgeoisie or bureaucrats or officers. (Smith, p. 132, original emphasis)

Smith also notes the variation in the phasing of nationalist movements in relation to industrialisation:

> . . . nationalist movements may overlap with the onset of industrialisation, or precede it altogether. In the latter case, the main adherents of the movement are various sections of the middle class and/or the peasantry, or sections of it, or even tribesmen. (pp. 123-4)

This breath-taking array in the variety of phasing and of social strata, does not appear to deter Smith from persevering with a general sociology of nationalism. Instead, he advances a typology of cases in terms of the phasing of movements in relation to industrialisation and the correlation between the phases and particular social strata. The only group which remains central and ubiquitous is the 'intelligentsia' on whom, ultimately, his thesis is based:

> . . . if we are interested in the explanation of the *recurrent origins* of nationalism, rather than its subsequent diffusion to other groups, we shall do well to stick to the crisis of the intelligentsia. (p. 134, original emphasis)

My argument with this position is not only that the social composition of nationalist movements is highly variable, but also that the designation of groups and classes by the same labels irrespective of the nature of the social formation in which they occur is a questionable practice. 'Middle classes', 'petty bourgeoisie', 'peasants', 'proletariat', 'intelligentsia', do these labels designate the same things in Argentina and Nigeria, Lebanon and Senegal, Iran and Papua? Clearly not. The ubiquitous 'middle class' alone logically requires an 'upper' and a 'lower' only specifiable in particular contexts. 'Proletariat' and 'petty bourgeoisie', with strong Marxist connotations (but not exclusively used by Marxists), these concepts, arguably, have a precise meaning in Marxism in relation to capitalism, the latter to only particular European contexts of capitalism. In so far as one is using 'proletariat' in this precise sense, it is possible, perhaps to refer to it in other capitalist or partly-capitalist social formations, but even then without assuming communality or identity of anything about this class across political/economic boundaries other than its relation to the 'means of production'. But with the other labels, what theoretical specification is there which can justify their use in this universalist fashion? Precisely none. 'Class' and various class designations are used extensively in the social sciences, but with little precision (other than the occasional *ad hoc* definition). In this way they only have vague, common sense meanings. It is in the various strands of Marxist theory that 'class' and class designations are theoretically specified. In this theoretical context, these concepts have precise meaning but only in relation to other theoretically specific categories, those of 'relations of production'. 'Classes' are constituted in terms of those relations of production. In this respect, class categories like 'peasant' do not have a universal significance, but are only precisely definable in terms of a particular mode of production. So a feudal 'peasant' and a 'peasant' in a social formation with capitalist social

relations, are not in these theoretical terms equivalent.[3] 'Peasants' are
only universally equivalent in terms of vague and *ad hoc* definitions
such as 'family household' or common cultural elements. 'Petty bourgeoisie' and 'bureaucracy' have even lesser claim to precision in
universal designation. With the 'intelligentsia' the arbitrariness of
definitions reaches new heights:

> For our purpose, the concept refers not just to the educational quali-
> fications and occupational structure of individuals, but more vitally
> to a set of problems and concerns which are known to agitate the
> members of this socially heterogeneous category. A certain circul-
> arity seems to be unavoidable; there is no firm line of demarcation in
> this instance. (Smith, 1971, p.135)

After this remarkable declaration, Smith perseveres with making the
intelligentsia the corner-stone of his sociology of nationalism! In effect
the 'intelligentsia' are the 'modern educated' and therefore the bearers
of all modern political ideologies including nationalism. Almost by
definition, all nationalism must start with them. This, of course, does
not carry with it any further sociological implications regarding the
social composition of the 'modern educated', their social organisation(s)
and institutions (if any) or their location within a social totality.

There cannot be a sociology of nationalism in general if the cross-
societal designation of groups and classes involved in the social processes in question cannot be shown to be equivalent.

Without being able to establish the operation of the variously designated world historical process, and without establishing the homogeneity, or at least basic unity of the effects of such a process on various
social formations and without demonstrating the comparability of social
classes/groups/strata invoked as actors in the socio-political formations
and processes of nationalism, we must conclude that sociologies of
nationalism have failed. Such sociologies denuded from their historical
props then appear as interpretations of sentiments, or more precisely
'resentment' of people (especially the educated, who are in a position
to know about foreigners) against domination or superiority of
wealthier foreigners or more successful neighbours. The various
attempts at analysis and typology in terms of various dimensions
judged relevant and classes judged important are no more than a
spurious show of precision when these dimensions and classes are themselves *ad hoc* concepts.

Marxism on Nationalism

There is no one Marxist theory or position on nation, nationality or nationalism. Many different and contradictory positions are represented in Marxism. The 'proletarian internationalism' of Rosa Luxemburg stands in strong contrast to variants of the 'national essence' theory advanced by Renner, Bauer and most notably, Stalin. Basically, Marxist arguments on nationalism have varied in relation to political contexts and positions.

For Marx and Engels, nationalism and nationality were not objects for a systematic theory, but a matter of *ad hoc* pronouncements and arguments relating to particular political problems. Abstracting from these various contexts, we can outline their main themes as follows:[4]

1. The formation of nation-states was essentially a bourgeois development aided by absolutist centralisation. National statehood is the favoured political form for capitalism.
2. That ultimately, the triumph of socialism will weaken national boundaries in favour of proletarian internationalism. There is some ambiguity in Marx as to whether the capitalist world market was already proceeding in the direction of internationalism by breaking up national boundaries or whether bourgeois mystifications thrived on chauvinism and national domination. It can be argued that both these tendencies can co-exist.
3. In the current political struggles, there is the problem of adopting positions and strategies with regard to nationalist movements or movements for national self-determination. Marx and Engels were not always consistent on these issues. In Marx's writings on Poland and Ireland, the overall tone is one of support for the oppressed nations in their struggle for national self-determination. National antagonisms can only be overcome by ending national domination and oppression, which, in any case, only strengthens the dominance of the bourgeoisie of the oppressor nations. These themes were later to be echoed more consistently by Lenin. For Marx, and certainly Engels were not consistent in this respect. As Lowy (1976) points out, one reason for their support of the Polish struggle was that it was against Tsarist imperialism, which they considered to be the most reactionary force in Europe. Consequently the national movements favourable to Russia (Czecks, Slovaks and Southern Slavs) were not accorded the same support. To justify his rejection of these national movements, Engels revived the Hegelian concept of 'non-historic nations', highly questionable in the context of Marxism. Of course, it presupposes the possibility of defining a true,

'historic' nation, which as we have seen can only be an arbitrary definition, the type of definition that Stalin was to introduce at a later stage.[5]

Lenin (1970) in his essays on the 'National Question', retained the explanation of nation-statehood in terms of bourgeois centralisation, and expected Eastern Europe and Asia to follow in the steps of Western Europe in the formation of nation-states associated with bourgeois-democratic revolutions. He also retained the expectation that proletarian rule will lead the way to internationalism. But the main focus of Lenin's work on the 'National Question' was on the current political struggles and the involvement of the socialist movements. His views on this matter were simple and clear: support all democratic movements for national self-determination; oppose nationalist movements aimed at national aggrandisement and subjugation of others. He was highly critical of Rosa Luxemburg and her colleagues who opposed the Polish struggle for self-determination on the grounds of internationalism and the benefits of alliance between Russian and Polish workers. Socialism cannot be achieved, he argued, in the context of imperialism and national oppression. To take a position against national self-determination is, in effect, to strengthen the reactionary forces of the dominant nations and therefore to strengthen the oppression of its (the dominant nation's) own proletariat. 'True' internationalism can only follow from the exercise of the democratic right to self-determination, and not from the dominance of particular nations over others. It should be noted that this position of Lenin's did not make it necessary for him to define a 'nation' and thus end up in the theoretical problems of arbitrary definitions. For Lenin, 'a nation' is defined by the democratically expressed 'common sympathies' of particular populations. That is, it is not a problem for Marxist theory to define 'a nation' — it is not a theoretical problem, but one of political practice. Similarly, a general theory of 'nationalism' does not feature in Lenin's work.

The first half of the twentieth century witnessed the most virulent reactionary movements with some form of nationalism as its central ingredient. Marxists and other leftist political forces were among the foremost adversaries and victims of these movements in government. In this context, nationalism was tinged with the threat of Nazism and Fascism and the internationalist tendencies of the left were enhanced and accentuated.

These sentiments regarding nationalism were to be subjected to a radical challenge in the context of the 'Third World' national struggles.

For most sectors of the international left were actively or sympathetically involved in the de-colonisation of independence movements, to
which, of course, various forms of nationalism were central. The fight
against 'neo-imperialism', 'economic imperialism' and international
capital would also seem to indicate 'national' solutions. The work of
Gunder Frank, Arrighi Emanuel and Samir Amin on the international
system of capitalist exploitation, through 'satellisation' or 'unequal
exchange', could have the implications that the struggle against the
forces of international capital has to be waged through national consolidation, and it has been thus read in many quarters (there is also an
internationalist reading in terms of 'Third World' solidarity, but even
that is ultimately a solidarity between various nationalisms united by
the fact of common oppression).

This context of sympathy for 'Third World' struggles on the left,
placed in the wider context of socialist internationalism, has led to a
characteristic ambivalence towards nationalism, one which has
questioned 'orthodox' Marxist positions and which has sought to confront nationalism with theoretical formulations and political analyses
more appropriate to the problems of the modern world and its recent
history. Let us consider an important recent statement of such a position, which seeks to formulate a Marxist theory of nationalism.

Tom Nairn (1975) starts with the contention that 'the theory of
nationalism represents Marxism's great historical failure' (p. 3). The
failure is both theoretical, in that Marxism has not generated an
adequate theory of nationalism and practical, in terms of political
positions and strategies in relation to nationalism. Nairn clearly perceives nationalism as a unitary phenomenon of which a Marxist theory
is possible: 'the task of a theory of nationalism . . . must be to see the
phenomenon as a whole . . . ' (p. 5). He then proceeds to advance such a
theory. Quite correctly, Nairn points out the difficulties in holding
nationalism and nation states to be a necessary stage in the internal
development of every society located between a 'traditional' past and
an internationalist future. It is not in the internal development of
particular social formations that the phenomen of nationalism has to be
located, but in the context of 'world history as a whole', ' . . . "nationalism" in its most general sense is determined by certain features of the
world political economy, in the era between the French and Industrial
Revolutions and the present day' (p. 6). The social origins of the
phenomenon 'do not reside . . . in the process of that (world political)
economy's development as such — not simply as an inevitable concomitant of industrialisation and urbanization. They are associated with

more specific features of that process . . . the *uneven development* of history since the eighteenth century' (p. 8, original emphasis). The fantasy of 'even' development lay in the various philosophies of progress (including, it seems, Marxism) which saw humanity going forth in a 'single forward march that would induct backward lands into its course'. But the reality of the matter was the domination of the 'core' industrialist-capitalist world over the 'periphery' of backward lands who were left behind and trampled underfoot in the competitive struggle. The 'peripheric elites', faced with huge expectations racing ahead of material progress 'had no option but to try and satisfy such demands by taking things into their own hands. "Taking things into one's own hands" denotes a good deal of the substance of nationalism' (p. 11). These elites had to mobilise their societies for a 'historical short-cut'. 'This meant the conscious formation of a militant, inter-class community rendered strongly (if mythically) aware of its own separate identify vis-a-vis the outside forces of domination' (p. 11). They had to do this in terms of language, ethnicity, race, etc. The picture thus far would suggest a theory of nationalism similar to Gellner's, quite favourable to nationalism as inevitable reaction to imperialist domination. But to Nairn this is not yet a complete picture. The process is dialectical. It is not only the impact of the core on the periphery which results in the nationalist reaction (the periphery included Germany and Italy in response to Britain and France as the core), but this reaction, especially when it is successful (Germany and Japan) reacts upon the core countries and brings them within the norm of nationalism (previously, it seems, they had developed nation-states, but not nationalisms – these were always developed on the periphery, but reacted upon and incorporated the core).[6] Within this picture, Nairn continues, we cannot divide nationalisms into good and bad – the 'good' of national liberation of Indo-China and Mozambique and the bad of dominant nations' chauvinism, of Fascism and American nationalism. All nationalisms contain the seeds of both, progress and liberation as well as atavistic regression and reaction:

> This ambiguity merely expresses the general historical *raison d'être* of the phenomenon which is the fact that it is through nationalism that societies try to propel themselves forward to certain kinds of goal (industrialisation, prosperity, equality with other peoples, etc.) by a *certain sort of regression* – by looking inwards, drawing more deeply upon their indigenous resources, resurrecting past folk-heroes and myths about themselves and so on. (Nairn, 1975, p.18, original

emphasis)

The irrational forces called upon in this societal *rite de passage* are parallel to the traumatic-repressed in the individual id! Hence the threat of atavistic eruption.

The imperialist spread of capitalism has insured that the 'dominant contradiction' was not that of the class struggle, as supposed in Marxism, but that of nationality. When capitalism destroyed the fabric of 'the ancient social formations surrounding it, these always tended to fall apart along the fault lines contained inside them. It is a matter of elementary truth that these lines of fissure were nearly always ones of nationality . . . ' (p. 22).

It would seem, however, that the forces of history have now reached a stage when Marxism itself can be transformed away from its Western Enlightenment origins into an authentic world-theory. Presumably, this is the status accorded to it when it can deal with the enigma of nationalism:

> It is in dealing with the enigma of nationalism that 'Marxism' is inexorably thrust against the limits of its own western origins, its Euro-centric nature. Yet it could never overcome these limits in theory, until they had been thoroughly undermined and broken down in practice − that is, by the events of the past decades, where the reflorescence of western capitalism was accompanied by its persistent defeat and degeneration on the periphery. It is in this sense perhaps much less fanciful than may appear at first glance to suggest that the years that witnessed the end of the great struggle in Indo-China, the oil-producers' revolt and the revolution in Portugal will appear in retrospect to mark a turning-point in the history of ideas, as well as in American foreign policy or international relations. (p.27)

It would seem that the forces of history do not only generate the great social transformations, but perform great feats of theoretical advance.

A relatively full summary of Nairn's argument is given here because I believe it to be an important one in the current international ideological/political conjucture, important for the Left in general and Marxists in particular in that it seems to articulate a wide-spread feeling that Marxism has failed in relation to nationalism and that to remedy this failure a theory of nationalism is needed which would contain adequate analysis for the formulation of political strategies. Our contention here is that such a theory is no more viable in Marxism than it is in sociology.

The basic structure of Nairn's argument does not differ significantly from that of the general sociological explanation outlined in previous sections of this paper and does not escape from the limitations of these sociologies. It is still the world historical process of the spread of capitalism, like Gellner's 'tidal wave' hitting different social formations at an uneven pace and breaking them up along the natural 'fault lines', those of nationality. Thus the course of world history would seem to proceed in terms of the struggle between nations and nationalities. Nairn's world historical process is just as open as that of the sociologists to questions of adequate theoretical specification and demonstration of the homogeneity or regularity of its effects, tasks which he does not perform. The passing remark that his theory should be situated within the same broad current of thinking as I. Wallerstein's *The Modern World System* and P. Anderson's *Passages from Antiquity* and *Lineages of the Absolutist State*, does not help very much. It is not clear how such a situation is to be effected. In any case the 'current of thinking' must be very broad indeed to incorporate both these authors. Perhaps what they have in common and what is shared by Nairn is a general historicist teleology, which raises many problems outside the scope of the present discussion, but which have been raised and discussed by others.[7]

Nairn's 'nations', the main actors on the historical stage, set in motion by the destructive and dominating impact of capitalism/ imperialism, raise many other conceptual problems. 'Nations' seem to be historical super-subjects with attributes of agency and action: they 'mobilise', 'aspire', 'propel themselves forward', 'react' and they even have atavistic, irrational 'ids' seething with traumas which explode periodically. In this respect, Nairn is not as careful as the sociological writers in distinguishing sectors, strata, interests, etc., within his nations. Theoretically he seems to surrender to the conceptual terms of the nationalist problematic of the national 'essence'. Without essential nations, how could 'nationality' constitute the 'fault-lines' of fissure contained within the ancient social formations? (See quotation above). There must be a way of systematically determining 'a nation' for the fault-lines to be considered to be those of nationality.

Nairn's nationalisms also seem to be always successful, at least internally. Nations operate as unitary entities. 'The masses' are success-fully mobilised by nationalism which provides them 'with something real and important — something that class consciousness could never have furnished . . . ' (p. 22). Here is another aspect of Nairn's participa-tion in the nationalist myths. As we have seen, nationalist movements are highly variable in their locations within the, in turn, highly variable social formations. At least the sociologists cited above have realised that some nationalisms never get anywhere near 'the masses' (whoever they are). The nature of the relationship between nationalist parties and 'grass root' or 'mass' support cannot be assumed, but has to be shown in relation to the particular case.

Nairn also seems to assume that all liberation movements and anti-imperialist revolutions are 'nationalist'. He clearly includes 'Indo-China' in this classification and would no doubt include China. It is perhaps, arguable that there are nationalist elements in communist revolutionary movements. If that is the case, it would constitute a very strong argument for abandoning the blanket designation of 'nationalism' for all liberation movements, for clearly this label would include both the Kuomintang of Chiang alongside the People's Liberation Army. A Marxist should perhaps be interested in making elementary distinctions of this nature!

To conclude, Nairn has not succeeded, any more than the sociologists, in establishing nationalism as a unitary object of theory. Neither theoretically, nor politically, does it constitute any general unity. Perhaps the most successful Marxist work on nationalism was that of Lenin, who refused to define 'nation' or to have a 'theory' of nationalism, but affirmed the general democratic/socialist principle of support for oppressed people's struggle for self-determination and opposition to the nationalism of the oppressors (principles which, alas, were not always followed by his successors). This is not to say that Lenin's general formulations constitute an adequate 'guide' to political analyses and strategies. These would surely have to be worked out for particular political conjuctures in particular social formations whose nationalist movements constitute a political force. The general designation of 'nationalism' as a unitary object or phenomenon and the general 'theories' of it considered here would not help very much in the task of adequate analysis of particular social formations.

Notes

1.   In his well-known works on Nationalism, Elie Kedourie (1960 and 1970) is clearly antagonistic to all nationalist doctrines and philosophies, not from an internationalist outlook, but, it would appear, from some kind of nostalgia for a 'pre-nationalist' world. One of the main concerns of his 'Introduction' to *Nationalism in Asia and Africa* is to demonstrate the absurdity of nationalist pronouncements in terms of the logic (or lack of it) of their arguments and the flimsiness of their historical constructions.

The point or the value of such an enterprise is not clear. The interest of nationalist doctrines for social or political science lies precisely in that they are 'ideologies' and not histories or theoretical discourses.
2.   For examples, see M. Crowder (1971) and Terry Johnson (1972).
3.   For a theoretical elaboration of this point see J. Ennew, P.Q. Hirst and K. Tribe, 'The Peasants as an Economic Category'.
4.   See Michael Lowy (1976) for a good survey of the various Marxist positions and debates on the 'National Question'.
5.   Stalin's well-known essay, 'Marxism and the National Question' (1970) is not discussed here because it does not raise issues of any special interest to this paper, except in that it advances a definition of 'a nation' as ' . . . a historically constituted, stable community of people formed on the basis of a common language, territory, economic life, and psychological make-up manifested in a common culture'. (p. 68). We have noted the problems of attempting systematic definitions of 'nation'.
6.   In this respect, Nairn's argument seems to contain a 'dialectical' parallel to W.W. Rostow's (1963) 'Reactive Nationalism'.
7.   See P.Q. Hirst (1975).

References

Crowder, M., (ed.), *West African Resistance: The Military Response to Colonial Occupation* (1971).

Ennew, J., P.Q. Hirst and K. Tribe, 'The "Peasantry" as an Economic Category', *Journal of Peasant Studies* (1977).

Gellner, Ernest, *Thought and Change* (London, 1964).

Hirst, Paul Q., 'The Uniqueness of the West', *Economy and Society*, vol. 4, No. 4 (1975)

Johnson, Terry, 'Protest: Tradition and Change', *Economy and Society*, Vol. 1, No. 2 (1972).

Kedourie, Elie, *Nationalism* (London, 1960).

—— *Nationalism in Asia and Africa* (London, 1970).

Laclau, Ernesto, 'Feudalism and Capitalism in Latin America', *New Left Review*, 67 (1971).

Lenin, V.I., and J.V. Stalin, Selected Works on the *National Colonial Question* (Calcutta, 1970).

Löwy, Michael, 'Marxists and the National Question', *New Left Review*, 96 (1976).

Nairn, Tom, 'Marxism and the Modern Janus', *New Left Review*, 94, (1975).

Rostow, W.W., *The Stages of Economic Growth* (Cambridge, 1963).

Smith, Anthony D., *Theories of Nationalism* (London, 1971).

Wolpe, Harold, 'Capitalism and Cheap Labour Power in South Africa', *Economy and Society*, Vol. 1, No. 4 (1972).

Worsley, Peter, *The Third World* (London, 1964).

3 CLASSES AND POLITICS IN MARXIST THEORY*

Barry Hindess

1.

This paper is concerned with the essentialist character of traditional Marxist conceptualisation of classes and class struggle in relation to the structure of the social formation. By essentialism I mean a mode of analysis in which social phenomena are analysed not so much in terms of their specific conditions of existence and their consequences for other social relations and practices but rather as the more or less adequate expression of an essence. Well known examples in Marxist thought are the works of Lukacs, in which cultural phenomena are interpreted as the more or less adequate expressions of an imputed class consciousness, and economism, in which political forces are effectively reduced to manifestations of class interests determined at the level of the economy. In political analysis essentialism leads to a reduction of political forces to 'interests' determined elsewhere (basically in the economy) and consequently to a political strategy that fails to take adequate account of the specific political forces at work in the social formation in question. In Marxist theory classes have been conceived both as categories of economic agent and as, or as represented by, political institutions and forces and ideological and cultural forms. This paper examines the main types of attempts to conceptualise this unity of classes in classical Marxist thought and it shows that each of them tends to generate essentialist modes of analysis. I argue in conclusion that political practice, institutions and ideologies must be conceived not as representing the interests of classes of economic agents but rather as providing certain of the conditions of existence of definite economic class relations.

Classes and the structure of the social formation

Classical Marxism has a definite conception of the necessary structure of society. A society is conceived as a social formation, an articulated structure of three interdependent structural levels, dominated by the structure of a particular mode of production consisting of an economic, a political-legal and a cultural (or ideological) level. The levels of a mode of production are supposed to be related in such a way that while the first always plays a primary role, that of 'determination in the last instance', the others are not simply reducible to it, they are 'relatively autonomous'. The economic level itself is structured by a definite combination of relations and forces of production. In a mode of production the relations and forces are supposed to correspond. Failure to do so signals the end of one mode of production and the beginning of a period of transition. Transition from one mode to another is effected by means of the class struggle which overthrows the structure of one mode of production and installs another in its place.

This conception of the structure of the social formation generates a serious problem with regard to the conceptualisation of classes. On the one hand classes are defined primarily in economic terms, as a function of the opposing positions specified in determinate relations of production: bourgeoisie and proletariat, lord and serf, slave-owner and slave, etc. Where the relations of production do not specify opposing positions there are no classes and therefore, according to the classics, no state and no politics either. It follows that 'the *existence of classes* is only bound up with *particular historical phases in the development of production'* (Marx to Weydemeyer, 5 March 1852). On the other hand classes are conceived as social forces, as participants in a struggle which takes political and ideological forms. In this sense classes are, or are 'represented by', political forces and ideological forms. The difficulty here arises from the problems of reconciling a conception of classes as categories of economic agents *and* as political forces and ideological forms with a non-reductionist conception of the autonomy (or relative autonomy) of politics, law and culture with regard to the economy. If politics and ideology are not simply reducible to the economy then what constitutes the unity of classes in these three respects? What mechanisms ensure the articulation of political forces and ideological focus on to the classes they are supposed to represent?

To illustrate the difficulty consider two passages from one of Marx's best known political analyses, *The Eighteenth Brumaire of Louis Bonaparte*. The first concerns what Marx calls 'the republican faction of the bourgeoisie':

> *It was not a faction of the bourgeoisie held together by great common interests and marked off by specific conditions of production.* It was a clique of republican-minded bourgeois, writers, lawyers, officers and officials that owed its influence to the personal antipathies of the country against Louis Philippe, to memories of the old republic, to the republican faith of a number of enthusiasts, above all, however, to *French nationalism,* whose hatred of the

Vienna treaties and of the alliance with England it stirred up per-
petually.(Marx and Engels, *Selected Works*, p. 105, first emphasis
added)

The points to notice here are first that a political faction is manifestly
not defined by reference to economic conditions and secondly that the
factors introduced to account for the strength of the republican faction
are non-economic in character. It seems then that Marx recognises the
existence of political forces and a field of political conflict that is not
immediately reducible to the effects of economic relations. But now
consider his comments on the two Royalist factions:

what kept the two factions apart was not any so-called principles, it
was their material conditions of existence, two different kinds of
property, it was the old contrast between town and country, the
rivalry between capital and landed property. That at the same time
old memories . . . convictions, articles of faith, and principles bound
them to one or the other royal house, who is there to deny this?
Upon the different forms of property, upon the social conditions of
existence, arises an entire superstructure of distinct and peculiarly
formed sentiments, illusions, modes of thought and views of life.
(ibid., pp. 118-19)

The contradiction between the positions advanced in these passages is
clear. If political forces are not reducible to effects of the structure of
the economy then 'two different kinds of property' cannot account for
what kept the Royalist factions apart. Alternatively, if political forces
are reducible to the effects of different forms of property then Marx
has no business treating the republican faction of the bourgeoisie as a
distinct and real political force. If political forces and cultural forms are
ultimately reducible to effects of class interests defined at the level of
the economy then nothing remains of the irreducibility of politics and
culture to economic conditions. If, on the other hand, politics and
culture are irreducible then the connection between classes, conceived
as categories of economic agents, and classes, or their representations,
conceived as political forces or as cultural forms must be extremely
problematic.

The difficulty here is endemic to the Marxist theory of classes and of
class relations. The irreducibility of politics is widely acknowledged in
practice in the classics of Marxist analysis of the conditions of concrete
political practice. In *The Agrarian Programme of Social Democracy in*

the First Russian Revolution, for example, Lenin argues that the balance of class forces cannot be read off from the structure of economic relations. Elsewhere he insists on the importance of analysing the concrete political forces at work in each 'current situation'. For example, with regard to the February revolution in 1917, he wrote:

> This, and this only, is the way the situation has developed. This, and this only, is the view that should be taken by a politician who does not fear the truth, who soberly weighs the balance of social forces in the revolution, who appraises every 'current situation' not only from the point of view of all its present, current peculiarities, but also from the point of view of the deeper-lying springs, the deeper relations between the interests of the proletariat and the bourgeoisie, both in Russia and throughout the world. ('Letters from Afar', *Selected Works,* Vol. 2, p. 36)

Here Lenin refers to the 'deeper-lying springs' of the current struggles, 'the interests of the proletariat and the bourgeoisie . . . ', but he absolutely insists on the analysis of the forces at work in the 'current situation'.

It is not enough to relate these forces to the 'deeper-lying' sources, they must be confronted in their specificity. In political practice the great Marxist leaders have come to terms with the specificity of the dominant political forces and issues of the day. But they have not confronted the theoretical problems posed by the recognition that political forces cannot be simply reduced to expressions of classes and class interests. If political forces and ideological forms are conceived as mere expressions of economic relations then there is no problem — and no necessity for the concrete analysis of the current situation. But once we acknowledge the autonomy of politics and ideology (however 'relatively') then the unity of classes as economic, political-legal and ideological as cultural agencies must be problematic.

Several distinct modes of attempting to conceptualise the unity of classes in this sense may be identified in the history of Marxist theory, but these can be reduced to variants of three basic types. Two attempt to establish the unity of classes in terms of a confrontation between the objective determination of class position on the one hand and the subjective unity of a consciousness on the other: *either* the unity of a class as the intersubjective unity of individual human subjects having similar class positions *or* the unity of a class-subject acting as an economic, political-legal and cultural-ideological agent — i.e. either Weber and sociology or Lukacs. In these positions classes are conceived in terms of the objective determination of economic position on the one hand and the will and consciousness of one or more subjective agencies on the other. The relative autonomy of politics and culture then consists in the possibility that the subjects may not recognise their true class position and their objective class interests. The counterposition of 'subjective' will and consciousness to 'objective' class position ensures that the unity of a class can only be conceived as essentially problematic. If forms of consciousness cannot be reduced to the effects of 'objective' class position then the formation of the unity of a class cannot be guaranteed by the objective structure of social relations. The third type subordinates the conceptualisation of class to the classical conception of the structure of the social formation as an essential unity of three 'relatively autonomous' levels governed by the 'determination in the last instance' of the economy. The economy plays a double role, first as determining the structure of the whole and secondly as a level represented in that structure. Classes may then be conceived as effects of the structure of the whole while the primacy of the economy in their determination follows as a consequence of its double role: classes are represented in the economy and also in the other levels as an effect of the matrix role of the economy. The most systematic and rigorous elaboration of this type can be found in the work of Althusser and his associates but it is also represented in a very different tradition of Marxist thought which represents the growth of the productive forces as the motor of history.

In spite of the considerable differences between these approaches to the conceptualisation of classes they can all claim significant textual support in the writings of Marx: in *The Communist Manifesto, The Eighteenth Brumaire of Louis Bonaparte,* and the other of Marx's political analyses on the one hand and on the other hand in the Preface to *A Contribution to a Critique of Political Economy* and those parts of *Capital* where Marx presents his conception of the structure of the social formation. The following examination of these types of conception aims to establish their theoretical and political consequences and to show, in particular, how they each entail essentialist and theoretically indeterminate modes of analysis. Following the discussion of these three basic types I shall comment briefly on the recent attempt in Poulantzas to present a systematic exposition of the Marxist theory of classes and politics. Although his position appears to be close to that of Althusser in several respects Poulantzas in fact adopts a very different type of theoretical position. We shall see that he merely adds an 'Althusserian' twist to the theoretical positions underlying the sociological and Lukacsian counterposition of subject and structure.

2. Class and Class Struggle as Effects of the Structure

The idea that classes and class struggle are called into being as effects of the structure of the social formation has a long history in Marxist thought. Perhaps the most rigorous elaborations of the position are to be found in the works of Althusser and his associates who argue that the structure of the social formation is governed by a 'structural causality'. A superficially similar position but with very different theoretical effects with regard to the conceptualisation of classes has been advanced by Poulantzas. His position is discussed in Section 5 below. However the conception of classes as effects of the structure can also be found in the famous quotations frequently cited in support of the classical Marxist conception of the structure of the social formation. I have referred already to Marx's claim 'that the *existence of classes* is only bound up with *particular historical phases in the development of production'* (Marx to Weydemeyer, 5 March 1852). Or again, consider the well known passage from the Preface to *A Contribution to the Critique of Political Economy* in which Marx outlines 'the guiding principle of my studies':

> In the social production of their existence, men inevitably enter into definite relations, which are independent of their will, namely, relations of production appropriate to a given stage in the development of their material forces of production. The totality of these relations of production constitutes the economic structure of society, the real foundation, on which arises a legal and political superstructure and to which correspond definite forms of social consciousness. The mode of production of material life conditions the general process of social, political and intellectual life. It is not the consciousness of men that determines their existence, but their social existence that determines their consciousness. At a certain stage of development, the material productive forces of society come into conflict with the existing relations of production or — this merely expresses the same thing in legal terms — with the property relations within the framework of which they have operated hitherto. From forms of development of the productive forces these relations turn into their fetters. Then begins an era of social revolution. The changes in the economic foundation lead sooner or later to the transformation of the whole immense superstructure . . . (*Critique of Political Economy*, p. 21)

The precise significance of this passage is not entirely clear. Marx presents a conception of society as structured by three loosely defined parts or levels, namely, the economic foundation, a legal and political superstructure, and definite forms of social consciousness. What is not clear is how these levels are supposed to be related. The relations referred to as 'on which arises', 'to which corresponds', are not rigorously defined and they are obviously open to a variety of interpretations. Or again, the assertion that 'changes in the economic foundation lead *sooner or later*' to transformations elsewhere suggests that there may in fact be real discrepancies between the foundation and the superstructure that is supposed to arise on it.

Nevertheless the primacy accorded to the connection between the relations of production and the productive forces does suggest that it is their precise interplay which determines the level of class conflict in any society. This conception has been taken up by an influential tradition in Marxist thought which presents the development of the productive forces as the motor of history. An excellent, if somewhat dry and pedagogic, exposition is given in Stalin's *Dialectical and Historical Materialism*:

> First the productive forces of society change and develop, and then, depending on these changes and *in conformity with them*, men's relations of production, their economic relations change . . . however much the relations of production may lag behind the development of the productive forces they must, sooner or later, come into correspondence with — and actually do come into correspondence with — the level of development of the productive forces, the character of the productive forces. (p. 31)

The teleological character of that position is evident. But its consequences for the conceptualisation of classes as effects of the structure reappear in the very different position of Althusser. Althusser's concept of structural causalty involves a sophisticated reworking of the classical Marxist conception of mode of production as consisting of three levels, economic, political and ideological, with the economic level determinant 'in the last instance' and the other two being 'relatively autonomous'. Thus while the political and ideological superstructures are conceived as being determined by the economic basis they are nevertheless relatively independent of it and able to react back on it. In *Reading Capital* a mode of production is represented as a structure of three levels in which the economy plays a double role, first it appears as a level in the struc-

ture and secondly it determines the character of the three levels and the
relations that hold between them. Classes can therefore be conceived as
effects of the structure while their primary location in the economy is a
function of its 'matrix' role in determining the structure. Althusser
therefore maintains:

> To conceive of the nature of a social class it is essential to bring
> together the determinations of the economic base, of the juridico-
> political superstructure, and of the ideological superstructure. It is
> equally essential to be aware of the interplay within this combined
> determination so as to account for the way in which dominance may
> shift between the different determinations . . . (quoted in Terray,
> 1972, p. 144)

The unity of these multiple determinations is itself the result of the
'structural causality' which, in Althusser's view, governs the structure of
the social totality. Structural causality means that the structure must be
conceived:

> as a cause immanent in its effects in the Spinozist sense of the term,
> that *the whole existence of the structure consists in its effects*, in
> short that the structure, which is merely a specific combination of its
> pecular elements, is nothing outside its effects. (*Reading Capital,*
> p. 189)

The unity of a class reflects the unity of the structure of which it is an
effect. Class may be conceived both as a unity and as represented at
each of the economic, political and ideological levels precisely because,
for all their 'relative autonomy', those levels are themselves just so
many effects of the structure of the whole.

Now, if the structure is indeed a cause immanent in its effects then
the existence of the structure secures the conditions of existence of its
parts (as effects of the structure) and the existence of the parts is
nothing other than the existence of the structure itself. Althusser therefore maintains that there is nothing in the structure of a mode of production which necessitates its supersession. On the contrary, each mode
of production must be conceived as 'eternity in Spinoza's sense' (ibid.,
p. 107): the mode of production secures its own conditions of existence
and is therefore capable of eternal reproduction. In *Reading Capital* the
transition from one mode of production to another is not conceived as
the necessary effect of the ever-forward march of the productive forces

but each period of transition is conceived as involving a definite non-correspondence between the relations and the forces of production. There are two types of structure of production: in a mode of production the relations and the forces correspond and in a structure of transition they fail to correspond. In the first case there is a reciprocal limitation between the relations and the forces such that each serves to reproduce the other. However;

> In the form of non-correspondence, which is that of the phases of transition such as manufacture, the relationship between the two connexions [the relations and the forces of production] no longer takes the form of a reciprocal limitation, but becomes the *transformation of the one by the effect of the other* . . . in which the capitalist nature of the relations of production . . . determines and governs the transition of the productive forces to the specifically capitalist form. (ibid, p. 304)

The essentialist and fundamentally teleological character of *Reading Capital's* doctrine of structural causality has been shown by Paul Hirst and me in Chapter 6 and the Conclusion of *Pre-Capitalist Modes of Production. Reading Capital's* conception certainly explains why a period of transition must come to an end: transition brings together in a single structure the *relations* of one mode of production and the *forces* of another and it comes to an end because the relations transform the forces – e.g. the transition from feudalism to capitalism ends in capitalism because the capitalist relations of production transform feudal forces into capitalist ones. But there is nothing in *Reading Capital's* argument and concepts to account for the possibility of transition from one mode of production to another for if mode of production is indeed an *eternity* then it cannot also be *finite*, it cannot end in transition to another mode. If a mode of production is an eternity then transition is impossible. If transition is possible then mode of production cannot be conceived as an eternity. This difficulty cannot be resolved within the framework of *Reading Capital*. In effect Althusser and Balibar, replace the manifest teleologies of the Hegelian theories of history as the ever-forward march of the productive forces by a covert and inconsistent teleology in which the conception of mode of production as stationary and repetitive is combined with a transformative conception of the structure of transition as being essentially finite.

The point to notice in the present context is the effect of the doctrine of structural causality on the conceptualisation of classes and class struggle. If the period of transition is brought to an end through the action of the relations of production in transforming the productive force, then the class struggle as such, the conflict of political forces, can have no independent effectivity. At most the class struggle merely performs the role assigned to it by the structure of production. In *Pre-Capitalist Modles of Production* Paul Hirst and I contrasted the teleological causality of *Reading Capital* and of the evolutionist conceptions in which the productive forces eventually come into conflict with relations of production to what we called the material causality of the class struggle. If transition from one mode of production to another takes place, we argued, that is not a teleological function of the mode of production itself or of Balibar's 'forms of transition'. It is a function of the material causality of the class struggle – that is, it is the outcome of definite conflict between definite political forces. Whatever the merits of our critique of structural causality it is clear that the invocation of the role of the class struggle in history merely returns us to the problem posed in the Introduction to this paper. It affirms that classes and class struggle cannot be reduced to effects of the structure but it does not offer any alternative conceptualisation of the unity of classes as economic-political-cultural agencies.

The theory of structural causality entails a manifest essentialism. For Althusser all social phenomena are effects of the structure – classes and the conflicts between them, political constitutions and practices and ideological and cultural forms are all alike effects of the one and the same essential structure. This conception provides no means of conceptualising the *differential* effectivity of specific political institutions and practices. The state, for example exists as a definite structure of institutions and apparatus which provide the means of action of state power. To confront state power and to attempt to overthrow it is always to confront specific agencies of control and coercive apparatuses and to attempt to subordinate them by means of other specific apparatuses. In the context of such an objective political calculation means to analyse the specific political forces at the disposal of both sides and the means and conditions under which they may be mobilised or prevented from mobilisation. These points may be obvious but they suffice to indicate the political impertinence of the doctrine of structural causality. To say that all political forces and institutions are equally the effects of the structure is to say absolutely nothing about the specific features and effects, the specific conditions of existence and the relative importance in relation to definite political objectives. In the world of structural causality all specificity vanishes into the overall determination of the structure itself. But what of Althusser's insistence in *For Marx* and again in *Reading Capital,* on the concrete analysis of the current situation? It is true that Althusser does insist on the analysis of specific social formations and of 'current situations' as 'conjunctures' within them. But those conjunctures cannot be theorised in terms of his conception of the structure of the social formation. Structural causality governs the structure of a self-reproducing eternity and in that context the notion of a current situation is an absurdity. The notion of definite political struggles with definite political forces engaged in them can have no meaning when all forces and struggles are merely the expressions of a single essential structure.

3. Class as an Intersubjective Unity

In marked contrast to the positions which conceptualise classes and their class struggles as called into being as effects of the structure of the social formation, two other approaches attempt to conceptualise the unity of a class by means of a counterposition of the objective determinate of a structure on the one hand and the subjective unity of one or more consciousness on the other. The unity of a class as an economic, political and cultural agency is dependent on a subjective or intersubjective unity of consciousness, and what makes that unity a class is the position of its members in the structure. Positions of this kind find their textual support in those parts of *The Communist Manifesto, The Eighteenth Brumaire of Louis Bonaparte* and other political writings which appear to counterpose economic class position on the one hand to class consciousness as a condition of class political action on the other.

Consider, for example, the contrast between the position of the proletariat as described in the *Manifesto* and that of the French peasantry described in *The Eighteenth Brumaire.* In the *Manifesto* the proletariat are described as going through various stages of development ranging from the struggle of individual labourers or the workers of a factory against their employer at one extreme to the class conscious organisation of struggle on the basis of national, if not international, political unity of the class at the other. At one extreme the class exists merely as a category of individuals organised, at best, into a multiplicity of local groups. At this stage the class does not organise for itself in pursuit of its own interests. If it unites at all 'this is not yet a consequence of their own active union, but of the union of the bourgeoisie, which class, in order to attain its own political ends, is compelled to set the whole proletariat in motion, and is moreover yet, for a time, able to do so' (Marx and Engels, *Selected Works*, p. 42). But the development of capitalist industry leads to the growth in size of the proletariat, to its concentration in particular workplaces and localities, and to improved means of communication which allow for the growth of contacts between workers in different localities. These factors together, above all, with their own experience of struggle result in the integration of the workers into a class. 'Now and then the workers are victorious, but only for a time. *The real fruit of their battle lies, not in the immediate results, but in the ever-expanding union of the workers'* (ibid., p. 43, emphasis added). The *Manifesto* adds that this development of the 'organisation of the proletarians into a class, and consequently into a political party, is continually being upset again by the competition between the workers themselves'. But now consider the small-holding peasantry:

> the members of which live in similar conditions but without entering into manifold relations with one another. Their mode of production isolates them from one another instead of bringing them into mutual intercourse. The isolation is increased by France's bad means of communication and by the poverty of the peasants . . . In so far as there is merely local interconnection among these small-holding peasants, and the identity of their interests begets no community, no national bond and no political organisation among them – *they do not form a class.* (ibid. p. 171).

The contrast is clear. Where the place of the proletariat in the capitalist organisation of production facilitates the development of class consciousness and class political organisation the position of the small-holding peasant tends to inhibit them.

It is easy to see how these passages, and the many others that could be quoted to similar effect, may provide the foundation for a conception of classes as first a category of similarly situated individuals and *secondly*, under suitable social conditions, as a cultural and political agency. A class *in-itself* is defined by a position in the organisation of production, a position that may be occupied by a mass of distinct individuals. But that class becomes a class *for-itself* only as a function of the growth to awareness on the part of these individuals, and later of groups, of the existence of a community of interests among them. This growth to awareness is facilitated by some social conditions and by the experience of action in common and it is inhibited by other social conditions. The unity of a class both as a category of economic agents and as a political and cultural agency is therefore conceptualised first in terms of the will and consciousness of individual human subjects and secondly in terms of social conditions leading to an intersubjective unity as the basis for communal action.

The most striking feature of this conception of classes lies in the affinity to Weberian sociology. Although they define class situation in rather different terms both treat it as providing a possible basis for communal action and both conceive communal action as a function of definite forms of consciousness. Action is a function of the will and consciousness of the human individual and class action is a function of the shared class consciousness of the members of a class. In view of this affinity it is hardly surprising that this interpretation of the Marxist theory of classes tends to be advanced more by sociologists than by Marxists themselves. Classical Marxism has always rejected any explicit conceptualisation in subjective terms. I have shown elsewhere that the emphasis on the will and consciousness of the individual actor as a basic explanatory princple can only lead to incoherence. However, in addition to the general problems with subjectivist forms of theory, this attempt to conceptualise the unity of classes in quasi-Weberian terms generates further severe problems for the classical Marxist conception of the structure of the social formation. First, to treat class action as a form of communal action, that is, as based on the recognition of common interests by a mass of individuals, is to admit that there may be other, non-class, forms of communal action. There is nothing about the concentration of workers in factories and large population centres as such, or in improved means of communication, to ensure that their interests as a class will be recognised and will form the basis for communal action. Shared experience of collective struggle is equally problematic as an explanation since it presupposes what has to be established, namely,that it is class interests which form the basis of collective action. The problem here is that once the *recognition of common interests on the part of individuals* is thought to play a decisive role in class action then, as Weber correctly maintains, there is no reason why other 'common interests', nationality, religious belief, 'race', etc., should not play an equally decisive role in non-class forms of communal action. To conceive of class as a form of communal action, therefore, is to conceive it as one among many of the possible forms of communal action. Class action cannot then be accounted for by refer- ence to class interests since some further explanation is required of why those interests and not others provide the basis for communal action. Short of some further explanation of the primacy of class interests over all others this conception must imply that politics and culture cannot be reduced to the expressions of interests formed at the level of the economy. To accept the conception of classes as communal agents is therefore to reject the classical Marxist conception of the social formation.

But, even if we assume that forms of consciousness are determined by the structure this conception must still conflict with the classical Marxist conception of the structure of the social formation. The proletariat would then be conceived in terms of an objective class situation on the one hand and a teleological process of formation into a class 'for-itself' on the other. But to say that the proletariat must evolve into a fully-conscious class 'for-itself' is to say that politics and ideology cannot be reduced to expressions of classes and class interests. This conception defines a direction in which working class politics is supposed to evolve, namely towards a political practice based on the self-conscious attempt to realise the objective interests determined by its class position. It follows that so long as that evolution remains incomplete working class politics must contain elements that cannot be explained by its class position. This conception therefore affirms the existence of non-class forms of politics and yet it provides no theoretical means of conceptualising them other than in terms of their difference from what a class-conscious politics would be. Political forms must therefore be conceived, not according to their specific conditions of existence and their effectivity with regard to other elements of the social formation, but merely according to the extent of their deviation from a different and idealised state of affairs. At most, then, this conception might seem to legitimise a culturalist and propagandist mode of political practice, conceived essentially as a form of consciousness raising, but it has nothing to offer with regard to the analysis of political forces and their effects in specific social formations.

4. Lukacs: The Class-subject as Subject of History

In *History and Class Consciousness* Lukacs has elaborated a sophisticated conception of classes and of history which combines a definite epistemological and ontological position with the traditional Marxist emphasis on the role of the class struggle in history and the significance of class-consciousness in that struggle. In common with the German neo-Kantian philosophies of history Lukacs argues for a radical distinction between the field of history and that of the natural sciences in terms of a difference in the nature of their objects and, consequently, in the form of investigation appropriate to those objects. Where the field

of natural scientific investigation is governed by an external and
mechanical causality the field of history is constituted by acts of
consciousness. Where Lukacs differs from the bulk of neo-Kantian
positions is in his conception of the decisive point of reference for historical investigation. It is not the will and consciousness of the human
individual that is crucial. Nor is it the role of a determinate spirit or
culture in constituting a distinctive mode of life. For Lukacs the
decisive point of reference for historical investigation is the will and
consciousness of a class. This emphasis on class consciousness provides
Lukacs with a means of integrating a neo-Kantian conception of history
as constituted by acts of consciosness with the conceptions of class
struggle outlined in Marx's and Engels' political writings on the other.
For Lukacs history is indeed constituted by acts of consciousness but it
is consciousness of classes rather than of individuals that count.

In addition Lukacs makes use of the idea of the class struggle as the
motor of history in his proposal to resolve one of the most fundamental
problems confronting any neo-Kantian conception of history, namely,
the problem of the radical separation of the consciousness of the
investigators from those constituting his object of investigation. It is the
problem of the interpretation of the meanings expressed by cultural
objects of various kinds by institutions and forms of social life. If the
cultural object is distinct from the meaning expressed in it then how is
an adequate interpretation of any cultural object to be established?

Lukacs finds the answer to this problem in the position of the
proletariat. First, since the class struggle is the motor of history it
follows that the consciousness of a class offers at least the potentiality
of overcoming the gulf between subject and object. Secondly, the position of the proletariat is uniquely privileged in that its coming to
power effects the total abolition of classes. Thus the proletariat can
appear as the identical subject-object of history since its own self-
knowledge and its knowledge of society is not limited by the effectivity
of other class-subjects:

> The self-understanding of the proletariat is therefore simultaneously
> the objective understanding of the nature of society. When the
> proletariat furthers its own class aims it simultaneously achieves the
> conscious realisation of the − objective − aims of society, aims
> which would inevitably remain abstract possibilities and objective
> frontiers but for this conscious intervention. (*History and Class-
> Consciousness*, p. 149)

History is the history of the effects of the consciousnesses of classes and it culminates in the growth to self-consciousness of the proletariat which simultaneously effects the abolition of classes and the true self-knowledge of society. In this conception of history the relation of subject to object is not an external mechanical one. It is a relation between and within consciousnesses and the products of consciousness — and it is for this reason that history is thought to require a method of investigation distinct from that of the natural sciences:

> For in the dialectics of society the subject is included in the reciprocal relation in which theory and practice become dialectical with reference to one another. (p. 207)

Lukacs therefore insists that the essence of Marxism lies not in this or that substantive proposition but in the dialectical method itself. An orthodox Marxist could, 'dismiss all of Marx's theses *in toto* — without having to renounce his orthodoxy for a single moment' (p. 1). In fact Lukacs' reduction of Marxism to the dialectical method is more than a little disingenuous since his 'solution' to the problem of historical knowledge depends crucially on several specific theses of Marx concerning the role of the class struggle in history and, in particular, the role of the proletariat in the abolition of classes. In his review of *History and Class Consciousness*, Revai has shown that Lukacs' solution to the neo-Kantian problem of historical knowledge cannot be sustained and Althusser has provided an effective critique of the attempted reduction of history to the actions of class (or individual) subjects.

But what is important for the present discussion is that Lukacs has provided one of the most sophisticated elaborations of the classical Marxist conception of the unity of class as both a category of economic agent and as a political and cultural agency. Two features of his conceptualisation of classes are particularly significant. First, Lukacs takes up a theme that recurs from time to time in Marx's political writings and is based on a particular formulation of the relation between base and superstructure. For example, in Marx's discussion of the Royalist factions of the French bourgeoisie in *The Eighteenth Brumaire,* we find:

> Upon the different forms of property, upon the social conditions of existence, rises an entire superstructure of distinct and peculiarly formed sentiments, illusions, modes of thought and views of life. *The entire class creates and forms them out of its material foundations*

and out of the corresponding social relations. (Marx and Engels, *Selected Works,* p. 118-19, emphasis added)

Here it seems that it is not the forms of property as such which create the superstructure but rather the class and its consciousness. It is this rather than the mechanistic form of the base-superstructure argument that Lukacs elaborates. On the one hand the superstructural forms express the consciousness and interests of a class to the extent that that class can achieve and maintain its hegemony over society. On the other hand the position of the class in society, its social conditions of exis- tence, limit the forms of consciousness that are possible on the part of that class. We have seen, for example, that the proletariat is supposed to be the only class whose social conditions of existence make true self- knowledge possible. Taken together these two aspects provide Lukacs with his basic principles of historical analysis and interpretation. Cultural objects are to be interpreted as more or less adequate expres- sions of the consciousness and interests of a class and therefore as expressing the necessary limitations of that consciousness. Lukacs treats the major social institutions of capitalist society, its forms of government and administration, its impersonal bureaucracies with their emphasis on rational calculation and technical efficiency, and so on, as expressions of a mode of consciousness characteristic of the social conditions of existence of the bourgeoisie as a class. Or again, in *Reification and the Consciousness of the Proletariat*, he attributes the specific antinomies and contradictions of modern, i.e. Kantian and post- Kantian, critical philosophy to the reified mode of thought specific to the social conditions of bourgeois society.

The second feature of Lukacs' conceptualisation of classes is that he insists on: 'the distance that separates class consciousness from the empirically given, and from the psychologically describable and explic- able ideas which men form about their situation in life' (p. 51). Empirically given ideas constitute 'merely the *material* of genuine his- torical analysis' but class consciousness must be imputed as a function of class position:

By relating consciousness to the whole of society it becomes possible to infer the thoughts and feelings which men would have in a partic- ular situation if they were *able* to assess both it and the interests arising from it in their impact on immediate action and on the whole structure of their society. That is to say, *it would be possible to infer the thoughts and feelings appropriate to their objective situation.*

The number of such situations is not unlimited in any society . . . there will always be a number of clearly distinguished basic types whose characteristics are determined by the types of position available in the process of production. (ibid, emphasis added)

There are several reasons for this discrepancy in Lukacs' theory between imputed class consciousness and objective class interests on the one hand and the empirical consciousnesses of the class on the other. The class consciousness of the proletariat is not a simple or automatic reflection of its class position. While, for Lukacs, the proletariat is 'the first subject in history that is (objectively) capable of an adequate social consciousness' (p. 199) that consciousness can be formed only in a dialectical process of evolution. The moments of that process represent no more than partial and inadequate expressions of imputed class consciousness:

These gradations are, then, on the one hand, objective historical necessities, nuances in the objective possibilities of consciousness (such is the relative cohesiveness of politics and economics in comparison to cultural questions). On the other hand, where consciousness already exists as an objective possibility, they indicate degrees of distance between the psychological class consciousness and the adequate understanding of the total situation. *These* gradations, however, can no longer be referred back to socio-economic causes. *The objective theory of class consciousness is the theory of its objective possibility.* (p. 79)

These last sentences give a further reason for the discrepancy between empirical and imputed consciousnesses. Following his rejection of the mechanistic conception of the relation between base and superstructure Lukacs insists that the development of class consciousness cannot be necessitated by class position. The 'point of view of the proletariat' may be given by its class position but there is nothing in the class position as such to ensure that it will be adopted by members of the class. Thus, while 'only the practical class consciousness of the proletariat' (p. 205) possesses the ability to transform bourgeois society and thus to eliminate the reified structures of existence:

it must be emphasised that the structure can be disrupted only if the immanent contradictions of the process are made conscious. Only when the consciousness of the proletariat is able to point out the road along which the dialectics of history is objectively impelled, *but which it cannot travel unaided,* will the consciousness of the proletariat become the identical subject-object of history whose praxis will change reality. *If the proletariat fails to take this step the contradictions will remain unresolved and will be reproduced by the dialectical mechanics of history at a higher level in an altered form and with increased intensity*. It is in this that the objective necessity of history consists. (pp. 197-8, emphasis added)

Lukacs reproduces at the level of the class subject all the problems of the subjectivist conception of history as a function of the will and consciousness of actors. If consciousness is not reducible to its social conditions of existence, if imputed class consciousness is not necessarily realised, then Lukacs' allusion to 'historical necessity' is no more than a rhetorical flourish expressing at best an assertion of blind faith with no possible basis in his argument. If, on the other hand, we were to take seriously the assertion of 'historical necessity' then we would have to conclude that class consciousness is ultimately necessitated by objective conditions — and in that case Lukacs' theory would be nothing but a complex and attenuated economic reductionism.

In either case Lukacs' argument entails the conclusion that politics and culture are not reducible to class determination. *Either* consciousness is ultimately reducible to class position at the end of a long process of development. It must then be irreducible to class position at all other points. *Or* consciousness is irreducible to class position: class consciousness may develop but there is no necessity for it to do so. Forms of politics and culture that do not express class interests and are therefore irreducible to class determinations are a real possibility.

Lukacs' theory therefore requires that there be non-class forms of politics and of culture but he provides no means whatever for conceptualising these forms except in terms of their discrepancy from imputed class consciousness. In effect, Lukacs' conception reproduces the theoretical and political effects of the conceptualisation of class as an intersubjective unity. Political and cultural forms must be conceived not in terms of their specific conditions of existence and effectivity with regard to other elements of the social formation, but rather in terms of the extent of their failure to reflect imputed class consciousness. While this conception may, too, serve to justify the culturalist and propagandist politics of consciousness raising it has nothing to offer with regard to the analysis of political forms and their effects in specific social formations.

5. Poulantzas: Structure and Social Relations

In *Political Power and Social Classes* Poulantzas polemicises against what he refers to as anthropologism of the subject 'whether in its historical or humanist forms'. On first reading it might seem that his conceptualisation of classes escapes the problems of those positions which conceive of classes in terms of a counterposition of subject and structure. Instead, at least in *Political Power and Social Classes*, he appears to rely heavily on the work of Althusser in *For Marx* and *Reading Capital*. In fact he merely provides an Althusserian gloss on a very different type of theoretical position. Where Althusser's use of the notion of structural causality implies that all phenomena are to be conceived as both elements and effects of the structure, Poulantzas makes a fundamental distinction between structures on the one hand and the field of social relations on the other. We shall see that while Poulantzas refuses to embrace an explicitly subjectivist position his counterposition of structures and social relations generates similar theoretical effects. In particular, his theory requires that there be forms of political practice and of ideology that do not represent class interests but he provides no theoretical means of conceptualising them.

Poulantzas argues against economistic interpretations in which classes are defined in terms of the position of agents in the production process and their relation to the means of production. Instead, they must always be conceived as the result of an ensemble of structures. This implies that they cannot be located at any particular level of the social formation. On the contrary, classes:

> do not manifest themselves inside the structure, but entirely as the *global effect of the structures in the field of social relations*, which in class societies, themselves involve the distribution of agents/supports to social classes. (*Political Power*, p. 64)

Classes are effects of the structure *in the field of social relations*. Where Althusser insists that the structure consists of 'nothing outside its effects' Poulantzas conceives of classes as effects that are outside the structure and in the field of social relations. It is precisely because he regards the two fields of structures and social relations as distinct and irreducible that Poulantzas can reject both economism, which reduces social relation to structures, and 'anthropologism of the subject', which reduces structures to social relations.

But while Poulantzas insists on the necessity of distinguishing structures and social relations the theoretical basis of that distinction is far

from clear. The nearest approach to a theoretical justification appears
in his distinction between relations of production, which belong to the
structure, and *social* relations of production, which do not:

> the relations of production do not denote simply interrelations
> between the agents of production, but rather these relations *in
> specific combinations* between agents and material-technical condi-
> tions of labour. On the other hand, social relations of production are
> relations among agents of production distributed in social classes:
> i.e. class relations. In other words, the *'social' relations of produc-
> tion*, class relations, manifest themselves, at the economic level, as an
> effect of this specific combination: agents of production/material-
> technical conditions of labour constituted by the *relations of pro-
> duction.* (p. 65)

Relations of production are relations between people and things whereas
social relations involve people only. Social relations of productions are
effects of relations of productions in the field of social relations. But
we can also talk of political and ideological social relations which 'manifest themselves as the effect of the political and ideological structures
on social relations' (pp. 65-6). What these and other passages suggest is
that Poulantzas conceives of the field of social relations as a field of
relations between subjects but the subjects themselves do not constitute
these relations. Social relations are relations between people and they
are constituted as effects of the structure, that is, they are not reducible
to the wills and consciousnesses of the people concerned.

But what concerns us in the present discussion are the theoretical
effects of Poulantzas' demarcation between structures and social relations. Classes and class practices belong to the field of social relations.
They are therefore subject to the effects of the structures but they are
not reducible to those effects:

> The determination of the practices by the structure and the inter-
> vention of the practices in the structure, consist in the production
> by the structures of limits of variation of class struggle: *it is these
> limits which are effects of the structure.* (p. 95, emphasis added)

and again: 'The effectiveness of the structure on the field of practices is
thus itself limited by the intervention of political practice on the structure' (Ibid). Class practices are limited by the effects of the structure
but they are not determined by them.

Thus Poulantzas counterposes the 'objective' determinations of the structures to the realm of human subjects and the social relations between them — and he insists that they are mutually irreducible. He presents class determination as an effect of the structures, economic, political and ideological, and it is this determination that defines the objective interests of a class. But class *interests* as determined by the structure, are not necessarily identical to the *positions* taken by the class in the concrete conditions of struggle. That follows directly from the irreducibility of social relations to structures. Thus the structure of the social formation gives class determinations which define class interests and the political and ideological positions which correspond to those interests. But in any particular conditions of struggle the position taken by a class may differ from its objective interests. In the conclusion to *Classes in Contemporary Capitalism* Poulantzas insists that there is no necessity for class position to correspond to class determination:

> We must rid ourselves once and for all of the illusions that have often affected the revolutionary movement, throughout its history, to the effect that an objective proletarian polarization of class determinations must necessarily lead in time to a polarization of class positions.(p. 334)

In effect we are presented with a principle of reduction of politics and ideology to class determinations as effects of the structure together with an insistence that political and ideological positions are irreducible to those determinations.

The parallel with Lukacs is evident. In both cases the structure provides an objective determination of class interests and in both cases those interests must be clearly distinguished from representations in the consciousness of agents. The structure determines class interests but it cannot ensure that they will be recognised. The theories of Poulantzas and of Lukacs therefore entail the existence of political and ideological practices that are strictly irreducible to class determinations. Nevertheless the two positions are not entirely equivalent for where Lukacs interprets superstructural forms as more or less adequate expressions of the consciousness and interests of a class Poulantzas sees them as expressing class relations. For example, in discussing political apparatuses Poulantzas tells us that they are 'never anything other than the materialisation and condensation of class relations' (p. 25). Thus: 'The State is not an "entity" with an intrinsic instrumental essence, but is itself a relation, more precisely the condensation of a relation' (p. 26). Poulantzas' equivocation over the discrepancy between structures and social relations is apparent in these formulations. On the one hand political apparatuses are reducible to class relations: they are *never anything other than* . . . On the other hand they are not reducible to class relations: they materialise or condense them and may therefore differ according to the forms of 'materialisation' and 'condensation'.

But in spite of these differences the fundamental consequences of the counterposition of subject and structure appear in Poulantzas' work as they do in Lukacs'. His theory requires that there be forms of politics and of ideology irreducible to class determinations but he provides no means of conceptualising these forms except in terms of what is required by objective conditions. Once again political and ideological forms must be conceived not in terms of their specific effectivity with regard to other social practices and relations but rather in terms of their failure to reflect the objective interests of a class.

For all that Poulantzas castigates sociological and Lukacsian conceptualisations of class in relation to the structure of the social formation his own theory must lead to similar theoretical and political consequences.

6. Summary and Conclusions

This paper has examined the conceptualisation of classes in Marxist theory and argued that the classical conception of the structure of the social formation gives rise to a fundamental ambiguity in the conceptualisation of classes and class relations. On the one hand classes are conceived as categories of economic agent and on the other they are, or are represented by, definite cultural and political forces. Three main types of attempt to resolve the ambiguity were examined and all were shown to be unsatisfactory. For present purposes these types may be reduced to two basic forms — with Poulantzas providing a minor variation on one of them. In one form classes are conceptualised in terms of a counterposition of subject and structure, subjective and objective conditions, social relations and structure, and so on — Lukacs, Poulantzas, left-Weberian sociology. The other form involves the conception of classes and class struggle as rigorous effects of the structure — Althusser and his associates and the very different tradition of Marxist orthodoxy represented in Stalin's *Dialectical and Historical Materialism*. In the first case the counterposition of subjective and objective (or structural) determinations entails the existence of political and cultural forms that are not reducible to the effects of class determinations. But the theory provides no means of conceptualising the effectivity of those forms. The second case involves a functional and expressionist conception in which cultural, political and economic forms and forces are reduced to effects of the structure itself. Political forces therefore have no independent effectivity: they merely perform the role assigned to them by the 'structural causality', the functional necessities, of the structure itself. These difficulties arise from the attempt to conceive of classes both as categories of economic agent and as political and cultured agencies. *Either* class as political and cultural agency is conceived in terms of a counterposition of the will and consciousness of the other to its objective, structural position – in which case there is no reason why politics and culture should reflect class interests. *Or* that counterposition is rejected and all social phenomena, including forms of subjectivity and consciousness, are reduced to rigorous effects of the structure – in which case there is no possibility of confronting the specifity of political conflicts and the forces active in relation to them.

But there is no reason why we should attempt to conceive the relation between economic classes, categories of economic agent, and political institutions, practices and ideologies in this way.

In Chapter 6 of *Pre-Capitalist Modes of Production* and again in *Mode of Production and Social Formation* Paul Hirst and I have shown that the doctrine of structural causality and of the determination in the last instance by the economy are both fundamentally essentialist and that they are the product of a particular type of rationalistic epistemological position.

We argued against these positions that the connections between relations of production and political, legal and ideological or cultural forms and relations must be conceptualised not in terms of determination in the last instance but rather in terms of conditions of existence and the forms in which those conditions may be satisfied. This means, for example, that while certain legal forms may be necessary as conditions of existence of capitalist relations of production this existence is not secured by capitalist relations of production themselves. Relations of production can be shown to have definite conditions of existence in other types of social relations (law, politics, culture, etc.) but they do not themselves secure those conditions and neither do they determine the forms in which they are satisfied. For example, there is nothing in the concept of capitalist relations of production to account for the differences between English and Japanese commercial law.

If the question of the connection between relations of production and other social relations and practices is posed in these terms then the classical conception of the social formation as a definite unity of three structural levels characterised by the determination in the last instance of the economy and the relative autonomy of levels must collapse. Instead the social formation must be conceived as a definite set of rela-

tions of production together with the social forms in which their conditions of existence are secured. Our argument on this point need not
be repeated here but it does have one significant consequence for the
present paper, namely, the dissolution of the problem of conceptualising
classes both as categories of economic agents *and* as political and
cultural forms. If the connection between relations of production and
political and cultural forces is conceived in terms of conditions of existence and the forms in which they are secured then there can be no
grounds for conceiving of political and cultural forces as generated by
or expressing the distribution of economic agents into classes by the
relations of production.

Now, it may be suggested at this point that the concept of representation provides Marxism with a genuine alternative to the economistic
reduction of political and ideological struggles to economic class relations; that political forces are not reducible to classes and the interests,
they *represent* them. Unfortunately that concept of representation
cannot be sustained. In effect it involves three distinct apsects: the
content of what is represented — class interests and the conflicts between them; the means of representation — political apparatuses and
institutions, etc., and the representation itself — the practices of
definite political forces. If the representation is not directly reducible
to the content of what is represented that must be because of the
specific effectivity of the means of representation. It follows that the
means of representation, political institutions and apparatuses, modes
or organisation and struggle, must be irreducible to classes and their
interests. Representation must always be a function of two independent
elements, the context and the means of representation — otherwise the
representation is directly reducible to the class interests represented and
we are back to economism again.

But, if the means of representation are not reducible to classes and
their interests how can they be constrained to function so that they do
indeed represent class interests? The problem is insoluble. Consider, for
example, the subjectivist interpretations of classes discussed earlier.
Class interests are supposed to be determined at the level of the
economy and the representation of these interests is a function of the
will and consciousness of a plurality of similarly situated actors. The
means of representation in this case are not determined by the interests
they are supposed to represent and we have seen that there can be no
necessity for representation to take place. But the example illustrates a
general feature of the problematic of representation. *Either*
economism: political and cultural means of representation are deter-

mined by the economy. *Or* the means of representation are not determined by the economy and there is no necessity for the political and
cultural representation of classes and their interests. Either political and
cultural forces are reducible to classes or class factions and their interests or they are not. To reject economism is to reject the classical
conception of the economic-political-ideological unity of classes. It is to
deny that political and ideological struggles can be conceived as the
struggles of economic classes.

The choice for Marxism is clear. *Either* we effectively reduce political
and ideological phenomena to class interests determined elsewhere
(basically in the economy) — an economistic reductionism coupled
perhaps with an acknowledgement that things are actually more complicated. *Or* we must face up to the real autonomy of political and
ideological phenomena and their irreducibility to manifestations of
interests determined by the structure of the economy. What is at issue
here is the choice between an essentialist mode of political analysis or
the rejection of economism. I have argued in this paper that the traditional Marxist conceptualisations of classes are fundamentally
essentialist: they are politically impertinent in the sense that they are
unable to confront the specificity of the dominant political stuggles of
the day and the political forces engaged in them. Some of the great
Marxist political leaders may have overcome the problems of economism
in this political practice but those problems have not been overcome in
Marxist theory. To reject economism is to maintain that the political
and ideological struggles cannot be conceived as, or as representing, the
struggles of economic classes. The social formation and the conflict of
social forces within it provides the conditions of existence of a definite
set of economic class relations. That is all.

This means that political issues and forces cannot be evaluated in
terms of their alleged representation, or failure to represent, the
essential interests of classes. They must rather be evaluated in terms of
their pertinence for definite political ideologies and their relevance for
the attainment of definite political objectives. It is not the ontological
position of the economy, its 'determination in the last instance', that
requires the discursive primacy of relations of production in Marxist
theory. On the contrary, it is the political objectives of a socialist transformation of economic class relations that pose the problem of relations
of production and their political conditons of existence as primary
objects of theorisation.

*This paper develops some of the arguments presented in A.J. Cutler, B. Hindess,
P.Q. Hirst and A. Hussain, *Marx's Capital and Capitalism Today*, Vol. 1.

4 ON THE SHAPE AND SCOPE OF COUNTER-INSURGENCY THOUGHT

Philip Schlesinger

Introduction

'Counter-insurgency' thinkers in the West are among the hired prize-fighters of the bourgeois state, to take liberties with a well-known remark. Their business: the prevention of revolution. Their vision of the world is Manichaean: here the Free World; there Communist Totalitarianism. The nets of the counter-insurgent are cast wide indeed. For where there is subversion, insurgency is likely to follow hard upon it. And from little insurgencies do revolutions grow.

Counter-insurgency thinkers may be regarded as intellectuals working within and/or for the repressive apparatus of the state. Their function is to produce ideas of a strategic and tactical kind for the use of that apparatus in winning counter-revolutionary wars. Such ideas, translated into repressive techniques are meant to be serviceable in assisting the security of the established order. However, it is not only the practical implications of counter-insurgency thought which are of sociological interest. Such thinking is also a significant form of ideology. A key feature of any counter-insurgency campaign is propaganda and 'psychological operations'. As the Americans put it in Vietnam: WHAM . . . Win Hearts and Minds.

This paper[1] sets out to analyse the ideological features of some contemporary British counter-insurgency writing. Given the recent growth of sociological interest in the state it is quite astonishing that this area of research should have been almost entirely neglected by sociologists in this country. Outside academic sociology itself, however, there has clearly been growing interest, particularly in Britain. Counter-insurgency and the related issue of 'political terrorism' have been discussed by historians (e.g. Laqueur, 1977a and 1977b; Iviansky, 1977) and political scientists (e.g. Wilkinson, 1974). The most insightful recent work has been produced by Marxist investigative journalists (Bunyan, 1977a; Ackroyd et al., 1977). In the USA, sociological interest in this field is a long-established one, and some substantial work has been produced there which greatly enhances our understanding of the integral role played by counter-insurgency in the American imperium and in the domestic class structure (CRCJ, 1975; Copans, 1975; Leggett, 1973).

Counter-insurgency is no innocent or neutral technical concept. Rather it carries its own ideological baggage with it. Such an approach to the world is a central element in the *Weltanschauung* of what Barnet has labelled the National-Security Managers, who, from their 'vantage-point in the national-security bureaucracy' of the USA see 'revolution in the under-developed world as a problem in the management of violence' (1972, p. 35). Consequently, as Eqbal Ahmad has observed, counter-insurgency as a practice

> involves a multi-faceted assault against organised revolutions. This euphemism is neither a product of accident nor of ignorance. It serves to conceal the reality of a foreign policy dedicated to combating revolutions abroad and helps to relegate revolutionaries to the status of outlaws. The reduction of a revolution to mere insurgency also constitutes an *a priori* denial of its legitimacy. In this article counter-insurgency and counter-revolution are, therefore, used interchangeably. (Ahmad, 1973, p. 325)

I follow Ahmad's usage here. A consideration of counter-insurgency thinking goes well beyond the area of foreign policy. It is currently highly relevant for an analysis of the *domestic* exercise of state power in numerous Western European states faced with 'terrorism' (Britain's Irish problem being just a case in point) and has been of notable importance in internal policing in the USA since the eruption of the 'new politics' of the 1960s.

Counter-Insurgency, Social Science and Imperialism

Counter-insurgency thought is a fairly modern invention. Of course, there is a sense in which it could be seen as being as old as the need for repression itself. But in the sense in which it is considered here it is very much the product of Western colonial and imperial expansion and the consequent relations of dominance imposed on the Third World. It is of some interest to note that the term 'pacification' was coined in the late eighteenth century by the British who then had some little local difficulties in India (Fairbairn, 1974, p. 46). The earliest codified counter-insurgency principles were later evolved — also in India — during the nineteenth century when a succession of 'small wars' broke out. The kind of knowledge developed by the army was 'political as well as military since the British were concerned to view pacification as a means of permanently consolidating power' (Fairbairn, 1974, p. 52). A further opportunity to develop counter-insurgency techniques came during the

Boer war when much was learned about concentration camps and cordoning systems. In the case of the USA 'pacification' of the indigenous Amerindians was a necessary concomitant of internal colonisation. And in Britain the problems resulting from a similar approach to its 'oldest colony', Ireland, are still with us.

Interestingly, recent critical historical re-appraisals of the rise of anthropology have illuminated, *inter alia*, moments in the history of counter-insurgency thinking.

Setting the scene, Talal Asad (1973, p. 16) has observed that anthropology is

> rooted in an unequal power encounter between the West and the Third World which goes back to the emergence of bourgeois Europe, an encounter in which colonialism is merely one historical moment. It is this encounter that gives the West access to cultural and historical information about the societies it has progressively dominated ...

It would be thoroughly mistaken to see the production of anthropological knowledge as simply constructed for the use of colonialist domination. The picture is complex and contradictory and merits the exhaustive discussion it has received elsewhere. However, by and large, anthropologists 'did not treat the total colonial situation in a scholarly fashion. Few studied settlers and administrators, for example, and this robbed their work of a vital dimension of reality' (Kuper, 1975, p. 147). Until the nationalist revolutions after the Second World War, it was possible for anthropologists to assume uncritically the legitimacy and stability of the imperialist social order which underpinned their object of study.

The thoughts of early counter-insurgents differed inasmuch as they *were* self-consciously designed to uphold the conquests of imperialism. What they did share with anthropologists of pre-war vintage was a set of assumptions about the legitimacy of the imperialist order. It is no historical accident, therefore, that *some* anthropologists came to perform a dual role, quite expressly using their skills to gain intelligence for the war efforts of metropolitan powers. Naturally, such actions raise ethical problems. Of central importance is the duplicity involved in gaining access to, and information about, a people ostensibly for the 'science of man' – while in actuality binding it to the uses of a power faced with an insurgency. It is of interest to consider one or two such instances, before confronting more contemporary material. *Plus ça change* ...

W.F. Wertheim (1972) tells of the Islamist and anthropologist,

C. Snouk Hongronje's activities on behalf of the Dutch colonial administration in Indonesia. The Dutch were faced with an insurrectionary war
in Atchin in the 1890s. Hongronje used his access to the Atchinese to
discover the leaders of the revolt and to recommend repressive tactics
to the authorities.

A more familiar example, perhaps, comes from British colonial
history and concerns the part played by various social scientists aiding
the Kenyan administration to deal with the Mau Mau insurrection. Work
conducted included research by the eminent pre-historian Louis Leakey
into the Mau Mau oath of allegiance in order to devise ways, in accordance with traditional Kikuyu ritual, to break the hold of the oath.
Leakey's express goal was to defeat the Mau Mau. Later on, several
researchers from the East African Institute for Social Research were
hired to investigate ways of changing the system of land tenure. The
political goal was to create a stable middle peasantry unwilling to
support the Mau Mau because it had something to lose (Buijtenhuijs,
1972).

Such enterprises are truly small beer by comparison with the research
currently engaged in by social scientists working in US counter-
insurgency programmes. The classic, most infamous, instance, is Project
Camelot. The project was devised by the US Defense Departments
Special Operations Research Office (SORO), and 'fronted' through the
American University of Washington. The pretensions of the project were
grand indeed — a complete science of counter-revolution for the use of
the American military. 'Document No. 1' made the purposes plain
enough:

> Project Camelot is a study whose objective is to determine the feas-
> ibility of developing a general systems model which would make it
> possible to predict and influence politically significant aspects of
> social change in the developing world. Somewhat more specifically,
> its objectives are
> *First* to devise procedures for assessing the potential for internal war
> within national societies; second to identify with increased degrees
> of confidence, those actions which a government might take to
> relieve conditions which are assessed as giving rise to a potential for
> internal war; and *finally,* to assess the feasibility of prescribing the
> characteristics of a system for obtaining and using the essential
> information for doing the two above things (Horowitz, 1974, p. 47-8)

At one and a half million dollars a year, for three to four years, success would have been cheap at the price. Leaving aside for the moment the questionable methodological assumptions, and the validity of Camelot's theory of counter-revolution, we might note that the revelations about the proposals sparked off an ethical debate concerning the rights and wrongs of 'strategic social science'.

The abandonment of Camelot did not end the story. It was, after all, a project designed to garner sociological knowledge for the purposes of state intelligence which was actuated by the success of the Cuban revolution. Since the problem of 'red subversion' in Latin America continues to exist so does counter-insurgency research. Camelot was followed by the setting up of think-tanks, this time funded 'privately' under the auspices of CRESS (the Centre for Research in Social Systems). Many projects are currently being funded by the US military-industrial complex taking in such diverse themes as population control, the psychological mechanisms of allegiance to guerilla groups, research into attitude changes, the creation and fostering of elites sympathetic to capitalist forms of ownership. In addition, there have been attempts to 'recover' the lessons of British and French operations (notably in Malaya and Algeria) with a view to applying them in the future.

Such thinking is not restricted to colonial and imperialist domination alone. It is of just as much significance in ensuring the maintenance of those domestic class structures which provide the social basis for imperialism itself. Indeed, as Leggett (1973, p. 322) has pointed out, there is an inescapable 'interlock' between domestic power relations in the USA and the uses of counter-insurgency both at home and abroad.

The Cold War and Counter-insurgency

In the contemporary world, all insurgencies, according to most Western military thinkers, are ultimately tied up with 'World Communism' in one or other of its hydra-headed manifestations. The logic of present counter-insurgency thought is shaped by the history and development of the Cold War, and whether it is crude or sophisticated, it faces the limits posed by a Cold War perspective.[2] This proposition may be concretely illustrated by reference to the most celebrated post-war French doctrine, and also to contemporary British thinking.

La guerre révolutionnaire

The French doctrine of *la guerre révolutionnaire* was forged from the experience of revolutionary war in Indo-China and applied in the context of the national liberation struggle in Algeria. The group of French military officers who constituted the doctrine's theorists had different tendencies in their thinking. Nonetheless, the broad outline of their vision may be taken as an ideal type for an examination of the shape and scope of Western Cold War perceptions of revolution. Current British thinking, as we shall see, has much in common with it.

For the French military thinkers of the 1950s revolutionary war in general was seen as part of a 'holy war' being waged on the West:

> Dominated by a resourceful ideology, one powerful enough to suppress and master its internal contradictions, the Communist nations are understood as a single entity which is threatening to storm the ramparts of the West. Traditional measures will in this instance be unavailing. *La guerre révolutionnaire* demands an antithesis that will in many respects resemble rather than differ from it, a *guerre contre-révolutionnaire*. It can only be found in the intensive study and critique of revolutionary tactics, and in the fastidious preparation of proper counter-measures. (Kelly, 1970, p. 424).

Revolutionary action must therefore be stood on its head. Or perhaps more exactly, a mirror image of its methods must be assembled to combat it. Such action is performed in the context of a set of clearly formulated assumptions about the international world order, and the role of revolutionary war in it. In his analysis of the *guerre révolutionnaire* theorists, Ambler (1966, pp. 309-10) has comprehensively summarised their assumptions:

> First, since the early 1950's a nuclear stalemate between East and West has rendered nuclear war most unlikely. In fact, the most probable form of war which the West will be forced to fight (indeed which it already is fighting) is subversive, revolutionary war. Second, the universal revolutionary war now in progress is unlike conventional war in that its primary object is not defeat of the enemy army but physical and moral conquest of the population. Third, that same revolutionary war is being conducted by international communism, and may be characterised as *permanent* and *universal*. It uses anti-colonial nationalism as a tactic to overwhelm the West by surrounding and weakening it. The battle for Algeria like that for Indo-China before it, is part of World War III; its outcome may well be decisive in the struggle between communism and Western civilisation. Fourth, in order to defend itself, the West must do the following: it must adapt to its own purposes some of the techniques of the enemy, especially in regard to propaganda, indoctrination and organisation;

and it must perfect a Western ideology with which and for which to fight.

There are a number of points which need to be added to this before turning to a consideration of present British thinking.

1. 'World Communism' is presented as a monolithic structure, even though when the *guerre révolutionnaire* school were writing the Sino-Soviet split was in progress or had taken place.
2. National liberation struggles are not seen as generated by factors internal to imperialist domination, but rather as the products of manipulation. A more sophisticated variant of this thesis acknowledges that nationalists are not necessarily *conscious* communists, or alternatively, that they are not aware of subterranean communist manipulation.
3. Methods and techniques are a central obsession of the school. The various exponents of the art of counter-insurgency, Col. Trinquier, Commandant Hogart, and Col. Lacheroy, to name but the most prominent, were exceedingly concerned to find a new method of response. A key concept was that of *action psychologique:* the *guerre révolutionnaire* school believed that revolutionary wars were conducted by skilful manipulators of the masses.[3] Thus it was a question of waging an adept propaganda campaign and imbuing the contended-for population with Western ideology. This 'injection' of the right modes of thought was to be supplemented by an extension of military control of the population and the imposition of a repressive apparatus on it to *pre-empt* subversion.

Current British Counter-insurgency Thought

The British State's 'Problem of Order'

In counter-insurgency thought it is the 'problem of order' which is addressed, from the standpoint of threatened power-holders. The theoretical assumptions implicit in such an approach have been made quite clear by Harry Eckstein (1964) in his discussion of 'internal war'. By this, he means action *against* the state, demonstrating thereby his conservative orientation. From this point of view, the sociology of revolutionary warfare is essentially the sociology of crises for state power. Looked at through Eckstein's functionalist spectacles, insurgency is disequilibrating, 'involving serious disruption of settled institutional patterns' (1964, p. 12). Above all, this orientation concerns itself with the maintenance and reproduction of the existing social order. Such an approach tends to take the legitimacy of the state for granted, and to be interested in the causation of revolutions as an administrative problem, rather than as one of sociological theory. As will be seen this perspective recurs in the writing examined below.

The recent spate of writing on counter-insurgency and 'terrorism' in Britain is not surprising given the present substantial urban guerilla war in Northern Ireland, one which has at times threatened the social order on the mainland itself. It would be intriguing, if space permitted, to explore some of the parallels between Franco-Algerian and Anglo-Irish relations. At all events, both have been stimulants to military thinking, and a corpus of British writings akin to those of the *guerre révolutionnaire* theorists is evidently building up.

It is not Ireland alone which has provoked counter-insurgency thought amongst British military intellectuals. The 'new politics' of the 1960s raised questions about the maintenance of 'law and order' on the streets. An enhanced security consciousness has also been brought about by the spate of hijackings and political kidnappings undertaken by various political groups, and the often related development of 'trans-national terrorism'. Of central importance in the calculations of counter-insurgents has been Britain's present economic crisis, and the extensive industrial and political conflict this has produced. It is important to relate this form of conflict and its possible containment to the way in which the British state has been dealing with the situation in Northern Ireland.

The British Society for Social Responsibility in Science has documented the growth of repressive technology — for example, water cannon, CS gas, rubber bullets, and sensory deprivation techniques — suggesting that 'Ireland's greatest value to the British Army may well prove to be that it provided a laboratory for the development of techniques soon to be needed at home' (BSSRS, 1974, p. 1; cf. Ackroyd *et al.*, 1977). It is clear that the British state is making preparations for 'internal defence' and it seems probable that the possibility of a show-down with the trade union movement has acted as a spur to these developments. It should not be forgotten that major strikes in the 1970s have been the occasion for declaring states of emergency. The 1970s have also been a period when plans for an 'alternative' structure of emergency government to that of liberal democracy have been refurbished, and when exceptional legal powers have been granted by parliament.

These plans are embodied in the Army Manual *Land Operations, Volume III: Counter-Revolutionary Operations*, which details the structure of a crisis 'working triumvirate' of the police, army and the civilian government in the event of a severe threat to national security (Bunyan, 1977b). A number of recent Home Office circulars also detail plans for emergency control, considerable emphasis being placed on information policy. Under this regime official news would be disseminated by a War Time Broadcasting Service (WTBS), run principally by members of the BBC's staff and others from the Central Office of Information (Bunyan 1977a, 1977b; Kelly 1976).

It has been suggested that such developments are moves towards a 'strong state'. Thus, for instance, Minerup (1976) has analysed the emergence of such a state in Western Germany (from whence the term derives) as only in part a response to terrorism. Among the features of this strong state are the extension of police powers, the notorious *Berufsverbot* (or 'extremists decree') prescribing political tests for employment in the state sector, and restrictions on the legal rights of political defendants at trials. The longer-term significance of such changes, Minerup argues, is that they furnish instruments of repression before they are actually needed.

On this point his analysis converges with that of Bunyan and Ackroyd, *et al.* who see the development of the strong state as to a large extent an anticipation of sharpening industrial and political strife as the West's economic crisis continues. With such a machinery of repression to hand industrial militancy could as a last resort be dealt with by techniques employed in the repression of terrorism. Naturally, this analysis is conjectural. It does, however, seem to make sense of many piecemeal developments.

Some British counter-insurgents

This section indicates in a very preliminary way some of the sources of military intellectual production in contemporary Britain (see Ackroyd *et al.,* 1977, ch. 11 for further details). A full picture of the institutional substructure of British counter-insurgency thinking would require a paper in its own right: relatively little is still known about its funding, personnel, the relationships between the various institutions concerned, links between counter-insurgents and various sectors of the state, and the uses of the media of communication.[4]

Any reader of literature in this field is bound to be struck by the number of items produced under the auspices of the Institute for the Study of Conflict (ISC). This body gained a certain notoriety in late 1976 due to revelations in the *Guardian* (20 December and 21 December) of apparent links between ISC's director, Mr Brian Crozier, and CIA personnel. According to Peter Chippindale and Martin Walker, authors of the reports, Mr Crozier's news service, Forum World Features (FWF) was funded by the CIA via an intermediary 'front' company in the USA. ISC was an outgrowth of FWF. When FWF ceased to exist in 1974 it was replaced by another company, Rossiter publications, which continued to receive funds from the same source. Mr Crozier denied these allegations (*Guardian,* 31 December 1976). Mr Crozier is author of numerous pamphlets on counter-insurgency, the editor of a book entitled *We will bury you: studies on left-wing subversion today,* and the author of several books, notably his *A theory of Conflict* which is discussed below.

A close associate of Mr Crozier is Mr Robert Moss, who edits the *Economist's* confidential subscribers-only 'Foreign Report', and who writes for that newspaper on guerilla wars. He was, for a time, the *Economist's* correspondent in Chile during the Allende period, and made a name for himself as a devout opponent of the Popular Unity's attempt to achieve a transition to socialism. His book *Chile's Marxist Experiment* was, according to the *Guardian,* published in a series indirectly funded by the CIA, the 'World Realities' series. Mr Moss is a member of the council of the Institute for the Study of Conflict, and together with Mr Crozier a member of the (far-Right) National Association for Freedom. Mr Moss worked for Forum World Features, has written pamphlets for both ISC and the International Institute for Strategic Studies (IISS).

Another NAFF activist is Sir Robert Thompson, who also wrote a book for FWF. He is perhaps the best known internationally of the British counter-insurgency writers, and is noted for his role as an adviser to the American war effort in Vietnam. Sir Robert is the author of *Defeating Communist Insurgency*. His general approach seems to have been influential on current thinking, but he seems to have little to say about contemporary Britain.

Another prominent figure is Major-General Richard Clutterbuck, who holds a doctorate in social science from London University, and is a lecturer in politics at Exeter University. He is a military intellectual in a university setting, and has written extensively on counter-insurgency. His book *Protest and the Urban Guerilla* is considered below. Dr Clutterbuck is apparently engaged at present in some research on terrorism and the mass media.

Major-General Frank Kitson is probably the best-known of recent counter-insurgency writers, and a figure in the Left's demonology. He too is a military intellectual, but this time one who writes from within the army. His book *Low Intensity Operations,* considered below, caused something of a *frisson* when it came out in 1971. Kitson has been taken most seriously, and with good reason, for he is clearly out to evangelise, believing that considerable change is necessary in military training. Others writing in the field include Mr Anthony Burton, author of *Urban Terrorism;* he has a military and journalistic background, and has written for IISS. Mr Geoffrey Fairbairn, an historian with a military background, is another writer on counter-insurgency who is a member of the Institute for the Study of Conflict. He has written *Revolutionary Guerilla Warfare* which is one of the less crude products of the ISC school. Fairbairn's base is primarily an academic one. So is that of Paul Wilkinson, Lecturer in Politics at Cardiff University. He has written a book entitled *Political Terrorism* which purports to be a theoretical essay in political science, but which is much more an undeclared counter-insurgency text. A full critique of this is presented later on. Wilkinson also has a connection with the ISC, having written a pamphlet for them entitled *Terrorism vs Liberal Democracy.*

As may be seen, interest in this topic lies very much on the liberal to far Right of the political spectrum. It would seem to be growing. Such a rise in interest is a reflection of the changing political situation in contemporary Britain, some elements of which were sketched out above. Intensive counter-insurgency thought is, at any time, a response within the state, and those who seek to influence it, to a perceived threat of revolution. Such a perception has evidently grown of late.

The Elements of Contemporary British Counter-insurgency Thought

What basically unites recent British writing is the 'scenario' it paints. It might best be characterised as a form of Right-wing catastrophism.

The Russians are coming

British counter-insurgency writers take it as axiomatic that ultimately all forms of protest are linked to a usually Soviet (sometimes Chinese) Communist Plot to Subvert the West. Their view reminds one strongly of the one inculcated into Philip Agee when he first joined the CIA:

> The central theory is that communist attempts to set up dictatorships around the world are really manifestations of Soviet expansion which in turn is determined by the needs to maintain CPSU power at home. (1975, pp. 34-5)

Within such a general framework recent developments in Western politics are interpreted as shifts towards soviet-style regimes. Thus Robert Moss in *The Collapse of Democracy* instances events in Portugal and Chile as ultimately linked to soviet plans for world domination. Moss concurs with Brian Crozier that, with the growth of Euro-Communism, 'the battlefields are located in our territory' (Moss, 1975, p. 19). Crozier depicts Euro-Communism as a 'more sophisticated approach to the problems of revolution' and the 'outcome of deep reflection in Moscow upon the extraordinary events of 1968'; as such it is part of the process of ripening the West for take-over (1974, pp. 114-15). This perspective is closely akin to that of Sir Robert Thompson, whose expertise lies in South East Asia. Thompson states: 'Just as within a country a communist insurgency cannot be dealt with in isolation, so, in a world wide context, it is not an isolated event, but an integral part of the continuing communist underground aggression by means of subversion and terror' (Thompson, 1972, p. 156). Kitson (1971, p. 19) perceives wars of national liberation as forms of subversion advancing the interests of the USSR, Cuba and China, and popular fronts as simply camouflage for the local CP.

Political change in the West, therefore, is seen as an extension of the Cold War. In *that* zero-sum game the West is portrayed as the likely loser. There are two positions in the World Revolution/Communist Take-over thesis, which are closely akin to those taken by theorists of the *guerre révolutionnaire* school. The crude version holds that the Russians/Chinese/Cubans are simply manipulators of unwary dupes. The other, more sophisticated, variant is that while there may be genuine nationalist insurgencies, these are always prone to perversion by the local branch of the Kremlin (Clutterbuck, 1973, p. 146).

Thompson inclines to the crude school and provides us with a typology of those involved in insurgencies. There is no genuine basis for revolutionary war, he argues, as is clear from the social composition of the insurgent movement. The 'naturals' (communists deep down) swell their ranks by drawing in the 'converted', and things really get off the ground when the 'deceived' (the congenitally simple) provide a mass following (1972, p. 35-6). Kitson operates with a similar motivational model, considering that the 'hard core' mobilise the 'politically conscious idealists' for protest and when confrontations with security forces occur, the 'hard core' capitalise to establish mass sympathy (1971, pp. 84-5). Conspiracy theories run through all of the writings considered here.

Subversion in Britain Today

As we know, the price of liberty is eternal vigilance. An axiom which frequently crops up in counter-insurgency writing is that the best insurgency is no insurgency at all. And the way to achieve this desirable state of affairs is to nip subversion in the bud. The counter-insurgents do not thereby put themselves out of business. Far from it. Once you decide to look out for subversion you have a permanent meal-ticket. It requires a formidable bureaucracy to scan the passing scene for signs of rot. There are always subversives. (One should perhaps look to the Grand Inquisitor or to the Jew-Detector in Max Frisch's *Andorra* for the appropriate models.) Signs of subversion may be found in many contexts. Consider the definition advanced by Kitson of subversion as

all measures short of the use of armed force taken by one section of the people of a country to overthrow those governing the country at the time, or to force them to do things which they do not want to do.(1971, p. 3)

Such 'non-violent subversion' includes activities such as political and economic pressure, strikes, protest marches, propaganda, small-scale violence. With the exception of 'small-scale violence', these activities look like the exercise of rights supposedly guaranteed the citizens of liberal democracies. Such a list provides a chilling insight into the counter-insurgent's view of liberal-democracy. The very functioning of 'normal' political life is seen as subversive. That the above pursuits, lawful in the terms prescribed by bourgeois legality, should be singled out underlines an essential point: that civil and political rights are at the centre of the terrain in which social conflicts take place, and that they are not static 'achievements', but rather the objects of continual struggle. In the counter-insurgent's scenario legitimate and legal dissent is re-categorised as subversion. Hence, no political activity can be above suspicion for there are always mind-benders waiting to pounce.

Students and academics

In Clutterbuck's vision the cause of 'protest' is to be laid at the door of a militant minority able to dupe the rest. He gives a 'statistical' breakdown of the student population, which contains: 1 − 3% 'activists'; 10 − 30% 'protestors'; 60 − 80% 'mainstream'; 10 − 20% 'hearties'; less than 1% 'fascists' (1973, p. 189). His book is almost entirely silent about the organised Right. At all events he does not give a detailed rundown on such organisations as the National Front and nascent British vigilantism. Rather he concentrates on the affiliations of Left radicals, providing potted material on the CP, SLL, IWC, Solidarity, IS, IMG, CPGB (ML), and suspect journals such as *New Left Review*. Even Amnesty International and the *Sunday Times* are taken to task for their unhelpful attitude to the Army in Northern Ireland. This is really an exercise in political rhetoric, which identifies all forms of left-wing thought and action (excepting the Labour Party moderates) as especially worthy of suspicion. 'Protest' and the 'urban guerilla' are linked in terms of guilt by association and not theoretically.

Crozier too sees the Left as the prime threat to social stability, arguing that the 'ideological extreme Right' are 'few and relatively unimportant' (1974, p. 107). It is important to be alert to the formation of clandestine revolutionary groups: 'The universities are breeding grounds for such movements. If students or faculty members become elusive or secretive in their movements or travel round to excess to other universities, it may well be they are engaged in incipient revolutionary activities' (1974, p. 144).

Strikes

There is impressive unanimity concerning industrial action and its dangers. Consider Kitson's much quoted scenario for the later 1970s;

> If a genuine and serious grievance arose, such as might result from a significant drop in the standard of living, all those who now dissipate their protest over a wide variety of causes might concentrate their efforts and produce a situation which was beyond the capacity of the police to handle. Should this happen the army would be required to restore the position rapidly. (1971, pp. 27-8)

Robert Moss is somewhat more direct in his approach, observing that

> Britain need not be governed in fear of strikes with adequate preparations — accumulation of stocks of coal and oil, organisation of private road transport, contingency planning for the use of resources and civilian volunteers — and with an intelligent political education campaign, a determined government can survive even a general strike. (1975, p. 117)

Mr Moss has learned the lessons of Chile, about which he has written so extensively. For Dr Clutterbuck strikes are one of his 'two particular flash-points' (student activity being the other). It is important, he

argues, for the 'strike weapon' not to be 'misused for other than industrial purposes'. He concedes the possibility of a 'Right-wing backlash'
resulting in a worrying spate of strike-breaking. One favoured solution
is the labour legislation of the 1960s and 1970s (1973, pp. 250-6).

The media and psychological warfare

Whether a particular exercise of force is legitimate or not is a central
theme in any discussion of counter-insurgency. Van Doorn has noted
how modern armies engaged in counter-revolution — and by extension
those supporting them ideologically — 'fall back on the legal form of
legitimacy by denying the legality of their opponents and emphasising
the need to maintain law and order. Referring to their opponents as
"subversive elements", "terrorists", "extremists", and "bandits" is part
of this general trend.' (1975, p. 103.) Such characterisations will be
more than familiar to those who have followed the evolution of the current
conflict in Northern Ireland. It is more important to recognise that
such concepts are ideological constructs. In everyday and mass media
discourses they tend to be handled without a critical awareness of the
ways in which they pre-manufacture a version of reality favouring those
in power. Harries-Jenkins has argued that in a liberal-democratic regime
the use of armed force in the maintenance of law and order provokes a
crisis of legitimacy for the military and the state more generally
(1976, pp. 48-51). This means that the management of information and
the organisation of propaganda become crucial weapons in the struggle
to justify military intervention and to gain public support. It is not surprising, therefore, that all counter-insurgency theorists have something
to say, if only in passing, about the role of the media, and it is generally
to their detriment. Burton (1975, p. 9) for instance notes their importance and considers that to publicise 'urban terrorism' is to risk an
imitation effect. In fact, most of the writers considered seem to be
paid-up subscribers to the long-discredited stimulus-response theory of
media 'effects': namely, that the content of a communication is
injected into a passive recipient who has no choice about how to interpret what he is told.

Given such a view, they are understandably worried when 'the television coverage of revolutionary wars — that of situations such as
Vietnam and Ulster — is invariably one-sided and detrimental to the
official side in the conflict' (Crozier, 1974, p. 30). For Crozier, it is
clear that subversive elements are at work when themes are presented in
the media which bring 'a regime into disrepute, causing a loss of confidence on the part of the ruling establishment, institutions, and govern-

ment' provoking a 'breakdown of law and order' (Crozier, 1974, p. 202). Kitson is on the same ground when he argues the need for 'the machinery for exploiting success in the minds of the people' (1971, p. 78). Fairbairn takes a more sophisticated line arguing that fellow-travelling has taken something of a hold in the West, and that there are lots of gullible people around who fit in with the objectives of 'totalitarian psychological warfare' and fall for such misleading concepts as 'national liberation front' without realising such notions mask the ambitions of power-hungry elites (1974, pp. 286, 290).

With this background it is easy to understand current anxieties in the British state about the effectiveness of the security forces' propaganda war in Northern Ireland. While counter-insurgency theorists seem generally to argue that uncensored media work against the interests of the state, recent research in Britain would tend to deny this view. It has been shown, for example that the British Army has had a positive portrayal in the media and that the state has been successful in systematically discrediting the Provisional IRA (Elliott, 1976). It has also been argued that, contrary to the myths, the British state has exercised considerable and generally successful indirect control over the BBC (Schlesinger, 1978). Chibnall (1977) has shown how in the past decade a number of themes have converged in British media coverage of 'law and order', particularly through a gradual conflation of the labels of 'criminal violence' and 'political violence'. These two media categories have in turn been subsumed under the broader media concept of 'the violent society'. Thus bank robberies, vandalism, anarchist and IRA bombings, and industrial conflict have all eventually come to be presented in terms of the same catch-all category of 'violence'. Given counter-insurgents' perception of industrial militancy as a threat to the established order, the depiction of strikes, picketing and so forth as forms of violence not fully distinct from, say, 'terrorism' or 'mugging' has important ideological consequences. In particular it tends to delegitimise trade union activity and its goals.

Given Crozier's significant role in this field, it is worth concluding this section by considering his advice on getting the right views across:

> All governments should have a department, or even several departments, specifically charged with authoritative but unattributable information. It should be the function of such departments to correct misleading or subversive allegations — not by distorting the truth, but by giving trusted journalists access to supporting evidence, under seal of confidence, and to trust them to write their own stories

unaided. It is not a question of censoring the news, but of making sure that one-sided versions of events that serve no other purposes than those of totalist groups and their foreign supporters do not go unanswered. (1974, pp. 206-7)

This type of policy bears precious little relationship to the classical liberal ideology of the freedom of the press. Its cynical approach to news management is in utter contradiction to Crozier's profession of concern for safeguarding democracy. It implies an incorporation of the media into the information policy of the bourgeois state which pre-serves democratic forms but converts their substance — hardly a strong position from which to attack 'totalists'. That is not to say that we should have any illusions about present-day news management practices in Britain. Indeed, police and military sources currently make use of the techniques Crozier describes, and have done so historically, as for example during the 1919-21 IRA campaign (Chibnall, 1977, Ch. 6; MacNally, 1977). It is perhaps no accident that Crozier's approach bears such a striking resemblance to the 'grey propaganda' line of the CIA according to which information 'is ostensibly attributed to people or organisations who do not acknowledge the US government as the source of their material and who produce the material as if it were their own' (Agee, 1975, p. 70).

Responses to Subversion and Insurgency

Counter-insurgency thinkers conventionally divide insurgencies into a number of phases. Subversion unchecked develops into isolated acts of terrorism. Terrorism becomes guerilla war. And finally, guerilla war becomes full-scale conventional war. At each stage the legitimacy of the incumbent government is under assault. Space does not permit a full discussion of this issue, and the 'graduated responses' the state is advised to make. However, it is possible to give some brief indications of the conventional wisdom to be found.

All the experts agree that if you can nip subversion in the bud then you will have no problems later. In order to do this an effective intelli-gence system is needed. Moss calls for 'a permanent anti-terrorist force' and 'centralised coordination of anti-terrorist planning' (1975, p. 235). He is echoed by Crozier who calls for 'Departments of Unconventional War' bringing together experts from security, special branch, intelligence, psychological warfare, interrogation, special operations, bomb disposal, trained anti-guerilla troops and also linguists and anthropologists (1974, p. 207). Kitson, who must be understood as an evangelist, calls for a profound change in army thinking, and the creation of a 'community of experts'. The underlying assumption present in current work is that the state needs to anticipate threats, as the 1970s will be characterised by 'civil disorder accompanied by sabotage and terrorism, especially in urban areas': in such a situation the 'tactical handling of information by operational commanders' is of the foremost importance (Kitson, 1971, p. 199). Such views express a particular view of military professionalism which tends to contradict liberal-democratic ideology. The creation of specialist cadres for improved social control is directly connected with the vision of a complete alternative structure of government outlined in the Army Land Operations Manual and the Home Office circulars.

There is wide agreement that the onset of an insurgency — 'the use of armed force by a section of the people against the government' (Kitson 1971, p. 3) — very likely entails the suspension or modification of normal legal practices. However, such changes have to be handled cautiously, as they are tied up with the legitimacy of the incumbents, and this has already been questioned. In the event of martial law being declared in some areas it is important to 'plan for peace, that is to pre-pare for the handing back to the civilian authority of areas and func-tions which have temporarily become the concern of the military' (Burton, 1975, p. 214). Kitson shrewdly argues that it is both 'morally right' and 'expedient' for an impartial legal system to be retained, but this must be married with tough anti-guerilla legislation (1971, p. 69). This line echoes Thompson's 'second principle' of counter-insurgency: 'The government must function in accordance with the law'. But the legal system is now on an emergency footing, with simplified laws of evidence and procedure, deportation laws, collective fines, imprison-ment for supporting insurgents, detention for suspects (1972, pp. 53-4).

Interestingly, Crozier and Moss part company with the rest by their explicit advocacy of an 'authoritarian solution'. Both argue with com-mendable candour that 'an authoritarian solution is preferable to a totalitarian solution' (Moss, 1975, p. 278). Authoritarianism is iden-tified with Franco's Spain, a regime where 'instead of ramming politics and ideology down people's throats, it confers upon them a benefit not to be despised — the freedom to opt out' (Crozier, 1974, p. 200). This is much to be preferred to the totalitarianism of Eastern Europe, or seemingly socialism of whatever variety in Western Europe.

When one considers the directly analogous ideology of the *guerre révolutionnaire* school, it becomes clear that ultimately, liberal demo-cracy must go by the board. This is *implicit* in Kitson's writing (as a serving officer he is presumably not permitted public heresies) where he

argues the need for 'counter-organisation' – 'a method by which the
government can build up its control of the population and frustrate the
enemy's attempts at doing so' (1971, p. 79). He has persisted in this
view in a subsequent book (Kitson, 1977, Chs. 23, 24).

Revolution has no objective social basis

This theme is an important one, and the questions it raises concerning
the causation of revolutions go well beyond the scope of this paper. The
position taken by British counter-insurgency thinkers is implicit in what
has so far been said. Their heavy reliance on manipulative/conspiracy
theory for explaining the origins of an insurgency makes small groups
of politically motivated men the key *explanans,* rather than objective
conditions. This view is dominant in the writings reviewed, and, as we
shall see, particularly open to attack in critiques of counter-insurgency
thought. Essentially, the writers examined here stress the intervention
of *consciousness* and *ideology* in a very Leninist way. True, there is
grinding poverty in the Third World, or an economic crisis in the
Capitalist West. But it takes some trouble-maker to stir things up. The
organisers of subversion *select* their cause in order to develop support
(Kitson, 1971, p. 29; Thompson, 1972, p. 21). A particularly blunt
statement of this view is to be found in Crozier (1974, p. 14): 'the social
environment in itself is not the cause of the rebellion, even if it is its
essential background. A rebellion begins when somebody feels strongly
enough about it to do something: in other words to rebel. What goes on
in the mind of the potential rebel leader is more important than what
surrounds him'. Fairbairn, in similar vein, has repudiated 'the spurious
argument that revolutionary wars erupt spontaneously out of conditions grown socially and economically intolerable', this view is
simply a 'propaganda weapon in the hands of sympathisers with revolutionary warfare' (1974, pp. 71-2). This view is also (not surprisingly)
to be found among American counter-insurgents such as Eckstein (1970)
who argues for the primacy of the *perception* of social conditions, and
is concerned to establish that there is no firm correlation between objective factors and 'internal war'. In a nutshell, it seems as though the
approach considered here is both voluntaristic and idealist.

From Counter-insurgency to Political Sociology

Most of the work discussed above does not present itself as 'academic'.
Certainly, it is dressed up with footnotes, and, in some instances, mani-
fests considerable erudition. However, its propagandist and ideological
purposes are not likely to be in doubt. This section takes a somewhat

different approach from the rest of the paper. It presents a critique of a book which in my view is counter-insurgency in sheep's clothing, namely Paul Wilkinson's *Political Terrorism*. The book is not important in terms of its intellectual content, as the critique which follows makes clear enough. Its significance lies in the fact that Wilkinson's academic standing permits him to give credibility to the doctrines of the ISC school, of which he is a member. The next few pages therefore should be read as a case study in revealing counter-insurgency doctrine masquerading as political sociology. If I have given Wilkinson a disproportionate place in this paper it is not because of his influence; Kitson is far more important in that respect. An academic audience, however, needs to be made aware of Wilkinson's kind of enterprise, particularly as his book is likely to be uncritically adopted as a basic teaching text in this important area, and as a further such offering, *Terrorism and the Liberal State,* is imminent.

A Shifting Object of Study

Wilkinson begins (p. 11) by arguing that the main concern of his text is with 'political terror: that is to say the coercive intimidation by revolutionary movements, regimes, or individuals for political motives.' In fact Wilkinson ends up looking at something rather different. Towards the end of the book, just before launching into an assault on 'terrorist' threats to liberal democracies, he draws the lines less generously. The study *now* attempts to contribute to 'a theory of revolutionary terrorism' (p. 129). Significantly, the idea of terror produced by regimes has entirely faded from the picture. This is no accident in terms of the logic of the book's development, which ends as a piece of tactical advice to the rulers of the liberal democratic capitalist state. What remains, then, as an object of study are small groups of politically motivated men *out of power:* the exercise of state power has ceased to be a question.

Defining 'Political Terrorism'

A linchpin in Wilkinson's definition is the idea that political terror must have an 'indiscriminate nature' (p. 13). In his condemnation of indiscriminate murder he is widely supported — and who could disagree? (cf. Rapoport, 1971; Finer, 1976). Further he sees all terrorist action as 'implicitly amoral and antinomian' (p. 17). This is rather different. To suggest that there can *never* be a moral basis for, say, selective terror against vicious oppressors is far from incontrovertible. Moreover, not *all* terrorism is, in fact, indiscriminate. Assuming the IRA were 'terrorists' in 1919-20 (rather than the military wing of a popular anti-colonialist movement), they were, in fact, highly selective in their targets, eliminating British agents and intelligence officers, rather than, as in the current campaign, setting off bombs in public places. To cite this instance raises terminological issues, of course. To define someone as a terrorist is to undermine his legitimacy. For this reason, if for no other, 'guerilla', 'freedom fighter' and 'commando' vie strongly for acceptance in the market-place of labels. Wilkinson does consider this point, and offers a caveat: 'moral and evaluative considerations are integrally involved. The student of terrorism, therefore, has to be on his guard against polemical uses of the term' (p. 21). The student of 'terrorism', it seems to me, has already made up his mind.

Wilkinson's definition cannot escape polemical consequences. He is aligned with the common sense definition of terrorism current today which presents it essentially as action taken against the state, rather than action taken by the state (Sobel, 1975). Consonant with this is his concern to 'identify what possible prophylactic political, social, or economic measures may be taken to prevent it . . . (and) . . . what effective anti-terrorist actions of a short-term nature should be taken, particularly by constitutional democratic governments which are already subject to terrorist attack.' These are the classic concerns of the counter-insurgency thinker. Instead of asking 'Why has this happened?' we are on the displaced territory of 'What can we do about it?'

Wilkinson's typology

Wilkinson claims to have made a typological advance over a book such as E.V. Walter's *Terror and Resistance* (1969), and argues: 'It is necessary to construct a more flexible typology which is not tied to the ruler-ruled dichotomy and which stems from motives other than revolution and repression' (p. 35). Accordingly, he distinguishes the following. 'Revolutionary terrorism' where 'many movements and factions have resorted to systematic tactics of terroristic violence with the objective of bringing about political revolution' (p. 36). The prototype here is the Terror during the French Revolution. It is worth noting however that this period was one of revolutionary action organised by the state (Hobsbawm, 1973). The relevance of this observation will be clear shortly.

The next category (and here Wilkinson claims to innovate) is 'sub-revolutionary terrorism' which is 'employed for political motives *other than* revolution or governmental repression' (p. 38) and is to be found where there are cultures of violence, feuds, and assassinations etc. Wilkinson considers this type of activity to have 'marginal political effects outside highly traditional autocracies' (p. 40). Whether, say sectarian murder in Northern Ireland, which is undoubtedly 'sub revolutionary', is so marginal in its effects is doubtful.

Just as Walter is only interested in state terror, so is Wilkinson essentially uninterested in his third category: 'repressive terror.' This is defined as: 'the systematic use of terroristic acts of violence for the purpose of suppressing, putting down, quelling or restraining certain groups, individuals, or forms of behaviour . . . It may be mainly directed at insurgents or suspected insurgents . . . ' (p. 40). That this is not a 'clean' category is obvious. The *revolutionary* Jacobins employed *repressive* terror against their enemies.

Wilkinson ignores the relevance of his last type — repressive terror — for an analysis of the liberal democratic state. His entire approach is based on the assumption that where the forms of liberal democracy exist, repression necessarily does not. For him repression is identified purely and simply with a military mobilisation in defence of the established order — shades of the night-watchman conception of the state. In such instances says Wilkinson 'If the government is provoked into introducing emergency powers, suspending habeas corpus, or invoking martial law, it confronts the paradox of suspending democracy to save it' (p. 109). But this seeming paradox melts away if we conceive of the liberal-democratic state somewhat differently. It should be related to the class relations which it acts to maintain and reproduce. Developments within the state towards overt repression are not simply expressions of concern to safeguard a threatened democracy, but also, more fundamentally, action taken in defence of the structure of underlying capitalist relations.

An analysis of the role of overt repression needs, therefore, to be more dynamic and processual. While the repressive apparatus of the liberal democratic state is most *visible* at moments of crisis, that does not mean it has suddenly sprung into existence. Every liberal state can be seen as in a process of tooling up for repression as it meets successive threats to its monopoly of violence and to its fundamental social relations. It is not therefore the *liberal* state which defends itself through tough measures, thereby, in effect, abolishing itself. Rather, it has become a repressive one. It is also important to note that a counter-insurgency capacity and a 'strong state' do not necessarily simply fade away when an immediate danger has passed. The central problem with Wilkinson's analysis is that it is based on the opposition of two static types. In actuality his repressive type (p. 40) must be placed in a continuum with his constitutional type (p. 109).

Applying an unsound typology

To be more precise I shall focus on one example in his sketchy reper-
toire. From evidence such as the British Society for Social Responsibility in Science's study *The New Technology of Repression*, and John
McGuffin's disturbing account of *The Guineapigs* (1974) in detention
centres, it is clear that within the British state machine's operations in
Northern Ireland what Wilkinson calls 'the systematic use of terroristic
acts of violence' have been part and parcel of administrative practice in
the Province in combating the IRA. In his preface, McGuffin describes
how fourteen 'men were selected as unwilling and unwitting subjects
upon whom army psychologists, psychiatrists and "counter-insurgency
strategists" could experiment in that particular field known as "SD" –
Sensory Deprivation.' Other special features of the British regime in
Northern Ireland are dirty tricks departments, and an impressive range
of hardware for uses ranging from crowd control to interrogation.

Now, is this evidence – not, incidentally produced by Wilkinson
when he discusses Northern Ireland and the IRA –not exceedingly
relevant for a discussion of what he terms a liberal democracy? While
the British mainland may make claim to this form of regime, there is
little ground for extending this characterisation to Northern Ireland,
where a state machine has made discrimination against and repression of
a large minority into a routine practice (De Paor, 1971; Downing, 1977).
By Wilkinson's own criteria, and not mine, any reading of recent history
in Northern Ireland should set that statelet into the repressive category;
for 'No repressive state appears to be able to dispense with a secret
police *apparat* whose members are specially trained in the methods of
murder, torture, forced confessions, denunciation, subversion etc.'
(p. 42).

It is often contended that Britain used murder gangs in Ireland in the
past, to say nothing of what is asserted today. Wilkinson specifically
mentions as repressive 'torturing and intimidating detainees to extract
information' (p. 42) – the very subject of McGuffin's book. And yet he
continues to classify British rule in Northern Ireland as that of a liberal
democracy:

> In so far as IRA violence has been directed against the British govern-
> ment since 1970 in order to force a British withdrawal from Ulster
> and the destruction of the Unionist regime it must be described as a
> campaign against a liberal democracy. But it must be admitted that,
> ever since the establishment of the Unionist regime in Stormont in
> 1922, the Northern Catholic population has suffered from political,

social and economic discrimination. Moreover the Special Powers
Acts introduced in Ulster in 1922 gave the government sweeping
powers to suppress any unwelcome forms of political opposition.
(p. 116)

This is an oddly incoherent set of statements. On the one hand the IRA
must be described as against liberal democracy, and on the other hand
it mounts a campaign against a regime which is described as lacking
both social justice and liberality, surely the defining ideas of liberal
democracy itself. Wilkinson has failed to analyse the *relationship* between Northern Ireland and the rest of the United Kingdom, which
stems from the Government of Ireland Act, 1920, and the Ireland Act,
1949. It is a double-think to divorce the regime in the Province from
that on the mainland. It is surely disingenuous for someone writing in
1974, after a lengthy period of Direct Rule (a phase incidentally,
straight from the handbooks of colonialism), to attempt to talk of *two*
separate political systems. And it is naive for a political scientist not to
observe the causal link between the indiscriminate violence presently,
and unjustifiably, being inflicted on innocent civilians in Britain, and
the British state's conduct of Irish policy. Wilkinson's handling of this
concrete case generally discredits his theoretical approach to the problem of terrorism in liberal democracies.

Sociologist or counter-insurgent?

Ever since Project Camelot the use of 'strategic social science' has been
much in question. Wilkinson's work is not quite of that order. He is
there to help government, but not funded by it. As an ideologist he
gives academic endorsement to the idea that terrorism is to be ruled out
ab initio from having any theoretical justification in a liberal democracy. But what if we are mistaken in our labelling of the regime? The
Stormont regime could hardly be said to have provided the full practical freedoms and benefits of a liberal democracy. Could it, because it
functioned within the wider framework of the United Kingdom, which
is more plausibly described as a liberal democracy, not therefore be
legitimately assailed — in the end by violent means?

What Wilkinson's approach to the concept of liberal democracy
leaves out is the theoretical possibility of considerable repression within
discrete *sectors* of a society governed by such a regime. Whare are we to
draw the line marking off the liberal from the repressive state? How
large does this sector have to be? What are the implications for the
legitimacy of liberal-democratic politics? These are the unasked ques-

tions. *A theory of 'terrorism' in liberal democracies, may, at the same time, in certain circumstances, need also to be a theory of sectoral repression.*

It is at this point that we necessarily enter counter-insurgency territory. Wilkinson here performs a function, and argues in a style, which is indistinguishable from the Thompsons, Clutterbucks and Kitsons. Thus he argues for governments to combine reform with strong security measures as part of a 'two wars strategy' (p. 138). This was a technique employed by Magsaysay in the Philippines, where it enjoyed success (Taber, 1972, pp. 120-3). Governments, argues Wilkinson, must strike a balance between repression and reform, and not be 'too soft with terrorists' (p. 139; note the popular phrase: is this Sociology or the *Daily Telegraph* speaking?). Further Wilkinson advocates special powers acts proscribing the membership of certain organisations and the banning of marches. He shows a political realism shared by Brigadier Thompson in advocating that 'impartial procedures of appeal and judicial review' be linked with special powers legislation. But he seems to be contradicting himself when he says: '*No democratic* government worth the name would deserve continuing public support if it went over to military rule for any length of time' (p. 141, emphasis added).

This extraordinary statement is most revealing. For counter-insurgents the administrative goal of defeating insurgencies overcomes the ostensible end: making democracy safe. Thus, for public consumption, what is important is to maintain democratic *forms*. Wilkinson is in fact working with the concept of a militarised 'democracy', and it is the logic of counter-insurgency thought which leads him there.

Critiques of Counter-insurgency

Counter-insurgency thought and practice have been the objects of sporadic criticism on various grounds. In conclusion, let us consider the recurrent questions.

Ethics and politics

Obviously, to engage in counter-insurgency research implies taking an ethical stance. Anti-revolutionaries make the maintenance of order and the demands of the state their first priority. If guerillas swim like fish in the sea of the people, as Mao puts it, counter-insurgents think up ways of catching the fish. In doing so they necessarily endorse the legitimacy of incumbent regimes (whether in an imperialist context, or in the domestic class structures of metropolises) often justifying this on the grounds of averting something worse. Lucian Pye has characterised the role of such a strategic social science in the Third World as one of 'accumulating insights on the art of controlling rebels who would destroy the prospects of democratic development and establish the rule of tyrants' (1964, p. 179). This is a more attractive sales pitch than arguing for active support for imperialist relations of domination.

It is an open question whether social scientists *ought* to lend themselves to this kind of operation. Project Camelot definitely posed the question of whether to adopt the problems of the state as one's own, and to work within paradigms not of one's own making. Subsequent revelations concerning the role of sociological advice on 'action programmes' in Thailand (Copans, 1975), and the Pentagon Papers' disclosure of social scientists' involvement in the formation of US policy in Vietnam, have only served to underline the fact that ethical choices remain on the agenda. Ethical choices in the area are indissolubly linked to political commitments, and the position which these entail on the desirability of violent social change in particular societies at particular times.

Fallacies of counter-insurgency

Most attention has focused on the question 'Does counter-revolution work?' Obviously, sometimes it does, sometimes not. To ask such a question opens up a Pandora's Box of theoretical problems concerning the causation of revolution. Does mounting an effective anti-revolutionary campaign necessarily presuppose an adequate theory of revolution? It seems doubtful. What is in question, though, is the long-term effect of such campaigns. W.F. Wertheim has noted a whole range of measures pursued in the interest of averting revolutions, and distinguishes three major forms of response taken by the state: reform, diversionary propaganda, and repression. His conclusion is that 'all known attempts to forestall revolutions are sooner or later abortive' (1974, p. 293). This is perhaps an article of faith rather than historical fact.

Critics of counter-insurgency have tended to share the position taken by Wertheim. One 'fallacy' which Robert Taber has identified is

the view that revolution is the (usually deformed) offspring of a process of artificial insemination, and that the guerilla nucleus (the fertilising agent so to speak) is made up of outsiders, conspirators, political zombies — in other words, actual or spiritual aliens — who somehow stand separate from their social environment while manipulating it to obscure and sinister ends. (1972, p. 19)

Undoubtedly, such an approach does characterise those considered in this paper. Conspiracy theories rarely, if ever, do justice to the complexity of social reality. Of course, it is true that a mechanistic and rather monistic theory of this kind *may* sometimes do the requisite work of explanation and assist the successful exercise of repression. However, counter-insurgency theorists do tend to have a somewhat metaphysical commitment to this line, and it is anyway no doubt good propaganda to maintain it. To talk of alien creeds is to legitimise home-spun common sense — which may well be a poor substitute.

Another 'fallacy' identified by Taber is the obsession with 'methods':

> The methods fallacy . . . is . . . the old-fashioned notion that guerilla warfare is largely a matter of tactics and techniques, to be adopted by almost anyone who may have need of them, in almost any irregular warfare situation. (1972, p. 20)

Without doubt, all the theorists considered here do have a strong commitment to the view that if the right techniques are employed subversion and insurgency can be repressed. If winning hearts and minds doesn't work their owners can in the last resort be subjected to some form of military rule without the dressing of civilian legitimacy. Obsession with methods may produce an awareness of the role of ideology. The *guerre révolutionnaire* school is a case in point: for them the manipulation of consciousness was a centrally important technique. But an obsession with the manufacture of a counter-revolutionary ideology may be self-defeating as it seems likely to exclude full consideration of those objective factors which, counter-insurgents attest, play so minor a role in revolution.

The Way Ahead

The analysis of counter-insurgency both as practice and as ideology is of particular importance when considering power in the contemporary state. The growth of counter-insurgency is particlarly interesting in the case of liberal-democratic regimes because of the contradictory pull between democratic forms and militarised practices, one which eventually creates a fundamental crisis of legitimacy. Hence, developments in the 'internal defence' of Britain and some other Western European states make the study of counter-insurgency of urgent relevance. In particular, attempts to forestall 'Euro-communist' advances and the response to continued economic crisis may well make the strong state a much more common form of regime.

A theory of 'political terrorism' in liberal democracy is likely to be misleading if it excludes a theory of state power. It must also consider the possibility that sectoral repression exists despite the existence of democratic forms. In fact, we cannot, as counter-insurgents do, simply take the state for granted and ask administrative questions about social control. We must make the state an essential part of the *explanation* of the origins and development of an insurgency. This has been done recently to some extent in the work of Kohl and Litt (1974) on Latin American guerilla movements. I have sought to show that the dominant way of thinking about insurgencies in liberal democracies is misleading because it ignores awkward questions about the nature of the bourgeois state.

Postscript

Counter-insurgency thought is organically related to the interests of power-holders and a species of service research, akin to that in other areas of state policy. In its discourse, 'insurgency', 'terrorism', 'sub-version' are the symptons of a disease. This paper has been a study of what C. Wright Mills called 'social pathologists', and the intellectual productions of those examined here contain the fairly cohesive domain assumptions of a professional ideology. Nothing stands still. And I hope that readers of this paper will not feel misled when I inform them that 'counter-insurgency' ceased to exist some time ago. Kitson notes how the US Army has now

> stopped referring to 'counter' insurgency and 'counter' subversion, and redesignated the business as 'Internal Defence and Development'. That part of 'Internal Defence and Development' provided by the armed forces to maintain, restore, or establish a climate of order is known as 'stability operations', a term designed to emphasise the fact that the purpose of destroying the insurgents is to provide the stability which the country requires so that it can progress and develop. (1971, pp. 52-3)

All those applying for posts in this area of social pathology take note.

Notes

1.   I am grateful to the following for helpful criticisms of this paper: Philip Elliott, Robbie Guttmann, Robert Peck, Adam Roberts, Roger MacNally

and Nira Yuval-Davis. I should also like to thank those who so constructively commented on the paper at the 1977 BSA conference, and at a subsequent presentation to the CSE Day School on Law and the State in May 1977. Any sins of omission are mine entirely. I hope to atone for them in a full-length treatment of issues raised here.

2. The general role of counter-insurgency thought in Western capitalist states needs to be examined in relation to *other* ideological currents. Why should a crass World Communist Conspiracy theory still be so vigorously propagated at a time of so-called *détente*? An explanation might well begin with the ideological division of labour. Ready-to-hand, stylised explanations are serviceable for mass consumption, and culturally supported by a wealth of symbolism delegitimising the revolutionary left. Simple theories are also functional in sustaining military morale. But elites need to know better: cf. *Problems of Communism* and *Foreign Affairs* for well-informed views. The question of variants of Cold War ideology is to be explored in a forthcoming study by Philip Elliott and myself.

3. Cf. Roberts (1977) for evidence of recent South African attempts to apply this thinking.

4. Fairbairns (1974) has documented some of the links between the armed forces and the higher education sector, focusing on 'defence lectureships' and research funded by the UK Ministry of Defence, US Department of Defence, and NATO at sixty-five universities and colleges in Britain; she has also pointed out the PR role of military education committees.

References

Ackroyd, Carol, Karen Margolis, Jonathan Rosenhead and Tim Shallice, *The technology of political control* (Harmondsworth, Penguin, 1975).

Agee, Philip, *Inside the Company: CIA Diary* (Harmondsworth, Penguin, 1975).

Ahmad, Eqbal, 'The theory and fallacies of counter-insurgency' in John Leggett, *Taking State Power* (Harper and Row, New York, 1973).

Ambler, John Steward, *The French Army in Politics* (Ohio State UP, 1966.)

Asad, Talal (ed.), *Anthropology and the Colonial Encounter* (Ithaca Press, London, 1975).

Barnet, Richard J., *Intervention and Revolution* (Paladin, St. Albans, 1972).

BSSRS (British Society for Social Responsibility in Science), *The new technology of repression: Lessons from Ireland* (BSSRS Paper 2, 1974).

Buijtenhuijs, Robert, 'Comment vaincre les Mau Mau. Quelques observations sur la recherche contre-insurrectionnelle en Kenya pendant l'état d'urgence' in Copans (ed.) 1975. Reprinted from *Sociologische Gids,* Sept-Dec 1972.

Burton, Anthony, *Urban Terrorism* (Leo Cooper, London, 1975).

Bunyan, Tony, *The History and Practice of the Political Police in Britain* (Quartet Books, London, 1977a).

―――― *Time Out,* No. 363, 4-10 March 1977b.

Chibnall, Steve *Law-and-order News* (Tavistock, London, 1977).

Copans, Jean (ed.), *Anthropologie et Impérialisme* (Maspero, Paris, 1975).

CRCJ (Centre for Research into Criminal Justice) *The Iron Fist and the Velvet Glove, An Analysis of the US Police* (Berkeley, 1975).

Crozier, Brian, *A Theory of Conflict* (Hamish Hamilton, London, 1974).

Clutterbuck, Richard, *Protest and the Urban Guerrilla* (Cassell, London, 1973).

De Paor, Liam, *Divided Ulster* (Harmondsworth, Penguin, 1971).

Downing, John, 'Northern Ireland: Beyond History and Religion' in *Thames Papers in Social Analysis*, Series 1: Northern Ireland (Thames Polytechnic, London 1977).

Eckstein, Harry (ed.), *Internal War: Problems and Approaches* (The Free Press, Glencoe, 1964).

—— 'On the etiology of internal war' in George A. Kelly and Clifford W. Brown Jr. (eds.), *Struggles in the State* (John Wiley, New York, 1970).

Elliott, Phillip, *Reporting Ulster* (Centre for Mass Communication Research, Leicester University, 1976).

Fairbairn, Geoffrey, *Revolutionary Guerrilla Warfare: The Countryside Version* (Harmondsworth, Penguin, 1974).

Fairbairns, Zoë, *Study War No More* (CND, London, 1974).

Finer, S.E. 'On terrorism', *New Society*, 22 January, 1976.

Harries-Jenkins, Gwyn, 'Legitimacy and the problem of order' in Gwyn Harries-Jenkins and Jacques van Doorn (eds.), *The Military and the Problem of Legitimacy* (Sage, Beverly Hills, London, 1976).

Hobsbawm, Eric, *The Age of Revolution* (Sphere Books, London, 1973).

Horowitz, Irving Louis (ed.), *The Rise and Fall of Project Camelot* (MIT Press, 1974).

Iviansky, Ze'ev, 'Individual terror: concept and typology', *Journal of Contemporary History*, 12 (1977).

Kelly, George A., 'The French Doctrine of la Guerre Révolutionnaire' in Kelly, George A. and Brown Jnr, Clifford W., *Struggles in the State: Sources and Patterns and World Revolution* (John Wiley, New York, 1970).

Kelly, Phil, 'Home Office prepares for War', *The Leveller*, December 1976.

Kitson, Frank, *Low Intensity Operations* (Faber, London, 1971).

—— *Bunch of Five* (Faber, London, 1977).

Kohl, John and John Litt, *Urban Guerrilla Warfare in Latin America* (MIT Press, 1974).

Kuper, Adam, *Anthropologists and Anthropology* (Harmondsworth, Penguin, 1975).

Laqueur, Walter, *Guerrilla: A Historical and Critical Study* (Weidenfeld and Nicolson, London, 1977a).

—— 'Interpretations of Terrorism: Fact, Fiction and Political Science', *Journal of Contemporary History*, 12 (1977b).

Leggett, John C., *Taking State Power* (Harper & Row, New York, 1973).

McGuffin, John, *The Guineapigs* (Harmondsworth, Penguin, 1974).

MacNally, Roger, 'News not Views: The Intelligence and the Press in Ireland' (Unpublished paper, 1977).

Minerup, Gunter, 'West Germany since the War', *New Left Review* 99, (1976).

Moss, Robert, *The Collapse of Democracy* (Temple Smith, London, 1975).

Pye, Lucian, 'The Roots of Insurgency and the Commencement of Rebellions' in Eckstein (ed.), 1964.

Rapoport, David C., *Assassination and Terrorism* (CBC Learning Systems, Toronto, 1971).

Roberts, Adam, 'South Africa Resorts to Psywar' *New Society*, 21 April 1977.

Schlesinger, Philip, *Putting 'Reality' Together: BBC News* (Constable, London, 1978).

Sobel, Lester A., *Political Terrorism* (Facts on File, New York, 1975).

Taber, Robert, *The War of the Flea* (Paladin, St Albans, 1972).

Thompson, Sir Robert, *Defeating Communist Insurgency* (Chatto & Windus, London, 1972).

Van Doorn, Jacques, *The Soldier and Social Change* (Sage, Beverley Hills, London, 1975).

Wertheim, W.F. 'La recherche contre-insurrectionnelle à l'aube du XXe siècle' in Copans 1975. Reprinted from *Sociologische Gids*, Sept-Dec 1972.

—— *Evolution and Revolution* (Harmondsworth, Penguin, 1974).

Wilkinson, Paul, *Political Terrorism* (Macmillan, London, 1974).

5 BUSINESS AND THE STATE: MANAGEMENT EDUCATION AND BUSINESS ELITES IN FRANCE AND GREAT BRITAIN.

Jane Marceau, Alan B. Thomas and Richard Whitley

Introduction

The aim of this paper is to contribute to an understanding of the role of high-level business education in the social reproduction of business elites. Examining this role involves not only the analysis of the mechanisms of reproduction but also of the way in which such reproduction is justified. Because education occupies the major legitimating role for inequalities within the socio-occupational stucture in modern capitalist societies, the use by business of the education system suggests the transformation of a mechanism publicly believed to be ensuring equality of chances into one aimed at the maintenance of the status quo. As has been pointed out in relation to France, by apparently delegating to the school system the power of selection to occupational and social roles, the privileged can appear to abdicate their own power to a neutral institution and so seem to renounce the more arbitrary hereditary transmission of privileges. By its verdicts on individuals, which virtually never work to the substantial disadvantage of the privileged classes, the school system contributes powerfully to the reproduction of the established order (Bourdieu, Passeron 1970, pp. 205-6; Bowles, 1972). By encouraging the establishment of graduate business schools, whether within the state university system or the state-recognised private system, business has been able to use the 'neutrality' of the state, and the presentation of the latter as essentially concerned with the 'public' interest, to refurbish its public image in the face of critical public attitudes while effectively retaining established recruitment patterns to elite positions and hence maintaining representatives of the most privileged groups in society in positions of economic power. We argue that the analysis of the context of development of business schools in countries such as Britain and France, of their 'publics', their student populations, and of the employers of the graduates of such schools suggests the principally 'conservative' role played by such schools and throws light on the relations between business and the rest of society through an understanding of those existing between business and the State as represented by the education system.[1]

The Context of the Development of Management Education: Economic and Ideological Change

Relations between the major economic institutions (business) and the state in modern European capitalist countries are essentially tinged with ambiguity and compromise. The relations at the basic level of the system of production, because of the constellation of wider social and political forces, have, if the system is to survive, to be 'disguised' and modified at the political and public level. For example, while the dominant ethos of the societies in many ways insists on the independence of business, the state increasingly shapes the conditions in which businesses must operate and, although the state upholds dominant business values, its policies nevertheless take account of those which other sections of the community have been able to impose. The action of such conflicting forces can be seen in the field of business education.

On the one hand there are the state-financed universities with their ideology upholding the tradition of independent learning and disinterested research.[2] On the other, the world of business, particularly in Britain but also to some extent in France, has traditionally emphasised practice over theory, and has preferred to recruit its own men to form in its own image and to hand on by apprenticeship methods the accumulated wisdom of previous generations.[3] That one could formulate abstract generalities from such experience and use them as a basis for formal education long remained an alien notion.[4]

In Britain, recruitment to senior managerial levels has been based largely on particularistic criteria with little reference to formal qualifications, using 'consensus' policies whereby a new incumbent 'emerged', as leaders of the Conservative Party were once wont to do, in cases where he was not the legal heir of the owners. In such a situation the state played little direct part and could not do much to modify recruitment patterns in line with ideas about 'careers open to talent' although these were the ideological basis of increased opportunities in education.

The French situation differs from the British in that most high-level managers in important firms have for long been graduates of the prestigious, though not always the most prestigious, *Grandes Ecoles,* mainly engineering schools, as well as the *Institut d'Etudes Politiques* and the Law, Economics and Science faculties of Universities. In France the ideology of the 'career open to talent', enshrined in such schools as the *Ecole Polytechnique,* provided a model of legitimacy for business while in fact training the heirs.

However, in both countries after 1945, and with growing momentum in the 1950s and 1960s, following significant changes in industrial structure and concentration, a new form of ideology legitimating business decision-making structures and managerial practices developed. This was institutionalised in a series of schools new in Europe — such as the Henley Administrative Staff College and the Business Schools at London and Manchester.[5] the *Institut Européen d'Administration des Affaires* (INSEAD) and later the *Institut Supérieur des Affaires* (ISA) in France — and in a thorough-going reform of the curricula and teaching methods of prestigious French undergraduate commercial schools. The State in both Britain and France, although in quite different ways, helped to create university-level management diplomas and degrees and to consecrate management as a discipline capable, if not entirely worthy, of study within the traditional university mould.

Although the pattern of industrialisation and economic growth in France, at least since the mid-nineteenth century, has been very different to that shown by Britain, certain important characteristics of the recent evolution of the productive base have been common to both. Those most important in relation to management education seem to be related to increased foreign competition (coupled in both countries to the loss of an empire, depriving them of privileged access to markets for finished products and sources of raw materials); to increased foreign investment in many crucial areas of industry and commerce; to concentration among firms such that a relatively few important concerns come to dominate many product markets,[6] and changes in the technological bases of whole industries such that many enterprises could not raise the capital necessary to meet increased competition and make the required product substitutions. In both countries, this last feature, the increase in industrial concentration, became an important focus for government policy, with the creation in Britain of the Industrial Reorganisation Corporation (IRC) and subsequently in France of the *Institut de Dévelopement Industriel* (IDI).

Increased size of firms, widened product ranges, greater technological complexity, a new emphasis on selling and on financial control increased the importance of certain functions, such as marketing, finance (as distinguished from traditional budgeting and accounting techniques) and forward planning.[7] These changes have led to new problems and, with the decline of the importance of economic capital as a means of ensuring the attachment of managers to their employers, a new problem of personnel control has arisen, the problem of managing managers. At the same time, changes in the political environment and prospects, coupled to a declining economic rate of growth in Britain, led to a new political emphasis on 'dragging British

industry into the twentieth century' and taking 'proper' advantage of
the 'white heat of technology'. In France, too, considerable stress was
laid on the failure of the controllers of French industry to modify their
traditional modes of recruitment to senior managerial positions, based
largely on particularistic attributes, and on the methods of management
and the assumptions upon which management decisions rested. In both
countries, the unsatisfactory economic performance (especially Britain)
and the failure to respond to new challenges (France) made industry
vulnerable. The need for a new ethos and for the presentation of a new
image of industry became matters of public debate.[8]

Similar economic and political processes in each country drew the
attention of the leaders of industry and the state enviously across the
Atlantic, where the American situation was seen as a model worthy of
emulation. Coinciding with academic theories of the period concerning
the evolution of societies which suggested a considerable convergence of
'industrial societies' and the suggestion that differences were due to
different levels of development, what had been done in America was
seen by public and private leaders not only as appropriate to the European situation, but also as essentially linked to the future progress of
European countries. As America was rich, and America had management
education of a high order, the latter seemed to many to be to a significant degree a contributory cause of the former. The logic of this argument pointed to an 'obvious' solution to the situation which British
businessmen, in particular, found discomforting.[9]

The proposed remedy seemed all the more appropriate because of a
further element of the belief system of the late 1950s which put much
faith in education as a panacea for a gamut of social ills, and in particular for failings in economic performance. The post-war period in both
France and Britain saw a widespread desire to reform the education
systems. The rise of management education can thus be seen as a
specific manifestation of this belief and as being linked to the society's
'manpower planning' provisions.

In brief, then, economic and political forces had both prepared the
ground and provided the conditions favourable for an ideological shift.
Although not specifically intended as such, the development of high-
level management education can usefully be seen in the context of this
process of adjustment: that education was to provide the manager with
a new, professionalised image.[10]

Management Education in Britain

There has been a long-standing attitude of apathy in Britain towards management education on the part of both business and the education system, expressed now and then as an active hostility.[11] Since the most prestigious sectors of the education system, the public schools and the universities, have traditionally oriented themselves, and their students, to careers in the professions and public service, thereby perpetuating the second-rate status of industry in relation to the professions, it is perhaps not surprising that industrialists have long been wary of committing themselves to an explicit alliance with the higher education system.

Given the traditional orientation of British management to on-the-job training rather than formal instruction in the education system, it is perhaps not surprising that, although companies express a belief in the professional manager, they have been unwilling to recognise the validity of formal management education, in the sense of subordinating their criteria of recruitment and promotion to the verdicts of the education system.[12] Qualificational restrictions on entry to certain levels of management remain almost totally absent.[13] The behaviour of industry in respect of management education indicates a strong desire to retain business based criteria in the selection of senior management. These criteria seem up to now to have consisted of an amalgam of practical experience and social acceptability rather than formal qualifcations.[14] Thus one of the principle reactions of industry to calls for a 'better-educated management' has been to support independent management colleges and internal management development schemes which lay outside the state education system, and which, by their very nature, have not been concerned to certify participants according to universalistic criteria. Hence, for example, the deleterious consequences of the designation of top managers as inadequate by a neutral examining body can be avoided, whilst a form of educational legitimation is obtained through attendance at a 'country-house' management college.[15]

The circumstances surrounding the creation of the 'high quality' business schools at London and Manchester reflect the ambivalent attitudes of industry, government and the universities to the creation of high-level institutions of management education within the state system. Even though the idea of establishing business schools in Britain on the American pattern had been proposed since at least the early 1950s,[16] these ideas took fifteen years to implement, and this implementation seems to have occurred largely as a result of the efforts of a small group of 'management intellectuals', who probably did not represent the views of major industrialists. Although it is difficult to pinpoint a single group or individual, Wheatcroft (1970, p. 94) indicates that in the early 1960s some senior businessmen, who were dissatisfied with the 'calibre' of their graduate intake to management, began to press for the establishment of business schools. At the same time, a House of Commons 'dining group', which included Sir Keith Joseph, began to discuss the question of high-level management education, and this resulted in the creation of the Foundation for Management Education (FME) which financed a number of teaching experiments in selected universities. A second group, known as the Savoy Group, proposed that a business school should be created at the proposed University of Warwick. The first 'official' reference to business schools came, however, in the second report of the newly established NEDC (NEDC, 1963) which advocated an increased provision for management education, and the establishment of at least one 'high-level' business school comparable to the renowned school at Harvard. This suggestion was also made by the Robbins Committee (Robbins Report, 1963, p. 135) to whom both the FME, FBI (Federation of British Industries) and BIM (British Institute of Management) gave evidence. Whilst the Robbins Committee was sitting, senior representatives of these last groups plus the Director General of NEDO, commissioned Lord Franks to produce a blueprint for British business schools which would resolve a number of controversies among the interested parties and bring matters to a head. The so-called Franks Committee was not therefore commissioned by the state, and operated in the face of an absence of government initiative, the state only later agreeing to implement business proposals. A report was issued by Lord Franks (Franks, 1963), under the auspices of the BIM, recommending that two business schools should be created in association with the universities of London and Manchester.

The tension between the universities and industry was clearly presented in Franks' Report.[17] Lord Franks noted that both academics and industrialists were deeply suspicious of each other's intentions. Industry feared that the universities would cast the business schools in the traditional academic mould, and that they would not, as a result, be concerned with what was 'practical'. The academics, on the other hand, believed that industry was only interested in short-term 'face-lifting', and were much concerned to ensure that the schools would be involved in post-graduate degree level teaching. Lord Franks, however, had decided that a business school was primarily an institution that was 'practical', and, in order to ensure that both the interests of the academics and industry were represented, proposed that the schools should be financed half by industry and half by the University Grants Committee, and that responsibility for policy should be equally shared by industry and the universities. The establishment of these two Business Schools thus represented a compromise between industry and the state educational system.

When it came to the possible sources of recruitment for students, the 'publics' of the schools, industry and academia were again divided. The industrialists wanted the emphasis of the school's provision to be on fairly young managers with some experience and those who had already been selected for managerial positions. This suggested an orientation to short-courses without certification. The academics, however, wanted the emphasis to be on post-graduate degree courses for those who had only just graduated or who were relatively inexperienced. In fact the distribution of resources, certainly in the case of Manchester Business School, has remained more or less evenly divided between post-graduate courses leading to a Diploma or Masters Degree, and post-experience courses for middle or senior managers. However, it is interesting to note that the willingness of industry to sponsor candidates for the post-graduate course has always been low[18] whereas the bulk of the costs of the post-experience courses are borne by industry.

Management Education in France

Commercial, and subsequently management, education in France, although its major institutions are private,[19] can only be understood in relation to the system of high-level technical education run by the state. The major engineering schools were founded by the state at various times during the nineteenth century to create a 'new' class of 'engineer-officers' for the French Army and technical-administrators for the high levels of the Civil Service.

They rapidly established a dominant position over recruitment to senior posts, not only in the state but also in private business. Towards the end of the century, the Chambers of Commerce, notably in Paris, reacted to this situation by funding a series of schools designed to produce the *cadres* of commerce and banking. The foundation of the *Ecole des Hautes Etudes Commerciales* (HEC) in 1881 coincided with a period of major economic and political change, with the development of financial institutions and commercial enterprises and the extension of the French colonies. From the beginning, the most prestigious commercial schools looked to the state to sanction their activities and identified themselves as closely as possible with the intellectual criteria for entrance used by the 'best' parts of the state educational system.[20] Gradually the *concours,* the selective entrance examination, has become more difficult, demanding from one to three years' study in special preparatory schools, exactly on the model of the state engineering institutions. The services rendered by HEC to French society, and hence to the state, have been recognised officially in the granting to the school of the Croix de Guerre and the Légion d'Honneur as well as in the formal opening of its new campus by President de Gaulle. The courses offered by this commercial school have also at times been geared to careers in public administration; as early as 1905 a section preparing for a career in the colonial service was founded and between 1910 and 1922 there were preparatory courses for entry to the diplomatic and consular corps. Prestigious undergraduate 'business' education has thus looked much to the state for its legitimation as well as, at certain periods, for outlets for its students.

Until 1955, however, no state institutions of higher education offering courses in management existed. The universities remained totally separate from business training of any kind. In France there have never been professorial chairs financed by industry, similar to those in the scientific faculties of British and particularly North American universities. Only in 1955 did the French Government introduce a certificate in management, obtained by university graduates after one year, part-time courses at small university institutes. It was not until 1968 that the business university of Paris IX, Paris Dauphine, was founded, at a time when the role and structures of all French universities were being called into question. The graduates of Dauphine, however, have never obtained the same recognition in financial and promotion terms as those coming from the major private schools, and its degrees have gradually become more and more oriented towards university standards of the most traditionally academic kind, enshrined in the new *Agrégation de gestion*.

The fundamentally ambivalent relationship between business and the state has thus been as evident in France as in Britain. In France, however, the private sector has retained control of its most prestigious educational institutions. This is important because it means that private business has thus retained control over admission procedures and curricula and can thus impose its ethos both in terms of who is selected for training and the content of what students are taught. Being outside the public system the commercial schools are not obliged to accept all students possessing the *baccalauréat* nor to gear their curricula and teaching methods to university norms. They benefit, however, from the state's sanction for their diplomas.[21]

The major post-graduate business school operating in France,[22] in
fact, is not part of the French system of education but is an international, principally European, school recruiting students from a wide
range of countries. This school, the *Institut Européen d'Administration
des Affaires* (INSEAD), situated at Fontainebleau, was founded in
1958, taking in its first students in 1959. The Institute was sponsored
by a group of businessmen belonging to the Paris and International
Chambers of Commerce and the European Productivity Agency, and
with technical assistance from the Harvard Business School.[23] The
1950s had seen considerable growth of industrial output and the
service sector in France, the beginnings of the Common Market and the
early stages of the opening-up of French industry to international
competition, principally American. These changes combined with, as we
said before, the concentration of firms into larger units and the previous
predominance of the engineer in management positions created a
demand for 'new' men, specially[24] prepared for international business
concerns. Presenting its *raison d'être,* the prospectus of the school for
1976 begins by saying that:

> INSEAD began in 1958 with a commitment to help in the building
> of a genuine European business community. It was considered then
> that the historical process of uniting Europe would have to start
> with the establishment of a new prosperity based on economic inte-
> gration and co-operation. To achieve economic prosperity would
> require the development of professional managers, and to build a
> European community would require that their training be European.
> (p. 10)

However, in spite of the interest of international business in an international institute, expressed by financial participation in the costs of
the school, there has been a marked reluctance on the part of enterprises to finance students on the one year programme.[25]

Tri-lingual — French, German and English — the Institute recruits
students from many countries but around one third of the students in
any one year are French who thus constitute the single most important
national group. In spite of its international orientations, INSEAD's
implantation on French soil, its recognition by the French Government
as, for instance, an *école d'application* for Polytechnicians and its close
contacts with French industry have meant that for the French it has
become almost a part of their national education system. For this
reason, the role the school plays for its French students is comparable

with that played for the British by the business schools at Manchester
and London. It should be noted though that the British constitute the
second largest nationality in the student body of INSEAD.

Elite Recruitment Patterns in Business: Economic, Social and Cultural Capital

Recruitment to elite (control) positions, and the career paths which
form routes towards them, may be understood as a manifestation of
the importance given to particular configurations of capital by the
dominant groups within the class structure of any given society.
Following Bourdieu's analysis,[26] significant forms of capital may be
grouped under the headings of economic capital (money and fixed
capital), social capital (networks of contacts, and social skills) and
cultural capital (educational qualifications and *culture générale*). Social
capital may take three major forms. First, kinship ties and connections
which can be expected to be mobilised on one's behalf to obtain
positions and exert influence, and which may be allied to the development of a network of personal contacts which are not based directly on
kinship ties but rather on a common educational experience and class
background. Secondly, there is the existence of social knowledge about
how the educational and occupational structures are related and positions allocated. This knowledge is highly inequitably distributed. This
form of social capital is linked to the first through the mobilisation of
the collective social knowledge of the kindship unit. The more members
of one's family that occupy elite positions the more social knowledge is
available. Finally, there is the set of social skills obtained from family
upbringing and attendance at certain educational institutions which
demarcate elite personnel from others by particular modes of speech,
dress and bodily movements. While these three forms of social capital
can be expected to be associated with economic capital, they also play
an important role on their own as means of co-ordinating and concen-
trating economic capital, centralising information and influence and
ensuring continued reproduction of elite personnel. Cultural capital
refers both to educational qualifications which confer right of access, or
facilitate access, to privileged positions in the occupational structure,
and to the more ethereal but nonetheless influential *culture générale*
which is often used as a criterion of elite membership. It also of course
implies acquisition of particular skills and expertise but these are not
always relevant to work subsequently undertaken or to acquiring control positions. In line with the new, technocratic ideology, particular
types of educational diplomas are becoming increasingly necessary to

obtain lucrative and controlling positions in the new very large firms whereas previously economic property rights were frequently sufficient to ensure access to control positions of dominant but medium sized businesses.

Within a social formation, configurations of these forms of capital change with changes in the economic foundation of the society and with specific social and economic circumstances. Such changes are linked to the ways in which elites justify their positions, but do not necessarily affect all groups in a harmonious way, creating 'lags' which frequently necessitate the use by existing or potential elite members of 'reconversion strategies', whereby a form of capital valuable in previous circumstances is invested in the acquisition of a new form which has currency under the new conditions. As business has been subject to a critique on the grounds of inefficiency, the development of management education, particularly as oriented to inculcating general managerial skills most appropriate to senior positions, can be seen as providing a new form of cultural capital and thus facilitating reconversion strategies. In connection with this the relations between business and the state become important, for the state provides a legitimation mechanism for recruitment patterns, either directly, because the state education system gives such recognition, or indirectly in that such a system stands as a model for educational arrangements in the private domain. The more closely a private system resembles the state model, the more readily it can claim a legitimating status. Relations in this area are, however, extremely delicate, for while the state may legitimate the capital its real value for recruitment is decided by business which provides its market. For instance, in France, business education provides an apparently highly effective reconversion mechanism for sub-elites where dominant members find that necessary, but it has never quite achieved the legitimacy conferred by the elite parts of the state education system. In Britain, on the contrary, the graduates of the predominantly state administered business schools, embedded principally in the universities, may, in spite of the expressed wish by industry for 'competent' high-level managers, not be on the fast tracks leading to the top.

These relationships can be illustrated by an examination on the one hand of recruitment patterns to the existing business elites, and, on the other, of the growth of management education and its links with the 'new' legitimation order in France and Great Britain.

Business Elites in France and Great Britain

Studies of top businessmen in France, Britain and the USA[27] indicate a considerable degree of social reproduction (with many businessmen being themselves the sons of businessmen), a high level of education in the case of France and the USA but a rather lower level in the case of Britain.

A study by Delefortrie-Soubeyroux (1961) of nearly 2000 *cadres dirigeants* (top managers) of French industry in the 1950s, showed that 41 per cent were the sons of industrialists while only 4 per cent were the sons of artisans, farmers or industrial manual workers and the bulk of the remainder had fathers who had been in either professional or managerial occupations. A later study, although restricted to the chief executives of the largest French firms, presented similar results (Hall and de Bettignies, 1968) and also showed that in terms of university attendance, France's top management in its biggest concerns was the most highly educated in Europe. Nearly 90 per cent of the chief executives had attended a university or *Grande Ecole*, although only a minority had studied economics or 'business'.

In these terms, Britain by comparison, had the least educated chief executives in Europe (Hall *et al.*, 1969)[28] In their study of chief exec-utives in 120 of the 500 largest British companies, Hall and Amado-Fishgrund (1969) also showed the high social origins of British business leaders; 70 per cent of the chief executives were sons of business owners, executives or professionals, whilst less than 10 per cent had fathers who were manual workers. Their educational backgrounds largely confirmed their high status. It appeared that about two-thirds of the sample had been to a public school, a finding also made by several other studies of directors. However, their higher education was far sketchier; less than half had attended a university and of these only three-quarters had actually obtained a degree. The researchers suggested that top manage-ment in Britain is characterised more by its social exclusiveness than in terms of high level education.

Whilst these findings were restricted to chief executives (i.e. mana-ging directors and chairmen), other studies of company directors in large companies present a similar picture. Whitley, for example, found that 65 per cent of the directors of the forty largest industrial com-panies had attended a public school, but only 58 per cent had attended a University. The dominance of public schooling as against university attendance was even more marked in the case of directors of major financial institutions. In general this suggests that high-level education has been relatively unimportant for gaining access to the highest-level positions in British business, ascriptive and particularistic attributes, connections and experience seeming to have played a much more important part. This confirms the conclusions of other commentators on the recruitment strategies implemented by British business.[29]

Comparisons between Britain and France suggest that the recruitment of business elites in each country has differed greatly in its use of state-recognised qualifications for elite positions in large businesses. In Britain business has traditionally preferred practical experience and social acceptability rather than formally certified qualifications. French business, on the other hand, has related career paths and promotion prospects relatively closely to the credits of the education system. Yet in both countries the result has basically been the same: those who have been selected to occupy controlling positions in business have largely come from the most privileged groups in society. Insofar as the education system has intervened at all, it has served largely to equip the heirs under the 'old' system of access with the new forms of capital necessary in the face of changed economic and ideological circumstances. Thus, while it might be thought that the emergence of new management education institutions, such as INSEAD and the London and Manchester Business Schools (LBS and MBS), would give grounds for supposing that business management has at last become a 'career open to talent' we suggest that such a judgement would, to say the least, be premature, as can be shown by an examination of the students of these schools and how they came to be there. Also, currently available evidence indicates that Business School graduates do not in fact quickly achieve top positions in large firms.

The Publics of INSEAD and the British Business Schools

Institut Européen d'Administration des Affaires (INSEAD)

The social origins of the French students at INSEAD are very high, notably higher than those of even the most prestigious schools of the purely French education system.[30] They are heavily concentrated in the top three INSEE[31] categories, and notably in the *patronat,* owners of businesses in industry and commerce. The backgrounds of the latter, however, do not place the families as members of the elite in the sense of the top firms but rather as members of the sub-elite[32] for not only are the firms owned by these families relatively small in terms of size of turnover or number of employees but they are frequently to be found in declining sectors of the economy, such as textiles. This is important for it means on the one hand that the fathers of the persons concerned (virtually all men) can no longer place all their offspring with their economic capital alone (especially because there tend to be several sons to place). In order, therefore, to maintain or improve the socio-economic position held by their families of origin some at least of the sons are thrown onto the 'public' labour market and therefore have to rely more on their cultural capital, principally, that is, on the educational diplomas they hold. Given the close integration between formal qualifications held and career possibilities in France it is important to acquire as high a level diploma as possible. As the tables below will show, many of the French students at INSEAD have not managed previously to obtain entrance to the most prestigious (mainly engineering) schools in Paris, but have been forced to accept the verdicts of the publicly-sanctioned education institutions which 'relegated' them to second place. Success in a prestigious post-graduate business school is seen by participants as compensating for previous inadequacies.

Many of the students (36 per cent) and particularly those from the *patronat* (53 per cent), had already been to private schools, the families having tried to ensure maximum benefit from the education system available.

Table 5.1: Socio-Professional Origins of Students at INSEAD 1959-1973

Socio-Professional Category	Number			% Known Origins		
Patrons (owners) of industry and commerce	135	)		36.5	)	
Liberal professions	49	)		13.2	)	
Cadres supérieurs[a] — public sector	45	) 86	) 270	12.2	) 23	) 72.5
Cadres supérieurs — private sector	41	)	)	11.1	)	)
Cadres moyens (middle executives)	50			13.5		
Artisans/small shopkeepers	20			5.4		
White-collar workers	8			2.2		
Manual workers	8			2.2		
Farmers	14			3.8		
Total	370			100		

[a] *Cadres supérieurs* are 'managers' or 'executives' in the widest sense and here include high level teachers and career officers, as in the INSEE classification, to whom we have added senior civil servants (very few). The second category, *cadres supérieurs* in the private sector includes only the managers in private business. The categories used here are adapted from those used by INSEE.

Source: J. Marceau, *The Social Origins, Educational Experience and Career Paths of a Young Business Elite*, (INSEAD, Fontainebleau, 1976)

The great majority of the students had passed the 'bac.C', the mathematics *baccalauréat* and those who were excellent at mathematics had gone on to prepare for entry to engineering schools (49 per cent), the others largely preparing for entry to commercial schools (39 per cent), with only a few going into university faculties (12 per cent). However, many of the students with an engineering background had not attended the most prestigious schools and 40 per cent had gone to provincial ones. To escape being 'relegated' to the provinces over a quarter (26 per cent) of the sons of the *patronat* had attended Swiss engineering schools. It should be borne in mind, though, that INSEAD students had by no means gone to *petites écoles* and the combination of high social origins, good if not excellent first diplomas and a prestigious management education stand them in good stead on the labour market.

Manchester Business School and London Business School

The social origins of British students on the graduate course at Manchester Business School (MBS) and London Business School (LBS) are shown in Table 5.2.[33] This shows that a majority of students at both London and Manchester have been recruited from the upper reaches of the social structure. Although the data for MBS show a substantial minority of 'working class' students, preliminary information on intakes for other years suggests that 1975 was unusual and that the more common distribution is rather similar to that found at LBS. A noticeable feature is the high proportion of students at both schools whose fathers were company directors or managers. At MBS, nearly half of the fathers within the managerial group were company directors or senior managers in firms which they did not substantially own, and a further quarter were substantial owners of incorporated business;[34] at LBS in 1976, 42 per cent of the managerial fathers were company directors or senior managers, and a further 42 per cent were owners; and for LBS 1966-73 approximately 45 per cent were directors or senior managers and a further quarter were owners. A sizeable proportion have also been drawn from professional backgrounds, predominantly from the 'higher' professions.[35] In the case of LBS about a third of those in professional occupations have been independent professionals.

The type of secondary school attended by the MBS and LBS students is shown in Table 5.3. The most striking feature is the substantial numbers drawn from the public schools. Indeed, 72 per cent of one year's intake at LBS were educated at public schools, and over the period 1966-73 more than 50 per cent were from public schools in six of the eight years. The bulk of those who attended public school had been to 'minor' schools, but 20 per cent of the 1966-73 LBS

Table 5.2: Socio-Professional Origins of British Entrants to the Graduate Course at MBS (1975) and LBS (1976, 1966-73)

	MBS 1975		LBS 1976		LBS 1966-73	
	n	%	n	%	n	%
Company Directors and Managers	25	49.0	19	37.2	151	36.0
Higher Professional	3	5.9	10	19.6	96	22.6
Administrative	4	7.8	6	11.8	63	15.0
Lower professional	4	7.8	3	5.9	21	5.0
Employers and Proprietors	3	5.9	2	3.9	26	6.2
'Routine' non-manual	1	2.0	6	11.8	21	5.0
Skilled manual	9	17.6	1	2.0	30	7.1
Other manual	2	3.9	4	7.8	13	3.1
Total	51	100.0	51	100.0	420	100.0

Source: Files and interviews

Table 5.3: Type of Secondary School Attended by Graduate Course Entrants at LBS and MBS

	1975 MBS Entrants		1976 LBS Entrants		1966-73 LBS Entrants	
	n	%	n	%	n	%
Clarendon school[a]	3	5.8)	6	11.1)	46	10.6)
'Well-known' Public[b]	1	1.9) 40.4	1	1.8) 35.1	53	12.2) 55.0
Other Public[c]	17	32.7)	12	22.2)	140	32.2)
Other Independent	2	3.8	4	7.4	9	2.1
Direct Grant Grammar	1	1.9	8	14.8	6	1.4
Local Authority Grammar	22	42.3	19	35.2	164	37.8
Secondary Modern	2	3.8	3	5.6	2	0.5
Comprehensive	2	3.8	1	1.9	11	2.5
Girls Public School	1	1.9	0.	0.0	1	0.2
Other	1	1.9	0	0.0	2	0.5
Total	52	100.0	54	100.0	434	100.0

[a] I.e., Charterhouse, Eton, Harrow, Merchant Taylor's, Rugby, St Paul's, Shrewsbury, Westminster, Winchester.
[b] As selected by David Boyd in his *Elites and their Education* (1973) pp. 41-2, partly in terms of Oxbridge Scholarships. The schools are: Bradfield, Cheltenham, Clifton, Fettes, Haileybury, Lancing, Loretto, Malvern, Marlborough, Oundle, Radley, Repton, Rossall, Sedbergh, Sherbourne, Stowe, Uppingham. It should be noted that this list excludes Gordonstoun and Wellington.
[c] Schools other than those in a and b having membership of the Headmaster's Conference.

students had been to one of the 'Clarendon Nine'.[36]

The family background of those who went to public schools was largely managerial. At MBS, 56 per cent of those with fathers who were directors or managers had been to public school, and this represented 67 per cent of all those attending such schools, whilst for LBS 1966-73, 67 per cent of this group had attended public school representing 43 per cent of all public school entrants. The higher professional and administrative groups had also made substantial use of public schools, so that for MBS and LBS 1966-73 the three groups of managers, higher professionals and administrators accounted for about 90 per cent of the public school attenders.

Business School students have also disproportionately attended Oxbridge. In the case of LBS, nearly half (47 per cent) the alumni had been either to Oxford or Cambridge, with Cambridge being predominant. In 1969, 58 per cent of the LBS intake had attended one or other of these institutions. At MBS the proportion of Oxbridge graduates has been lower, being about a quarter of those entering with degrees between 1965 and 1974 and with a peak figure of 34 per cent in 1969, but it is clear that the contribution of these elite universities to both schools has been far from inconsiderable.[37]

The Career Paths of Business School Alumni

The social origins and educational paths previously followed by students of the three business schools considered here show them as members of the upper classes of French and British society but probably from sub-elite rather than elite backgrounds. The career paths followed after business school suggest that the alumni will follow successful business careers and will certainly, by a form of 'horizontal' social mobility into posts appropriate to the changed economic structure, reproduce the socio-economic positions of their parents and hence reproduce the personnel of the sub-elites of British business. The available data on INSEAD and preliminary data on Manchester and London alumni suggest that they earn high salaries relative to non-business school personnel from similar backgrounds and that they enter the 'new' streams of managerial functions (finance, consulting, marketing, corporate planning). In the early stages of their careers they go predominantly into large businesses, in many cases in manufacturing, frequently American or multi-national. However, by the time the INSEAD alumni were in their third firm, only 19.5 per cent of these employed over 10,000 people compared with 42 per cent of the first firms. At the other end of the scale, the proportion working in firms employing less than 50 people had more than trebled (5 to 17 per cent) in the move from first firm to third firm. Similarly, 19 per cent of those in their third firm were running their own business compared to half of one per cent of those in their first firm. The data for the MBS alumni do not show such a radical shift but they graduated more recently than the INSEAD group. Roughly the same proportion, just over half, of alumni from all three schools went into manufacturing industry for their first job although there was a slight decline to just under a half for INSEAD and MBS alumni for their current job in this sector. The next largest sector for the INSEAD graduates was services (especially consulting) with 21 per cent of the alumni taking their first job there and 26 per cent their third post. By comparison 23 per cent of LBS alumni and 27 per cent of MBS alumni took their first post in banking, insurance and financial services and this was still the second largest employment sector for MBS graduates in 1976.

As might be expected the bulk of business school graduates are first employed in fairly specialist posts although the emphasis differs between the British and the French. Marketing and sales was the main function for the INSEAD alumni first job (39 per cent) and remained so for their third (49 per cent). This was followed by a variety of functions but in later firms the second place was taken by 'general management' (20.5 per cent) which is usually considered to be on the major route to the top. The British graduates' first jobs were less concentrated in marketing and the largest category for both LBS (21 per cent) and MBS (26 per cent) was in fact finance, with marketing being in third place (14 per cent) behind management services (19.5 per cent) for LBS and being the second largest function (20.5 per cent) for MBS. A sizeable group of British graduates worked in 'corporate planning', a major 'new' function — 15 per cent of MBS alumni took their first jobs in this function. Comparable data for the proportion entering the 'general management' stratum are not yet available for the British but an impressionistic examination of the earlier MBS graduates — i.e. those with at least 5 years' post-Business School work experience — suggests that most are still in upper middle management positions which are fairly specialised while a small minority has moved into senior management posts in large companies — e.g. managing director of a substantial subsidiary of a very large business firm.

Although salaries are not always the best indicator of level of managerial responsibility there is no doubt that many business school graduates are earning substantial sums of money. In 1974, 36 per cent of INSEAD alumni reported that they were earning over 110,000 French francs while in 1976 28 per cent of MBS alumni said they were earning more than £9,000. These figures refer to basic salary and do not include bonuses and fringe benefits. In some firms, profit related bonuses can make a substantial difference as, for example, in the case of one MBS graduate whose basic salary in 1976 was £12,000 and bonus in 1975-6 was £10,000. INSEAD students are also paid more than graduates with diplomas from other French schools (cf. Marceau, 1976, pp. 78-80). In general terms, the effect of going to business school seems to be to increase British students' salaries by roughly 50 per cent although inflation makes comparisons difficult over the whole period 1966-76. However, salary increases are due rather to the changes in function and firm's activity that going to business school made possible, than simply to having a post-graduate business qualification. For instance, nearly all LBS students who had worked in production and R & D departments before business school took their first job after business school in more highly paid functions, particularly finance and management services, a move otherwise difficult or even impossible.

On the evidence obtained so far it does appear that business schools do function as 'reconversion' opportunities for many students – especially in terms of department. Furthermore, opportunities for employment and finance and marketing do not appear to be available to the small proportion of sons of clerical and manual workers among business school students. However, it is not clear that business schools enable the sons of business elites to obtain top positions in large firms; rather they seem to attract sons of senior managers and business owners in medium sized firms who then move into comfortable and privileged, but not top, jobs in large firms and subsequently obtain general management posts in smaller – but still substantial – companies. Although many business school graduates in their own words 'aim for the top', the moves they make, from larger to smaller firms, may mean that many disqualify themselves from membership of dominant businesses and hence of the business elite.

Conclusion

In this paper we have argued that the establishment of graduate business schools under the auspices, or with the sanction, of the state in Europe is likely to perpetuate the status quo in terms of recruitment to important positions in business rather than to modify existing practices according to the principle of the 'career open to talent'. The effect of the creation of such schools has been primarily to consecrate a new legitimating ideology in relation to practices of recruitment to positions of responsibility in business rather than to create new paths of upward social and professional mobility – the new form of legitimation became important in the face of social, political and economic changes which called into question the efficacy (and hence legitimacy or justice) of existing practices. As the continuing development of monopoly capitalism has posed new problems for its administrators, business has looked increasingly to the education system to provide highly trained personnel, especially for 'man management', and as a means to rebut incipient public criticism.

However, because of the essentially different principles on which selection in education and business is based, such use of the education system has posed problems for business. Thus, at the same time as they have used the education system's verdicts as a mechanism of selection to certain managerial strata, senior persons in business have stressed the system's failure to persuade the public of the 'legitimate' needs of capitalism[38] and its failure to distinguish and develop the non-intellectual criteria implied in notions of 'managerial ability'. Moreover, although for technical personnel, and indeed for access to some levels of the recruitment stratum, business has had little reason to ignore the verdicts of the education system, the potential encapsulation by educational institutions of the skills of *management* threatens to weaken industry's control of management succession, and in consequence of access to the controlling elite. The flirtations of industry with 'public' management education are manifestations of the dilemma which the formal certification of managerial skill poses for the existing elites. The recognition which they give to more technical qualifications, coupled with the formalisation of managerial expertise, entails in theory their giving as much weight to this new form of cultural capital as they do to its technical counterparts, but as the education system is, at least in principle, open to all, its use could make existing senior managers vulnerable where they lack the cultural capital publicly considered necessary[39] and encourage the 'wrong' people, those armed only with cultural capital, to feel they are eligible for promotion to the 'top'. The latter, sharing the ethos of the education system to which they owe all, may not share the dominant values of business. Business, therefore, has tended to react by preferring 'in-house' training where the 'company view' can predominate and the use of private, high-level, short courses for men of 'proven managerial ability' to the more formal and general intellectual criteria used by academic, especially university-level, institutions.[40]

In this sense the 'bureaucratic potential' of business, increased by recent developments, has not been realised in the sense that formal educational criteria are now used as the basis of promotion. Lord Franks himself emphasised that 'most training for business, *and specifically m)st training for management*, must always be "on the job" in the factory or office' (Franks, 1963, para. 4, emphasis added). Top management has continued to emphasise traits such as 'calibre' or 'personality', that is to say attributes which are not taught by the education system (except perhaps in the 'best' schools with suitable playing fields) but inculcated through non-formal institutions such as the family. Thus, except insofar as they can satisfy the potential employers of their graduates that the latter have not only cultural capital but also social and perhaps even economic capital, the business schools of Europe are unlikely in themselves to modify recruitment patterns to the top. In spite of the fact that these institutions emphasise that they inculcate the skills of the generalist over the specialists[41] and see themselves as producing an elite corps of managers or the 'leading Europeans',[42] we suggest that analysis of their publics indicates that in fact, for the foreseeable future, they will reproduce more the personnel of sub-elites in business, and hence probably reinforce the structure of the latter than they will constitute a mechanism permitting access to the 'fast tracks', leading to the elite in the largest corporations. Insofar as any of the students do reach such elite positions they will probably do so for reasons which largely lie outside the education system and *a fortiori* outside the business schools.

The state, by sanctioning education and more particularly education for business, will by that token continue to contribute to maintaining the invisibility of the true criteria used by business in recruitment to controlling positions and facilitate the production and continued credibility of a new legitimating ideology.

Notes

1.   There are numerous problems surrounding the concept of 'elites'. For the
      purposes of this paper, we will use the term 'elite' largely as suggested by
      Giddens (1974, p. 15), and include in the business elite only the top per-
      sonnel of the few hundred biggest companies. The socio-economic origins
      of many students from the business schools we consider are taken to be
      those of 'sub-elites'; that is to say we see them as members of families
      holding important positions at local or regional level, but lacking the
      national or international dimensions of elite groups as such, having rela-
      tively few interconnections with such groups and controlling fewer
      resources.
          We refer principally in this paper to the *Institut Européen d'Admini-*

stration des Affaires (INSEAD) at Fontainebleau and the Manchester and London Business Schools (MBS and LBS). A major study of the French students at INSEAD, one of the premier continental business schools, was carried out by Marceau during 1973-5, financed by SSRC (See Marceau, 1976). LBS and MBS can fairly be treated as the British business schools *par excellence*, although it should be noted that several other institutions have sizeable intakes of post-graduate management students, such as the Bradford University Management Centre, the Cranfield School of Management and the University of Lancaster School of Business and Organisational Studies. The graduate course at MBS began in 1965 and awards either a Diploma of Business Administration (Dip.BA) after one year, or a Master of Business Administration (MBA) after two. Although LBS was also founded in 1965, its first intake of graduate students was in 1966, and it awards a two year MSc. The MBS/LBS study, also financed by the SSRC, is still in progress and is due for completion in late 1978.

2. In recent years some holes have appeared in this representation of the universities' situation, *Warwick University Ltd.* (Thompson, 1970) being a case in point.

3. Mosson (1965) indicates that the first major state initiative in British management education embodied this notion of managerial apprenticeship: 'The National Diploma Scheme reflects the British apprenticeship tradition; a lengthy period must be served before the apprentice manager receives his diploma, and he must attain a specified age' (p. 190).

4. Writing in the late 1950s, McGivering (1960, p. 135) suggested that there was no systematic body of knowledge relevant to management *per se,* a view that was echoed by Nichols (1969, p. 85) nearly ten years later. Nichols also indicated, with the support of evidence from his own study of directors, that many top managers did not accept the existence of management theory, and that 'a sizeable proportion of modern-day directors are anti-management education and, above all, anti-management theorists' (p. 90).

5. The Administrative Staff College was founded in 1947 as a result of a private initiative and with private finance. In the public sector, technical colleges had long offered a variety of courses in management subjects but very little provision for management education was made by the universities until the 1960s. The establishment of two business schools at the universities of London and Manchester in 1965 was associated with a marked increase in the number of universities offering post-graduate management courses (BIM, 1974). By 1972, 25 universities produced 806 graduates. Heller (1973, p. 83) describes this period as one of an 'explosion in management education'. These institutions were the first to be styled as 'Business Schools', and unlike many of their counterparts exist as quasi-autonomous bodies within their 'host' universities.

    Other major business schools, closely following the American, especially Harvard, model were founded in Europe in the 1950s and 1960s, notably the *Centre d'Etudes Industrielles* at Geneva and the IMEDE at Lausanne which is aimed at an international audience and other more 'national' ones such as the *Institut Supérieur des Affaires* (ISA) near Paris and the IESE at Barcelona. The development of Business School curricula and their links with industry at a European level have been facilitated by the European Foundation for Management Education, established in Brussels.

6. In relation to industrial concentration in Britain, see Everly and Little (1960), Utton (1970), Hart, Utton and Walshe (1973), Aaronovitch and

Sawyer (1975) and Hannah (1976). For France, see Claude (1965), Didier and Malinvaud (1969), Diman (1972), Carré *et al.* (1972) and Morin (1974). A useful summary of the factors surrounding the development of management education in the 1960s can be found in Mosson (1965), Chester (1965) and Wheatcroft (1970, pp. 6-19).

7. The increasing importance of the former type of position can be seen as linked to the increased participation of banks in industrial enterprises, most clearly seen in France, whilst the development of forward planning is associated with the concentration phenomena. The bigger a firm becomes in the market, the more it becomes possible to exercise control over that market and institute planned processes of investment and expansion.

8. See the Robbins Report (1963, p. 134) for reference to public debate on high-level management education. Rose (1970) describes the critical atmosphere of the early 60s as follows:

> The slow rate of economic growth of this country as compared with that of others and the frequence balance of payments crises have led to a general feeling of national economic malaise in which no set of institutions has been free from criticism. In consequence, the view has developed over the past decade that, whatever the faults of government policy in general and whatever the failure of government policy to assist management in particular, the relatively poor performance of British industry is attributable partly — but to a significant degree — to inadequate managerial performance. There was discernable in government thinking in the 1960s some increase in the degree of emphasis on the improvement of managerial quality as a factor in economic growth as against others such as direct stimulation of capital investment. (p. 6)

McGivering (1960) noted the need for top managers to adopt a new legitimating ideology:

> Theoretically, appeals to a Divine Right are unlikely to be widely accepted, and the substantial separation of ownership from control makes the appeal to traditional property rights less valid. Thus the justification must be made in terms of the senior managers being the most able persons for the position in the community, and of their ranks being open to all who can demonstrate the requisite competence. (p. 70)

For a national criticism of French industrial management see, for instance, J-J. Servan-Schreiber (1967).

9. Lupton (1972), who was critical of this argument, indicates that it was one of those put forward by businessmen who favoured the establishment of business schools in Britain. Openness to American ideas was enhanced by French and British participation in 'productivity missions' to the United States in connection with the Marshall Aid Scheme. The British teams were particularly impressed by American business education. See AACP (1951), Hutton (1953, pp. 43-4), and for France, Mosson (1965, p. 57), and Wheatcroft (1970), p. 92). The influence of such missions from France on the curriculum and teaching methods of the leading commercial schools was also considerable (see the recent doctoral thesis by H. Le More).

10. The role of high-level management education in the 'professionalisation' of management is mentioned, albeit in an oblique fashion, at several points in the Franks Report (1963) which was instrumental to the creation of the British Business Schools. Thus

These convictions spring from the fact that business management is an intelligent form of human activity, not intellectual nor academic, but practical in nature. Just as nowadays a surgeon has to know many things, possess a range of skills, and be disciplined, exercised and trained in how to apply his knowledge and skills competently in the moment of action, so increasingly the manager of to-day and to-morrow has quite simply to know a lot more things, to be familiar with a much wider range of skills, know how to apply the knowledge and the skills in a practical and enterprising fashion in bringing different ideas together to form a sensible policy, in making his decisions and in communicating them to those who have to carry them out. In short, he has to be a much more knowledgeable and skilful person if to-day he is to be judged competent. (para. 6)

Further, the habit of going to a university is spreading rapidly in Britain and will become even more widespread in future so that soon many more entrants into industry and commerce will have degrees. It will seem strange to these young men and women if it is allowed to appear that for industry and commerce, almost alone among the important careers in this country, no form of intelligent preparation is needed. (para. 29)

11.   See BIM (1971) and Weston's comments (1972). The BIM investigators reported widespread discontent with post-graduate management education.

12.   The lukewarm attitude of industry to management education through the state education system has by no means been restricted to provisions made at university level. One of the earliest attempts by the state to formalise management education took the form of the National Scheme of Management Studies, instituted as a result of a report issued by the Ministry of Education in 1947 (Min. of Ed. 1947), but which, by the late 1950s had fallen into disrepute, was much criticised for its low level of attainment and generally ignored by industry. The low prestige of the technical colleges, principally associated in the eyes of business with the training of young workers and with unprestigious technical courses, meant that industry was unwilling to recognise the Diploma as an indication of suitability for a managerial career, and that the colleges were unable to attract senior managers from industry to act as teachers, thus helping to perpetuate their low-status position.

It might be thought that industry's distaste for management education provided through state institutions would be to some extent assuaged by the involvement in the field of those institutions whch stand at the apex of the state system. Yet in the late 1950s and early 1960s both industry and the universities were predominantly opposed to any expansion of the then meagre provision of management courses. At post-graduate level only a handful of universities offered full-time courses in management subjects leading to a university diploma or certificate. They attracted less than 200 students a year (Mosson, 1965, p. 178) and only a tiny minority of these were sent by companies.

13.   There are, of course, a number of professional bodies associated with business, but these are generally either concerned with technical functions (e.g. accountancy, engineering) or with only quasi-managerial functions (e.g. personnel). Wheatcroft's assessment of the situation in 1970 seems unlikely to have changed.

No formal qualifications were required for entry into the career of business and none still are. Many professionally trained men are needed in business but it is still possible for the managing director or chairman of a vast international business, advised by professional accountants, lawyers, engineers, scientists and economists, to have himself left school at fifteen and had no further formal education. (Wheatcroft, 1970, p. 2)

See also Mosson (1965, p. 199).

14.   For a review of the relation between technical qualification and board membership, see Nichols (1969, pp. 80-3) who concluded that the argument that top management had become technocratic was unconvincing.

15.   The BIM reported the 'growing unease and the doubts in industry about some developments in the rapid expansion of undergraduate and post-graduate courses in business studies' (BIM, 1971, p. 2). Their unease, however, was largely related to courses involving certification, where their control of recruitment is limited:

Whereas most of the people we met were, in varying degrees, perplexed, worried or angry about postgraduate education, the question of post-experience education found them much more relaxed . . . Industry, however, feels that it can control the selection of people to go on post-experience courses reasonably well so that it can ensure that the people selected are the right basic management material and are going on the courses for a clearly defined purpose; and it sees the post-experience courses at the business schools as one only relatively small part of a total range of management development tools in which commercial institutions, consultants, internal training, career planning and many other initiatives are both proper and effective. (BIM, 1971, p. 12)

'Country house' management colleges appear to be a favourite form of finishing school for those in, or about to enter, the highest levels of management. 'In certain cases there is an attempt to offer the amenities and the cachet of an exclusive club. Given the social bias of British management it is not surprising that participation in such courses is highly sought' (Mosson, 1965, p. 194).

16.   'In 1950, for example, at a British Institute of Management national conference, Colonel Urwick called for the immediate establishment in this country, in connection with an existing university, of a residential school of business administration on the American pattern' (Wheatcroft, 1970, p. 3). See also AACP (1951).

17.   The report was commissioned by Lord Rootes, Sir Norman Kipping (Director General, FBI), Cecil Mead (Chairman, BIM), J.W. Platt (Chairman, Foundation for Management Education) and Sir Robert Shone (Director General, NEDO). The mutual suspicions of industry and the universities are graphically presented in paragraphs 17, 18, 19, 28, 29 and 34 (Franks 1963).

18.   The proportion of graduate-course students at MBS sponsored by employers has rarely exceeded 50 per cent and has declined steadily over the last ten years. Less than 25 per cent of entrants to LBS between 1966 and 1973 expected to receive employer sponsorship and although we do not yet know how many actually received sponsorhip, it is probably less than this. This suggests at best a rather limited enthusiasm on the part of industry for this type of post-graduate management education. Weston (1972, p. 10)

cites figures for 1969-70 which show that more than two-thirds of those receiving some form of management education were attending independent centres or were on courses provided by employers.

19. Most commercial schools are financed by local Chambers of Commerce and student fees. Some institutions such as INSEAD are 'more' private in the sense that they are supported directly and almost exclusively by industry and commerce and by student fees.

20. For example, at one period the entrance *concours* was based on the same curriculum as that of the Military Officer School, St Cyr. Also, the idea of the *concours* itself aped that of the State schools and has followed the latter in an increasing attention to the mathematical ability of candidates.

21. This can be seen in their statutes and the 'control' of teaching standards.

22. The other major business school in France, ISA, is part of the French system of education and was founded in 1969. A study of its population and role is planned for the next two years.

23. No detailed data are as yet available on the precise circumstances leading to its foundation.

24. See the analysis of this change, exemplified in employment offers in *Le Monde* made by Bourdieu and his colleagues (1973).

25. INSEAD's post-graduate programme lasts one academic year. The curriculum covers organisational behaviour, accounting, financial analysis, marketing, business policy and a course on the 'European Environment'. Only approximately 8 per cent of the French students are sent by the firms they work for.

26. See, for example, Bourdieu and Passeron (1970), Bourdieu (1971) and Bourdieu, Boltanski and de Saint Martin (1973).

27. Recent studies of British directors include Whitley (1973, 1974), Heller (1973), Stanworth and Giddens (1974) and Fidler (1976). For a brief review of several earlier studies, see Mosson (1965, pp. 147-60) and Nichols (1969, pp. 112-20). For France, see Delefortrie-Soubeyroux (1961), Girard (1961) and Hall and de Bettignies (1968 and 1969). A recent study of American top executives, which also summarises a number of previous studies, is Sturdivant and Adler (1976). This study shows an increasing homogeneity among the American business elite.

28. Data for this study were obtained by mail-questionnaires sent to 2,400 chief executives of the largest companies in Europe. Base figures for individual countries are not given by the authors, but the overall response was 24 per cent. French *Grandes Ecoles* were counted as universities.

29. A recent indication of the probable importance of 'social acceptability' is given by Coventry (1973) in his popular text on management. With reference to selection for top management positions, he writes:

> The group approach extends to such organised procedures as so-called 'psychological week-ends' or 'country house' conditions, where candidates take part in public-speaking sessions, group discussions, debates, exercises etc., and are closely studied by specialists from all points of view. This includes an assessment of their social ability to mix well, to take part in intelligent conversation, and to conduct themselves correctly at table. (p. 240)

The characteristics of the British business elite have, perhaps, been nowhere better summarised than by Heller (1973): 'middle-aged, upper

middle class sons·of businessmen, of no particularly high academic achievement, brought up primarily with others from the same background' (p. 83).
30.   See Marceau, 1976, p. 24.
31.   The French National Statistical Agency.
32.   Evidence gathered on professions and diplomas held by members of the extended families of these families suggests the lack of inter-connections between them and other fractions of the bourgeoisie.
33.   The classification of father's occupation uses a scheme based on the OPCS system, incorporating certain modifications suggested by Routh (1965). It should be noted that the 'employers and proprietors' category excludes owners of incorporated firms, who are classed as directors, and independent professionals, who are allocated to one of the professional categories, usually 'higher professional'.

   Data for LBS entrants prior to 1976 were obtained from application forms rather than by interview. We are not yet in a position to say whether the intakes at LBS and MBS differ from each other in significant ways. Data on MBS alumni are still being collected and analysed, so the figures given later for this group are based on preliminary returns to a lengthy questionnaire. MBS data for 1975 are based on 52 of the 57 British entrants in that year; 1976 LBS data on all 54 British entrants, and 1966-73 LBS data on all 442 British entrants. MBS interviews are being conducted by Thomas and those at LBS by Mrs Janet Cabot, Research Associate.
34.   The categorisation of fathers as business owners as opposed simply to directors or managers, was based on interviewees' accounts of their father's position in terms of whether a father's employing organisation was 'his own business'. 'Business owners' are often those owning family-firms, and we do not include small businessmen owning unincorporated concerns in this category. For the LBS alumni, the information given on application forms made the identification of owners more difficult, and in cases of doubt fathers were regarded as non-owners. It is important to emphasise that exclusion from the category of 'business owner' does not necessarily mean that insignificant numbers of shares were held in the employing company or other companies, nor, of course, a lack of other kinds of economic capital.
35.   I.e., those in OPCS Order XXV with Social Class I, which includes doctors, dentists, professional engineers, barristers and university teachers. The figures for professionals for MBS in 1975 are probably unusually low. In 1976 the proportion with fathers in the professions rose to 34 per cent, three-quarters of whom were higher professionals. The manual group, however, fell to 9 per cent.
36.   The association of the Business Schools with public schools is not entirely 'accidental'. In its early years, MBS employed an ex-managing director of Shorko-Metal Box Ltd to act in a senior capacity liaising between the School and business. In a talk given in 1967, he is reported as having said that he had 'interested several well-known public schools – Glenalmond, Marlborough, Eton and Harrow among them – in preliminary business studies – and had introduced them to the thought that business is worthwhile' (Quoted in *Credit Trader*, 18 November 1967). For some evidence on financial links between the public schools and industry, see McGivering (1960, p. 66). It is perhaps worth noting the finding of an Institute of Directors survey in respect of the education of directors' children: ' . . . over a third of the children are or were at

public school' (Institute of Directors 1966, p. 272).

37.   For instance, in 1974, Oxford and Cambridge produced 8.5 per cent of all graduates from British universities (DES, 1974).

38.   A 'confidential document' prepared by the Departments of Education, Employment and Industry in 1976 is reported as having proposed a 'cultural revolution' to change the attitude to industry of young people, especially schoolchildren'. Its proposals included:

> . . . tax incentives and differentials starting next July to end the nine to five attitude among industrialists and to prevent further emigration from Britain; Home Office monitoring of emigrants; pressure on national newspapers — either by encouraging them to report industrial success stories or encouraging firms to complain about bad stories; and encouraging links between schools and industry by appointing industrialists as school governors. (*Guardian*, 9 December 1976)

39.   Commentators on business are aware of this and anxious that 'those in the seats of power' should not ' . . . feel themselves likely to be at a disadvantage because of the enhanced knowledge of those at a lower level . . . ' (Coventry, 1973, 242).

40.   In Britain, for example, a recent guide to employers indicates, under the heading 'What the Interviewer is looking for', that the recruitment of technical specialists is based on degree class, qualifications and interests which are 'all important' whilst other factors are 'almost irrelevant'. However, for future general managers 'attitudes and personality attributes are the key issues' (*Daily Telegraph*, 1975). In France, a quick examination of undergraduate-level business schools shows the importance as criteria for admission of tests of 'personality', 'motivations', 'general culture', 'qualities of elocution and presentation', 'maturity', 'ability to work in groups', 'vocabulary', 'character analysis' as evidenced in 'non-directive tests' or 'interviews with a psychologist'. Also examined are the 'sense of organisation', 'dynamism' and 'perseverance' of the candidates (data taken from the schools' presentation of themselves in the dossier drawn up by the French Management Education Foundation, FNEGE).

41.   In this they have followed the model of leading American business schools. The MIT brochure, for example, in the early 1960s emphasised that the 'emphasis in all courses is NOT to prepare a man to take on a specific role in business but to give him the intellectual and social skills he needs in order to perform effectively in any job or any situation'. It is interesting that in this they also follow the model of elite French schools such as Polytechnique.

42.   See INSEAD's recent advertisements in the British Press.

References

Aaronovitch, S., and M.C. Sawyer, *Big Business: Theoretical and Empirical Aspects of Concentration and Mergers in the United Kingdom* (Macmillan, London, 1975)

Anglo-American Council on Productivity, *Education for Management*, (London, 1951)

Bourdieu, P. 'Reproduction Culturelle et Reproduction Sociale', *Social Science*

Information 10 (1971).

Bourdieu, P., and J.C. Passeron, *La Reproduction: Eléments pour une Théorie du système d'Enseignement* (Minuit, Paris, 1970)

Bourdieu, P., L. Boltanski and M. de Saint Martin, 'Les Stratégies de Reconversion', *Social Science Information* 12 (1973).

Bowles, S., 'Unequal Education and the Reproduction of the Social Division of Labour', in M. Carnoy (ed.), *Schooling in a Corporate Society: The Political Economy of Education in America and the Alternatives Before Us* (David McKay, New York, 1972).

Boyd, D., *Elites and Their Education* (NFER, Slough, Bucks, 1973).

BIM *Business School Programmes: The Requirements of British Manufacturing Industry* (London, 1971).

—— *Business Graduates in Industry* (London, 1974).

Business Graduates Association, *The Business Graduate in Britain 1973* (London, 1973).

Carré, J-J., P. Dubois and E. Malinvaud *La Croissance Française* (Paris, 1972: also published in abridged form 1973).

Chester, T.E. 'Industry, Management and the Universities: Trends and Problems of a Changing Relationship', *District Bank Review* 156 (1965).

Claude, H., *La Concentration Capitaliste: Pouvoir Economique et Pouvoir Gaulliste* (Editions Sociales, Paris, 1965).

Committee on Higher Education, *Higher Education (Robbins Report)* (CMND 2154, HMSO, London, 1963).

Coventry, W.F., *Management Made Simple* (W.H. Allen, London, 1973).

Daily Telegraph 'Which Company: The Daily Telegraph Guide to British Employers' (Kogan Page, London, 1975).

Delefortrie-Soubeyroux, N., *Les Dirigeants de l'Industrie Française* (A. Colin, Paris, 1961).

Department of Education and Science, *Statistics of Education* (HMSO, London, 1974).

Didier, M. and E. Malinvaud, 'La Concentration de l'Industrie s'est-elle accentuée depuis de Début du Siècle?' *Econ. et Stat.* 2 (1969).

Diman, D., 'Evolution des Structures de Bilan des Entreprises Industrielles entre 1961 et 1969', *Econ.et Stat.* 36 (1972).

Egon Zehnder International *Survey of Business School Graduates in Europe* (London, 1975).

Everly, R. and I.M.D. Little, *Concentration in British Industry* (Cambridge University Press, London, 1960).

Fidler, J., 'The British Business Elite: Recruitment and Attitudes to Social Stratification', unpublished paper presented at the EGOS Conference on the Sociology of the Business Enterprise, December. 1976.

Franks, Rt. Hon. Lord, *British Business Schools,* (BIM, London, 1963).

Giddens, A., 'Elites in the British Class Structure', in P. Stanworth and A. Giddens (eds.), *Elites and Power in British Society* (Cambridge University Press, London, 1974).

Girard, A., *La Réussite Sociale en France* (PUF, Paris, 1961).

Hannah, L., *The Rise of the Corporate Economy* (Methuen, London, 1976)

Hall, D. and H.C. de Bettignies, 'The French Business Elite', *European Business* 19 (1968).

Hall, D. and G. Amado-Fischgrund, 'Chief Executives in Britain', *European Business* 20 (1969).

Hall, D., R.-C. de Bettignies and G. Amado-Fischgrund, 'The European Business Elite', *European Business,* (October 1969).

Hart, P.E., M.A. Utton and G. Walshe, *Mergers and Concentrations in British*

Industry (Cambridge University Press, London, 1973).

Heller, R., 'The State of British Boardrooms', *Management Today* (May 1973).

Hutton, G., *We too can Prosper: The Promise of Productivity* (London, 1953).

Institute of Directors, 'The Director Observed Away From His Desk', *The Director,* May 1966.

Lewis, R. and R. Stewart, *The Boss: The Life and Times of the British Businessman* (Phoenix House, London, 1958).

Lupton, T., 'Business Education, British Style', *Centre for Business Research Newsletter* (Spring 1972.)

Marceau, J., 'Education and Social Mobility in France', in F. Parkin (ed.), *The Social Analysis of Class Structure* (Tavistock, London, 1974).

—— *The Social Origins, Educational Experience and Career Paths of a Young Business Elite* (INSEAD Monograph 1/76, Fontainebleau, 1976).

McGivering, I.C., D.G.J. Matthews and W.H. Scott, *Management in Britain: A General Characterisation* (Liverpool University Press, 1960).

Mills, C.W., *The Power Elite* (Oxford University Press, New York, 1956).

Ministry of Education, *Education for Management, Management Subjects in Technical and Commercial Colleges* (HMSO, London, 1947).

Morin, F., *La Structure Financière du Capitalisme Français* (Calmann-Levy, Paris, 1974).

Mosson, T.M., *Management Education in Five European Countries* (Business Publications, London, 1965).

National Economic Development Council, *Conditions Favourable to Faster Growth* (HMSO, London, 1963).

Nichols, T., *Ownership. Control and Ideology* (Allen and Unwin, London, 1969).

Rose, H.R., *Management Education in the 1970s: Growth and Issues* (HMSO, London, 1970).

Routh, G., *Occupation and Pay in Great Britain 1906-60* (Cambridge University Press, London, 1965).

Servan-Schreiber, J-J., *Le Défi Américain* (Denoel, Paris, 1967); translated as *The American Challenge* (Penguin, London, 1969)

Stanworth, P. and A. Giddens, 'An Economic Elite: A Demographic Profile of Company Chairmen', in P. Stanworth and A. Giddens (eds.), *Elites and Power in British Society* (Cambridge University Press, London, 1974).

Sturdivant, F.D. and R.D. Adler, 'Executive Origins: Still a Gray Flannel World?', *Harvard Business Review* (Nov-Dec 1976).

Thompson, E.P. (ed.), *Warwick University Ltd: Industry, Management and the Universities* (Harmondsworth, Penguin, 1970).

Urry, J. and J. Wakeford (eds.), *Power in Britain* (Heinemann, London, 1973).

Utton, M.A. *Industrial Concentration* (Harmondsworth, Penguin, 1970).

Weston, R. 'Management Education and Research — Survey of Comments and Issues', *Centre for Business Research Newsletter* (Summer 1972).

Wheatcroft, M., *The Revolution in British Management Education* (Pitman, London, 1970).

Whitley, R.D., 'Commonalities and Connections Among Directors of Large Financial Institutions', *Sociological Review* 21 (1973).

—— 'The City and Industry: The Directors of Large Companies, their Characteristics and Connections', in P. Stanworth, and A. Giddens (eds.), *Elites and Power in British Society* (Cambridge University Press, London, 1974).

Willig, J-C, 'Organisation Man or Entrepreneur? Europe's Business School Managers.' *European Business* 27 (1970).

6 THE FAMILY-EDUCATION COUPLE: TOWARDS AN ANALYSIS OF THE WILLIAM TYNDALE DISPUTE

Miriam E. David

Introduction

'Happy schools, like happy families, are similar and unremarkable.'
Gretton and Jackson (1976) − after Tolstoy − used this remark to
introduce their recent journalistic critique of the educational controversy over London's William Tyndale's school. This débâcle is the
subject of exploratory analysis in this paper, to illustrate a theory of
the relationship between education and the family in advanced capitalist society. It also develops, in particular, the political economy of
women, and explores the connection between parents, especially
mothers, and schools in their relationships with children. In a situation of compulsory schooling, such as in advanced capitalist societies,
both parents and schools share the responsibility for the rearing of
children. Yet this issue has been relatively uncharted from either a
feminist or a specifically Marxist perspective. There is a conspicuous
lack of theoretical articulation of class relations with sex relations.

Althusser (1971) whose notes have provided the initial inspiration
for this investigation argues that the 'family-education couple' has
replaced the family-church couple in being the dominant ideological
structure in late capitalism. He adds that there is a need for more
detailed investigation of that link. The intention here is to explore
the mechanisms which link the family and the English education
system, through the state, to understand how they contribute to the
reproduction of aspects of the social formation and to class struggle.
Other Marxists have analysed the function of education in the processes of reproduction but they have traditionally focused on the
links with the economic system narrowly defined and not the part
played by the state, repressively. They have looked at how education
contributes to either the technical division of labour, namely the skills
necessary for jobs or positions in the labour market, or the maintenance of the social division of labour, namely the relationships of
exploiter to exploited or class relations. They have not looked at how
education reproduces familial relations and hence the relations
between men and women as husbands and wives or fathers and

158

mothers, that is as parents. They have also ignored the sexual division of labour within the economy and the part of the family within it. Two sociologists of education, working within a Marxian framework, have alluded to this question, but not as part of a wider analysis of the reproduction of the socio-economic system, or the role of the state.

Marxist-feminists have tried to locate the function of the family in the processes of reproduction but their investigation has ignored the connection with the education system and the rearing of children. It has been limited to an understanding, albeit vital, of *domestic* labour and not of *mother-child* relations and how they articulate with the socio-economic system. An analysis of the wider political economy of women, and its relation to generational reproduction, is required.

Feminists, on the other hand, who study the education system have rarely looked at either the articulation with the family especially in terms of sexual differentiation or, within the education system itself, how the form of relationships are predicated upon a patriarchal ideology and are sustained by the state. They have been more concerned to demonstrate that the content of the education system, either through official ideology or practice, is sexist and contributes to the unequal sexual division of labour in adult life. Their analysis has been focussed upon women's predominant adult roles as wife and mother and how these are initially produced and not how the family-education couple sets together the broad conditions for the reproduction of both class and sex relations.

Thus there are basic concerns in this concrete analysis.

1. *Reproduction*

I am interested in the question of how capitalist societies are maintained and hence reproduce themselves. There are several aspects to reproduction; the system is primarily sustained through the economic system. Nevertheless important components of that are class relations and the sexual division of labour. These are not automatically reproduced by the economic system but have to be sustained by ideology. The question is therefore raised about how notions of class and sex relations are developed and reproduced, through education, the family and their interconnections. The use of the concrete example will be to explore the form and legal specification of these links which reproduce the relations on a daily and generational basis.

2. *Role of the State*

Althusser's Marxist analysis develops Gramsci's theory of the state to distinguish between types of state apparatus. On the one hand, there is the one repressive state apparatus namely the politico-legal system. It is through this, for example, that the education system is designed. On the other, there are several ideological state apparatuses such as the family, education, church, media etc. These do not function chiefly by repression, or by the enforcement of rules and law, but through their ideas. In this analysis of the particular controversy, I shall attempt to distinguish the contradictory aspects of the role of the state, first in the definition of the participants in the system, second in the ideological function of education and third in how to control crises in education.

3. *Class Struggle*

Although traditional Marxist concerns in education have concentrated on the maintenance of the economic system, I shall attempt to show how struggle over both social and sexual division of labour has occurred within the education system. The class analysis used as a basis is very tentative since there is particularly little theoretical clarity on the class location of teachers and whether they are agents of the state, and hence bourgeois, or not. I will try to rely on Poulantzas' formulation (1974) of the working class who produce use values, the mix of the new petty bourgeoisie and fractions of the middle class and the bourgeoisie or ruling class; locating teachers initially as of the middle classes.

The central *thesis* is that education links with the family in advanced capitalist societies and is crucial to both the reproduction of class and sex relations. This may be achieved by ideology but, in times of crisis, the state may resort to the use of repression, that is the rule of law, in order to maintain the system. Traditionally, the ideology operates not only through, in education, the content of curricula but through the *form* or organisation of relationships both between parents and schools and also teachers and pupils. They are organised upon a patriarchal ideology. I look first at the theoretical literature and locate its limitations and second explore the concrete example of the William Tyndale's dispute to develop this thesis and illustrate these three issues.

Theories of Education

Althusser's theory of the dominant role, in advanced capitalist

societies, of education in the reproduction of the relations of production, provides the most composite Marxist framework for analysis. It
must be expanded. There are, however, several problems with this
theory. First is the problem of his general theory of ideology. I shall
ignore this as the issue has been explored extremely well by Hirst
(1976) and rather more sketchily by McLennan, Molina and Peters
(1977, pp. 77-106). Second, since the theory is only claimed to be
notes towards an investigation, several crucial issues remain unexplored. In particular, the family is presented as a homogeneous entity
and is not subject to rigorous analysis. The sexual divisions within the
family are not identified. Moreover, Althusser does not, of course,
provide a feminist perspective. He also ignores the whole question of
the sexual division of labour, and how that articulates with the reproduction of either labour power, generations or broadly social reproduction. Nevertheless, the framework is useful as a basis for the
analysis of the concrete educational controversy in that Althusser is
not limited to trying only to understand reproduction. He also raises
the questions of the role of the state and class struggle. This is mis-
understood in Erben and Gleeson's (1977, pp. 73-93) critique of
Althusser. They claim that the theory is purely functionalist, and
therefore determinist.

Althusser states first that any society, to ensure its maintenance,
must reproduce all its productive forces. There is, in fact, some confusion of terminology but he includes here three aspects: the means
of production and labour power as the conditions of production, and
the social relations of production. In capitalist society, the means of
production are reproduced solely within the economic system through
the realisation of surplus value. Labour power is reproduced in a
rather more complicated way but Althusser does not detail all its
complexity. He states that, according to traditional Marxist theory,
it occurs through the giving of material means to each wage-labourer
with which to reproduce himself, namely wages 'to enable the
wage-earner to present himself again at the factory gate the next day'.
He adds later, almost as an aside, that the family has other functions
than ideological reproduction since 'it intervenes in the reproduction
of labour-power'. Moreover, 'in different modes of production it is
the unit of production and/or consumption'. It is important to note,
here that, although Althusser does not make much of it or does not
spell it out the family in capitalism links the two forms of reproduction – that of the means of production and, as we shall see later, the
social relations of production. The nuclear family in traditional

Marxist writings has been seen as crucial to capitalist relations of production. It is still a source of controversy in current Marxist theory
as to whether the family is concerned only with reproduction or,
directly or indirectly, produces surplus value (Secombe, 1974;
Gardiner, 1975). Yet the family is responsible, according to Althusser,
for the reproduction of labour power, daily, and for the reproduction
of generations which then generates the need for daily maintenance.
Althusser also adds that wages are 'indispensable for raising and
educating the children in whom the proletarian reproduces himself . . .
as labour power.'

Here Althusser begins to detail the complexity of the reproduction
of labour power in advanced capitalist society. He argues that
labourers do not only need to be healthy: they also need to be
competent, 'suitable to be set to work in the complex system of the
process of production'. He adds that this 'is achieved more and more
outside production: by the capitalist education system'. The question
is therefore raised about what children learn in school. He presents
two topics: 'know-how' and 'the rules of good behaviour'. Children
need to learn certain broad skills to fit them for the socio-technical
division of labour in terms of jobs and posts: and they also need to
learn the attitudes to enable them to submit to the rules of the
established order. It is here that ideology enters the analysis, for
ideology concerns these rules for the socio-economic system.

The way that social and ideological reproduction occurs is through
a set of complex machinery, namely the State apparatus. Althusser,
drawing out the Marxist thesis of infra and superstructure, postulates
that the state, as superstructure, functions by both relative autonomy
of, and reciprocal action on, the economic system. He relies
heavily on Gramsci's theory of the state. He argues that Gramsci
claimed the state to be 'a more complex reality' than merely the
political apparatus which includes the law, the head of state, government and administration. Gramsci saw the state as elements of both
political and civil society but, Althusser argues, he did not develop
it. Indeed, in most of Gramsci's concrete work he uses only the
political system as the state although he tries to develop the wider
notion of hegemony (1971).

The state is vitally important, not only from the point of view of
descriptive theory, that is 'the edifice metaphor'. Politically it is vital.
The purpose of class struggle is to seize and take control of state
power and change the apparatus. This entails not only the apparatus
that is the government, administration, law, police and army but also

the apparatus that functions by ideology. Althusser therefore distinguishes, as did Gramsci, the one repressive state apparatus from ideological state apparatuses (ISAs). He claims that there is a plurality of
ISAs which include education, the church, the family, the media
whereas there is only one repressive apparatus. As Gramsci did, he distinguishes the public/private dimension of state apparatuses but claims
it not to be significant to their functioning. He argues that the distinction arises from bourgeois, legal definitions and that only ISAs can be
private. The key distinction between state apparatuses is not this but
that the repressive functions 'by violence' whereas the ISAs function
primarily by ideology.

Using Lenin, he adds that no class can hold power for long periods
without the ISAs. Thus the ISAs become 'not only the stake, but also
the *site* of class struggle, and often bitter forms of class struggle'. The
ISAs become vitally important, not only because they function as
agents of reproduction but also because they are a locale of vital class
struggle. Althusser claims, however, that

> the ruling class (or class alliance) in power cannot lay down the law
> in ISAs as easily as it can in the (repressive) State apparatus not only
> because the former ruling classes are able to retain a strong position
> there for a long time, but also because the resistance of exploited
> classes is able to find the means and occasion to express itself there,
> either by the utilization of their contradictions or by conquering
> combat positions in them in struggle.

The ISAs are important because it is possible for class struggle to occur
within them; the ruling class holds state power and wields it through
both the repressive state apparatus and also ultimately through the
realisation of the ruling ideology in the ISAs, 'precisely in its contradictions'.

Althusser argues that the social relations of production are reproduced in a complex way through the state apparatus. Both the legal-
political and ideological superstructures function to maintain and
reproduce the existing socio-economic system. Reproduction is complex
both because the ISAs are multiple and relatively autonomous and also
because it is more difficult for the ruling class to sustain its ideological
hold over these apparatuses. He also adds that the ISAs function only
primarily by ideology. They function secondly by repression 'even if
ultimately but only ultimately this is very attenuated and concealed,
even symbolic'. He adds that schools, churches and even the family 'use

suitable methods of punishment, expulsion, selection, etc., to 'discipline' not only their shepherds, but also their flocks'. Thus there is a 'double functioning' of ISAs of which there are innumerable examples. Moreover, Althusser specifies a research programme at this point, which was the inspiration for this paper. This double functioning 'must be studied in detail if we are to go further than this mere observation'.

When Althusser spells out how the *educational* ISA operates as reproduction, he does not present such a complex process. He states that education has replaced, after a long and bitter struggle, the church as the dominant ISA, adding that its dominance is still maintained in concert with the family. Yet he now claims that its dominance is so great that it is not recognised: 'This ISA certainly has the dominant role, although hardly anyone lends an ear to its music; it is so silent! This is the school.' Its power is strong because of the monopoly hold over all children through compulsory schooling. Althusser states firmly: 'no other ISA has the obligatory (and not least, free) audience of the totality of the children in the capitalist social formation 8 hours a day for 5 or 6 days out of 7'. Compulsion, therefore, is central to the achievement of this new hegemony, which Althusser claims is, nevertheless, a universally reigning ideology of the school. He spells out what he believes the content of this ideology is, and this, again, shows the vital links with the family. It

represent the school as a neutral environment purged of ideology (because it is . . . lay) where teachers respectful of the 'conscience' and 'freedom' of the children who are entrusted to them (in complete confidence) by their 'parents' (who are free, too, i.e. the owners of their children) open up for them the path to freedom, morality and responsibility of adults by their own example . . .

He is claiming sarcastically that the bourgeois ideology, linking the family and education, is not controversial. Moreover, he frequently refers to this couple without further explication. In describing the obligatory nature of education it is stated that the ISA

take children from every class after the infant school stage, and then for years, the years in which the child is most vulnerable, squeezed between the family SA and the educational SA it drums into them 'know-how' and ruling ideology.

Although the obligatory nature of schooling does make education pre-

eminent, the fact that education, as for other ISAs, is the *site* of class
struggle may make this relationship between the family and education
more contradictory than Althusser asserts. The principle of the relationship, in bourgeois ideology, is that of 'trust' by parents, in teachers'
ability to inculcate the values of adulthood and individualism to their
children. He does argue that there is now a crisis in education which is
also shaking the family system but does not specify its content.
Indeed, he refers only very briefly to the struggles in schools since it
effects, in his view, only a minority of those teachers, who in
'dreadful conditions attempt to turn the few weapons . . . [to] 'teach'
against the ideology . . . '

What Althusser sees as crucial both to the reproduction of the social
relations of production and also to class struggle is the 'family-education
couple'. He does not detail the mechanisms by which it operates but
asserts its importance and, indeed, pre-eminence. Without going into
some of the difficulties which Althusser's theoretical position poses and
which he addresses in that same paper, I wish to explore the operations
of the 'family-education couple' in England today. The project which
Althusser designs of detailing both the 'double-functioning' of ISAs,
through ideology and repression, and of examining class struggle within
the 'family-education couple' have not been explored. However, his
framework does not pose adequately the nature and form of the link
between the family and education. It asserts that parents 'trust' the
teachers to instil appropriate values into their children. Parents are not
differentiated into mothers and fathers who also have different posts
and positions within the socio-economic system, which, moreover, have
to be sustained. Neither does Althusser explore how the education
system actually operates 'in loco parentis' and thus sets the conditions
for the reproduction of the sexual division of labour both in the family
and the economic system. Some of these issues are explored by other
theorists.

Benton, however, tries to apply the Althusserian framework to the
English education system, albeit very briefly (1974, pp. 9-38). He
extends the analysis by the statement that

> even more importantly, the education system plays a large role in
> the inculcation of the relevant skills and subjection to the relevant
> ideological dispositions of women in preparation for their role in the
> division of labour within the capitalist family. (ibid, p. 27)

Yet he does not extend this assertion but tries to explain a particular

conjuncture: the ideological role of the Labour Party in developing
equality of educational opportunity over the last decade or so. This
leads him to show that a changing governmental ideological position is
not sufficient as a basis for a change in state power. In trying to expli-
cate how state power may be changed through education, he develops a
class analysis of the education system. He refines Althusser's theory
and argues that the education system is only indirectly reproductive
since it only reproduces agents and not positions (using Poulantzas'
concepts) within the economic system. Teachers are in a complex
location within the class structure. Benton explores the two current
theories that they are either members of the working class or agents of
the bourgeoisie. He does not extend this to a concrete situation.
Benton's own analysis is but a sketch and does not take us much
beyond Althusser's own notes towards an investigation.

Other recent Marxist analyses of education have not touched upon
the complexities of the processes and yet do develop important aspects
of the theory. Bowles and Gintis (1976) who apply a Marxist analysis
to the history of American education, start from very limited postulates.
They have no theory of the state and are concerned only with the ways
in which education contributes to the reproduction of the economic
system and the social relations of production. They argue that this
occurs only through the form and not the content of schooling and 'the
inculcation of the rules of good behaviour'. Their use of the term form
is very narrow: it does not refer to the political structure of schooling or
its relations with the family but merely to the organisation of *learning*.
Moreover, they argue that this comes about through the 'correspondence principle': that is the organisation of learning mirrors that of
economic life, defined as work.

> Specifically, the relationships of authority and control between
> administrators and teachers, teachers and students and students and
> their work replicate the hierarchical division of labour which domin-
> ates the work-place.

Although the analysis is highly functionalist, they begin, towards the
end, to provide an explicit causal analysis of the relationship between
education and the economy. For example, they add

> The pattern of social relationships fostered in school is hardly
> irrational or accidental. Rather, the structure of educational ex-
> perience is admirably suited to nurturing attitudes and behaviour

consonant with participation in the labour force.

Even so, they focus on particular, narrow aspects of schooling, namely the system of authority relationships and how they provide special character traits such as industriousness or authoritarianism. This is a useful starting point. They do not discuss how the actual curricula of schools have particular effects and contribute to the reproduction of 'know-how' or broad skills for the socio-technical division of labour, even if only in terms of providing appropriate agents. They are only concerned with how the rules produce 'good workers'. Although they see a parallel between work and school organisation, they do not analyse the nature of that system of authority. In particular, they do not recognise how it is a system of patriarchal authority. Yet this analysis has been briefly provided by Lightfoot (1975, pp. 105-43). Nor do they explain how schools reproduce the sexual division of labour in the economy. Indeed, they appear to believe that schools are 'sex-blind' and do not contribute to that reproduction, but that it is achieved within the family. They actually assert that 'the family's impact on the reproduction of the sexual division of labour, for example, is distinctly greater than that of the education system' (1976, p. 143). They go on to argue that sexual divisions are reproduced through the correspondence principle: this time it is the parallel of the family with the capitalist system of production. They have both a narrow view of the economy as the work-place, which therefore excludes the family for all purposes. They also have a narrow view of the family itself and here argue a contradictory point. They now claim that the family diverges drastically from the capitalist system of production.

> The close personal and emotional relationships of family life are remote from the impersonal bureaucracy of the wage labour system . . . Indeed, it is precisely because family structure and the capitalist relations of production differ in essential respects that our analysis sees schooling as performing such a necessary role in the integration of young people into the wage labour system. (1976, p. 144)

Although they talk of young people this would appear to imply that they are concerned only with the production of male workers. They do not provide an understanding of how schools provide different experiences for boys and girls which will help them encounter such experiences in the labour force or in the family. Yet they argue that the experience of schooling prepares children for the experience of the labour force.

The family, on the other hand, cannot achieve this because its ideology is counter to that experience. Given that there is a sexual division of labour in the economy, and Bowles and Gintis nowhere try to contradict that, and given their functionalist analysis, this division has to be reproduced. Their analysis cannot provide an explanation, nor does it show the actual links between the family and education. They are seen as entirely separate, and with different ideologies.

The other issue that is virtually ignored is that of class struggle. Bowles and Gintis show that the developments in education are not all smooth but are subject to conflict. However, that conflict is attributed to the contradictory needs in the productive system for capital accumulation. Bowles and Gintis also examine alternative forms of schooling but do not investigate the nature of conflict within education itself. Moreover, they do not attempt to distinguish the repressive role that the State may play either to resolve conflcts within education or to reproduce the social and/or sexual division of labour. Their analysis is confined to the question of the reproduction of the social relations of production and in that it is limited in its extent to a theory of correspondence which, only with difficulty, accounts for contradictions. It is useful to the extent that they develop the notion of what constitutes the ideology that schools impart. They stress authority relations. They only ignore the feminist perspective on them.

Hussain's (1976) brief analysis also ignores the links between the family and education in preparing for the socio-economic system. He argues generally against both economists and sociologists of education. He claims that economists have seen the role of education in too narrow a light, focussing only on its contribution to the technical division of labour. On the other hand, sociologists, he claims, have only looked at the social and technical aspects of education separately and independently. He asserts that 'once the economy is conceived not only in terms of its technical relations but also its social relations, the relations between the economy and the education system in capitalist society appear in a different light'. He goes on to argue that educational qualifications do not prepare individual workers for specific skills or occupations. He claims that 'what is crucial is that educational qualifications determine access to not one but a wide variety of occupations'. He, therefore, gives primacy to the economic system in determining the function of education, but only in terms, first, of the range rather than specificity of jobs and second of class and social relations. He ignores completely the family, the sexual division of labour or the links between the family and education, in this process. But it is clear that the education system does not reproduce men and women for the same broad range of occupations. Women as Benton asserted have to be imbued with ideology for their roles in both the family and work force. Yet Hussain does indicate that the schools can do this only indirectly by setting the conditions for such roles and not specifying them in detail.

Two sociologists of education, although not Marxists, have developed the notion of the family-education couple in a quasi-Marxian framework. They have not been concerned with its contribution to the reproduction of the social or sexual division of labour but rather with spelling out the mechanisms of the relationship. In this, they provide insights into how the links may be specified to understand the processes of reproduction. They, however, ignore the repressive role of the state and do not discuss whether the education system or the family can be conceived of as state apparatuses.

Bernstein (1975, p. 3) argues that it is 'important to keep together in one analysis the inter-actions between the family and the school, and to show the variations in this relationship — both within and between social classes.' In this crucial paper he tries to show (p. 13) how the 'variation in the development of class structures affect the classification and framing of educational knowledge.' What is both useful and exciting in this paper, when it is dredged of its virtually incomprehensible sociological jargon, is the idea that women's role has changed in both the family and the economy and therefore affected the ways children are treated within the infant or nursery school. Bernstein, however, is less concerned with the structure of reproduction than with what he calls the process of cultural transmission. This central thesis is 'the notion that educational transmissions embody class ideologies which are crucial to the cultural reproduction of class relations' (ibid.). The main focus is upon the 'new middle class' and how they control both the form and content of cultural transmissions. Using a Durkheimian framework, Bernstein postulates two family forms — personal and individual — which have increased with the increasing division of labour and which have led to a change in emphasis in the form of socialisation. 'The major argument of the paper then is that conflicting pedagogies have their origins within the fractions of the middle class and so an unreflecting institutionalising of either pedagogy will not be to the advantage of the lower working class.' Specifically, Bernstein claims that 'historically, under individualised organic solidarity the mother is neither important as a transmitter of symbolic or physical property'. He adds that she was 'a domestic administrator' and served therefore only as a role model for her daughters. Moreover, this gener-

ated only two models for cultural transmission: the abstracted mother
was a model for the nanny-babyminder and the governess the model for
the teacher of elementary competences. On the other hand, the mother
'under personalised organic solidarity is transformed from an agent of
physical to cultural reproduction and unable to get away from her
children'. Bernstein goes on to argue that this latter is the model of
'invisible pedagogy' which underlies the form of cultural transmission in
new infant and nursery schools. Yet he ends up with a very agnostic
conclusion that 'the form of reproduction of class relations in education
has been *interrupted* but not changed' (my emphasis).

The importance of Bernstein's work, notwithstanding the difficulties
with the conceptual scheme, is that it acknowledges the crucial connections, in social reproduction, between the family and in particular,
the mother, and education. Nevertheless, Bernstein omits to stress that
these links are crucial for the reproduction of the social relations of
production. Yet it has been argued that the family and the sexual division of labour are fundamental, within class relations, to the capitalist
system.

Bourdieu, from whom Bernstein draws his intellectual inspiration for
the paper above cited, is more explicit about the importance of the
family and education to cultural reproduction. He argues, in various
places, that the family is crucial because the education system demands
a cultural competence that it does not itself provide and which is part
of the 'cultural unconscious' which can only be acquired through the
family (1971). Bourdieu's main fascination here is with the *bourgeoisie*
and how its influence affects the culture which is transmitted through
schools and particularly to *sons*. However, although Bourdieu is interested in the family-education couple, he is preoccupied with the
mechanisms of cultural reproduction, rather than their contribution to
the socio-economic system. He is concerned with the broad contours
of culture such as literature and the arts. In this pre-occupation, he
ignores completely the differential role of men and women in the
family and the sexual division of labour in the economy. It is only in
one very obscure aside, placed in parentheses, that he mentions that the
sexual divisions within the bourgeois family may affect cultural reproduction (1971, p. 170):

> The gradual rationalisation of a system of teaching could threaten
> the cultural integration of the educated class if, so far as that class is
> concerned, education and more particularly what is known as general
> culture, were not at least as much a matter for the family as for the school.

for the family in the sense of parents and their progeny and also in
that of the fields of knowledge (*many scientists are married to
women with an arts back-ground*) and if all types of training did not
allot a place, always a fairly important one, to classical liberal education. (my emphasis)

To paraphrase him, he is claiming that the integration of society would
not be sustained for the educated classes, if crucial socialisation did not
take place in the family as well as in the school. Moreover, he assumes
that it is women, as *mothers,* who maintain this relationship because of
their educational backgrounds. He therefore assigns a critical role to
women, and does not, in fact, ignore them.

Although both Bernstein and Bourdieu make much of the relationship between the family and the school, they do not show how this
links with socio-economic reproduction. Bourdieu virtually ignores the
sexual division of labour: Bernstein's contribution *is* important but does
not go far towards an understanding of the structure of reproduction.
On the contrary, Bernstein denies the importance, at this point in the
analysis, of the links to the social relations of production. Neither of
these two sociologists sees the inter-connections as crucial to class
struggle, but rather as Bourdieu (1966) argues 'as a conservative force'.
However, Bourdieu, although eclectic, does have an intellectual debt to
both Marx and Althusser and considers education broadly in terms of
its contribution to the social relations of production. From his scattered
writings it is possible to see that, for example, he considers the working
class family disadvantaged with respect to cultural and economic
capital, and therefore in a particular position in the processes of reproduction.

Feminist studies of the education system provide little insight into
the ways education contributes to social reproduction or the links with
the family. Wolpe (1974) and Marks (1976) and Blackstone (1976) all
concentrate on the ideological *content* of the education system and
how it enables women to fulfil their predominant role of being a wife
and mother in adult life. They show this through an investigation of
recent official ideology, historical practice and the development of
special educational institutions and current practices. Given, however,
that women, even as wives and mothers, participate in the economy
they do not show how this process comes about, and is reproduced. Nor
do they develop a view of the contribution of the state, through the
legal system, or class struggle to changes in the system. Their analyses,
contrary to Bowles and Gintis, are overly concerned with the explicit

rather than implicit assumptions contributing to reproduction. They also ignore the organisation of schooling and its links with the family, especially mothers, over the rearing of children. This may provide the conditions for the reproduction of social and sexual relations.

Another focus which is here ignored is taken up by other feminists. It is the way in which familial relationships are developed within the education system. Shaw (1976) tries to develop an understanding of the ways in which the legal clause 'in loco parentis' has been applied within the English education system and its implications for both parents and teachers currently in the system. Lightfoot (1975) looks at American sociology of education from a feminist perspective. She analyses both the studies of the role of the teacher and classroom interaction between teachers and pupils for they are 'areas of the field in which women have a significant and dominant presence' (1975, p. 109). She argues that teachers are seen as having either womanly or child-like qualities irrespective of either whether they are predominantly female, or how they actually behave. Secondly, she shows how classroom experience is different for boys and girls and yet how lacking any analysis is in specifying the effects of, to use her term, the 'sexuality' of the teacher. But women deliberately choose teaching as a career because it is 'work devoted to the problems and concerns that the woman herself faces in her private capacity with her family ... [Yet to] social scientists ... The teaching profession is seen as a woman's secondary role, which competes with her primary role as a mother of a family' (1975, p. 134). She argues basically that the subject is replete with familial analogies.

This same thesis is present in English, non-feminist studies of the workings of schools. Richardson (1973, pp. 214-18) for example makes the point that the head in a secondary school takes a paternal role and that the senior mistress a pastoral care function. She adds 'family and tribal imagery was powerfully present in the Nailsea culture'. Musgrove (1971) argues that secondary teachers derive their authority from that of the father whereas Bernstein (op. cit.) has argued that primary teachers have women as mothers as role models.

Although some studies of education have concentrated on either how education provides for women's adult role in the family or what the continuities are between education or schools and families, especially for women,there is no general framework for analysis of the relationships between education, the family, the sexual division of labour and the economic system.

Curiously Marxist-feminist studies of the family, whilst predicated on the assumption that the nuclear family is essential to capitalism, do

not explore adequately the contribution it makes to generational reproduction or the rearing of children. The most recent debate has focussed
upon the character of domestic labour and its part in production. The
main discussion has been over whether it is directly or indirectly productive, and not over its reproductive contribution. Whilst it is axiomatic that domestic labour involves tasks for the housewife in caring for
children as well as husbands, the question of the mother's ideological
and material role in rearing children is not addressed. Indeed, the only
reference is to the problems of understanding the present situation of
pre-school child-care (Gardiner, Himmelweit and MacIntosh, 1975).
Although this is crucial to interpreting the sexual division of labour, it
is not the only or major issue that must be addressed. On the other
hand, the rest of the debates on the political economy of women have
addressed the important question of women as wage-labourers and tried
to understand the reasons for their predominant location in the secondary labour market. Again, the question of the links with women's role
in both the family and education as mothers has not been raised fully.
(Beechey, 1976; Barron and Norris 1976). Thus there are a number of
extensions or improvements to the Althusserian framework but they are
all partial or incomplete. It is necessary to try and explain the educational dispute through this framework and the additions to it that have
been specified.

The William Tyndale's Dispute

The analysis of this dispute is to illustrate the three concerns outlined at
the beginning of the paper: the role of the family-education couple in
the reproduction of sex and class relations, the double-functioning of
state apparatuses by ideology and repression and education as the site
of class struggle.

In order better to understand the issues that underlie the controversy,
it is necessary to demonstrate briefly the ways in which the education
system in England, as an example of an advanced capitalist society,
functions habitually both by ideology and repression. The general links
with the social and sexual division of labour in the economy and family
also need to be sketched in to interpret how the conflict was resolved
in an attempt to sustain social and sex relations of production.

First, it can be argued that compulsory education, as now defined
under the terms of the 1944 Education Act, illustrates the functioning
both by ideology and repression. Education is the dominant ISA
because all children, in England between the ages of 5 and 16, are as
Althusser argues, to partake of it. Moreover, the state has developed a

complex machinery to enforce its rules. Tyack (1976) in exploring the
reasons for the origins of compulsory schooling, mainly relying on
American evidence, presents as one argument the state's ex-post legitimation of the actions of the majority of parents who were already
educating their children in collective settings. The extension of compulsion may be viewed in the same way. Moreover, parents may have
objected to the form if not the fact of schooling (Musgrove, 1964, 1966).
The state needs to determine the form to ensure both a differentiated
labour force and social relations of production and also to limit
resistance or class struggle. Simon (1960, 1965) tries to develop this
latter type of analysis of the English education system. Indeed, many
aspects of the education system and its links with the family are determined by the law. Thus Althusser's 'universal reigning ideology of the
school' is reproduced not only by ideology but also by the enforcement
of the law. In the first place, the law on education confirms that children are the private property of their parents. Parents have a legal *duty*
to ensure their children's education, and, as a corollary, the state provides financially 'free' schooling to enable parents to exercise their
duties. Parents are, however, not committed to one form of education.
They have three choices: one to use the publicly financed system, two
to use the private system or three to educate their children themselves.
In fact, in 1975 over 90 per cent of children attended state maintained
schools. These latter two choices are not viable for the parents of the
working or middle classes. The costs may be prohibitive. Moreover,
most parents do not any longer have the time or skills to exercise this
responsibility. On the other hand, some bourgeois parents do still buy
such skills and use the services of a governess or private tutor for their
children (Howe, 1955). Leila Berg, in commenting on another of the
Inner London Education Authority's (ILEA) educational controversies,
shows how this system is indirectly reproductive of both the sexual and
social division of labour:

> Under the 44 Act, parents can keep their children at home provided
> they educate them. What a mockery! Hardly any parents have any
> education . . . Even if the mothers were educated, they are most of
> them working. Sometimes they are the only wage-earner. How could
> they keep the children at home, giving up their job? (1968, p. 72)

Second, parents are responsible for ensuring their children's attendance
at school and they are ultimately responsible if their children fail to
attend school. Non-attendance is a legally punishable offence and the

state has built up a complex machinery, including Education Welfare
Officers, to ensure the attendance at school of children. However, as
Shaw (1977) points out this system is designed to ensure boys' rather
than girls' attendance. Girls' absences are deemed to be rather more
legitimate since they are assumed to be contained within the family.

Third, if parents choose to opt into the publicly maintained system
they have very limited controls over that system. They only have very
circumscribed choices of schools. Although Local Education Authorities (LEAs) are charged with the responsibility of providing schools 'in
accordance with parental wishes', this is muted by the fact that they
have to do so 'with regard to reasonable public expenditure' (Saran,
1973). Parents only have the initial choice of school, within their geographical area. There are very few legally defined channels of communication or influence over the schools, and these are all based upon the
relationship between individual parent and school. There are no legally
defined collective mechanisms (Kogan, 1976). Parents do not have a
special status in the daily, regular or ultimate control of schools. At this
point the system is based upon the assumption that, as Althusser argues
they do, parents will entrust their children to the schools. Even channels
of complaint are not legally defined. Parents, however, may withdraw
their children from one particular school and ask for them to be
placed elsewhere.

Fourth, the organisation of schooling is predicated upon a particular
partnership with parents and there is, here, an assumption of a sexual
division of parental duties. The state does not take over complete
responsibility for children's education and replace parents (David, 1976).
It regulates and supplements their actions. But the organisation of
schooling does not, contrary to Bowles and Gintis' argument, mirror
the conditions of the labour market, but rather the wider socio-
economic system. For example, children do not attend school for a
working day or working year. Thus their experiences in school are not
exactly as they would be in the labour force. Moreover, a parent, usually
the mother, is assumed to be available to ensure children get to and
from school and are cared for in school holidays. This form of schooling
does not facilitate married women's full or complete participation in
the labour force on an equal basis with men. However, as the needs for
different kinds of labour have developed the organisation of schooling
has been modified. For example, school meals have increased the
possibilities of some participation in the labour force. On the other
hand, there are also ideological constraints on such participation. Avon
LEA (1977) and the annual conferences of the Association of Head-

masters and Headmistresses (June 1977), for instance, blamed the
problems of school truancy and bad behaviour on mothers' labour force
participation, confirming Benton's point that women are prepared for
their ideological role in the family. This behaviour is not enjoined for
bourgeois parents and those who send their children to private schools.
Indeed, the head of one prestige boarding school, about the
same time, praised those mothers who participated in the labour force
to make sacrifices to send their children away to boarding schools.
Bourgeois mothers are not expected to have daily charge of their children, although they do have ultimate responsibility (Lambert, 1974).
Working class parents are expected to be so responsible and, indeed,
there have been recent attempts to engage mothers' more regular
involvement in primary and nursery schools (Midwinter, 1975; Halsey,
1972).

Thus, the education system does not only function through the
values it imparts through the curriculum but through the enforcement
of particular rules and forms of organisation. However, these rules and
forms are neither immutable nor subject to question both by parents or
teachers within the schools. Yet the political organisation of schooling
is based upon the 'democratic' assumption that neither parents nor
teachers are ultimately responsible for the design of schooling. The
1944 Education Act set a legal partnership between central and local
government (David, 1977). Although the law has not since been
changed, legal interpretations and judgements have altered that partnership of 'reciprocal inequality'. The Tameside incident has set limits to
the powers of Central Government to control policy implementation
and given such powers to the judiciary (Griffith, 1976). This again
illustrates its repressive functioning. Local Authorities are responsible
for the daily provision of education and, here, the main provider has
been found to be the educational administrators rather than politicians
(David, 1977). Schools also are governed by bodies of managers who
have limited powers over discipline, curriculum and teacher appointment. These bodies, traditionally moribund, were composed of political
appointees (Kogan, 1976). Since the early 1970s, they have changed
constitutions with certain LEAs allowing one place to a parent.

Teachers' responsibilities have only been vaguely defined in law. Yet
they are expected to act 'in loco parentis'. Indeed, there is plenty of
evidence to suggest that their interpretation of this duty leads them to
mirror familial relationships. (Richardson, op. cit.; Lightfoot, op. cit.).
Moreover, there are few legally defined sanctions against teachers.

In sum, the habitual workings of the family-education couple reveal that it functions both by ideology and repression. Parents entrust their children to schools, but within a strictly defined context. That context reveals the conditions for the reproduction of both the social and sexual division of labour. The state, as a legal apparatus, is very active in defining the workings of the system. Yet, aspects of the system reveal the potentialities for class conflict. It is to this that I now turn.

Although the controversy to be examined was over only one small junior school, containing about 150 pupils and 7 teachers, in Islington, an inner city area of London, it has wide implications. There may, of course, be more significant and deeper struggles taking place within education. The significance of this dispute lies in its wide coverage in the media and the attention it attracted as a dispute both about 'teaching method' and 'parental rights' over a lengthy period of time. Each aspect of the dispute was widely reported in the popular and serious press and on television and radio. The reason for this national interest was partly the connection that some of the parents, teachers and managers had to the national media. Some were, indeed, journalists. Others were professional educationists or politicians.

What needs to be explained, however, is *why* the issue nevertheless attracted this attention. Part of the explanation lies in the preeminence, as Althusser argues, of the family-education couple as an ideological apparatus. The dispute raised the questions about how that form of ideology should be sustained. The conflict centred upon the controls that both mothers and fathers could have over educational practice, and their commensurate rights. It also therefore focussed upon the appropriate sexual division of labour to be reproduced. It highlighted the roles that teachers play in social and familial reproduction, setting and implementing the conditions for such. The dispute does indicate, albeit in stark and crude form, the boundaries of the relationships between parents, teachers, taught, government and administration which can be tolerated within the present system if social and sexual reproduction is to be maintained. More important to the explanation is that it illustrates that education is a site of class struggle. It pinpoints what struggles can be engaged in by teachers, or parents, acting as agents of the working class and the lengths to which the repressive state will go to prevent such conflict. Here, the ILEA ended by settling the dispute by direct legal means rather than through the traditional informal system of disciplinary procedures, presided over by educational experts. It, therefore, spent a very long time (almost nine months) and a lot of money (set at £55,000 in the Auld Report) on the legal inquiry. This excludes the costs of teachers' salaries. The five teachers were suspended on full salaries throughout the inquiry. There were also the costs, of time and money, of the witnesses giving evidence. In addition, the disciplinary hearings of the teachers have taken a further six months, with the teachers on full salary. The appeals against sentence still continue. Thus, the legal interpretation of the dispute has taken over 18 months. The dispute must, therefore, be seen to have ramifications that extend beyond that of the particular school and its relations with the children's parents, the local authority and its managing body. It is, indeed, about how social reproduction should be sustained and class struggle contained.

According to media characterisation, the dispute concerned parental attitudes to teaching methods. A more detailed reading of even the evidence of the two journalists and the teachers who wrote up their stories reveals that this was not so (Gretton and Jackson, op. cit., p. 33; Ellis *et al.*, 1976; Walker, 1977). The two key substantive issues were, first, the ways in which teachers and their superiors – administrators, inspectors and politicians – in the local authority were to act 'in loco parentis'. Second, the extent of parental – fathers' and mothers' – involvement and choice in schooling for their children was the other issue. The public dispute, from the summer of 1975, centred upon conflicting definitions of teacher and parental involvement in the determination of the educational process. Auld, chairman of the inquiry and author of the official report, called it a 'demarcation dispute' (Auld, 1976). Teacher *method* was but one aspect to be determined; curriculum and rights were others. More important were the implicit ways in which children were to learn, both from the teachers, and their mothers and fathers, about how to behave, in adulthood both in work and in the family. The majority of the teachers, at that point, saw themselves as agents of the working class but the most involved parents were members of what Poulantzas terms fractions of the middle classes. Neither group was allied with the working class parents. The conflict was, therefore, over class representation and alliances in the 'family-education couple'.

The history of the William Tyndale dispute needs to be told, briefly. The origins of the dispute are, in fact, not clear. The five teachers party to the dispute start their account (Ellis *et al.*, op. cit.) with the difficulties experienced by the school in the late 1960s and early 1970s with a falling pupil population and its changed character. The population altered through the gentrification of the housing in the locality, to contain more predominantly of the middle classes. The teachers claim that the previous headmaster and chairwoman (significantly) of the school managers, both of whom resigned in 1973, were aware of difficulties in

running the school, including conflicts with one new part-time remedial
teacher. They cite the specific difficulties as through the slow move, via
new teacher appointments, to less formal techniques, and the types of
children to be taught who constituted a changing mix of the middle and
working classes. The increases in children from the middle classes posed
particular educational problems. Ellis adds that he, therefore, 'inherited
parental anxieties'. But difficulties were already being experienced over
education for the working class children.

   Auld, in his report of the official inquiry to ILEA, starts with the
detail: the resignation of the headmaster after being there six years,
from the end of term, summer 1973. He goes on to detail the
controversy surrounding the new appointment and the two-stage process that occurred. In the first instance, the man who subsequently
became head, was not appointed although short-listed. The post remained vacant, and was readvertised. The appointment was therefore
made by a newly constituted body of managers. This was a result of a
number of resignations (which are nowhere explained; one can surmise
that the resignations were no chance occurrence and may indeed have
contributed much to the subsequent conflict). The journalists' account
(Gretton and Jackson, op. cit) also refers, but only briefly, to problems
prior to the new appointment. They claim, however, that the conflict
might not have occurred had the chairwoman of the managers either
not resigned or had her proposed successor accepted the proposal. This,
however, is pure speculation. It is interesting to note that the chairwoman was seen as a powerful figure, and potentially able to control
the politics of that educational controversy. She was not a current
mother for the school.

   Critical events followed fast upon the changes in both the composition of the teaching staff and the managing body. The crises related to
defining the boundaries of the responsibilities of those now in charge.
In essence the new teachers — not only the headmaster but also a *man*
appointed in 1973 by the previous team of managers and head — began
to adopt new working styles, such as staff meetings to discuss their
philosophy and what has subsequently been termed 'co-operative
teaching'. In their own words, they were keen to adopt more egalitarian
relationships with their pupils. They state (Ellis, op. cit., p. 44) 'the
teacher who had been a strict parent now becomes the occasionally
severe aunt or uncle'. In this they make clear the fact of their changed
definition of acting 'in loco parentis'. Nevertheless, the change, as they
espoused it, is not to abolish the distinctiveness of childhood, particularly at the primary stage of schooling, but to give it a new flavour. It is

interesting that in modifying the notion of patriarchal authority they move to a concept of avuncular authority as being less authoritarian. It does include the potential of femininity.

Both their style of operating, in terms of meetings, and their new approach to children, were objectionable to one of their five colleagues. She acted both in her capacity as the school's part-time remedial teacher and as self-professed concerned mother/parent, although her children were not in this school, and were of secondary school age. She began to make public her disquiet. First, she objected to the teachers themselves through a series of written comments and second, voiced her criticisms to individual parents and to members of the managing body, some of whom were parents of children at the school. She made a written denunciation of the school's approach entitled a black paper, at a parents' evening meeting called for another purpose. (In her reappraisal of the conflict she calls the paper 'green' (1977, p. 39).) Clearly, she had a notion of the proper conduct of teachers 'in loco parentis' which she attempted to share with some parents. It is argued, by Gretton and Jackson, and the teacher herself (ibid) that she singled out working class parents. However, the mother-managers and other managers with whom she also shared her fears were wives of professional men — civil servants, university teachers, management consultants, etc. They were clearly of the middle classes.

The managing body of the school also began, slowly, to assume a new style of working. Since 1971, the ILEA have allowed for, first, individual schools to have managers and, within them, two parents to be elected from the body of parents, one for infants and one junior, to serve as managers. The other (15) managers are appointed by the major and minor political parties of the LEA and its administrative division to serve, along with the two heads — one each from the infants and juniors — and a teacher appointed by the school staff. Some of these politically appointed managers may, in fact, be parents of children in the schools. At this school, this was the case. Moreover, the managing body reflected the sexual division of labour in the organisation and runnings of schools. Gretton and Jackson make this point again, now almost inadvertently. They state (1976, p. 33) that 'while the husbands made hay in the town hall, the wives (and sometimes the husbands as well) provide some new more active blood in managing and governing bodies of schools'. They had argued that the previous chairwoman would have contained the dispute. Clearly here the first level of political control of education was assumed to be a feminine activity. The managing body of the school was predominantly female (13 women and 8 men, over a two year period) and, moreover, contained some mothers of children in the two schools. The duty of the managing body was 'the oversight of the curriculum' and this was assumed to be a relatively infrequent activity of about once a term, through a formally constituted meeting. However, three of the managers, all married women who were not in full-time employment because of their childcare responsibilities, began to take a more active interest in the day-to-day running of the school. As Ellis adds of the two mother-managers 'both were educated women, unable to pursue careers, because of young families' (Ellis, 1976, p. 23). Gretton and Jackson now make a contradictory point and argue that 'the school was unusual in the links between managers and the playground.' Indeed, the two managers who were also mothers had a 'dual role' and, according to the journalists, this led them to a 'confusion of managerial and parental hats' (1976, p. 61). It may be the case that although management was allowably a feminine activity it was to be confined to women who had already completed the 'primary' rearing of their own children. This was certainly the case for some of the female managers, and the previous chairwoman who was avowedly a legitimate authority.

The three mother-managers in any event, began to make obvious and frequent visits to the school. One reason was their concern with the running of the school: the other was the necessity to get their children to and from school. In that, they began firstly to voice their concern and secondly, acting individually and as mothers concerned about their own children's future and the skills they were not learning, rather than as a corporate body of managers, they began to demand admittance to the school. This coupled with the strident actions of the part-time remedial teacher, upset the head and other full-time teachers and they objected to the 'interference' with their professional responsibilities. They went so far as to refuse their admission, when finally requested by some of the managers. They argue that 'they wanted to be left in peace, to work through their educational plans, to liaise with parents without interference and provide for the children a relevant educational experience' (1976, p. 38).

By the end of the summer term 1974, when the new head had been in post for two terms, a tension between teachers, parents and managers, and within each of these three groups, had been created. The clarity about their various responsibilities and duties — daily, regular or ultimate — towards the children in primary education had evaporated. Each began to take individualistic action. In particular, some parents began to remove their children from the school, including the mother managers who had become actively involved in the school. This caused them to resign from the managing body. Gretton and Jackson argue that this is one of the only channels of complaint open to parents. However, the grounds for complaint were at this stage not at all clear: they were based upon rumour rather than evidence. The rumours continued to abound as the conflict within the teaching staff was exacerbated by the continuing criticisms by the remedial teacher of the other staff. The teachers summarise the media characterisation of the teacher as 'a woman determined to help parents who could not speak for themselves to secure an acceptable education for their children.' She herself argues that she wanted parent power (1977, p. 41). Indeed, it has frequently been asserted that she canvassed the working class parent who, it was presumed, would intuitively support traditional authoritarian and rote methods. In fact, throughout the whole of the case, there was little canvassing of these parents and their attitudes to different educational strategies are not well known. They were perhaps most evident by their absence. Nevertheless, the public focus of the dispute was upon both the methods and subject-skills or 'know-how' favoured by different classes of parent for their children. The middle class parents, largely represented by the managing body, on the contrary did object to the teachers' exercise of their responsibility, wanting to believe that the Tyndale teachers were unusual or even unique in their incompetence or indifference to 'know-how'. As the teachers (1976, p. 41) argue, the ILEA, especially its professional staff, supported this critique, because it did not wish the problems of all ILEA's inner city schools, especially for the working class children, to be exposed to the same publicity and public scrutiny. The ILEA did try to sustain the belief that the school was not typical, publicly. On the other hand, the local inspectors acknowledged this typicality in internal memos for future appointments.

The conflict escalated still further in 1975 depite the resignation and departure of one of the main perpetrators – the remedial teacher. By this time attitudes had hardened. The teachers, for example, argue that 'do parents know what is best for their children? . . . What should teachers do if what they believe to be best for the development of the child is at variance with the beliefs of the parent?' Gretton and Jackson confirmed this point: 'Like some medieval priest, the teacher is still wanting the parents to commit their children unreservedly to him just as they were committed to their teachers by their parents – and on the same grounds, i.e. "the teacher knows best".' No allowance is made for any diversity of views among the parents, nor even for any expres-

sion of any views which might be allowed to 'influence the teacher.'
Parents, too, of younger children in the infants who were to transfer to
the junior school were becoming concerned since rumours circulated of
'educational incompetence'. Many considered taking, and did take, their
children to other schools. The school roll at the beginning of the year
was considerably reduced to about 100 children. The managers, seven
of whom were new because of the resignation of the mother and other
managers, became more active in their duties. Now the male members
of the managing body, two new men who replaced the women, tried to
intervene politically. But instead of the managers acting as a corporate
body vested with authority over the school, each began to take individual action and make secret visits to the school and the LEA. These
actions further escalated the distance between parent, manager and
teacher. The head firmly refused to tolerate more uninvited visits. The
teachers also tried to enlist the support of the local teaching association
for them to maintain their autonomy in the control of the curriculum.
The association was unwilling to give full support. The female managers
and some of the mothers, all of whom as Gretton and Jackson argue
were 'on children's tea-party if not dinner-party terms' further escalated
the problems by enlisting the advice of, first, the unusually constituted
borough education committee and, second, the borough's members of
the ILEA. Then, they went to the ILEA's chairman of the schools committee, carefully trying not to appear to be 'middle class trendies.' He
was at first reluctant to intervene since neither the professional educ-
ators, such as the divisional education officers, nor the inspectors conveyed any sense of disquiet. The managers in any event were acting
individually and not corporately. Finally in the summer of 1975, when
some of the managers close to the media had succeeded in precipitating
a crisis by advertising the problems in the national press, the schools
committee took action. It agreed to provide an internal inspection of
the school and an internal inquiry into the reasons for the dispute. The
five teachers did not accept these terms of reference, since both were
based upon the assumption that the managers were not part of the
dispute. The blame could only rest with the teachers and not their
political masters. They also felt that an inspection would be used to
provide evidence against them in the inquiry. They, therefore, went on
strike in September 1975, to object to the inspection and demand an
inquiry, independent of ILEA and its politicians: preferably by the
Department of Education and Science. The teachers did not get the
backing of the National Union of Teachers and their strike remained
unofficial. It was also unusual for the teachers set up, and taught about

half the pupils in, an alternative school until October 1975.

The ILEA continued with its intention to hold its own inquiry into the running of the school, but modified its composition. The inquiry was not conducted by the elected members of ILEA but by an outside *barrister,* initially assisted by two members of the schools committee. It was to investigate 'the teaching, organisation and management of, the William Tyndale's Junior and Infant Schools'.

The inquiry degenerated into a *trial* based upon the traditional methods of prosecution and defence, rather than remaining an investigation. It lasted for four months and was based upon both oral and written evidence, in which written evidence was only used with oral testimony and with each party represented by a barrister. The full proceedings lasted longer, for the teachers remained suspended, and the children provided with education in other ILEA schools, for the whole school year. The report of the inquiry on which decisions were based, was not published until the end of the academic year, four months later. It consisted of both a statement of the events and a series of condemnations of most of the parties to the dispute — managers, all the junior school teachers, borough and ILEA politicians, inspectors and local administrators. As a result, a number of resignations followed — all the managers and the chairman of the school committee. None of the administrators resigned although it must be remarked that,coincidentally,the Chief Education Officer of ILEA retired at the end of that year. It is indeed curious that no blame attached to him over his lack of conduct in the whole affair.

The ILEA instituted disciplinary proceedings against the teachers which lasted a further two terms. The teachers were found guilty and dismissed because they had gone on strike illegally and created an alternative school. Although they are, at the time of writing, appealing against the judgement and sentence they do not have the support of their union, the NUT. The school has since been amalgamated with the infants' school and is headed by the infants' headmistress, who was seen, by Auld, to be exemplary in her behaviour. The replacement of the head by a woman may be of deep significance. Most important, however, is that ILEA chose to use this as a test case and devoted many resources — time, manpower (sic), and financial — to confirming the present organisation of the system both in terms of teaching positions, and the links between schools and parents. It thus set the conditions for the reproduction of the social and sexual division of labour.

In sum, the dispute nicely encapsulates the three issues that Althusser proposes for a research project — the double functioning of ISAs for social reproduction, the role of the state and education as a site of class struggle. Moreover, the dispute can be analysed from a feminist per- psective for it illustrates the importance of the sexual division of labour in the family, school and economy and how that is reproduced. The issues may be summarised thus. First, the dispute shows how education, and its links with the family, sustain social and sexual relations of production through ideology. Children are clearly the private property of their parents, both fathers and mothers. This ideology both underlies the organisation of schooling and was responsible for the final settle- ment of the dispute. However, the tacit expectation, in education, is that parents entrust their children to schools where they will both learn broad skills for participation in the socio-economic system and rules of the established order. Both parents and teachers operated on this assumption. Indeed, the dispute occurred because of the break-down in the shared assumptions about teacher and parental responsibilities for children. The teachers were continually disappointed in the lack of trust felt by some of the parents and their demands for more accounta- bility. These parents, on the other hand, felt that their children were acquiring neither skills nor know-how to fit them for the established order and could therefore not trust the teachers. They had difficulty making their feelings heard because of the ideological assumptions on which schooling is organised. There are indeed few channels of parental communication with the schools. They could only act individually, con- firming the assumption of the possession of their own child alone, or through the parent representative on the managing body. Even this latter had few powers of influence except in concert with the other managers. Then the managers' powers are heavily circumscribed, and to be able to act effectively they have to have recourse to their political superiors. This form of organisation confirms Bowles and Gintis' general thesis of the importance of authority relations for social reproduction. Moreover, the more authoritative the body, the less feminine it was in composition. It was only the managing body that was predominantly female, confirming women's position in the social and educational hier- archy. It is only the first tier of authority that can legitimately be feminine. The main ways in which parents were allowed to communi- cate with the schools were either through support and ad hoc parents' meetings with the teachers or informally through mothers' contacts in the playground. Again this confirms the role that mothers are to play both in the economic and educational system. They are assumed and expected to have daily responsibility for their children. This has to be on an individualistic basis. There were no mechanisms for collective, maternal support for, or complaint to, the schools, or even more important, maternal influence.

As a corollary, the teachers were expected to establish authoritarian relationships with the pupils, which were based on forms of patriarchal authority, and also to teach about the prevailing social order. When the teachers attempted to 'teach against the ideology' to quote Althusser they were castigated for not preserving the social order. Here Bowles and Gintis' thesis is again confirmed. The authority relationships were clearly important to the maintenance of the social system, and to the reproduction of class relations. Indeed, the parents' objections to the teachers were precisely because they appeared to be ignoring class differences within the school. Moreover, the teachers on the whole did not adopt appropriate familial positions vis-à-vis the children. As Bernstein has argued, at the primary or elementary level, the appropriate model is the mother. The teachers tried to be neither mothers nor fathers and indeed were not mainly female. They tried to be avuncular. This also resulted in friction and confusion. Lightfoot, using American evidence, argues that whether teachers actually are female or not is not important to the assumption that they should behave in feminine ways. This was clearly the problem.

On the other hand, although the overt concern and anxiety of the mothers about their own children's futures led to the rapid escalation of the conflict, it did not indicate a radical change in social reproduction. Rather, it confirmed Bourdieu's argument about bourgeois families; that mothers are essential for cultural reproduction. The mothers who became involved politically and in the playground were pursuing their expected social role more actively than is habitual. But they were acting within the ideology. They were anxious only about their own children's futures. Bernstein has argued that changes in the economy have affected the family and cultural reproduction. But he claims that the form of reproduction has been interrupted, not changed. Clearly here the middle class mothers faced a dilemma. They have been educated to expect to be more deeply involved in their children's rearing. This has affected the ways in which they behave with respect to the schools. But they did attempt to confirm bourgeois ideology and protect their own children's interests. Here the form of reproduction has not altered. But mothers are now more actively involved with the schools and attempt to share with or complement their responsibilities. Bernstein's view seems to be borne out that reproduction of the social and sexual division of labour has not changed but has merely been interrupted. This situation also affects theories of domestic labour.

Women's position in the family is clearly linked with the rearing of children in school. It does not just concern ensuring the health and physical protection of husbands and children. The changes in the economy have led to changes in the sexual division of labour in that mothers are now more clearly expected to nurture and rear their children in concert with the schools. This was one of the issues that was highlighted in the dispute.

The second issue that can be illustrated is that education is the site of class struggle. In this case, the identification of the classes involved is complicated. As Benton has argued (1974, p. 36) teachers are usually regarded as agents of the ruling class, teaching ruling ideology. They may, however, be part of the middle classes and able to form alliances with the working class to struggle against the ideology. In this dispute, the teachers all attempted to act as agents of the working class. The remedial teacher even argued that she was their representative although it is nowhere confirmed that she did have any support from the working class parents. The other five teachers tried to help working class children and, since the school had a mixed class composition which was a root cause of the problem, discriminated against middle class children. They focused their attention on the children from poor and minority backgrounds. They did not, however, set out to form alliances with the parents of these working class children. They tried to act 'in loco parentis'. Nor did they try to obtain the support of the parents of the middle class children. Indeed, the dispute occurred over this very problem. It was both about the teachers' allegiances and the ways in which they put them into practice. The middle class mothers became concerned that their own children would not learn their appropriate position in the social order. They went so far as to fight to maintain this ideology. The teachers, however, did not establish their position very strongly. They did not try and ensure the support of their administrative or political masters. This was partly because their counter ideology not only attacked social relations of production but also partriarchal ideology. They did not try to continue authoritarian relationships in school. This was reflected in their teaching methods, their choice of curricula and their relationships as colleagues. However, they did hope to work within the ideology to the extent that they expected that the parents would entrust their children to the school, whatever its style. This is where their problems began. They had not prepared themselves to struggle against parental resistance which was predictable and almost inevitable.

However, parental resistance was more effective than either they or

the teachers could have predicted because of the change in the form of
the organisation of schooling. This enabled the parents to establish
organised·resistance. Both the fact that the school had a newly acquired,
and its own, body of managers and that it also contained one representative parent manager were important. The teachers were perhaps justified in their expectations that the managers, as a body, would support
their actions, virtually without question. They had been led to believe
in their own autonomy. Their hurt, anger and defensive behaviour as a
response to the managers' individualistic actions can be seen in this
context. Nevertheless, they might have calculated that their own actions
did require a modicum of explanation to a new body, with new powers
and a desire to be seen to be politically active. However, they could
perhaps be excused for not calculating the effect of the changes in the
sexual division of labour and its repercussions on the organisation of
schooling. The change in the constitution of the managing bodies in
order to contain a parent-manager exacerbated the conflict. The traditional remit of such bodies was to have overall concern for the running
of the school and not for individual pupils. Although such bodies are
legitimate places for women to be active, they have traditionally been
composed of women who are not mothers of children in the school
concerned. Indeed, the women have generally completed their child-
rearing activities. The representative parent-manager appointed was a
mother-manager and she, not unexpectedly, experienced considerable
conflict in her position. This was also the case for several of the ordinary managers. They, too, were concerned mothers. Thus they were
confused about whether to defend their own children or act on behalf
of the whole school. They ended up by struggling individualistically.
This was because of their aspirations and expectations as educated
middle class women. They have, as Bernstein (ibid, p. 125) argued become more closely concerned with the direct rearing of their children.
Moreover, they have been educated to assume that they may play a
more active role than is traditional within the socio-economic system.
They may be called upon to participate, as married women, in the
labour force. However, they may have to pursue their activities as
mothers and workers sequentially rather than simultaneously. They still
face structural as well as attitudinal barriers to full-time labour force
participation as mothers of young children. The organisation of the
school day does not mirror that of the working day and, moreover,
child-care facilities after school hours are not easily available. The
ideology also teaches that these women should have a direct and articulate concern in their primary school children's education. Many mothers

who were articulate in this dispute were middle class, new to the area, educated to expect to be involved.

This changed socio-economic situation meant a reversal in the class composition of the teachers and those taught in the school. The children fought over were middle class and their mothers sought to preserve their position. They did so on the managing body and as individual parents. The teachers, although themselves middle class, tried to act as agents of the working class and oppose the ideology of the active mothers. The mothers of the middle class children were perhaps more successful than they even expected because of their coincidental connection with the media and the fact that this compounded the problem and led to the ILEA's strong reaction.

The third issue that is thus highlighted is how the state may act repressively within education to suppress class conflict. In this dispute the conflict was settled by very severe means – the use of the formal, legal system rather than the informal, disciplinary procedures. Invoking the legal system has not been unusual in situations of economic crisis. The William Tyndale dispute was, however, the first recent example: the Tameside controversy followed fast upon it. Here the law reaffirmed the authority of representatives of the ruling classes, in this case the judiciary, to determine the educational process (Griffith, 1976). In the case of the William Tyndale's Inquiry, the teachers were eventually castigated and, in effect, the mothers' anxieties were supported and condoned. In fact, the mothers were also chastised for their particular actions. The teachers essentially were condemned because they tried to alter fundamentally both their position and the ideology they taught. They did not take on the traditional role 'in loco parentis' but tried to establish benign, avuncular authority. They also tried to limit actual parental rights in education. They prevented both parents, or mothers especially, and managers from too frequent and overbearing a concern with the school. More important, perhaps, but not explicit, was the fact that although they were men they did not act paternally or maternally. In addition, they did not even make any concession to teaching traditional skills.

Moreover, the teachers did not engage in class struggle effectively and the conflict was relatively easily contained. They did not build alliances either with any of the parents or other teachers. They did not obtain the support of their trade union – the NUT – or the local teachers' association. On the other hand, they were caught within a local political conflict over the areas of control of the various political bodies in education. The Labour Party in Islington was struggling for more regular control of education with ILEA, itself Labour, and the teachers became the eventual scapegoats.

The mothers, however, were not struggling against the ideology. They were not demanding a change in form but only more regular individualistic and personal involvement. They, unlike the teachers, still regarded the children as their personal property and wanted to have more influence over them. They felt threatened because their children did not seem to acquiring either skills or know-how about the established order. Moreover, they could not understand or accept the change in classroom relationships. They wanted to retain maternal authority in the primary school.

The law was used to confirm the existing social and sexual division of labour both in and outside school. Although Auld reprimanded most of the participants in the dispute, the only people really to suffer were the teachers. They were eventually dismissed despite the lack of clear procedures for this. The grounds for dismissal were not the teachers' school behaviour and methods but their going on unofficial strike. This may serve to confirm that the system is generally based on trust between parent and teacher. It is only rarely that the system collapses. Disputes are generally containable and do not require the use of the law.

The Inquiry led to immediate changes in the local school system. As a result of the findings these have been confirmed. They point to the ways the education system has been preserved and maintained. Children remain primarily the property of their parents and their futures are to be determined by them. The teachers have to teach an ideology both of 'freedom' and parental authority and cannot diverge from it. Moreover, they are expected to be particular types of people and establish particular authority relations with the children. It is no accident that it was only the headmistress of the infant school whom Auld did not reprimand but praised, and that she has been confirmed as headmistress of the new amalgamated primary school composed of the junior and infant schools. The mothers' position in the school system has not been altered administratively but the expectation is that they may be regularly involved in schooling. The political masters of the ILEA were also reprimanded and have been compelled to resign. The reprimand was over their laxity and lack of precision and decision in applying authoritarian rules. It is argued that the dispute could have been contained if the teachers had been disciplined earlier by the inspectors, administrators or politicians. Thus, this ruling implies that the education system should function more routinely by repression, and not only ultimately. In addition, the implication is that the strict hierarch-

ical system of authority in schooling, not only in the classroom but in
the political organisation must be preserved to reproduce social relations. Of course the sexual division of labour is sustained within that
since the first tier of authority is now legitimately composed mostly of
women, mainly mothers.

The dispute arose from a complex mix of factors which show the
repercussions of changes in the economy on the school system and the
family. The most important factor was the change in the position of
middle class women. The contradictions in the educational ideology,
the structure of economic life and the family have not enabled women
to participate equally in any of these spheres. The way the dispute was
settled also served to confirm the social and sexual division of labour
and the boundaries of women's position in the family, schooling and
the economy. Primary schooling remains a feminine area where mothers
and women teachers must work under strict conditions of authority to
reproduce the capitalist order.

Conclusions

The analysis of the William Tyndale's dispute has enabled us to fill out
Althusser's sketch of the role of the family-education couple in advanced capitalist societies. It is now clear that the links between the
family and education, both formally specified in law and informally in
action, are vital to the reproduction of the social relations of production. To summarise, first, those links confirm that children are the
private property of their parents in the first instance. Second, the relations between schools and parents confirm the class position of parents,
and this view is passed on to their children. Third, the organisation of
the relationship sets the conditions for its reproduction. It confirms the
rules of the socio-economic system. Reproduction of the social formation is more complicated than the reproduction of the economic
system. Both schools and families contribute to general reproduction.
They do not just prepare children, as Bowles and Gintis,and Hussain,
separately argue, for the work force or wage-labour system but for
their various posts and positions in adult-life. Life in the family is one
of these positions.

Second, the family-education couple contributes specifically to the
reproduction of the sexual division of labour. Althusser ignores this
point and Bowles and Gintis confuse it. They argue that such reproduction only occurs in the family and not the school system. The example
has highlighted how it is the two ISAs, in concert, that sustain this division of labour. They do so through several mechanisms. First, mothers

and fathers have different parts to play in the rearing of their children and this is written into the organisation of education. Second, the teachers act as particular role models for the children when performing 'in loco parentis'. They are expected to use familial relationships. Third, the system of authority relations in education locates women in special positions, such as at the bottom of the political hierarchy of control.

Third, the family-education couple reproduces the social and sexual division of labour simultaneously. Thus we can begin to develop a theory of the articulation of class relations with sex relations of production. Women in both the working class and middle class, as mothers, have prime responsibility for the rearing of children. How they do so, does depend upon their class location and hence their position in the economy. In this example, Bernstein's theory that changes in the economy have affected the position of women in the family and hence middle class women are now more directly concerned with the rearing of children is an important contribution to understanding these complex relationships. He argues that reproduction has been interrupted not altered. However, it is important to make explicit the specific contribution that women make to reproduction and how their positions are themselves reproduced. This has habitually been ignored in the literature. The emphasis has been on understanding the reproduction of the economic system. This is normally conceived narrowly and ignores the sexual division of labour, or rather considers only men. If we look at both class and sex relations we have a clearer understanding of the reproduction of the whole social formation. Women as wives and mothers are important links between the reproduction of labour power and the social relations of production. They maintain reproduction both within the home and with their relationships with the school system. The nurturance aspect of their labour has been much underplayed in the theory of domestic labour where there has been overmuch concern with what kind of labour, productive or unproductive, housework is. It is clearly of vital importance in the maintenance of the class system, with education. Moreover, it plays a crucial part in providing the conditions, with education, for its own reproduction and hence that of the sexual division of labour.

Fourth, we may begin to understand how class struggle may be engaged in, in education, and particularly the part that women may play. Women clearly have a separate, and specific, place in class struggle. As mothers they may struggle within the ideology for a particular form to their relationship with children as their private property. They can also struggle over the established links between the family and school system and hence the nature of their involvement in the economic system. In order for women to play an equal part in the labour force, their relationship to their own children both within the family and the school system, needs to be radically transformed. Moreover, education is a vital locale for transforming the whole social relations of production. Here mothers may be able to form alliances with teachers to work towards transforming the social order. Although the teachers at the William Tyndale's junior school were unsuccessful, they have located the constraints and potentialities for such action.

The way in which the state, as the politico-legal apparatus, reacts to such struggle is now clear. Struggle in education is not only repressed in a concealed or symbolic way, as Althusser claims. In particular conjunctures it may be tackled by the repressive State apparatus. This indicates, however, how tenuous the ruling ideology is and how it may be countered. In order to reproduce both the social order and patriarchal ideology, the state has to take vigorous and explicit measures. In so doing, the form of reproduction is not altered but sustained. The bourgeois family is reinforced within the family system, in its links with education, and through the system of authority relations in education itself. This system needs to be maintained through structures which may function both by ideology and repression. Ideology alone is not sufficient to maintain the social order and, in particular, the sexual division of labour. Repression may occur within the school system itself or, in the last instance, through the rule of law. Sustained struggles over the position of women in the family, education and the economy will continually threaten the easy maintenance of the social and sexual capitalist relations.

References

Althusser, L., 'Ideology and Ideological State Apparatuses' in *Lenin and Philosophy and Other Essays* (New Left Books, London, 1971).

Aries, P., *Centuries of Childhood* (Penguin, 1975).

Association of Headmistresses Conference, ' "Inadequate" Parents Blamed for Classroom Rebels',*TES,* 10 June 1977.

Auld, P., QC, *William Tyndale Junior and Infants Schools Public Inquiry* (ILEA, 1976).

Barron, R. and G. Norris,'Sexual Divisions and the Dual Labour Market' in D.L. Barker and S. Allen,*Dependence and Exploitation in Work and Marriage* (Longmans, 1976).

Beechey, V., 'On the Political Economy of Woman',unpublished paper given at the Communist University on Feminism, Bristol, April 1977.

Benton, T., 'Education and Politics' in D. Holly (ed.), *Education or Domination?*

(Arrow, 1974).

Berg, L., *Risinghill: Death of a Comprehensive* (Penguin, 1968).

Bernstein, B., *Class Codes and Control* Vol. 3, *Towards a Theory of Educational Transmissions* (Routledge and Kegan Paul, 1975).

Blackstone, T., 'The Education of Girls Today' in J. Mitchell and A. Oakley (ed.), *The Rights and Wrongs of Women* (Penguin, 1976).

Bowles, S. and H. Gintis,*Schooling in Capitalist America* (Routledge & Kegan Paul, 1976).

Bourdieu, P., 'Systems of Education and Systems of Thought' in E. Hopper (ed.), *Readings in the Theory of Education Systems* (Hutchinson, 1971a).

—— 'Intellectual Field and Creative Project' in M.F.D. Young (ed.), *Knowledge and Control* (Collier-MacMillan, 1971b).

—— 'Cultural Reproduction and Social Reproduction' in R. Brown (ed.), *Knowledge, Education and Cultural Change* (Tavistock, 1973).

—— 'The School as a Conservative Force: Scholastic and Cultural Inequalities' in R. Dale *et al.* (eds.), *Schooling and Capitalism* (Routledge & Kegan Paul, 1976).

Pamphlet No. 2 *On the Political Economy of Women* (Conference of Socialist Economists, 1977).

County of Avon Education Service,*External Influences and Pressures on Schools* (unpublished mimeograph, 1977).

David, M.E., 'Education and the Reproduction of the Social and Sexual Division of Labour'. Paper given to *Sexual Divisions and Society Study Group,* BSA Annual Conference, Manchester, April 1976.

—— *Reform, Reaction and Resources: The 3 R's of Educational Planning* (NFER, 1977).

Ellis, T. *et al., William Tyndale's Junior School: The Teachers' Story* (Writers and Readers Collective, 1976).

Erben, M. and D. Gleeson 'Education as Reproduction: A Critical Examination of Some Aspects of the Work of Althusser' in M.F.D. Young and G. Witty, *Society State and Schooling* (Falmer Press, 1977).

Gardiner, J., 'Women's Domestic Labour', *New Left Review* 89, Jan-Feb 1975.

Gardiner, J., S. Himmelweit and M. MacIntosh, 'Women's Domestic Labour' in *Bulletin of the Conference of Socialist Economists* Vol. 4, No. 2 (II) June 1975. Reprinted in CSE Pamphlet No. 2,op. cit.

Gramsci, A., *Selections from the Prison Notebooks* (Lawrence and Wishart, 1971).

Gretton, J. and M. Jackson,*Collapse of a School or a System?* (George Allen and Unwin, 1976).

Griffith, J.A., 'The Tameside Opinion', *New Statesman* 29 October 1976.

Halsey, A.H. (ed.), *Educational Priority Vol. 1 Problems and Priorities* (HMSO, 1972).

Hirst, P.Q. 'Althusser and the Theory of Ideology' in *Economy and Society* Vol. 5, No. 4 (Autumn 1976).

Hussain, A., 'The Economy and the Education System in Capitalistic Societies' in *Economy and Society* Vol. 5, No. 4 (Autumn 1976).

Kogan, M., 'Democratically Does It', *TES* No. 3207, (19 November 1976).

Lambert R., *et al., The Chance of a Lifetime* (Weidenfeld and Nicholson, 1975).

Lightfoot, S. Lawrence, 'Sociology of Education: Perspectives on Women. In M. Millman and R.M. Kanter (eds.), *Another Voice: Feminist Perspectives on Social Life and Social Science* (Anchor, 1975).

Marks, P., 'Feminity in the Classroom: An Account of Changing Attitudes' in Mitchell and Oakley, op. cit., 1976.

Marx, K., *Capital*, Vol. 1, Book 1 (*Dent, Everyman*, 1976).

Midwinter, E., *Education and Community* (Allen and Unwin, 1975).

McLennan, G., V. Molina and R. Peters 'Althusser's Theory of Ideology' in *Working Papers in Cultural Studies 10 On Ideology* (Centre for Contemporary Cultural Studies, 1977).

Musgrove, F., *The Family, Education and Society* (Routledge and Kegan Paul, 1966).

—— *Youth and the Social Order* (Routledge and Kegan Paul, 1964).

—— *Patterns of Power and Authority in English Education* (Routledge and Kegan Paul, 1971).

Poulantzas, N., *Classes in Contemporary Capitalism* (New Left Books, 1975).

Richardson, E., *The Teacher, the School and the Task of Management* (Heinemann, 1973).

Saran, R., *Policy-Making in Secondary Education* (Oxford University Press, 1973).

Secombe, W., 'The Housewife and her Labour under Capitalism' *New Left Review* 83 (1974).

Shaw, J., 'In Loco Parentis',unpublished paper presented to Anglo-French Seminar at Maison de Science des Hommes, Paris, April 1976.

—— 'School Attendance: Some Notes on a Further Feature of Sexual Division', unpublished paper presented to *BSA Sexual Divisions and Society Study Group,* Coventry 11 June 1977.

Simon, B., *Studies in the History of Education,* Vol. 1, 1780-1870 (Lawrence and Wishart, 1960).

—— *Studies in the History of Education,* Vol. 2, 1870-1920 (Lawrence and Wishart, 1965).

Sutherland, G., *Policy Making in English Elementary Education 1870-95* (Oxford University Press, 1974).

Tyack, D., 'Ways of Seeing: An Essay on the History of Compulsory Schooling' in *Harvard Ecucational Review* V. 46, No. 3 (August 1976).

Walker, D., 'William Tyndale' in C.B. Cox and R. Boyson (eds.), *Black Paper 1977* (Temple Smith, 1977).

Wolpe, A.M., 'The Official Ideology of the Education of Girls' in A. Flude and M. Ahier (ed.), *Schools, Educability and Ideology* (Croom Helm, 1974).

7 THE POLICE AND THE STATE: ARREST, LEGALITY AND THE LAW

Doreen J. McBarnet

1. The Problem of Legality

In the ideology of the liberal democratic state, the rule of the state over the individual is closely circumscribed by the notion of legality. Citizens should be subject to the rule of law not of men, to established law not individual whim or retrospective decision, with all citizens equal before the law and free from arbitrary arrest or imprisonment. An essential ingredient is that state officials, especially the police, operating the most explicitly oppressive of routine state powers, criminal law, should themselves be subject to laws that protect these civil rights. This imposes recognised limitations on the effectiveness of police work, but the rhetoric goes that it is better for ten guilty men to go free than for one innocent man to be wrongly convicted.

Hence the basic protection against arbitrary arrest in English, Scots and American law in the principle that a person may be arrested or searched only in relation to a specified offence: 'a citizen is entitled to know on what charge or on suspicion of what crime he is seized' (*Christie* v. *Leachinsky*, 1947 AC). Otherwise policemen 'cannot compel any person against his will to come to or remain in any police station', to answer questions or be searched. Hence too civil rights under arrest: first, the right of the accused to remain silent, indeed to be cautioned that: 'You are not obliged to say anything unless you wish to do so but what you do say may be put into writing and given in evidence', and the right to be protected from induced confession by the principle of admitting only voluntary statements; second, the general right to legal advice: 'every person at any stage of an investigation should be able to communicate and to consult privately with a solicitor.' These points are referred to in the English Judge Rules (HO circular 1964 no. 31)[1] but Scots Common Law and American constitutional rights involve similar maxims for controlling police behaviour. The warrant, the caution, legal aid, and the duty solicitor are all symbols of legality.

Sociologists of the police have tended to treat the notion of legality as unproblematic, not because they assume the police operate according to these principles, but rather because they assume the opposite, that they are largely irrelevant in practice. Thus Skolnick notes that the purpose of his book is 'not to reveal that the police violate rules and regulations. That much is assumed' (1966, p. 22). Rather, he seeks to show how the work conditions of the police produce pressures and preconceptions that lead to a presumption of guilt rather than innocence, to an emphasis on catching criminals, if necessary at the expense of the civil liberties embodied in legality. The same emphases permeate the literature on police behaviour vis-a-vis citizens. The dominant *issue* is the law in action − how the police *do* behave − rather than the law in books − how they should. The dominant *approach* is via the discretionary and discriminatory side of the policeman's role, how the police come to select for arrest particular individuals who tend to be male rather than female, working class rather than middle class, black rather than white. The dominant explanation is in terms of non-legal influences on the policeman − family, colleagues, bureaucratic demands, personal ambitions (Cain, 1973) − and in terms of informal interaction − police interpretations of behaviour, stereotyping, perceived lack of deference sparking off hostility on both sides (Skolnick, 1966; Piliavin and Briar, 1964, Kadish, 1962; Young, 1971; Sykes and Clark, 1975). Not surprisingly, then, with police studies dominated by interactionist rather than structuralist sociology, the key to police action is found in the informal, the situational and the subjective. If the police conduct arrests in a way that contradicts the spirit of legality, this is merely a byproduct of informal interaction: the role of formal law and the potential constraints of legality are barely touched on.

Yet ironically the idea of legality is almost always taken for granted as embodied in a formal legal standard from which practices deviate. Cain quotes the policeman's view that 'You can't play it to the book. You'd never get anywhere in a job like this' (1971, p. 88). Skolnick bases his work on a dichotomy of law versus order on the same assumption; Reiss and Bordua refer to the trial's 'institutionalised distrust of the police' and talk of the suspect who 'demands all the safeguards of due process' (1967, pp. 31, 49), assuming thereby that they exist. So much is the law itself assumed to incorporate real rights, indeed, that Skolnick argues fairness and efficiency would result if only practice could be brought into line with existing law.[2] More generally it is almost mandatory to refer to Packer's two ideal types for describing law enforcement, 'Due Process' (or legality) and 'Crime Control' (1964). The point is made that in practice policemen veer towards the Crime Control approach to enforcement, which is empirically scrutinised for all the non-legal reasons involved. Due Process, meantime, remains simply the other half of the dichotomy, the assumed legal standard, unproblematic and unexplored.

If sociologists have tended to take it for granted that the law on criminal procedure embodies legality so too have those making policy proposals to widen police powers. Working with an unproblematic conception of due process means working on assumptions, and the dominant assumptions at the moment are framed by those with a vested interest in assuming the law not only *does* provide safeguards for the citizen vis-a-vis the police but provides so many safeguards that the police task is impossible; in short, that due process *prevents* crime control. Sir Robert Mark's views are the obvious example.[3] These opinions in turn become the basis of proposals for policy changes in favour of wider police powers, such as the recommendation of the Thomson Report to move away from arrest only on a specific charge to detention on suspicion: 'We recommend, therefore, a form of limited, or temporary arrest — arrest on suspicion' (1975, p. 12).

Indeed, interactionist research on the police has lent support to such arguments exactly because it presents the views of policemen on due process, rather than investigating it. Take, for example, Skolnick's dichotomy of law (legality) versus order (crime control) or his testament that policemen see procedural rules as making their jobs more difficult by requiring them to prove to legal standards the guilt of someone they 'know' to be a criminal, a point Mack makes too (1976). West Coast sociologists and the police lobby may make strange bedfellows but they share the same blind spot. Indeed, even the National Council for Civil Liberties accepts that civil rights are lost by police *abuse* of the law without scrutinising the law itself:

> All policemen are under the same pressure; *bend the rules to* deliver the goods in the form of convictions . . . It is the *abuse* of police powers in these circumstances — arrest, search and questioning — that has created the most intractable police/civil liberty problem in recent years. (Cox, 1975, p. 164, my emphases)

But the issue remains an empirical one. Are legal procedures distorted by informal police interaction? Do legal procedures safeguard the principles of legality at the expense of crime control? A straightforward need for information, then, is the first reason for subjecting due process to empirical scrutiny.

The second reason is more explanatory. Sociologists studying arrest have concentrated on asking why policemen want to make arrests; the rules seen as significant have been not the abstractions of law but those informal rules constructed *in situ* for practical purposes. But there is another question: why may policemen make arrests? That involves looking at the formal rules of the law itself and at what judges treat in court as acceptable, accountable or sanctionable exercises of police power. Sociologists have focussed so far on studying police behaviour on the beat, but we must also study it in its legal and judicial context. This perspective is significant in two ways.

First, there is the potential causal influence of the law on police be-haviour. To say this is not to fall into naive role theory; it is not just to suggest that what people ought to do affects what they do, but rather that what they can get away with affects what they do. The elements of accountability and sanctions introduced by formal rules make them more than just abstractions. Courts, after all, are taken for granted as sanctions on the police, in 'the book' and the safeguards for defendants mentioned by the police and those who study them. It may even be that the police take heed of the formal rules of admissibility they may have to face in court not only *retrospectively* in the accounts of their behaviour that they give in reports and court testimony, but also *prospectively* in their behaviour and decisions. There is, for example, some indication that a change in the District of Columbia rules of admissible interrogation in 'Mallory' which the Chief of Police predicted would make the collection of evidence impossible and lead to a 'complete breakdown in law enforcement', led instead to a redefinition of the possible and a new set of methods involving more investigation and less interrogation (Sowle, 1962, p. 167).

In short, if abstract rules are redefined and used according to practical purposes, then practical purposes, the 'needs' of crime control, may also be redefined according to the demands of formal rules. Rules and practice interrelate. Sometimes, of course, the sanctions are empty. Most studies on the police have paid scant attention to the judicial sanction exactly because most police work is 'justice without trial', where the police settle or punish disorder themselves taking it no further and where most cases that do come to court are guilty pleas with no trial involved. But as argued elsewhere (McBarnet, 1976) justice without trial is not just a product of informal police activity: it is also a product of the legal system itself. Police decisions are taken in a legal context which is significant as one formal parameter to add to the informal ones on why particular decisions are made in the process of law enforcement.

But what the police may do is significant from a second point of view and that is the main interest of this paper. Studies of the police so far have in fact been less about the law than about an occupational group who happen to operate the law and incidentally impinge on it, a significant issue but not the only one. Law enforcement analysed instead from the perspective of how it is meant to operate provides a more direct entrée into the nature of the law itself and the judicial and political elites of the state who make it. Here, methods scorned for studying the police become vital for studying the law. Observation in court and study of police records may not tell us much about the actuality of police behaviour but do tell us what kind of police behaviour is acceptable in law. Analysis of the 'law in the books' on police behaviour does not tell us what the police do, but a good deal about what the police are legally allowed and legally expected to do. Law enforcement, in short, is not exclusively an area for interactionist study at the micro level; it is also an issue in the politics of law at the macro level. This means a change of focus, shifting attention from the routine activities of petty officials of the state to the top of the judicial and political hierarchies where rules are made and sanctions operated, switching our question from the effectiveness or otherwise of rules and sanctions (assuming they were intended to be effective) to the intentions themselves. *Is* the law formulated to control the police? *Does* the law incorporate civil rights as in the ideology of legality it should?

Posing the question at this level indicates that 'Due Process' is a more complex concept than Packer's dichotomy might suggest. Compressed into the vague concept are two quite distinct aspects:
1. the general principles around which the law is discussed, and
2. the actual procedures by which legality is operationalised.

In short, between police practices and the rhetoric of legality lies the state — judges and parliaments, the actuality of legality in common law and statute. If police behaviour deviates from the rhetoric of legality therefore, we cannot just assume it does so despite the law; we must also investigate how far the law itself incorporates its own rhetoric. *Is* deviation from the standards of legality merely a product of informalities and unintended consequences at the level of petty officials, or is it also institutionalised in the formal law of the state?

Shifting the question like this raises a whole array of potentially significant issues on the state, the law and dominant ideology, on contradictions within dominant ideology and the mechanics of its operation. The first step towards these wider theoretical issues, however, is the practical one of describing empirically the current procedures of legality governing arrest. The main focus will be on the law of Scotland

where court observation was carried out.[4] But English law is covered
too and despite the much referred to variations in the two systems, it
shows remarkably little real difference on the basic points argued in this
paper. Indeed, significant judicial decisions, taken though they are in
relation to specific cases and according to two apparently independent
bodies of law, are often strikingly parallel and contemporary: a point
which is not only ironic in these days of devolution but perhaps relevant
to any study of the relative autonomy of law.

2. The Law on Arrest

Arrest, that is, the detention of a person against his will, may be legally
carried out only in relation to a specified offence. Otherwise attendance
at the police station is purely voluntary. This is the spirit of the Judge's
Rules. Barry Cox points out succinctly the gap between this ideology
and practice: 'Detention for questioning is therefore in theory
impossible; in practice "helping the police with their inquiries" is a
daily event' (1975, p. 172). How is this possible? Partly because of the
simple fact that if such arrest is impossible in theory it is nonetheless
perfectly possible in *law*. Although they are much referred to as a
symbol of legality, the Judges' Rules are *not* law, only principles for
administrative guidance. Authoritative law on arrest is rather different.

For example, the *voluntary* nature of helping the police with their
inquiries has been interpeted in law, to say the least, very widely. Consider the Scottish case of *Swankie* v. *Miln* in 1973 which defines the
current situation. This was deemed not only not to be an *illegal* arrest
but not to be an arrest at all. The judges accepted that the police had
stopped the accused in his car, taken his keys away, waited with him
and would have prevented him from leaving if he had tried to. However, they concluded that the accused had remained voluntarily and had
not therefore been arrested. What their judgement would have been if
he had tried to leave is unclear. But since one can also be arrested according to the 1964 Police Act for obstructing the police in the execution
of their duty,[5] since this has been interpreted as: 'the doing of any
act which makes it more difficult for the police to carry out their duty'
(Parker L.J.) and since this might include simply refusing to answer
questions and any sarcasm[6] in one's manner (*Rice* v. *Connolly,* 1966), it is
difficult to see how someone can avoid being arrested if the police have
a mind to do so. Furthermore, refusing to co-operate is not a far cry
from resistance, which is, of course, subject to arrest, nor is resistance far from another offence, assault.

Indeed, in court, resisting arrest tends to be presented by prosecutors

as indicative of guilt and therefore a justification of the arrest on the
first charge anyway. Only the guilty take advantage of civil rights is the
line taken. On the other hand, with the nice skill lawyers have of
always holding the winning trick, failing to resist is also suspicious.
Witness case 8:

The prosecutor was suggesting that the accused *must* have been
committing the offence or he would not have allowed himself to have
been seized (uncharged) by two men (the police were in plain clothes)
without resisting:

Prosecutor	You didn't do anything?
Accused	I couldn't.
Prosecutor	You didn't say 'What are you doing?'
Accused	No, it was all too quick.
Prosecutor	And no explanation was given at all?
Accused	No.
Prosecutor	When did you gather they were policemen?
Accused	I asked them — they said they were taking me to the station.
Prosecutor	But why assume they were policemen? There *are* railway stations.

In his summing up the prosecutor considered it doubly suspicious that
the accused's companion had not fought off the two policemen if his
friend was being innocently seized:

Prosecutor	According to his story, his companion made no protest while the accused was dragged out by two unknown men. This is quite incredible. He is clearly guilty of this charge.

The companion in question might, however, have been relieved that he
had *not* intervened if he had heard the accused's mother's account of
her night in jail charged with Breach of the Peace when she went to
protest, or if he had witnessed case 13:

Policeman	One youth ran towards us saying 'What are you taking him in for? It's a fucking liberty. He's done fuck all!' He was cautioned and charged with Breach of the Peace

— and fined £10.

In any case, the prosecutor's argument was only about the credibility of the accused not the legality of the arrest. Indeed, in cases of resistance or assault, even if the arrest was unfounded and illegal it is still, in English law, 'open to the jury to convict of common assault' (Halsbury, p. 634) and the charge sticks even if the resister did not know the person seizing him was a policeman. In short, the law itself does not encourage standing on one's right to freedom from arbitrary arrest.

Given this, the warrant system provides a potential method for safeguarding the citizen against *arbitrary* arrest since it involves a specific charge and acceptance by a neutral judge that there are grounds for suspecting the accused. However, in *R.* v. *Kulynycz,* 1971, it was agreed that arresting without a warrant while pretending to have one was not fatal to the case, while the Criminal Law Act of 1967 allows a member of the public or a policeman to arrest without warrant 'anyone who is, or whom he reasonably suspects to be in the act of committing an arrestable offence', while a policeman may also arrest someone whom he reasonably suspects is *about* to commit an arrestable offence.[7] So in most serious cases a suspect can be arrested without warrant. The same is true of the all-embracing Breach of the Peace, while specific acts often have specific powers of arrest without warrant attached, e.g. in drug offences, immigration offences and motoring offences. Under Scots law, the police may arrest without warrant for all common law crimes (most crimes being based on common law) and for statutory offences, categories which can cover most incidents.

In any case, the control function of the warrant seems rendered redundant by the view expressed in the authoritative manual on procedure that 'such petitions, being presented by responsible officials, are assumed to be well-founded' (Renton and Brown, 1972, p. 28). This is rather at odds with Lord Hewart's rhetoric on the rule of law over officials too:

> One of our most priceless possessions is the liberty of the subject. If once we show any signs of giving way to the abominable doctrine that because things are done by officials, some immunity must be extended to them, what is to become of our country? (Ludlow, 1938)

However, the view that officials can be trusted was upheld by the Thomson Committee in the face of requests for change and it was on this basis that they found it 'satisfactory' for judges to 'rubber stamp' rather than investigate requests for warrants (1975, p. 20). Lafave and Remington's American study of the warrant system (1975) points to informal judicial laxness as the source of its ineffectiveness, but from these views, expounded by a legal authority and a committee set up by the government and Crown Office and chaired by a High Court Judge, it would seem in the Scottish case to be formally endorsed common law and policy.

With or without the symbolic warrant, however, an arrest is accountable and there must be grounds for it, although of course it is accountable only if challenged, and, as Renton and Brown point out in discussing arrest without warrant, 'it is not often challenged' (1972, p. 28). Given the methods available for challenging an arrest (in the course of a criminal trial, by a civil action or by a complaint to the police) and given that most cases do not come to trial (Criminal Statistics), that most defendants are unrepresented and unversed in law (Dell, 1971; Bottoms and McClean, 1976), that civil cases are costly and legal aid limited, and that police complaints are rarely effective (Box and Russell, 1975) this is hardly surprising. If challenged, however, an arrest is accountable on two aspects:[8] first, on whether there is enough evidence to charge the suspect under a specific law with a specific offence, since an arrest must be accompanied by a charge (*Chalmers* v. *HM Adv.*, 1954), and second on whether it is necessary to arrest, i.e. to keep him in custody after the charge rather than releasing him on bail until he comes to court.[9]

The legality of custody is defined in terms of reasonableness or the interests of justice (Renton & Brown, 1972, p. 30), neither of which sets the parameters very clearly, allowing wide scope for subjective discretion. Indeed, common law merely offers a post hoc check on the 'reasonableness' of the policeman's *belief* that arrest was justified. The law also accepts the belief that people ought to be taken into custody if they have a past record (*Carlin* v. *Malloch,* 1896) or are jobless or homeless. Lord Deas in *Peggie* v. *Clark* made it clear that the arrest of a member of 'the criminal classes' or of someone with no means of honest livelihood or fixed abode is easier to justify than that of someone who 'even although expressly charged with a crime by an aggrieved party, be a well-known householder – a person of respectability – what, in our judiciary practice, we call a 'law-abiding party'. This statement by a judge in 1868 remains the criterion today. (Renton and Brown, 1972, p. 29). What is more, the requirement in Scots, though not in English, law, of a cash deposit for bail rather than just a promise that the money will be paid if the accused fails to turn up in court, leads to the detention of the same type of people – the jobless and homeless – regardless of the trivial nature of their offence. Even the *Ludlow* case, noted above, which found for the complainant in his action against the police for abuse of their powers of arrest and search and is full of civil rights rhetoric, nonetheless draws its indignation from the *status* of the citizen so affronted: 'Is it easy to imagine a more gross indignity offered to a perfectly innocent and respectable professional gentleman?' (1938).

Note the parallels in law with the practical grounds for arrests used informally by Skolnick's policemen, that the homeless or jobless were most likely to abscond, with King's account (1971) of police objections to bail (the two most frequently mentioned were that the accused had previous convictions or no fixed abode) and with Cain's account of the arrest of vagrants. In two police stations she found that 20 per cent and 27 per cent respectively of those arrested for marginal offences were of no fixed abode. She links this to their vulnerability as 'a small, exposed and powerless section of the population' who are therefore particularly at risk to the policeman's interests in making arrests, especially during 'the long cold haul between supper break and dawn' (1971, pp. 74, 5). 'But it is not just informal motivations and assessments that are involved, subverting equality before the law. Given the law's attitude to the homeless and jobless we could not expect equality anyway. Pragmatics and rationalisations at the informal level – with the consequence, intended or otherwise, of class and racial bias – are also endorsed in formal law.

As for having sufficient evidence on a specific offence, there is also plenty of scope for legally circumventing that principle. The specific offence may itself be rather unspecific: breach of the peace (whose peace?), loitering with intent or being on premises for unlawful purposes (how does one determine purpose or intent?), possessing goods for which one cannot satisfactorily account (how many people carry receipts and what is satisfactory?), carrying implements that could be used for housebreaking (where does one draw the line?) or as weapons. Even an empty milk bottle has been defined as a dangerous weapon (Armstrong and Wilson, 1973). If the police operate at this level with wide discretion (Bottomley, 1973) it is not just because they surreptitiously take it into their own hands but because they are formally allocated discretion on what constitutes an offence via vague substantive laws and wide procedural powers.

So, in vague cases like Breach of the Peace, the offence exists *because* the police say they observed someone loitering, drunk, 'bawling, shouting, cursing and swearing', to quote the daily menu for the district courts, or more unusually but nonetheless an observed case, 'jumping on and off the pavement in a disorderly fashion' (case 30). These offences may be, in Maureen Cain's term, marginal. They are, as described, amazingly trivial. Recognising the marginality of such offences, but recognising too their numerical significance (76 per cent of the arrests she observed) Cain probes the non-legal reasons for police making such arrests (1971, p. 74). But what is also important is the formal structure which makes such arrests, whatever their motivation, legal. Likewise, one must refer to more than informal stereotyping to explain the arrest of two young boys, a 'known thief' and his companion, who, according to the police evidence, were 'touching cars', according to the boys 'just pointing at Volvos and things, expensive cars'. Whatever the informal motivation of the police, the legality of their action is indusputable and the stereotyping more than informal. The General Powers Act 1960[10] lays down the law that known or reputed thieves in suspicious circumstances are subject to arrest. A known thief is someone with a previous conviction for dishonesty: previous convictions become therefore not just informal leads for narrowing down suspects on committed crimes but legal grounds for arresting them. A reputed thief is someone who keeps bad company and has no known means of honest livelihood: stereotyping and assuming the worst are thus written into the law. Suspicious circumstances are left to the police to define. Thus police evidence in this case (9) is expressed purely as subjective interpretation:

> they were touching them *as though to* open them
> he *seemed to say* to Craig to stand back
> they *appeared to be* watching and waiting (my emphases)

Note that it is not just police practice but the formal law here which deviates from the ideals of legality, replacing arrest for a specified offence with arrest on suspicion or for prevention; replacing established law with arbitrary definitions; replacing the doctrine of trying each case on its merits with the relevance of previous convictions. Personal and bureaucratic motivations may explain why the police want to make arrests; the law itself explains why they may.

What is more, judicial sanctions on police arrests at this level are meaningless. Vague laws and wide powers effectively sidestep standards of legality and proof by equating the subjective police decision with the substantive law and requisite evidence. The police are given the

statutory powers to define the limits of the behaviour that constitutes
public order. It is not necessary to prove intent in cases like these, by
for example, reference to:

> any particular act or acts tending to show the purpose or intent; he
> may be convicted if, from the circumstances of the case and from his
> known character, the court is of the opinion that he was intending to
> commit a felony. (Vagrancy Act, 1824, s. 12)

Nor is there any need to prove effect, e.g. in a Breach of the Peace, that
anyone was offended or even affected: a breach has occurred 'where
something is done in breach of public order or decorum which *might
reasonably be expected* to lead to the lieges being alarmed or upset . . . '
(*Raffaeli* v. *Heatly*, 1949, SC). So the refusal of members of the public
to say they were offended in witnessing the incident, a point regularly
made in police reports, is rendered irrelevant, as indeed judges point out
to juries, reading out the legal definitions and emphasising: 'Note that
"might be". There need not be evidence that anyone was actually upset'
(case 93).

Since the offence presupposes a specified offender and eyewitnesses,
there is nothing left at issue but the credibility of the police versus the
accused. In Scotland corroboration is required, but since the police (as a
result of this legal requirement rather than the hostility of the natives)
tend to go around in pairs, this is rarely a problem. The magistrate
who sums up: 'I see no reason to disbelieve the police' (case 8) is not
informally ignoring his right to sanction police behaviour but recognising that there is at law nothing to sanction. The openness of the law
means that there are few grounds for judicial control in such marginal
cases. It is hardly surprising then that they dominate police work and,
since less marginal cases requiring harder proof are more likely to be
dropped in the early stages (Mack, 1976) it is not surprising that trivial
cases dominate the courts even more. In petty offences judicial control
of the police is abrogated by the law.[11]

The significance of police powers on such petty offences, however,
does not stop there. Defining as arrestable offences behaviour as indeterminate as these examples gives the police wide powers of legal detention, and these powers may be used to establish evidence for a different
suspected offence, which the policeman is really interested in but has
no evidence on which to charge and therefore arrest. Once arrested, the
person, and the premises he is in, can be legally searched, and if evidence relevant to another charge is unearthed, the search is quite lawful

and the evidence admissible. This is despite the principle that such search should not take place until there are grounds for charging on a specific offence. Even in more general instances of search, urgency excuses the police from the principle 'urgency being widely interpreted in favour of the police' (Renton and Brown,p. 36; *Bell* v. *Hogg*; *Hay* v. *HM Adv.*).

Indeed, even the seizure without warrant of perfectly legitimate goods has been deemed acceptable in English law. In *Chic Fashions*, 1968, Lord Justice Salmon pointed out that the police had reasonable grounds to suspect that the goods seized might be stolen, and since in the law of arrest 'reasonable grounds to suspect' legitimises seizure of the *person*, he could scarcely hold that the same did not apply to mere *property*:

> If a man's person is not so sacrosanct in the eyes of the law, how can the goods which he is reasonably suspected of having stolen or received be sacrosanct? Only if the law regards property as more important than liberty and I do not accept that it does so.

Thus did common law justify illegally invading personal liberty to recover property by the principle that personal liberty is more significant in law than property. In doing so of course it set up a new precedent that reversed its own justification, making the right to recover *possibly* stolen property outweigh the right to individual freedom from interference from the police.

It is not just search that is opened up by the holding charge. Although interrogation is forbidden after a charge, questions regarding a different charge are quite legal. The holding charge thus allows a suspect to be questioned in private and in custody until a confession is elicited. In the 'touching cars' case, according to the evidence of the defendants, it was exactly this motivation that prompted the police to invoke the General Powers Act to arrest them. The boys, defending themselves, tried to use this point to lend credibility to their story that they were lifted for nothing, that they 'were not touching cars' but 'playing football and he came up and asked us about a tv set'. However, because this referred to another offence on which they had not been charged it was deemed legally inadmissible:

Magistrate	(to policeman) Did you apprehend him on another charge of stealing a television set?
Policeman	No sir.

Magistrate   (to accused) Then he can't answer that.

When the second accused brought in the same point the magistrate stopped him:

Magistrate   I'm sorry. I'm not prepared to listen to information about a television.
Accused   But he said he didn't ask us about a tv set and he did.
Magistrate   It's irrelevant to this charge.

When he pursued it further:

Magistrate   Look, this charge is nothing to do with a stolen television. You're doing yourself no good telling me you're involved in another charge. Understand?

But, of course, the suspicion of involvement with a stolen television set might have had everything to do with the use of the holding charge and be absolutely relevant to the defendant's alleged innocence. The police may indeed drop both the holding charge and the other case so that the chance to raise the matter in court at all is denied unless the defendant takes out a suit for wrongful arrest.

The Judges' Rules specify as an overriding principle and fundamental condition that only voluntary statements are admissible, with a veto on questioning after charge precisely in recognition of the unreliability of 'confessions' in such circumstances. So the holding charge is quite contrary to the whole underlying spirit of the Rules. But it is perfectly legal. Indeed, Renton and Brown point out that 'The police could presumably arrest an offender on this charge and hold him until they obtained a warrant on the charge in which they were really interested. (1972, p. 32), while Lord Simonds declared in the House of Lords, that, while a man should be told the charge against him, it could not

> be wrongful to arrest and detain a man upon a charge, of which he is reasonably suspected, with a view to further investigation of a second charge upon which information is incomplete. (*Christie* v. *Leachinsky,* 1947, AC 593)

Indeed, he went on to assert,

> . . . it is not an essential condition of lawful arrest that the constable

should at the time of arrest formulate any charge at all, much less
the charge which may ultimately be found in the indictment.

Holding charge practices do not then require abuse but simply use of
the law. They are not informal subversions of due process: they are due
process as defined by common law and statute.

Lawful arrests and legitimate police treatment of citizens under
arrest are therefore defined very much more broadly in legal procedure
than the principle of legality might suggest. What is more, an *unlawful*
arrest does not of itself damage a police case if it can be justified after
the event. Likewise, evidence acquired by an unlawful search can itself
by legally admissible, since there is no equivalent in Scots or English law
of the American doctrine that the fruit of the forbidden tree is itself
forbidden — inadmissible (*Mapp* v. *Ohio US*, 1961).

Scots law on exclusion of evidence is sometimes described as clearer
and fairer to the accused, much more geared to disciplining the police
via the power of exclusion than English law. Heydon suggests this (1975,
p. 230) citing Lord Justice General Cooper's exclusion of unwarranted
search evidence in *Lawrie* v. *Muir* in support. But the same judge has
regularly admitted illegally obtained evidence, for example, because it
was taken 'in good faith' (*Fairley* v. *Fishmongers of London*, 1951, JC),
although he had ruled out good faith as a good reason just the year
before. Indeed Lord Justice General Cooper has made it clear that the
evidence he declared inadmissible in *Lawrie* v. *Muir* was defined as such
mainly because it was *not* the police who obtained it:

> It is especially to be noted that the two inspectors who in this
> instance exceeded their authority *were not police officers enjoying
> a large residuum of common law discretionary powers,* but the
> employees of a limited company acting in association with the Milk
> Marketing Board, whose only powers are derived from contracts
> between the Board and certain milk producers and distributors, of
> whom the appellant is not one. Though the matter is narrow, I am
> inclined to regard this last point as sufficient to tilt the balance
> against the prosecution. (1950, JC, my emphasis)

This is hardly a raising of the standards of civil rights against illegal
police activity. However, the image of Scots law as fair and operating
tight controls on the police, may be understandable if it is compared
with the extremes in English law. In *Kuruma,* a 1955 case of illegally
obtained evidence (the evidence itself being rather dubious anyway),

English judges went so far as to justify their decision by citing a judicial opinion of 1861 that effectively declared anything goes: 'It matters not how you get it; if you steal it even it would be admissible.' Ducking the inadmissibility issue means that even the principle of post hoc control of police behaviour via the courts' power to exclude evidence is avoided.

In short, according to case law the police may with impunity make an arbitrary arrest, arresting not on a charge based on some kind of proof of specific implication in a specific offence, but arresting in order to acquire that proof or find out if there has been any activity that could be defined as an offence. ('That could be defined' is important. Remember we are not always talking about finding sacks marked 'Swag', but, for example, left wing posters and pamphlets.) Authoritative common law thus unceremoniously turns the basic principle governing arrest on its head.

Prohibitions on interrogation after charge and the right to a solicitor are similarly interpreted at common law in such a way that the police can ignore the principles of the Judges' Rules where they conflict with the practical purposes of crime control. And, indeed, it is exactly with this reasoning that police behaviour deviating from the spirit of legality is justified by the judges themselves. Implicit or explicit in court decisions, textbooks, legislation and commissions on criminal procedure lies a recognition of the dilemma between the liberty of the citizen embodied in the rhetoric of legality and the effective control of crime. We are back to due process and crime control not just as a dichotomy for *explaining* the law but as a dilemma in the law itself, summed up, for example by Lord Wheatley in *Milne* v. *Cullen* in 1967:

> While the law of Scotland has always very properly regarded fairness to an accused person as being an integral part of the administration of justice, fairness is not a unilateral consideration. Fairness to the public is also a legitimate consideration, and in so far as police officers in the exercise of their duties are prosecuting and protecting the public interest, it is the function of the Court to seek to provide a proper balance to secure that the rights of individuals are properly preserved, while not hamstringing the police in their investigation of crime with a series of academic vetoes which ignore the realities and practicalities of the situation and discount completely the public interest.

Lord Wheatley explicitly used this case as 'an opportunity for clearing

up certain misapprehensions which may have arisen in the minds of the
legal profession, the police and the public' to the contrary. In short, it
is not just the police who informally point to the practical needs of
crime control to justify ignoring the principles of legality: that same
justification is writ large and indeed offered as guidance for the police,
in the cases, textbooks and government reports which formulate the law
itself. Police justifications may be a distortion of the spirit of legality
but they are an exact replica of the spirit of the law.

3. Conclusion: law, legality and dominant ideology

In conclusion, this review of the law on arrest suggests a first simple
point. There is a clear gap between the rhetoric of legality and the
actuality of law in both the procedures laid down and the reasoning
behind them.

Legality requires equality; the law discriminates against the homeless
and jobless. Legality requires that officials be governed by law; the law
is based on post hoc decisions. Legality requires each case be judged on
its own facts; the law makes previous convictions grounds for defining
behaviour as an offence. Legality requires incriminating evidence as the
basis for arrest and search; the law allows arrest and search in order to
establish it. Legality embodies individual civil rights against public or
state interests; the law makes state and the public interest a justification
for ignoring public rights.

Any gap between how the police should behave according to democratic principles and how they do is not simply a by-product of informal abuse and non-legal motivations among the police themselves,
the administrators of justice; it exists in the law as defined in court
decisions and statutes by the judicial and political elites of the state.
Deviation from legality is institutionalised in the law itself. The law
does not need to change to remove hamstrings on the police: they exist
only in the unrealised rhetoric.

Indeed the police are in a sense the fall guys of the legal system,
taking the blame for any injustices in the operation of the law, both in
theory (in the assumption like Skolnick's that they break the rules) and
indeed, in the law. The law holds the individual policeman personally
responsible for contraventions of legality that are successfully sued,
while at the same time refusing to make clear until after the event
exactly what the police are supposed to do. It is no coincidence that the
police themselves asked for the Judges' Rules.

Coming back to Packer's two polar types for describing law enforcement, due process and crime control, empirical analysis of due process

reveals them as a false dichotomy. The law on criminal procedure in its current form does not so much set a standard of legality from which the police deviate as provide a licence to ignore it. If we bring due process down from the dizzy heights of abstraction and subject it to empirical scrutiny, the conclusion must be that due process is *for* crime control.

It is, however, a conclusion that implies a whole complex of further issues. If the contradictions between rhetoric and practice in law enforcement cannot simply be explained away as the unintended consequences of petty officials, then we are faced with contradictions within the core of the state between the ideology and structure of the law. Why does such institutionalised deviation occur? It might, of course, just be an example of a crude ideological disguise for dominant interests. But that's an answer that needs to be posed in turn as a question and analysed. It might also involve something rather more complex, contradictions within dominant ideology itself. There are 'how' questions too: how is the gap between legality and law managed and legitimised? And questions of change: why does the gap vary? For it does. All I have described is the law in its current form. It is endemic in judicial discretion that cases *can* be used in court to sanction the police. Indeed it is endemic in common law that it changes, swings away from crime control to legality — and back again. The swings are patterned of course and historically located. Why do they occur and how are they accomplished within the concept of a single body of law?

Finding the law does not live up to its rhetoric then is not just the end of a piece of indignant exposé research (Taylor, Walton, Young, 1975, p. 29) but the beginning of a new series of questions. Far from implying that the rhetoric should simply be dismissed as necessarily empty, it implies rather that the rhetoric (and the relationship between the state and the rhetoric) requires analysis too. This has implications beyond the bounds of the sociology of law. Probing how and why notions like legality and justice are constructed currently and historically provides a case study in the wider issue of the sources and mechanics of dominant ideology.

Notes

1. Note particularly the statement of principles unaffected by the rules.
2. This may in fact be truer in the USA than in Britain. See particularly *Miranda* v. *Arizona*, 1966, US; *Mapp* v. *Ohio*, 1961, US.
3. For example his charges that the jury system and magistracy lead to too many acquittals of the guilty. See e.g. Sir R. Mark, 'Social Violence' in

J.C. Alderson and P.J. Stead, *The Police We Deserve* (1973, p. 16); *The Disease of Crime: Punishment or Treatment* (Royal Society of Medicine, 1972); 'Minority Verdict', The *Listener,* 8 November 1973.

4. This article is drawn from a larger project based on observation of 110 cases in the district and sheriff courts of a Scottish city, informal interviews and analysis of statute and case law.

5. J.D. Devlin in 'Police Charges', 1968, asserts there is no such power but it is assumed and used in the courts, e.g. *Stunt* v. *Bolton,* 1972, RTR 435 (Leigh, 1975, p. 72).

6. In *Rice* v. *Connolly* the conviction was in fact quashed but the possibility kept open that failure to answer questions *plus* some other circumstances could be grounds for arrest.

7. An 'arrestable offence' is a serious one for which the accused may be imprisoned for five years.

8. This is the situation in Scots law, but in England there is a similar control in principle: 'If the police cannot demonstrate that there was a reasonable ground for arrest, they will in theory be liable in an action for false imprisonment.' (Leigh, 1975, p. 35) And see *Christie* v. *Leachinsky,* 1947, AC. On the face of it this requirement in Scots law that an arrest must be accompanied by a charge seems to incorporate far more protection from arbitrary arrest than the English rule that 'the constable, before arresting, must have reasonable grounds for suspicion. *This does not mean . . . he must have evidence sufficient for a prima facie case*' (Leigh, 1975, p. 34, my emphasis). Nor indeed need there be a charge formulated on arrest at all (*Christie* v. *Leachinsky,* 1947, AC). However there may be less difference here than at first sight appears, since in Scotland there are two stages of charging involved, the police charge and the procurator fiscal's. Thus the case required for a police charge is merely evidence sufficient to report to the procurator fiscal, a rather lower standard of 'prima facie case' than that required of the procurator fiscal in Scotland and, of course, with no such middleman, of the English police, in making out a charge for the court. The different uses of terms like 'sufficient evidence', 'prima facie case' or 'charge' may thus disguise an actual similarity of conditions pertaining to arrest in the two systems.

9. ' . . . There are many cases where arrest is competent but not justifiable in the particular circumstances, since the interests of justice can be sufficiently served by methods not involving arrest'(Thomson, 1975, p. 11).

10. This example is a local act specific to the Scottish city in question and thus the relevant context for this particular case but other acts operate on similar stereotypes and fulfil similar functions in other parts of Scotland and England e.g. The Vagrancy Act, 1824, or the Prevention of Crimes Act, 1871.

11. This is not to say that the rules of evidence have no effect on police decisions to arrest or prosecute. Mack has pointed out that cases, ironically major cases rather than the petty ones mentioned here, are frequently dropped because the evidence would not stand up in court (1976). Major criminals *are* major criminals exactly because they can keep themselves clear in strict legal terms. That does not, however, detract from the points made here on what the courts *do* allow.

References

Bell v. *Hogg,* 1967, JC.
Carlin v. *Malloch,* 1896, 2 Adam 98.
Chalmers v. *HM Advocate,* 1954, JC.
Chic Fashions (West Wales) Ltd. v. *Jones,* 1968, 1 All E.R.
Christie v. *Leachinsky,* 1947, AC.
Fairly v. *Fishmongers of London,* 1951. JC.
Hay v. *HM Advocate,* 1968, SLT
Kuruma v. *R.,* 1955, AC.
Lawrie v. *Muir,* 1950, JC.
Ludlow v. *Shelton,* 1938, *Times* 3 and 4 February.
Mallory v. *US,* 1957, 354 US 449.
Mapp v. *Ohio,* 1961, US.
Milne v. *Cullen,* 1967, JC.
Miranda v. *Arizona,* 1966, US
Peggie v. *Clark,* 1868, 7M 89.
R v. *Kulyncz,* 1970, 3 All E.R.
Rafaeli v. *Heatly,* 1949, SC.
Rice v. *Connolly,* 1966, 2 Q.B.
Swankie v. *Miln,* 1973, JC.
Armstrong, G. and M. Wilson, 'City Politics and Deviance Amulification', in L. Taylor & I. Taylor (eds.), *Politics & Deviance* (Penguin, 1973).
Bottomley, A.K., *Decisions in the penal process* (Martin Robertson, 1973).
Bottoms, A.E. and J.D. McClean, *Defendants in the Criminal Process* (Routledge and Kegan Paul, London, 1976).
Box, S. and Russell, 'The politics of discreditability: disarming complaints against the police', *Sociological Review,* May 1975.
Cain, M., 'On the beat', in S. Cohen (ed.), *Images of Deviance* (Penguin, 1971).
Cain, M., *Society and the Policeman's Role* (Routledge and Kegan Paul, 1973).
Cox, B., *Civil liberties in Britain* (Penguin, 1975).
Criminal Law Revision Committee, *11th Report: Evidence* (HMSO, Cmnd. 4991, 1972).
Dell, S., *Silence in Court,* Occasional Papers in Social Administration, 42 (Bell, London, 1971).
Halsbury's Laws of England, 3rd edn., Vol. 10.
Heydon, J.D., *Cases and materials on evidence* (Stevens, 1975).
Kadish, S.H., 'Legal norm and discretion', 75 *Harvard Law Review* (1962).
Home Office Circular, 1964, no. 31.
Lafave, W.R. and Remington, 'Controlling the police: the judge's role in making and reviewing law enforcement decisions', 63 *Michigan Law Review* (1975).
King, M., *Bail or custody?* (Cobden Trust, 1971).
Leigh, L.H., *Police powers in England and Wales* (Butterworths, 1975).
McBarnet, D.J., 'Pretrial procedures and the construction of conviction', in P. Carlen (ed.), *Sociological Review Monograph on the Sociology of Law* (Keele University, 1976).
Mack, J.A., 'Full-time miscreants', *Modern Law Review,* May 1976.
Packer, H.L., 'Two models of the criminal process', *University of Pennsylvania Law Review* 113 (1964).
Piliavin, I. and S. Briar, 'Police encounters with juveniles', *American Journal of Sociology* 70 (1964).
Reiss, A.J. and D.J. Bordua, 'Environment and Organisation: A Perspective on the Police', in Bordua (ed.), *The Police* (Wiley, 1967).

Renton, R.W. and H.H. Brown, *Criminal Procedure According to the Law of Scotland,* 4th edn. (Green, 1972).

Skolnick, J., *Justice without trial* (Wiley, 1966).

Sowle, C.R. *Police power and individual freedom* (Aldine, 1962).

Sykes, R. and J. Clark, 'A Theory of Deference Exchange in Police-Civilian Encounters', *American Journal of Sociology* 81, 3 (1975).

Taylor, I., P. Walton and J. Young, *Critical criminology* (Routledge and Kegan Paul, 1975).

Young, J., *The Drugtakers* (Paladin, 1971).

8 VIOLENCE AND THE SOCIAL CONTROL OF WOMEN

Jalna Hanmer

This paper is concerned with the social phenomenon of male violence to women.[1] It is not concerned with explaining variations in the amount and type of violence, in when, where and among whom it occurs, or with explaining why it occurs. Nor is the concern with explanations of individual violence, but rather the focus is on the significance and meaning of violence from the male to the female at the social structural level.

To understand this phenomenon requires a re-assessment of the role of violence in male-female relations. The universality of the subordination of women is considered first and then the definition, forms, and incidence of violence. Sociological explanations of inter-personal violence are criticised, followed by an examination of the role of the state in creating 'symmetrical' dependency between the sexes. The relevance of an analysis of violence in male-female relations for an understanding of the relationships between sex and class is raised. And the final question is, can male violence be successfully challenged?

Male Violence and Female Subordination

To the extent that the issue of male versus female power and authority in society is considered cross culturally, the dominant view today seems to be that women always, everywhere have less power and authority in society than men.[2] Male activities, whatever they are, are always, everywhere more highly esteemed than those of women. Two materially based reasons are usually given to explain this phenomenon. One is that the female reproductive function limits their social participation. Bearing, nursing and looking after young children is seen as the basis for the exclusion of women from the most highly valued (and violent) activities of many societies, i.e. hunting and warfare. This sexual division of labour is also a division between the public and private spheres of cultural life, which may be embryonic or highly developed, and the rigidity of the separation further affects the access of women to power and authority. The second material factor is the role of women in economic production, but it has been found that even in societies where their share is in excess of 50 per cent women never achieve full

217

equality.[3]

The relation of force and its threat to other variables is rarely examined but a recent paper attempts to assess the relative importance of the institutionalised use of violence, ideology and economic stage of development in ensuring women's acquiescence in their own subordination.[4] K. Young and O. Harris argue that in societies with the least control over nature the dominant mode of control is the institutionalised use of force, where men collectively punish individual women who have violated social rules, for example through group rape. At a somewhat higher degree of control over nature ideological mechanisms dominate, 'there is a proliferation of lived, repressive institutions,' and violence is restricted to the individual use of force.[5] At a still higher level of production, the dominant mode of control becomes the economic. 'Women are denied access to the means of production, no longer control even their own household surplus, have no access to labour etc.'[6] Ideological control weakens and violence is further masked.

Certainly within our own society neither men nor women are eager to acknowledge the importance that force or its threat play in the daily drama of everyday life. Hostile feelings and behaviour towards the opposite sex are often carefully concealed, even from the self, as a matter of everyday routine. Within the family, violence from men to women has the character of a tabooed subject that occasionally surfaces in at least a proportion of public consciousness. For example, in our immediate past in Britain public discussion of marital violence in the late nineteenth century led ultimately to a change in matrimonial law enabling a wife to gain a legal separation from a persistently violent husband.[7] The issue then sank into obscurity to surface again during the time of the struggle for women's suffrage, to sink and resurface again today. Thus women have from time to time become conscious of the use of force against them as a group; but more important sociologically, most of the time the use of force and its threat has not been recognised, except possibly as a problem limited to a few individuals. Thus efforts to reinterpret marital violence and also rape and other assaults on women in the public area of life as activities carried out by individual men on behalf of all men may strike one as novel, daring, perhaps ludicrous, so individualised is our consciousness of these important phenomena.

Given the difficulties of comparison and lack of data no attempt will be made to argue that the quantity or quality of violence is less or greater in other societies than in our own. What will be argued, however, is that the use of force and its threat, even though highly masked, is of sufficient importance in our own western industrialised society to be recognised as a major component in the social control of women by men. Further, I will argue that force and its threat is the basis for the extraction of all benefits that men make from women; that is, economic, sexual and prestige gains. As with subserviance based on social class, ethnic group or third world country, that of sex, too, rests ultimately on force and its threat.

Violence and the fear of violence moulds behaviour. The phenomenon is pre-eminently sociological but in order to further sociological insight the definition must include the perceptions ofthe recipient as well as that of the aggressor and society at large.

Violence Defined

In a woman's life fear of violence from men is subtle and pervasive. At a subliminal level, fear is experienced as unease, a concern to behave properly, worry that one may be laughed at or ridiculed. Fear can be activated by knowledge of actual violence to oneself, to known or unknown others, or by deviating from accepted social behaviour or even contemplating doing so. What deters one woman may not deter another and the sense of unease that may accompany deviation, for example, walking home alone late at night, may totally eliminate violations of 'living safely', or limit them to unusual occasions. Even if women define 'living safely' somewhat differently, each woman knows emotionally and intuitively the location of the boundary that leads into a grey area, like the no-man's land of World War I, that could lead to a serious and losing battle. These same boundaries exist in the domestic sphere.[8]

At its most covert, the threat of force, or force itself may proceed from behaviour which on the surface may appear friendly or joking. For example, Anne Whitehead in her account of rural life in a parish in Herefordshire gives several examples of abusive joking behaviour; one effectively served to remind a woman of her exclusion from the local pub, the meeting place of the male clique to which her husband belonged, while another conveyed disapproval of a wife's extra-marital interest in another man.[9] Alwyn Rees' account of life in a Welsh parish contains several accounts of the joking role of the young men's group in controlling the behaviour of others within the community, but such behaviour is remarkedly under-examined in community studies.[10]

Moving on to 'joking' among strangers there are the common urban phenomena of wolf whistles and 'invitations'. Dominque Poggi and

Monique Coornaert explore the ways in which the city is off-limits to women reminding us that 'it wouldn't be far fetched for a cartoonist to sketch out a "street guide for the ladies" '.[11] Joking with its *double-entrendre* represents the most subtle form of the threat of force and is at one extreme of the continuum of violence.

A sociological definition of violence needs to include both the use of force and its threat as both compel or constrain women to behave or not to behave in given ways. Death is at one extreme of the continuum while the threat of force is at the other. Lying in between are a variety of everyday occurrences from wounding and grievous bodily harm to indecent assault and rape. A definition of violence should include the legal categories and move beyond to include all modes of behaviour that coerce compliance. This definition is a feminine one; based on the perspective of the victim.

The Extent of Male Violence to Women

The importance of force and its threat is argued for, even though the extent of male violence to women is unknown even if we limit our attention to indictable offenses. There are two issues; official statistics inform us about what police and courts do, not necessarily about the incidence of violent behaviour, and statistics are not available on the sex of the victim except for homicide. But given these major limitations a few conclusions still can be drawn. One is that almost all violent crime is committed by men. Few women compared with men commit violent acts against women or men. Another is that given the description of the crimes, women clearly are the vast majority of victims of sexual offences, with indecent assault accounting for 50 per cent of the indictments in this category.[12]

But the sex of the victim is totally hidden within the other major category 'violence against persons', where 'other woundings, etc' accounts for 90 per cent of the indictable offences. With homicide the major fact emerging from the analysis of the relationship of the offender and victim is that a woman is more likely to be killed by someone she knows than by a stranger. It is likely that the same conclusion would be drawn for physical injuries and sexual assaults if comparable statistics were kept.

Some harder data, however, are available. In 1974, R. and R. Dobash examined the initial charge sheets for all offences in all precincts in Edinburgh and one in Glasgow.[13] Violence and its threat was a small proportion (11.10 per cent) of the offences reported to these police stations. Of this violence and its threat within the family was slightly less (4.79 per cent) than non-family violence. (6. 31 per cent).

Within the family wife assault accounted for almost half of the offences (47. 25 per cent). If husband assault (0.79 per cent), husband and wife disputes, and alleged and threatened wife assault are added to wife assault, 84 per cent of all family violence and its threat was between the marital pair, and almost all of it flows from the male to the female. Child assault (6.69 per cent), parent assault (4.26 per cent), sibling assault (3.04 per cent), and non-violent disputes with other family members (1.94 per cent) account for the remainder. Of non-family violence only 13 per cent was from men to women thus lending substance to the view that for a woman to marry or cohabit is to court the greater danger of physical attack.

This, however, does not begin to give a true picture of the degree of assault and wounding women suffer, particularly in the home. The police admit that they are less likely to arrest a man beating up his wife than if he is physically abusing a child of the family or someone other than his wife in the street or other non-home setting.[14] Evidence to the Select Committee on Violence in Marriage produced no hard data on the amount and kind of violence within the home, and to one's knowledge no research projects are in hand to discover this.[15]

This is a crucial issue. Why is information on the direction of violence not kept, and further, given the attention the Select Committee focused on this area, not sought? In my view this indifference does not reflect the infrequency of the behaviour so much as its acceptance as a form of social control. The phenomenon in both the public and domestic spheres is unrecognisable, except as an individual problem so that even in this golden age of the sociologist, computer and statistician, establishing incidence is not seen as a priority.[16]

Structural Stress and Socialisation

Within sociology the role of violence in structuring and maintaining male-female relations is inadequately considered. In apparently relevant documents the use of force may be completely ignored or underplayed.[17] And when sociological efforts are made to explain some aspect of male violence to women the social fact that violence usually flows from the male to the female is not taken theoretically into account. The response of the state through its various officials and departments is often ignored, but even if mentioned is not seen as integral to an understanding of the violent act.

But even with these omissions the researcher confronting individual case material still concocts a *pot-pourri* of explanations as no one theory can account for the remaining phenomena. At crucial moments there seems to be a tendency to individualise and psychologise. The use of social structural theory of frustration, stress and blocked goals to explain individual behaviour and the development of categories unconnected with social structure, such as irrational and expressive violence, are examples of this practice. In theories of socialisation, at their worst sociologically, norms and values of violence are seen as deviant, affecting either sub-cultures or some individual families while society as a whole remains unaffected.[18] At best violence is seen as widespread and the family described as a social institution providing basic training in norms, values and techniques of violence. Sub-cultures of violence then become the tip of an iceberg arising from an underlying social structure with norms and values that approve of violence.

For example, this is the stance adopted by Gelles in a recent and unique analysis of eighty violent American families.[19] He combines socialisation theory with theories of frustration, stress and blocked goals to account for variations in the behaviour of his respondents. With socialisation theory he attempts to explain present behaviour by past events while present behaviour is accounted for by theories of frustration, stress and blocked goals. A multitude of explanations are necessary as not all the violent adults in the study were exposed to or treated with violence as children (also we know from other sources that not all who are grow up to be violent while others from apparently nonviolent backgrounds become so in adulthood). The relationship between violent behaviour in adulthood and childhood socialisation is statistical and an unknown correlation at that as we do not know what proportion of the population observe or experience violence in childhood, even if we could agree on how it is to be defined. This same point applies to theories of frustration, stress and blocked goals. Further these theories are used to explain individual behaviour and thus the proposed explanations of social phenomenon equals the simple sum of individual characteristics. To change the emphasis to sex role socialisation does not resolve these difficulties even though both past and present socialisation (including reinforcement or its lack) can be included in the same concept.[20]

Dominant ideology states that female submissiveness and dependency on the male is self-chosen. The liberal challenge to this view does not blame women so obviously for their difficulties, as female submissiveness and dependency, like male aggression, is said to be taught through childhood socialisation into sex-roles. While these explanations may have some validity in that they potentially expose the role of ideology in human conduct, as well as describe aspects of learned behaviour, on their own they are inadequate explanations of social structure and process based on dominance and submission.

Resource Theory

W. Goode with resource theory hovers on the edge of a new analysis but safely turns away with the view that violence is used when other resources, which he defines as economic, prestige or respect and friendship or love, are lacking.[21] Goode, however, recognises that marriage is a power relationship and that force or its threat is a resource usually held by the husband/father (as, it can be added, is the economic and a general higher status position). Only in the area of friendship or love has the woman a good chance of gaining more of a resource, and then only by lifelong devotion to husband and children.

Love and sexuality is an aspect of male-female relations that has been widely written about within the Women's Liberation Movement. A common theme is that through love and sexual relations with men, women are oppressed psychologically and materially. Women are turned against women in their competition for men and alienated from their sexuality; hence the furore in the Movement when the biological basis of the female orgasm was finally established.[22] Love is seen as double-edged. It is all a woman can hope for yet once received and given it confirms a woman's subordinate social position. Through love of husband, home and children they are inducted into a relationship characterised by dependency on the male. Thus love, too, becomes a mechanism of control of women by men.

Asymmetrical Reciprocity + the State = 'Symmetrical' Dependency

But in industrial societies we cannot discuss modes of social control and particularly the use of interpersonal force without considering the role of the state, as the organisation, deployment and control of force and its threat is incorporated within it. The question to be considered is for whose benefit is this force used? This is partly exposed by how the state deploys its force and controlling function and partly by how the state reacts to those outside the state apparatus who use force.

E. Marx in a recent study of an Israeli township analyses a number of violent encounters within the family and community and relates these to the organisation of the state.[23] He divides violence against officials of the state as coercive and that against other family members or general public as appealing (for help). When interpersonal assaults are carried out in public they receive the attention of the police but when carried out in the privacy of the home they may not be treated as offences even if the participants sustain injury and the matter becomes public knowledge as ' "public interest" is not at stake, and the law organs tend to apply a more restricted definition of violence to them.'[24]

For example in the Ederi family the husband regularly attacks his wife physically, the children accept it matter-of-factly, and no one intervenes. The analysis focuses on Mr Ederi's blocked goals. He was said to have beat his wife this time because of the prospect of being unable to provide for his family. There was an unexpected debt and Mrs Ederi wanted to give up her job. But Mrs Ederi suffered severe leg pains, was nearly exhausted, finding it difficult to run a large household and keep her part-time job. After the attack Mrs Ederi 'muttered under her breath: "What he wants is that I should go out (to work) so he can stay at home and attend to the children." '[25] The author, in the following sentence interprets this to mean 'She realised, then, that her husband's concern was not this particular debt, but the prospect of being unable to provide the family's minimum requirement in the near future.'[26]

Another interpretation is that Mrs Ederi is imputing an instrumental motive to the attack which if taken seriously would do more than call into question the acceptability of so-called non-instrumental categories of violence. If the action was coercive, designed to keep Mrs Ederi in paid employment against her will and to reduce her spending does she not have blocked goals as well?

But Mrs Ederi's position is analysed differently from that of Mr Ederi's. The explanation is of why she cannot alter her situation in any way. She can expect no help from the police, the welfare officials or the general public with her marital situation. Therefore when she stood in front of her house, blood oozing from the back of her head, no one approached her. She also can expect no help in leaving her marital situation. Relief work and welfare assistance are only given to women when no able-bodied man is in the household and should Mrs Ederi attempt to relinquish responsibility for the household by breaking up the marriage, 'She could not count on the support of the welfare officials, who would find themselves saddled with so many children.'[27]

While recognising that Mrs Ederi is trapped within her situation, 'when a man assaults his wife, who is bound to him by their joint tute-lage over the children and by enduring ties, he is liable to use greater force, as he does not fear a rupture in their relationship',[28] the state is not seen as an institution helping to create and maintain Mr Ederi's supraordinate position in relation to his wife. Rather violence from husband to wife is said to not threaten the interests of the state, as would violence to an official which would therefore be dealt with more seriously. In this view the state is an institution of rulers, who respond to the degree their power is threatened. Mr and Mrs Ederi are not principals in this theory of the state; but stand outside (or are oppressed by it?).

I argue that this is an incorrect view of the relation between the Ederis and the state. Mrs Ederi is presented as someone without blocked goals that need understanding or call for the sharing of responsibility. To see the issue as one of sex bias is too narrow; the question is why can the same analysis not be applied to the victim of the physical attack? I argue that to do so would be to expose privilege, and not just the privilege of relieving feelings by beating up another without fear of retaliation either from the victim or the larger community, but also the privilege of not fulfilling what E. Marx describes as the major expectation of male provider.

He argues that interpersonal violence arises from the mutual dependency of the sexes, unlike that of the state where violence arises from a challenge to its power. It is a means of altering the balance of the relationship so that the husband beats his wife to remind her that their dependence is mutual. The view presumably is based on Levi Strauss who attributed the universality of the sexual division of labour to the requirement that dependency between the sexes be reciprocal. I argue that in the case of the Ederis the dependency was reciprocal only because of the intervention of the state. It is the intervention of the state that *forces* Mrs Ederi to be dependent upon her husband and thus she must accept his beatings and lack of financial provision while she must bear the children, look after them and work in paid employment.[29]

To be able to fulfil or not fulfil social expectations is the language of power and dominance. It is the actions of the state that both give Mr Ederi this power and deny it to Mrs Ederi, *and thus public interest is defined and served*. That the state can be treated as irrelevant to an understanding of domestic violence is a measure of the power of men to define social reality. In this and in the following examples state power takes the form of a restraining force, what Backrach and Baratz call non-decision making.[30]

In our own larger, more anonymous society where the local community is often less able to impose a limit on the degree of violence, the full brutality of the state (and husbands) is exposed. For example, variations on this personal account can be repeated *ad nauseam*:

'My face was so swollen from being punched that I was not recog-
nizable. I lost a front tooth. He stripped me naked. He banged my
head against a brick wall for an hour as he repeated "Who was the
bloke?" Six ribs were broken from being kicked. I was black all
down one side from being punched and kicked. I was dragged down
stairs by my hair. He repeatedly stamped on my bare toes with cuban
heel shoes. He was still repeating "Who was the bloke?" He then
fetched a knife and said he was going to kill me if I didn't tell him
who I had been out with. He tried to stab me but I managed to stop
the blow by raising my arm and received a long gash under the arm-
pit. All this took place in front of my daughters aged 5 and 9. Eventually the police arrived after a neighbour had called them eight
times. They would not enter the house although the front door was
open. He went out and told them that he was beating me up because
I had left the children alone. I pleaded with them to take me to the
hospital but they would only do so if I charged him. They left telling
him to keep the noise down as the neighbours were complaining.
They didn't ask me whether what he said was true or give any other
assistance. He came back into the house and told me and the children
to get dressed. He took us up to his girl-friend's house to show her
what he'd do to her if she ever was unfaithful. He then asked her if
she still wanted him after she had seen what he'd done to me. She
said yes – that she'd had worse than that from her first husband. I
said she must be mad and he kicked me in the mouth. They then
put my daughters to bed in her house and he told them that she was
their new mum from now on as I was a whore and not fit to look
after them. They made coffee but not for me and then he took me
to the hospital, threatening all the way that if I didn't tell him
who I'd been out with he would crash the car. In the hospital car
park he told me to tell them that I'd been beaten up on my way
home after going out for the evening. When we got inside he told
them his story, but I told them that he had done it, and he spat in
my face calling me a bastard. I thought they would keep me but they
said they were short of beds and sent me home with him. On the way
home he drove the car off the road into a ditch to try to scare me. I
had to walk home.'[31]

Male Power and the State

The view that the purpose of male violence to women is to control them
parsimoniously explains both acts of public and private violence. It also
accounts for what might appear to be an excessive use of force. It may

be, or seem to be, necessary to kill, mutilate, maim or temporarily reduce a woman's ability to carry out services, etc. in order to be in control. Prestige, self-esteem, a sense of personal worth is gained, expressed and made public by the acquiescence of others.

In this perspective the state represents the interests of the dominant group, i.e. men, in confrontations with the subordinate group, i.e. women. Thus it is consistent that in domestic disputes the status of the victim determines the response of that section of the state given the task of controlling violence.[32] That men unknown to the woman (the policemen) would back up the man known to her (the husband) in pursuit of their joint state-defined interest is to impartially enforce the law for in practice the state defines women as less equal. This knowledge, however, comes as a shock to most women when they seek protection from the police for the first time. Women lack consciousness of the rights they surrender on marriage or cohabitation but once in a violent domestic dispute the contradiction between their interests and that of their husband and men in general begins to become apparent.[33]

The pre-eminent interests of men are expressed through explicit policies, for example in Britain a major plank of the welfare state is to maintain the family and within this unit the woman is defined as the dependent of the male.[34] To create 'symmetrical' dependence between the sexes the state aids the man by making it difficult for a woman to leave marriage. Law and law enforcement, housing policies, income maintenance, employment and earnings, interlock to trap the woman in dependency. For a woman and her children to leave a violent husband she must have protection from violence, and in common with all other women she must have somewhere to go and an income. The Select Committee raised the issue of state induced dependency by asking rhetorically, 'Why should it be the wife and children who have to leave and not the husband? . . . Why should we not create hostels to receive the battering husband? . . . '[35]

On both an ideological and practical level the problem is the victim's. Women passing through women's aid refuges provide examples of how their husband's violence becomes 'their problem' i.e. is turned back upon them, by all the relevant departments of the state (health workers, social workers, voluntary and statutory, as well as the police and legal services). In turning the problem back upon the woman it is individualised, the direction of violence is ignored, and the ideology supporting male dominance is confirmed.

This process is clearly illustrated by the earlier examples of marital violence. The police, welfare and hospital workers saw the problem as strictly that of the injured women. Further, the state bears the financial burden of the man's excessive use of force in that it provides the services that patch-up the wife and cares for any children the couple may have if requested to do so. It picks up the pieces through residential services and through social work with the family.[36]

But if a woman with dependent children manages to leave her husband, the state often bears the burden through social security until the woman marries again. Seen in relation to the man, the state takes over his financial responsibility. As the Finer Committee Report makes clear, in practice men are only financially responsible for women living with them.[37] This is another direct substantial state benefit to males who thus are enabled always to have the services of a woman and one who is defined by the state as dependent. Meanwhile, the woman dependent on the state (her husband surrogate) is kept at a low financial level to encourage her to begin servicing yet another man. In this way the policies of the state are designed to force women back into marriage should they manage to leave it.[38]

In the public sphere state support for male interests is exposed in how the state reacts to the violence of individual men. It is apparently impossible to make the streets a safe place for women or to guarantee their entry into all parts of the city and community on the same basis as that of men. Our western industrial arrangement of the city parallels that of many settled non-capitalist societies where the men's house or area occupies the centre and the women and children live around the periphery. In our cities the centre is composed of public buildings, centres of masculine activity. As D. Poggi and M. Coornaert explain the central institutions, the places of power, prestige or influence where the most significant transactions of the community are carried out are effectively closed to women as a group.[39] At the same time, there is only limited entry to the areas of urban activity, of production and work, leisure and pleasure. Women are tolerated, but with restrictions. Women do not have full use of the city rather 'their paths are studded with keep-out signs and danger signals.'[40] Women must avoid certain neighbourhoods or streets and parks and open spaces unless fulfilling a domestic child-caring role during the day, and never at night. In shops the only urban space women have free access to, and their homes women are isolated from each other. Urban space for women is compartmentalised; to deviate from women's allotted space is to run the risk of attack by men.

The violent act that has received the most public attention is rape. There is a growing exposure of police and court procedures and

reactions. as the NCCL explains rapists are more likely to be acquitted
if the rape is socially possible and if the victim's life style, even if unknown to the rapist, expresses autonomy.[41] Thus to live alone, to walk
alone, to hitch-hike, to wear 'indecent clothing' to have talked or drunk
with a rapist are acts likely to make rape possible. To be celibate, a
divorcee, an adultress, to have an illegitimate child, a lover, to have had
an abortion, all irrelevant to the act of rape, may absolve the rapist of
guilt. As Feministes Revolutionnaires explain 'only a married woman,
locked in her home, in company and fully clothed can be recognised as
a victim. Then rape is not only physically impossible, but above all,
socially unjustified from the point of view of the patriarchy.'[42] Thus
men apparently unconnected with the organisation of state force and
its control can be seen as fulfilling that function. Men who pester,
attack or rape women in the streets of the city can be described as
'these inquisitors, the cops, the warders, of the patriarchial system', and
not demented, ill-socialised, or sex crazed, 'for woman-hunting season
is 24 hours a day all the year around.'[43]

The pervasive fear of violence, and violence itself, has the effect of
driving women to seek protection from men, the very people who
commit violence against them. Husbands and boyfriends are seen as
protectors of women from the potential violence of unknown men.
Women often feel safer in the company of a man in public and the
home and marriage is portrayed, and often feels, the safest place of all,
even though statistically speaking women are more likely to be violently
assaulted in marriage and from men known to them. Fear created by
violence in public places is another factor underwriting female dependency on the male. The fact that many husbands do not beat their
wives, and many men do not attack women in the streets, either regularly or ever, is not proof that wife beating and other assaults are
irregular, unsystematic practices limited to a few unfortunates either of
birth, or training, or low economic resources, but merely that it is not
necessary to do so in order to maintain the privileges of the superior
group.[44]

The main argument of this article is that force and its threat is never
a residual or secondary mode of influence rather it is the structural
underpinning of hierarchical relations; the ultimate sanction buttressing
other forms of control. While this is not a unique view, it is rarely
applied to male-female relations possibly in part because to do so is to
raise the issue of the relation between sex and class exploitation.

Sex and Class

The black analogy is useful in making explicit the role of force in maintaining a particular social structure and process. J. Dollard's analysis of
black-white relations in a Southern American town and the economic,
sexual and prestige gains whites make at the expense of blacks parallels
that of the women's liberation movement in the sense that movement
writers focus on the areas of sexuality, waged and unwaged work, and
status or prestige to describe exploitative relations between men and
women.[45] But Dollard goes on to show how these gains to whites are
maintained by ideology backed up by force and its threat. Deference is
continuously exacted from blacks and infractions of social rules are
punished primarily by force, although economic sanctions may be used.

While the analysis of exploitative relations between men and women
is not as developed as that between blacks and whites, marriage and
family life has been identified as the primary form of control. Love and
'a woman's nature' have been explored as ideologies of oppression.
There is also a growing body of literature on the domestic economy of
women that examines the economic value of the unpaid labour of the
wife, but who benefits is disputed; the husband, the capitalist, or
both.[46]

The role that male violence plays in economic exploitation, which
includes lower incomes for women in paid employment, is discussed
tangentially, if at all. One argument is that capitalism, not men, benefit
from male aggression to women. For example, R. Frankenburg in his
reinterpretation of relations between miners and their wives in 'Coal is
Our Life' argues that there is an economic gain, but not to men.[47]
Capitalism is the beneficiary because men take out their frustrations on
their wives and not their bosses. Although the emphasis differs this is
also the position taken by the Wages for Housework campaign.[48] Every
act of servicing the male worker is seen as work for which wages are
due, not from the man, the wage slave, but from the capitalist. Men are
never held accountable for the gains they make by virtue of their wives'
unpaid work. Sociologically these views ignore the reality of marriage
as a power relationship and the meaning that control over finances and
the ability and will to use force has for the marital pair. D. Barker's
analysis,in this volume,of marriage as a labour relation does not make
this mistake.[49]

But the relation between the use of force and economic output in
the marital situation is not direct. If the purpose were to extract maximum labour from women then force and its threat should be finely
administered to ensure it, much as it needs to be in industry in order to

maintain profit. For example, Harris in describing the generality of wife beating among the Peruvian villagers she was studying noted that the degree of beating did not relate to the skill of women in fulfilling their marital role which included agricultural production, but rather appeared to be random.[50] The 'best' wives were among the most beaten while the lazy and incompetent might well escape. Closer to home in the experience of women's aid, physical violence by husbands and cohabitees does not seem to be related to competence in domestic work. The force is too often counter productive, not only may the woman be seriously injured but she may suffer nervous disturbance that makes it even more difficult for her to look after the children, prepare the meals, manage on the housekeeping allowance etc. and she may end up in hospital, medical or psychiatric, thus depriving the man of her services at least for a time.

Peruvian males said they beat their women in order to control them, as do British men, and, in my view, this rather than the economic stage of development of society, or economic relations between the sexes in society, or between individual pairs should be accepted as the reason.[51] But to do so is to view force and its threat as more fundamental to the inferior position of women in society than the role women play in economic life. Economic exploitation becomes only one benefit men gain at the expense of women. As the control men exercise over women is more extensive there are also benefits to them in the areas of sexuality, reproduction, status, and internalised feelings, for example of superiority.

But to return to an earlier theme, the remaining level on which the relationship between economics and male violence to women can be considered is that of the organisation of the sexes in societies through history. Engels' view on violence in marriage, while virtually an aside, is relevant to this discussion.[52] Engels argued that 'no basis of any kind of male supremacy is left in the proletarian household'[53] as they have no property, bourgeois law does not apply to their marriage relations and the woman's ability to gain economic independence by entering production means that the proletarian women, unlike the bourgeois, can separate from her husband if she wishes. This rosy picture of female proletarian domestic life is then qualified slightly, 'except, perhaps, for something of the brutality towards women that has spread since the introduction of monogamy'.[54] For Engels family organisation varies directly with economic conditions. He argues that with increasing economic surplus men imposed monogamy on women and that women accepted that the surplus belonged to men because it had been created outside the home in the male sphere of labour. 'The very cause that had formerly made the woman supreme in the house, namely, her being confined to domestic work, now assured supremacy in the house for the man; the woman's housework lost its significance compared with the man's work in obtaining a livelihood'.[55] Engels believed this new economic power enabled men to overthrow the reckoning of descent and right of inheritance through the mother in favour of doing so through the father. Engels then describes a move from pairing to monogamous marriage (at least for the bourgeoisie); from a position where the woman could easily separate and retain control over at least part of the matrimonial assets to one where neither was possible.

Rosiland Delmar in a recent relook at Engels' essay points out that neither a spontaneous and clear cut division of labour, women in the home and men outside it, nor a historical progression of societies from matriarchy to patriarchy have been verified by later anthropological work.[56] Further, anthropological findings are that male violence to women predates monogamy and thus this behaviour is not an unfortunate vagary of human nature called forth by class society. However, to the extent that women have lost social power over time, male use of force should be considered at least as part of the explanation of how this occurred as a better reason is needed to explain why women accepted that the surplus belonged solely to the male and male progeny.

Unfortunately we do not have the information which would permit an informed discussion of whether male violence to women became greater once monogamy had been instituted among the bourgeoisie, but Delmar reminds us that in Engels' view the most oppressed women in the society of his day were the wives of this class. A century later the experience of women's aid in providing refuges for battered women has established that violence continues to occur in all social classes. Public violence, too, is not class specific.

For these reasons I argue that violence operates independently (if not totally then substantially) from the economic organisation of society.

Exclusion and Compulsion

The male use of force or its threat towards women has two currents; one is to exclude participation or restrict behaviour while the second is to compel particular responses. The two interact so that achieving one is an aid in achieving the other.

Women are excluded from, or have restricted access to, male social, economic, and political groups. Men have the power to define social reality because they can exclude women while women cannot exclude men without appearing unreasonable or deviant (witness the difficulties Women's Aid has 'explaining' why there are so few men in their organisations and their inability to exclude them totally).[57] The power to exclude is the langugage of dominance; and thus men's groups become public groups while those of women are on the whole private or seem less permanent as they lack the social validation that flows from a supraordinate position. Because men's groups are public women are excluded from, or have restricted access to, certain buildings, or parts of the city. Exclusion carries with it the threat of retaliation (i.e. use of force) should women become 'uppity' and attempt to gain admission to forbidden areas.

The second current in the male use of force or its threat to woman is to compel them to behave in given ways or to undertake certain tasks; particularly nurturative and housekeeping work. The more women are excluded from social, economic and political areas the easier it is to enforce domesticity. But even if there is little exclusion from the public sphere, deferential servant-like roles for women can be enforced through ideology and material control, both economic and violent, and state policies that favour this type of family organisation. In its harshest form there is isolation from other adults and total economic dependency so that the smallest material wants and even conversation depend on male largesse.

It is interesting to note that the women's movement at the end of the nineteenth and early twentieth century was largely concerned with the power of men to exclude women (from education, employment, political process) while that of today is largely concerned with the power of men to compel a particular kind of domesticity. A focus on violence, the social cement ensuring female dependency, offers an opportunity to unify these two concerns.

Challenging the Use of Force by Males

While from time to time there are examples of men as a group physically attacking women as a group, almost all violence is to individual women carried out by individual men or groups of men.[58] The major point seems to be that it is very rarely necessary physically to attack women as a group in order to control them. The only recent British examples that I know of are attacks on lesbian women, for example a group of men attacked the women who attended the last National Lesbian Conference. Within the women's liberation movement this group offers the

greatest challenge to males as of all women they are the most independent of men, but it is worth noting that no National Lesbian Conference has been held since then as the women concerned say no safe
venue can be found. That women as a group rarely challenge male
dominance sufficiently to call forth the ultimate sanction on them as a
group may be partly the result of fear and partly that they are too well
controlled by other means to make this necessary.

Challenging male dominance is like running a gauntlet or breaking
through a series of barriers beginning with a consensual acceptance of
the sexual social system, moving on to overcoming a fear of deviating,
of breaking cultural norms and possibly unleashing a violent response, to
an acceptance of possible violence and finding ways of surmounting
state supported dependency in the areas of income, housing, and law
and its enforcement.

Clearly we are in a period of renewed consciousness of male violence
and in a small way it is being challenged by women. In the early analyses
of female subordination during the present wave of the women's
liberation movement, violence was one of a number of factors. In the
United States help for victims subsequently developed around rape,
while in Britain the original focus was on women assaulted in marital
relationships and both have been taken up elsewhere in the Western
world. But we cannot know what this will mean for the future. Will
consciousness be lost again, the 'problem' individualised once more,
or will the knowledge of the social meaning of male violence continue
to spread and the analysis and response be extended?

The 'problem of men' has yet to be raised theoretically and with it
the question of the extent to which men can be re-educated.[59] Psycho-
logy, anthropology, sociology have served largely as publicists and
apologists for the male view of society, culture, women and ideal male-
female relations.[60] A new perspective is needed to right the balance;
one that focuses on force and its threat as an elemental factor holding
together a social structure and social process based on female subordination. An analysis of violence in the maintenance of male power and
authority, individually and collectively on varying levels of organisation
from local informal groups through to the national formal operation of
the state also should clarify, relative to social class, the independent
basis and functioning of sexual divisions in the exploitation of women.

Notes

1.   This paper arises out of an Anglo-French seminar on violence in male-female relations sponsored by the SSRC in 1975.

2.   See for example, M. Rosaldo and L. Lamphere (eds.), *Women, Culture and Society* (Stanford University Press, 1974); E. Friedl, *Women and Men* (Holt, Rinehart & Winston, 175); R. Reiter (ed.), *Toward an Anthropology of Women* (Monthly Review Press, 1975).
    In the introduction to F. Engels, *The Origin of the Family, Private Property and the State* (Lawrence & Wishart, 1972), E. Leacock makes the point that we know of no societies untouched by western society. Anthropologists carried their viewpoint with them and nowhere more than in areas they viewed as unproblematic, i.e. the sexual division of labour and the invisibility of violence.

3.   Ibid.

4.   K. Young and O. Harris, ' The Subordination of Women in Cross Cultural Perspective', *Papers on Patriarchy* (Women's Publication Collective, 1977).

5.   Ibid.

6.   Ibid.

7.   J. Young, *Wife Beating in Britain: a Socio-Historical Analysis 1850-1914*, ASA Conference paper, 1976). In ranging between 'the personal troubles of milieu' and 'the public issues of social structure' the women's movements have expressed the sociological imagination. This time will academic sociology do as well? C. Wright Mills, *The Sociological Imagination* (Oxford University Press, 1959)

8.   B. Jones, 'The Dynamics of Marriage and Motherhood', in R. Morgan (ed.), *Sisterhood is Powerful* (Vintage, 1970) pp. 46-61, describes some of the ploys a husband can use to consolidate his position of dominance. The threat of force need not be blatant to create fear of a violent outcome.

9.   A. Whitehead, 'Sexual Antagonism in Herefordshire', in D. Barker and S. Allen (eds.), *Dependence and Exploitation in Work and Marriage* (Longmans, 1976), pp. 169-203.

10.   A. Rees, *Life in a Welsh Countryside* (University of Wales Press, 1951).

11.   D. Poggi and M. Coornaert, 'The City: Off-Limits to Women,' *Liberation*, July-August 1974, pp. 10-13.

12.   Home Office, *Criminal Statistics England and Wales*, 1975 (HMSO, 1976).

13.   R. and R. Dobash, *The Nature and Extent of Violence in Marriage in Scotland* (Scottish Council of Social Service, 1976).

14.   *Report from the Select Committee on Violence in Marriage Together with the Proceedings of the Committee, Vol. 2, Report, Minutes of Evidence and Appendices* (HMSO, 1975), pp. 270-90, 361-91.

15.   Ibid, Vol. 1. Report, p. xiii recommended that as an initial target there should be one family place (for the woman and her children) per 10,000 population. At present approximately 15 per cent of the needed places are available through voluntary projects, most of which are affilated to the National Women's Aid Federation.

16.   After the Select Committee reported the DHSS made several research grants for studies of marital 'crisis management systems' and how agencies do or could respond to marital violence. The Home Office is now considering separate recording of the incidence of domestic violence. *Observations on the Report from the Select Committee on Violence in Marriage* (HMSO, 1976).

17. For an example of violence underplayed see W. Goode, 'Force and Violence
     in the Family', *Journal of Marriage and the Family*, Vol. 33, No. 4 (1971),
     pp. 624-36. For examples of violence ignored see C. Bell and H. Newby,
     'Husbands and Wives: the Dynamics of the Deferential Dialectic', in Barker
     and Allen op. cit., pp. 152-68; P. Berger and T. Lucknann, *Marriage and
     the Social Construction of Reality* (Penguin, 1967); R. Blood and D. Wolfe,
     Husbands and Wives: The Dynamics of Family Living (Free Press, 1960).
18. While this paper is not concerned with psychological explanations, psychi-
     atrists do seem to make the most unsophisticated use of sociological
     theory: for example P. Scott, 'Battered Wives', *British Journal of
     Psychiatry* 125 (1974), pp. 433-41; and also of method, for example,
     J. Gayford, 'Wife Battering: A Preliminary Survey of 100 cases', *British
     Medical Journal*, 25 January 1975, pp. 194-7 and 'Ten Types of Battered
     Wives', *The Welfare Officer*, No. 1 (January 1976, pp. 5-9. For an excellent
     critique of Gayford's research see *The Existing Research into Battered
     Women* (National Women's Aid Federation, 1976). Even E. Maccoby and
     C. Jacklin, *The Psychology of Sex Differences* (Stanford University Press,
     1974), pp. 264-5, succumb to statements of belief when discussing marital
     violence: 'Although incidents of this kind exist as an ugly aspect of marital
     relations in an unknown number of cases – an aspect that tends to be
     unseen, or deliberately ignored and denied, by outsiders – there can be
     little doubt that direct force is rare in most modern marriages . . . let us
     simply say that we believe that any man-woman pair usually forms a coali-
     tion in which in the interests of maintaining the mutually rewarding aspects
     of the relationship, aggression is deliberately minimised.'
19. R. Gelles, *The Violent Home* (Sage Publications, 1972). A study of
     battered wives in Scotland is nearing completion: R. and R. Dobash,
     Violence Against Wives: A Case Against the Patriarchy (Free Press,
     1977).
20. See S. Steinmetz and M. Straus, *Violence in the Family* (New York, Dodd,
     Mead & Co, 1974) and D. Martin, *Battered Wives* (Glide, 1976).
21. Goode, op. cit.
22. The work of Masters & Johnson established that the physiological site of
     the female orgasm is the clitoris and not the vagina: W. Masters and V.
     Johnson, *Human Sexual Response* (Little, Brown, 1966). Jill Johnston's
     perceptive comment was that the movement reacted 'As though the case
     for an insensitive vagina provided women with their first legal brief for the
     indictment of phallic imperialism.' J. Johnston, *Lesbian Nation* (Simon and
     Schuster, 1973), p. 169.
23. E. Marx, *The Social Context of Violent Behaviour* (Routledge & Kegan
     Paul, 1976).
24. Ibid, p. 18.
25. Ibid, p. 79.
26. Ibid, p. 79.
27. Ibid, p. 79.
28. Ibid, p. 102
29. The crucial question, as in the campaign to overthrow feudalism among the
     Chinese, *is who depends on whom?* Through consciousness raising sessions
     what looked initially to be the greater dependence of the peasant on the
     landlord was exposed as false consciousness and a system of relations main-
     tained by force. See W. Hinton, *Fanshen* (Vintage, 1968).
30. P. Backrach and M. Baratz, 'Two Faces of Power', *American Political
     Science Reveiw,* Vol. 56, 1962, pp. 947-52.
31. This was one of a series of violent episodes during this woman's married

life. Eventually she found refuge with women's aid.

32. Since the Select Committee on Violence in Marriage has reported one potentially important legal change has taken effect. Police are required to enforce injunctions if a judge grants a power of arrest whereas previously this was the responsibility of the court officials. However, this should be seen as one move in a complicated game of psychological warfare as the police have always had the power to arrest felons.

33. For a fuller discussion of these issues see J. Hanmer, 'Community Action, Women's Aid and Women's Liberation Movement', in M. Mayo (ed.), *Women in the Community* (Routledge & Kegan Paul, 1977).

34. For a fuller discussion of how the state enforces female dependency on the male see H. Land, 'Women: Supporters or Supported?' in Barker and Allen, *Sexual Divisions and Society: Process and Change,* op. cit., pp. 169-203 and R. Lister and L. Wilson *The Unequal Breadwinner* (National Council for Civil Liberties, 1976).

35. Select Committee on Violence in Marriage, op. cit., p. 190.

36. An analysis of sexual divisions within social work is long overdue. The significance of the fact that the client and the basic grade social worker (but not higher up) are more often than not women has yet to be explored. Nor has the literature been analysed for its presentation of the sexual social system.

37. *Report of the Committee on One-Parent Families* (HMSO, 1974).

38. The reclassification of women from independent to dependent does not involve legal marriage. See *Living Together as Husband and Wife,* Supplementary Benefits Administration Paper 5 (HMSO, 1976).

39. Poggi and Coornaert, op. cit.

40. Ibid, p. 10.

41. A. Coote and T. Gill, *The Rape Controversy* (National Council for Civil Liberties, 1975). The seminal work is by S. Griffin, 'Rape: The All-American Crime', *Ramparts,* September 1971, pp. 26-34.

41. Feministes Revolutionnaires, *Justice Patriariale et Peine de Viol,* unpublished, 1976.

43. Ibid.

44. J. Dollard, *Caste and Class in a Southern Town* (Yale University Press, 1937), sympathetically writes of the good white people of Southerntown who stand above the cruel and mean practices of some of the others to blacks. But the point is that any white man could beat, rape, or murder any black with very little fear of state prosecution, just as any man can physically abuse his woman if and when he wants to. He also writes of how blacks seek white protection, i.e. the need for a black man to have a white 'angel'.

45. Dollard, op. cit.

46. For examples see C. Delphy, *The Main Enemy* (Women's Research & Resources Centre, 1977); J. Gardiner, 'Political Economy of Domestic Labour in Capitalist Society', in Barker and Allen, op. cit., pp. 109-20, W. Secombe, 'The Politics of Housework', *New Left Review* 83 (1974), pp. 3-24.

47. R. Frankenburg, 'In the Production of their Lives, Men (?) . . . Sex and Gender in British Community Studies', D. Barker and S. Allen, *Sexual Divisions in Society: Process and Change* (Tavistock, 1976), pp. 25-51. A similar point is made by R. Titmuss, *Essays on the Welfare State* (Allen and Unwin, 1958), who concludes that the man's reaction to modern industrial techniques may lead him to behave in an authoritorian and punishing way within his family.

48.   For example W. Edmond, and S. Fleming, *All Work And No Pay* (Power of
      Women Collective and Falling Wall Press, 1975).
49.   This point is developed on page 239 and in footnote 2 of her article. See
      also C. Delphy's debate with D. Leger in C. Delphy, op. cit.
50.   Personal communication.
51.   This view is not unique. For example, R. Whitehurst, 'Violence in
      Husband-Wife interaction', in S. Steinmetz and M. Straus, op. cit., pp. 75-
      81; D. Russell, *The Politics of Rape* (Stein and Day, 1975); and S. Brown-
      miller, *Against Our Will* (Secker and Warburg, 1975) argue that the purpose
      of male violence to women is to control them.
52.   F. Engels, *The Origin of the Family, Private Property and the State,* op. cit.
53.   Ibid, p. 135.
54.   Ibid, p. 135.
55.   Ibid (Pathfinder Press edition) p. 521.
56.   R. Delmar, 'Looking Again at Engels' *Origin of the Family, Private Property
      and the State,* A. Oakley and J. Mitchell (eds.), *The Rights and Wrongs of
      Women* (Penguin, 1976), pp. 271-87.
57.   At the National Women's Aid Federation Conference in October 1976, it
      was agreed that while men are active in local groups their role should be a
      minor one and that they should not reinforce sexual stereotypes as the
      Federation is an organisation of women for women.
58.   J. Mitchell, *Women's Estate* (Penguin, 1971), pp. 85-6, gives several
      examples of the threat of and violence to women in the Women's Libera-
      tion Movement from male radicals.
59.   Gold Fower's story in J. Beldon, *China Shakes the World* (Pelican, 1973),
      pp. 367-421, illustrates how the dominance of men over women in pre-
      revolutionary China was sustained ultimately by violence and partly broken
      by female violence in post revolutionary China. But present efforts by the
      Chinese and Western analysts to explain why women remain subordinate to
      men after almost 30 years of revolutionary leadership do not consider
      force and its threat as a relevant variable.
60.   An interesting contribution to the discussion on biological reductionism is
      that of N. Mathieu, 'Homme-Culture et Femme-Nature?', *L'Homme,* Vol.
      XIII, 1973, Cahier 3). She calls for the study of the sexual social system on
      the same basis as that undertaken in the economic, religious or political
      system.

9 THE REGULATION OF MARRIAGE: REPRESSIVE BENEVOLENCE

Diana Leonard Barker*

Almost everyone in Britain gets married at least once, and the majority of the adult population at any one time are married.[1] The state controls the entry into marriage, regulates what marriage should involve and punishes those who default. It also, increasingly, treats those men and women who go through some of the motions of being married (i.e. co-habitation, having children) 'as if' they were married. Why should this be?

The usual reasons advanced to justify legal regulation of, support for, and intervention into marriage and the family are: the protection of women and children (assuring support obligations and assigning responsibility for child care), ensuring family stability (for the psychic good of all its members, and hence the stability and well-being of the polity), and the promotion of public morality. A more important reason for regulation of marriage – indeed *the* most important reason – is that in supporting marriage the state supports a particular, exploitative relationship between men and women in which the wife provides unpaid domestic and sexual services, childbearing and rearing, and wage-earning and contribution to the household income when convenient (i.e. her labour for life – with limited rights to quit, and herself as an instrument of production) supposedly in exchange for protection, assured upkeep and some rights to children (cf. Benston, 1969; Delphy, 1970, 1976).[2]

The law is presented as supporting the weaker party in the marital relationship. In the past the husband, and now whichever partner is better off (still almost invariably the man), has the officially imposed duty to support the other during and after the termination of the marriage. Women are seen as benefiting from marriage as a state-supported institution, and it is they who are more likely to feel a vested interest in the maintenance of their 'rights', i.e. in the *status quo*. Thus state support for marriage acts (as do the various elements of the welfare state, in a different context) to stabilise a potentially disruptive (class) struggle. It helps to mute or silence women's demands for equality of treatment in the labour market; to ensure that they continue to accept the assignment to them of the care of the young, the sick and

239

the elderly, and that they are prepared to drop out of paid employment to provide such care; and to encourage them to put their energy, and occasionally even the money for their own food or clothing (Young, 1951; Rowntree, 1954; Oren, 1974; NCC, 1975), into the maintenance of their husband (their current provider) and children.

But the protection provided by marriage is illusory. As Jalna Hanmer's paper in this volume shows, women are more likely to be assaulted in their homes by their husband than outside by anybody else; in the event of marital breakdown relatively few ex-spouses pay even the low maintenance awarded (see McGregor *et al.,* 1970); and women actually have fewer rights to their children when they are married than when not married (Barber, 1975). In any case, the argument that women need the protection provided by marriage could not be sustained were it not for male violence towards women, the assignment to women of child-care, and their disadvantaged labour-market position (cause and consequence of their domestic exploitation).

This is a very different view of marriage from that presented in most existing accounts of the family. Sociologists have generally accepted the phenomenal view and commonsense functionalist explanations of the family of the society they were supposed to be analysing. They have taken for granted the equation of biological and social categories and have often staunchly defended the separation of the home from the rude, commercial world, stressing domestic affection and consensus (see among others, Fletcher, 1966; Rapoport and Rapoport, 1971; Pahl and Pahl, 1971; Young and Willmott, 1973). In so doing they have directed attention away from the material relationships which bind the domestic group and exist between generations, presenting not a group with a differential distribution of power, where members have their relationship to other institutions affected by their situation in the family (and vice-versa), but an a-economic domestic unity.

It is of course not just the law and sociology but the entire society which is profoundly supportive of marriage. Marriage and parenthood are universally presented as inseparable, inevitable and highly desirable (see Busfield, 1974). Not to get married is not an option which most people see as available, let alone attractive. One does not *choose not* to get married, one *fails* to get married. A whole 'battery of neglect, suspicion and derision' (Comer, 1974, p. 208) is directed at the non-married and the childless, and they are stereotyped as shirking their duty, selfish, immature, lonely, bitter, abnormal and unattractive, or pathetic.

Marriage however, is not just a 'natural' or social necessity — though

these are the terms in which marriage is frequently seen by the participants, by sociologists and by the judiciary. The interrelationship of
unwaged domestic labour and the wage-labour market make marriage an
economic necessity for nearly all women, and a wife is an economic
asset for a man. Most women cannot earn enough to keep themselves at
the same standard of living as they can enjoy as the wife of a man from
the same class background as themselves, since women earn roughly half
as much as men in the working class and are discriminated against in
middle class occupations: they form the bulk of the secondary labour
market (Baron and Norris, 1976). Men can support themselves economically when single, but benefit from their wives' domestic, sexual and
procreative services within marriage, particularly if they want children.

It bears repeating that what marriage involves for a man is very
different from what it involves for a woman (Bernard, 1972) — though
this may easily be overlooked when the 'function' of marriage is seen
exclusively in terms of security, companionship and ego-stabilisation
for the individual. When women get married they not only attain an
important element of adult status, they also chose a husband/'boss'
from whom it is very difficult to separate, and a 'job' whose 'organisational embrace' is near total. A man chooses a wife/'worker' and it is
important to him that he gets a good, devoted, competent, sexually
appealing one. But the woman takes her husband's name and is still
largely absorbed into his legal persona; she has her standard of living
determined by his income, however hard she works; her rhythm,
pattern and place of living are dictated by his; and what is required of
her as a wife will be in considerable measure determined by his occupation. As the church service says: they become *man* and *wife* (not husband and wife, or man and woman, and certainly not woman and
husband). To ignore this (see, for example, Berger and Kellner, 1964) is
equivalent to talking about the relationship between a farmer and farm
worker while overlooking the fact that the one employs the other. While
the relationship between husband and wife differs from that between
gaffer and man — i.e. from wage labour (or indeed from serfdom and
slavery, though as Marx and Engels and J.S. Mill have commented, it
contains elements of these) — and is *sui generis* in a number of respects, the
deferential nature of the husband-wife relationship, the importance of
romantic love as ideology, and the odium of homosexuality in our
society, cannot be understood without a clear recognition of the sexual
division of labour and the fact that there is a *labour relationship*
between husband and wife.

Working then with the proposition 'that marriage is the institution by which gratuitous work is extorted from a particular category of the population, women-wives' (Delphy, 1976, p. 77), let us return to a consideration of the state's regulation of marriage. We are at once faced with the problem that there has been almost no consideration of judicial (and very little of religious or welfare agency)[3] regulation of marriage by sociologists.[4] The bulk of the sociology of law relating to marriage and kinship, like most textbooks of family law (e.g. Bromley, 1976; Hall, 1966) is concerned with divorce and legal separation, not with how the state via the legal system affects the start of or ongoing family life, and not at all with the regulation of sexual behaviour. Perhaps sociologists have simply accepted the lawyers' view that

> English practice . . . has been to refrain from formulating general principles as to how families should be managed. It has preferred to wait until something has gone wrong and then to provide some form of remedy for the aggrieved party. (Eekelaar, 1971, p. 76)

However, it seems more likely that this neglect of the juridical structure is a result of sociologists' concentration on interpersonal relationships (or at best interpersonal-cum-community relationships) of family members, and neglect of the family as an institution.

One reason why lawyers can assert that the law does not interfere in or regulate ongoing marriage is that there is no place where one can find written down the rights and duties of husbands and wives. But this is not to say that there is not judicial consensus about the general nature of the marital relationship. Rather the lack of specification reflects the totality of the relationship — of the husband's appropriation of his wife's labour, time and body — and that it is a relationship of *personal* dependency. The couple work out together what the husband wants her to do — based on his needs and his ability to control her — within certain general parameters. The lack of specification also reflects the fact that there is no rigid segregation of tasks within marriage. What is specific is the relation of production. Husband or wife may cut the lawn or cook a meal, but the wife does it as a dependent — gratuitously, for the head of the household.

Since there is no direct assertion of our law's views on marriage (cf. for example the Civil Code of Switzerland) the judicial perspective must be worked out from a small mountain of statute and case law.[5] In this article the focus will be on that sector which concerns the establishment of whether a marriage exists or not (with a view to the courts enforcing duties of husband, wife or affine, parent or child). This will

involve an outline of the history of the process by which the Church
(gradually from the third or fourth century) and then the State
(especially in the eighteenth century) established what constituted a
valid wedding ceremony and what capacities were needed to contract a
marriage, together with some general comments on changes in the treatment of marriage dissolution and of unmarried couples.

The Development of State Regulation of the Process of Getting Married

1. The Nature of the Ceremony Required for a Valid Marriage

Our present wedding derives from Roman practice. Under early Roman
civil law there were three types of formalities (*confarreatio, coemptio*
and *usus*) by which patricians could enter into a *manus* marriage. All
required that the formalities be conducted openly. Later, free marriage
was used in place of the more formal types of wedding and all that was
required was that the parties had the right to contract a Roman civil
marriage (i.e. were Roman citizens) and that they had the intention to
marry (James, 1957, p. 25). No particular formula or ceremony was
required to contract a valid marriage and there was no requirement that
any sort of public official attend, nor that the marriage be registered.
The woman was delivered by her father and kin into the control of her
husband and his kin in a way very much analogous to *traditio,* whereby
property was transferred. This form of marriage became established
throughout most of Europe.

   According to Helmholz (1975) the English church achieved control
over marriage only very gradually and its courts sought not so much to
enforce the principles of Christian law and doctrine on the laity as to
try to settle actual legal quarrels, with a lesser concern for theological
aspects. He claims the ecclesiastical courts and canon law stood for
the maintenance of a *bona fide* contract, publicly entered into after
due time for consideration and for any impediments to come to light,
for the legitimation of children and the restoration to deserted
spouses of their rights. To this we might add, the security for a women's
kin of her property, since on marriage all she owned passed into her
husband's control and he might dispose of it, rather than it passing to
her children (her kin's descendants) or it reverting to her kin should she
die without issue.

   In order to clarify who was and who was not married, the medieval
church stressed the need for a betrothal and wedding ceremony *in facie
ecclesiae* (at the church door). While non-church weddings were recognised as binding they were illicit and forbidden on pain of excommuni-

cation or penance,and a priest blessing such a marriage might be suspended for three years. This notwithstanding, throughout the Middle Ages many marriages continued to be celebrated with or without a priest, in gardens and houses or even at the wayside, sometimes with no public ceremony and few or no witnesses, either *per verba de futuro,* which was binding as soon as the union was consummated, or *per verba de praesenti* (using words in the present tense), which made the marriage binding immediately. Consent not consummation was the essential element. The stress was on exchanging words deliberately referring to marriage, not on conduct (e.g.intercourse or cohabitation would merely mean concubinage was intended, though calling each other 'husband' or 'wife' was evidence of consent to marriage), and while consent of parents or kin and the giving of a dowry were desirable, they were not necessary (Helmholz, 1975, p. 27).

In addition to its stress on consensuality and its desire for publicity, canon law also emphasised the indissolubility of marriage and its Christian sacramental aspect: marriage was a 'natural state' (governed by natural law) for the security of patrimony, but also a 'holy estate', a source of supernatural blessing and for the safeguarding of sexual morals (hence under the jurisdiction of the Church). Weddings should take place in church so as to seek God's blessing on the union.

Although there were obvious advantages associated with marriage in church and such marriages were favoured in common law (e.g. the wife was not dowable unless she were endowed at the church door), over time the publishing of banns and the presence of witnesses came to be considered unnecessary. What was then stressed was the presence of a priest,[6] and he did not need to say the whole service, so long as at some point the two parties declared that they took each other as spouse. Indeed, if a couple – the boy needed only to be 14 and the girl 12 – simply announced that they were married – not in church and not in front of a priest – they were married for certain purposes.

While the ecclesiastical courts afforded full protection only to those marriages in the presence of a priest and according to the full regulations of the church, and civil courts dealing with the property elements of marriages also accorded the full civil privileges of matrimony only to those married in church, civil lawyers were continually hamstrung because by common and canon law they accepted any marriage as binding – especially one in front of a priest. They could not undo a dubious marriage, given the doctrine of indissolubility. They could only proceed for malpractice, or against the upholding of marital rights.

The problem of clandestine marriages became acute in the seven-

teenth century when *centres* for the solemnisation of such marriages
arose. Unbeneficed clergy became 'attached' to 'marriage houses' —
often the upper rooms of alehouses, brandy shops or coffee houses —
and they went out to private houses for the weddings of the wealthy.
By the first decades of the eighteenth century marriages performed in
or around the Fleet prison 'had become part of the common consensus
of London life and so people (especially from the lower orders) arrived
to be married there as a matter of course' (Brown, 1973, Ch. VII). They
sought cheap, quick, private weddings. However, there were frequent
abuses (tricked, fabricated, predated and forced weddings) and
particular concern was occasioned to the upper classes by the
seduction of heiresses.[7]

When the church failed to take action against the rogue clergy involved, a Bill to end the confusions and abuses was sponsored by a
lawyer, the Lord Chancellor, Lord Hardwicke. His Act of 1753 changed
England and Wales from a nation where marriage was based on consent
alone to one based upon a public contractual identity — that contract
to be sealed in a minutely prescribed manner. The Act was Draconian,
going from extreme laxity as to formalities to extreme rigour. It
insisted that no marriages (except those of Jews or Quakers) should be
valid unless they were solemnised according to the rites of the established Church, in the parish church of one of the parties, in the presence of a clergyman and at least two witnesses. Unless a 'special
licence' was obtained from the bishop of the diocese, banns had to be
read in the parish church of both parties for three Sundays; and if either
party was under 21, parental consent had to be obtained as well. (If
this consent were unreasonably withheld the consent of the Lord
Chancellor might be sought instead.) The penalty for altering or forging
or counterfeiting an entry in a register, or for procuring such an entry,
was death, and other 'technical' errors could carry 14 years' imprisonment. Any marriage which did not fulfil these prescriptions to the
letter was null and void. In sum, the Act was preventative, not construc-
tive. It sought to deal with clandestine marriages by refusing them any
state support whatever. It was unchanged for fifty years, after which a
series of statutes amended it to make it less harsh and inflexible.[8] In
essentials it still stands today.

A Marriage Act of 1836, together with the Births and Deaths Registration Act which was passed immediately after it, brought into existence local Superintendent Registrars and the centralised system of
state registration of marriage. Its other most significant feature was that
for the first time since the Middle Ages it was possible for anyone to

contract a fully valid marriage by civil ceremony. Initially the civil
equivalent of banns was a reading of the notice of marriage to three
weekly meetings of the Poor Law Board of Guardians (followed by a
wedding in a register office, which was usually the room in the work-
house used by the Guardians' Clerk), but after amending legislation in
1856 civil weddings were removed from the Poor Law machinery.
There was then a simple posting up of notices of intended marriages in
a Superintendent Registrar's Office for 21 days. In this way civil
weddings came to provide a means of getting married which, like the
Fleet weddings, was cheap and free from publicity (no one went into
the register office except on business).

> No one intended this. The legislation of 1856 was simply yet
> another bargain between political nonconformists determined to
> remove the stigmas associated with marriage in chapel, and anti-
> erastians anxious to spiritualize the Anglican marriage ceremony,
> and the law of civil marriage was altered almost incidentally as part
> of a package deal. Civil marriage had no pressure groups behind it,
> and seemed too unpopular to be of any importance. (Anderson,
> 1975, p. 66)

Nationally the incidence of civil weddings remained low during the
second half of the nineteenth century (only in 1874 did they comprise
10 per cent of all weddings).[9]
 A further aspect of the 1836 Act was that it took cognisance of
growing religious tolerance and established the right of Roman Catholics
and Protestant dissenters to conduct their own wedding ceremonies in
their own place of worship, under certain conditions[10] – they still do
not have the same rights as the Established Church.
 During the second half of the nineteenth and the first half of the
twentieth century there were a series of minor amendments to the 1836
Act, and in 1949 a new Marriage Act consolidated all the forty or more
statutes and the case law which had accumulated, but itself contained
few substantive changes. There have since been some half dozen
amendments, and the Law Commission (established in 1965) has, as
part of its review of all statute law, produced a *Report on the Solemniz-
ation of Marriage in England and Wales* (1973), many of whose recom-
mendations (all relatively minor) can be expected to be accepted.
 Our current marriage formalities thus express a longstanding
church and state concern to establish who is and who is not married so
as to determine property rights, legitimate children, get deserted spouses

some redress and to secure public morals and stability. The contract of marriage we make is based primarily on verbal assent followed by sexual intercourse, but this assent must be made in front of a suitably authorised person (vicar, priest, minister, secretary or registrar) in a registered place (church or register office). However, while the object of Lord Hardwick's Act was to prevent secret marriages, today provided both parties are of age (i.e. 18), they can marry within 48 hours of giving notice, effectively without the knowledge of their parents, friends, relatives or neighbours, and certainly without the knowledge of a wider public (e.g. the press) and with little ceremony. With central registration of births, marriages and deaths there is no longer dispute as to whether a particular marriage has occurred or not, and reliance that there is no impediment to the marriage depends not on publicity, but upon the requirement that the parties to the marriage give their oath that the information they give is true, and the heavy penalties attached to perjury and forgery. This is related to changes in women's property rights and the nature of wealth within the society which mean that the seduction of heiresses is not the profitable business it used to be.

Marriage is now a very easy contract to make (contrast it with, e.g. the legal formalities of buying land or property, or setting up a business or a trust) – but it is a difficult contract to end. It used to be virtually impossible to break. Until 1857 an Act of Parliament had to be passed for a specific marriage to be dissolved, and from 1857 till 1937 the only grounds for a husband to ask for his marriaged to be ended was adultery by his wife. (No women's marriages were ended by Act of Parliament before 1800, and for a wife to seek the end of her marriage from 1857 to 1923 she had to provide evidence of her husband's adultery plus some other intolerable conduct – e.g. that the adultery was incestuous, his cruelty, desertion, etc.) Only in 1971 did it become possible to end a marriage simply because it had broken down irretrievably, and only then was discretion removed from the judiciary as to whether or not they *agreed* to accept the marital fault being put forward and to give a divorce. Even today the three year moratorium on divorce remains so that there is still no 'quick and simple return to square one' (Eekelaar, 1971, p. 73.)

Concern is consequently quite frequently voiced about the ease with which young people can 'rush' into marriage (see Eekelaar, 1971, p. 63), but the Committee appointed by the Lord Chancellor which recently considered the question came down against 'any formal betrothal (or cooling-off period) required by the state' (Latey Report, 1967, paras. 178-83).

2. Capacities Needed to Contract a Marriage

Marriage differs from all other contracts we may make not only in that to make the agreement peculiar formalities must be carried out, but also in that the law relating to 'capacity' is special. For a marriage contract to be valid:

(a) the parties must be of opposite sex;
(b) neither party must be already married;
(c) both parties must be over 16;
(d) the parties must not be closely related to each other;
(e) both parties must be of sufficiently sound mind to be able to understand the nature of the contract they are entering upon; and
(f) the parties must be acting freely and under no fear or duress.

(a) The parties must be of opposite sex. Heterosexuality in marriage is taken to be so obvious that most law texts merely cite Lord Penzance's edict in *Hyde* v. *Hyde and Woodmansee* (1866) that 'marriage, as understood in Christendom . . . (is) the voluntary union for life of one man and one woman, to the exclusion of all others . . . ', and make no further comment. While for many people there is no problem, what is 'a man' or 'a woman' can occasionally be in doubt.[11]

A man who had been married and had had three children underwent a NHS sex change operation after his divorce and lived as a woman (during this time he used to carry with him a certificate 'saying he was a woman'). He then stopped living as a woman and resumed the name of John. He was married again in the Kidderminster register office as a man. The registrar 'said he was satisifed that the parties were of opposite sex'. (*Observer,* 23 December 1973)

Some lesbians and homosexuals find this capacity restrictive and seek to contract openly homosexual marriages or to pass as heterosexual couples.

Two women married in Manchester after making a false declaration. The 'marriage' was struck from the record and the magistrate gave both an absolute discharge. (*Guardian,* October 1971)

More generally, since the society is organised around couples — married couples — in respect of everything from social acceptance to housing and tax allowances, restriction of marriage (and its privileges) to heterosexual couples is a powerful statement of the deviant nature of any other relationship.

(b) Neither party must be already married. Marriage in Britain has been monogamous since at least Roman times, but again this has been so taken for granted that its significance for the relationship of husband and wife has not been explored.

Anthropological discussion of monogamy and polygamy has focused predominantly on the significance of marriage as creating alliances or producing heirs and has stressed that getting affines or heirs is generally as important as getting a spouse.[12] It is suggested that the advantage of polygyny (by far the most common form of polygamy) is that a man can make several useful alliances which create and sustain a position of influence, and take a second wife if the first is barren. Of course, 'at a given moment the majority of men (in a polygynous society) are married to only one wife . . . and a very small proportion (of older, wealthy) men have more than two' (Mair, 1971, p. 154). Young men may have to wait till their mid-twenties to get their first wife. (Women are married around puberty.) Within such systems the first wife almost invariably has a superior position and is married with more ceremony. She cannot be repudiated without divorce, whereas junior wives are less secure, and concubines may sometimes be dismissed at any time.

It is usually also noted that a man who holds or seeks office and influence needs several wives as a work team to produce more food and surplus beer etc. for his visitors. Hence polygyny is the means to increase wealth and authority as much as it is the privilege of office. 'Sexual variety', on the other hand, 'is the least of the reasons why polygynous marriages are sought in societies which allow them' (Mair, 1971, p. 152).

In the European system of marriage, in contrast, women married late (in their mid to late-twenties) and the husband and wife would be of roughly the same age at first marriage (see Hajnal, 1965). Unmarried male and female servants and apprentices were used to provide the work team in the wealthy older man's household, rather than junior wives. Thus the number of alliances which a man could contract would be limited (except perhaps in so far as he took other men's children into his household as squires etc.). However, given the high mortality rate (especially in childbirth) many ex-spouses (in particular widowers) remarried swiftly and sometimes several times.[13] (At some periods as many as a third of all marriages were remarriages for one or both parties. Lawrence Stone has wryly remarked that divorce is the twentieth century substitute for death).

Certainly monogamy as such has rarely meant a restriction on men's sexual relationships. Some of the servants in the houses of the upper and middle classes 'gave' sexual services to the master (and his sons) (see Davidoff, 1973), and wealthy men have maintained women — from mistresses who were effectively 'junior wives' to prostitutes — whose sexual, domestic and social, and even procreative services they have used on a casual or permanent basis.

(c) Both parties must be over 16.[14] From Roman times to 1929 young people were able to marry when they reached the legal age of puberty — 12 for girls, 14 for boys — which were also the ages of sexual consent. The Age of Marriage Act, 1929, made any marriages contracted under 16 void (previously underage marriages could be ratified when the child reached puberty) and also made this the age at which a girl could legally give her consent to heterosexual intercourse. (There is no corresponding age of consent to heterosexual intercourse for boys.)[15] This raising of the age of marriage was almost certainly but a part of the general trend of extending the formal duration of childhood (cf. Musgrove, 1964).

(d) The parties to be married must not be closely related to each other. Prior to the Reformation, English law followed the vagaries of canon law on prohibited relationships (see Simon, 1965; Helmholz, 1975). A major change came with the break from Rome — not surprisingly given that the precipitating factor was concern with the validity of Henry VIII's marriage to his dead brother's 'wife'. Regulation of what were to be prohibited degrees of consanguinity and affinity passed from the church to civil statutory control, and the new English Law, like that of Calvinistic Europe, reverted to the rules set out in Leviticus (the third book of the law of Moses), which had been those of the early church. The new laws were modified in a series of statutes during the reigns of Henry VIII, Mary and Elizabeth I. They were in some respects vague, especially the reference in a statute of 1540 to 'God's laws' — not surprisingly since the 'mythical charter' for a bilateral European kinship system was drawn from a patrilineal Semitic society. The exact prohibitions remained a subject of litigation till 1861, although it was generally agreed that the prohibited degrees were those laid down by Archbishop Parker in 1563 and included in the *Book of Common Prayer.*

Only some three hundred years later did there start to develop a significant pressure for change. Dissatisfaction was expressed with the stringent rules relating to affinity: that not only could one not marry one's own relatives, one could not marry one's spouses's relatives even after the spouse was dead. Gradually during the course of this century laws have been passed allowing marriage with, *inter alia,* a deceased wife's sister and a dead brother's widow.[16] Since 1960 it has even been possible to marry such 'affines' when the former marriage is dissolved or annulled, even if the previous spouse is alive. This probably relates to a change in the social structure and value system (Farber, 1970) whereby affinal ties have become more restricted and impermanent. Ties of marriage end with death or divorce. The elementary family recognises few obligations to those who marry its members – and fewer still which continue after the marital link is severed. (Nor, since the final ending of the Poor Law with the National Assistance Act of 1948, has the state seen support obligations as extending beyond spouses – and ex-spouses until they remarry – and parents for dependent children.)

(e) Both parties must be of sufficiently sound mind to be able to understand the nature of the contract they are entering upon. This covers not only being drunk or under the influence of drugs at the time of the ceremony, but also being able to understand what marriage entails. However, the mental capacity judged necessary to make a marriage is not high: Puxon (1967, p. 20) cites a case where greater capacity was seen as necessary to make a will than to get married. (An elderly person attempted both in one afternoon. He was adjudged to have been capable of getting married but not of sound enough mind to make a will.)

Cases cited in law textbooks show occasions when people have claimed that they were mistaken as to the nature of the ceremony – e.g. thinking it was a betrothal or the induction into a religious sect – due to fraud and/or language problems. In such cases the courts have set great importance by whether or not intercourse occurred afterwards; it being implicit that intercourse is so restricted to marriage that if the defendant permitted intercourse she or he *must* have realised the nature of the ceremony.[17]

Mistake as to the nature of the ceremony may be grounds for the annulment of a marriage, but mistake as to the effect marriage will make is not (e.g. thinking that, if married, one's wife/husband will be allowed into a country and then finding she/he will not be; or thinking a marriage polygamous when it is in fact monogamous). Mistake as to the person married likewise applies only to mistake as to identity, not as to fortune, health, status or moral quality.

3. Voidable Marriages

A third (and relatively minor) difference between marriage and other
contracts that ordinary people may make is that even after the wedding
(assuming it was validly conducted) and even if the couple have the
capacities to marry listed above, the contract may still be voidable if
certain other conditions prevent it being sealed. These conditions throw
further interesting light on the judicial view of what marriage involves.

A marriage is voidable if either party:

is unable, or wilfully refuses to consummate the marriage;
is at the time of marriage suffering from VD in a communicable form;
is at the time of marriage suffering from mental disorder of such a
kind as to make the party unfitted for marriage and the procreation
of children,[18] or subject to recurrent attacks of insanity or epilepsy;
or
if the bride, at the time of marriage, is pregnant by another man.
(NB however that if another woman is pregnant by the groom it
affects the marriage not one jot.)

A voidable marriage is at its inception a valid marriage, but the existence of an impediment (not the fraud of concealing an impediment)
allows one (or occasionally either) spouse to go to court to turn it into
a void marriage by decree. But the injured party must have been un-
aware of the circumstances at the time of the wedding, he or she must
act swiftly and there must be no condonation[19] – specifically no intercourse – after the discovery. However, if the couple agree they can continue the marriage and it will be fully binding. No one but the spouses
can challenge the validity of such a marriage (cf. a void marriage where
any interested party – e.g. someone who stands to get property if the
marriage is null – can challenge), and a voidable marriage can only be
annulled during the lifetime of both spouses. Once one spouse has died,
the marriage stands.

Since inability or wilful refusal to consummate is far and away the
most common plea for nullity there has been considerable (and to some
lawyers, e.g. O'Neill (1974), distasteful) discussion of what constitutes
consummation. It is 'full and complete intercourse'; penetration and
ejaculation – 'full and complete' for the man. From one such case,
Baxter v. *Baxter* (1948), where the husband sued for wilful refusal to
consummate on the grounds that his wife has always insisted on the use

of a contraceptive (to wit a sheath) arose the ruling, now a principle
'apparently established in English Law' (Royal Commission 1956) that
procreation is not a principal end of marriage. This is contested by the
Anglican Church, which in its report to the Royal Commission points
out that 'the court never reviewed a wealth of judicial authority to the
contrary' (Royal Commission, 1956, p.16). The Commission, while
accepting that 'some who enter marriage. . . attach more importance to
the ability to have children than to the ability to have intercourse'
(p.17), concluded that to include sterility as grounds for voiding
marriage would lead to all involuntarily childless marriages and all
marriages entered into by post-menopausal women being at risk. However, this stress on consummation (and our other stress on the sexual
exclusiveness of spouses – especially that of the wife) rather than
procreation within marriage, and our acceptance that it is better to die
childless rather than adulterous,is odd by most societies' standards
(Mair, 1953).

A final point about the law's view of marriage which is shown by its
treatment of pleas for nullity deserves mention. 'The courts do not look
favourably' (Hall, 1966, p.60) on petitioners who, knowing the facts
and the law, approbate a void or voidable marriage, or who derive
benefits and advantages from it, and who then try to treat it as if it had
never existed. Thus decrees have been refused in voidable marriages
when couples have adopted a child, or where the petitioner has previously brought proceedings before other courts which implied that the
marriage did exist (e.g. asking for restitution of conjugal rights or
maintenance). Where the marriage is void and the couple knew this when
they married, or if they continue together long after discovering the
impediment, they may get a decree, but also a reprimand, and no costs.

> In Pettit v Pettit (1963) the husband sought a decree of nullity on
> the grounds of his own impotence. It was held that his wife had
> given him the best years of her life, had borne him a child (con-
> ceived by *fecundatio ab extra*), had been deprived of intercourse
> through no fault of her own, and might lose her pension rights, etc.
> Thus it would be 'unfair, inequitable and unjust to grant this husband
> a decree against the wishes of his wife'.

Time and the acceptance of services thus help to seal a marriage.

The Right to Quit and the Nature of the Agreement

Not only must people go through particular, precise procedures in order to get married, and possess various capacities if they are to form a valid contract, as has been mentioned, marriage differs from most other contracts in that it cannot be broken off, nor a voidable marriage declared void, simply by mutual consent. In the past the couple had to go to a court of competent jurisdiction (County Court or High Court) and *ask* for a decree of dissolution (divorce) or nullity (annulment). There is no need to labour the point of how expensive, time-consuming and traumatic this process used (and for some still continues) to be — due in no small part to the activities of legal and welfare agents (see Dezalay, 1976). This has changed, however, and, since 1973, although a couple must go to court to end the marriage, the judiciary no longer has discretion as to whether or not to grant a divorce if the couple agree that they want it. (However legal machinations continue to make the distribution of property and children into a contest). Dissolving a marriage may now be no more complex than dissolving various kinds of trust.

Marriage differs from trusts and commercial contracts, however, in that while the parties to such agreements may make such terms as they think fit (provided they do not offend against rules of public policy or statutory prohibitions), the parties to a marriage are much more limited in this respect. In some cultures various forms of marriage and concubinage coexist, being entered into in different ways and with different rights and duties,[20] but in Britain there is but one type of marriage. There can be no bargaining between spouses since the state decrees what marriage shall be. It is not, in fact, a contract between the spouses, but rather they agree together to accept a certain (externally defined) status.

This is because marriage is regarded by both church and state as a 'natural institution', of unquestioned form, to which they merely give support and blessing.

> Marriage is an honourable estate, instituted of God in the time of man's innocency . . . a mystical union . . . not to be enterprised . . . lightly; ordained for the procreation of children to be brought up in the fear and nurture of the Lord . . . to avoid fornication, for . . . mutual help and comfort, in prosperity and adversity (Book of Common Prayer)

> a marriage involves more than . . . a relationship between two indi-

viduals . . . [it] is the most important social group in the community
. . . The law has not created the family. The family is a social
organism which arises to fulfil certain needs of society and of individuals . . . [and it is upon this organic unit that the law] confer[s]
special recognition . . . (Eekelaar 1971, p. 11)

Both agree that the nature of marriage, and what is involved in the
change of status from single man and woman to husband and wife, is
not negotiable. One chooses to change status, and one chooses who to
marry, but one does not choose what 'marriage' is to be. Having
accepted 'to be married' a couple are free to work out an individual
slant. It being preeminently a relationship of personal dependence, the
husband works out an accommodation with his wife (e.g. he may or
may not 'stop her' going out to work, he may require her to do housework or he may provide servants to release her for entertaining, etc.)
But a couple cannot drastically modify the relationship in law — e.g.
the spouses cannot contract out of their mutual duty to maintain, nor
can the woman demand payment for her domestic work, nor can they
be of the same sex, nor can it be a relationship between three people,
etc.

    While a commercial agreement between two parties does not, as such,
confer rights or impose duties on any other person(s), the fact of being
married affects the spouses' rights and duties with respect to other
persons in many ways. For example, marriage affects (or may affect)
the parties' nationality and domicile; they become 'next of kin' and
acquire legal rights to participate in each other's estate on death over
and against other individuals; it affects taxation, insurance and rights to
certain welfare benefits; the wife customarily and the children legally
take the husband's surname; and it may affect the rights and duties of
third parties — e.g. neither spouse can agree to marry another while still
married since the existing spouse is entitled to undivided consortium.

    The support given to marriage — be it God's blessing in church, or
the blessing of the Inland Revenue in the shape of the married man's tax
allowance (Land, 1976c), or the ability to change a spouse's nationality
— is not extended to any other domestic group or relationship between
adults.

Recent Changes

It has been suggested that we should recognise marriage as a particular
and peculiar unpaid labour relationship which preexisted industrial
capitalism and which continues in this society dominated by the sale of

labour power. This paper has shown that the existence and nature of this relationship between men and women (or more precisely, between *a* man and *a* woman) has been regulated by the church and the state in Britain for centuries. However, the means of extracting gratuitous work from women-wives has changed somewhat over time.

In the early nineteenth century the union between a man and a woman was virtually unbreakable (except, of course, by death). The woman (and her property) were delivered into her husband's physical and legal control and there was no way she could get out of it. However, with the feminist struggles and changes in the rest of society, from the mid-nineteenth century onwards there were substantial changes in regard to married women's rights to property and their children, to divorce, and in their access to the labour market. These changes have loosened the bonds of marriage and the law has become (technically) less sex discriminatory. From the turn of the century, and particularly since the Matrimonial Causes Act of 1973, family law has been in a state of flux.

The nineteenth century tendency which was, in Maine's terms, that of a 'progressive society' moving from status to contract, with 'The Individual steadily substituted for the Family, as the unit of which civil laws take account' (Maine, 1965, p. 99), affected many aspects of marriage(e.g. the law relating to married women's property in 1857, 1870, 1874, 1882-1907, and their rights to children in 1839, 1873, 1886), but did not touch the core of the labour relationship between husband and wife. The dominant interpretation of Individualist philosopy in the nineteenth century itself would be better named Familialism — or simply Patriarchy. It envisaged full legal citizenship extended to all heads of households and 'individual obligation' as being between household heads. The possibility of dependants (married women and children — and at an earlier date, servants) being seen as rational, contract making, independent individuals was not considered in most political thought of Maine's day.[21] When all adult men were recognised as full and equal citizens (albeit some more equal than others), there was a shift to a retrenching doctrine: Nuclear Familialism.

. . . on 1 January 1971 family law faced in two directions. Many of its doctrines were survivals from the era of individualism. But more were directed towards new paths . . . [recent] reforms . . . reflect the acceptance of the view that many individual problems are the symptoms of a malfunctioning family unit. They direct the legal and administrative response . . . towards trying to sustain family life and to salvaging as much of it as possible when a crisis situation occurs. The philosophy might be expressed, crudely, in these terms: look after the family and this will take care of the individuals. (Eekelaar, 1971, p. 9)

On the one hand there can still be found many legal texts and judicial pronouncements which (re)assert that marriage is a 'natural institution'; that it is the 'natural right' of any adult to get married (see e.g. the European Declaration of Human Rights); and that family members are/ should be a 'natural community' and not a 'rational association'. An example is the 'romantic' viewpoint of Lord Evershed who approved of 'sentiment not law continuing to regulate the distribution of property among the family', and who declared himself very averse to 'husband and wife in law and in form becoming partners in the firm of marriage' (Foreword to Graveson and Crane, 1957, p. ix). This is also of course an essential element in the Christian doctrine of marriage, the Anglican variety of which 'until recent years . . . dominated all discussion of marriage and divorce and determined the standards of accepted behaviour' (McGregor 1957, p. 101).

It is this view of marriage which helps to justify the law and its agents (police, lawyers, social workers) being so loath to intervene in family life:

The normal behaviour of husband and wife or parents and children towards each other is beyond the law — as long as the family is 'healthy'. The law comes in when things go wrong. (Kahn-Freud and Wedderburn in Eekelaar, 1971, p. 7)

This unwillingness to 'interfere' continues indeed even when things have manifestly gone wrong (e.g. in cases of assault of husband upon wife, see Pizzey, 1974, Ch. 5; rape within marriage; and husbands' failure to pass on wage increases in periods of rapid inflation, see NCC, 1975).

On the other hand, there have been clear moves in law towards making marriage more contractual, associated within changes towards equality of treatment of the sexes.

1. It is now very much easier than it used to be to get married and unmarried. The lack of formality, notice and expense needed to start a marriage in a contemporary register office wedding was noted earlier. At the other end, it is now possible to get a divorce at will when there is mutual consent and there are no children. It is not necessary to use a lawyer and it is not even necessary to attend the court. Even when there

are children and the divorce is contested, the process is no longer anything like as fraught and costly as it used to be. A major support for
marriage — the difficulty and unpleasantness of divorce *pour encourager
les autres* — has thus disappeared.

2. The effects of marriage are now in law largely the same for both
sexes. While the words of the Established Church's marriage service
continue to stress differences between the roles of husband and wife
(although the extent of the differences has been substantially reduced
in the new liturgy[22]), the words of the civil ceremony have long suggested that the obligations of the spouses are identical. However,
statute law and judicial practice used to follow and reinforce common
law and customary practice in seeing the man-husband as household
head and breadwinner, and the woman-wife as financially dependent
and responsible for domestic duties, child-bearing and rearing, the care
of the sick etc., only a peripheral wage-earner, and much more
culpable if adulterous. The same grounds for divorce for both sexes
were established in the 1920s, and since the late 1960s other elements
have also changed (see the consolidating legislation in the Matrimonial
Causes Act, 1973). For example, the duty to maintain is now placed
equally on the husband and wife — depending on who has the greater
income; domicile is no longer presumed to be that of the husband
and it is not desertion if the wife will not move with the husband; and
either sex can bring a foreign spouse into the country. The process of
removal of sex discrimination from family law is nearly — but not quite
— complete (e.g. children born abroad to British women married to non-
British husbands do not have the same citizenship rights as children
born to British men with non British wives) and it could be said that the
special protection the law afforded to women-wives has been removed;
men-husbands have been given the same rights. However, of course,
in most cases factors outside marriage and marriage law continue to
make the positions of men and women within marriage very different,
and *de facto* the woman-wife continues to be the weaker party: the
party who is protected.

3. There is less differentiation of the married and the unmarried couple.
The history of the process of entry into marriage which has been outlined shows the gradual take-over by the Church and its formalisation
and regulation of the rite of passage, followed by a further, drastic,
formalisation by the state in the mid-eighteenth century and slow subsequent liberalisation. The church and state both sought to make a
clear distinction between those who were and those who were not
married so as to determine who owed whom what rights and duties,

who owned and who should inherit what property, and so as to control public morals.

Today, while the process of getting married is clearly defined, the division between the status of being and not being married in Britain is sharper in theory than in practice.Expediency is invoked. For example, void and voidable marriages are increasingly treated as having existed until they are officially annulled (e.g. as regards legitimacy of children and rights in property and to maintenance) because of the anomalies and hardship which are otherwise produced. In addition couples who live together and who present themselves as husband and wife without having gone through the ceremony are colloquially described as having 'common law marriages', and if someone claims they are *not* married the onus is on him or her to prove they are not, not on the couple to prove they are. Such 'spouses' have some rights as next of kin – e.g. visiting in prison (Coote and Gill, 1974, p. 285), and the 'husband' can argue for certain rights to the children if he acknowledges paternity and provides support (Barber, 1975).

The justification of expediency for treating the unmarried as if they were married is most marked, however, in what McGregor and Finer (1975) call 'the third system of family law' – that for the 'destitute', now social security provision. The whole system of welfare benefits assumes that when any man and woman live together the man will support the woman, even if the couple assert that they are not, and do not wish to be seen as husband and wife, or that they wish to organise their lives differently. There is still no possibility of role reversal here (cf. the system of family law for the 'rich'). If a cohabiting woman is or becomes unemployed she cannot claim supplementary benefit or draw a widow's pension for herself or her children. Even when they are not the children of the man with whom she is living, he is held responsible for their support, though he cannot get national insurance benefits for the mother. If the man is unemployed, he must claim supplementary benefits for the woman and her/their children as his dependants. If an unmarried but cohabiting mother is employed but earning a low wage, she cannot draw family income supplement, since eligibility is determined by the level of her cohabitee's income and he must claim[23] (see Land, 1976a and 1976b; Lister and Wilson, 1976).

In addition, the tendency to treat men and women living together *as if* he is supporting her financially, and to treat 'common law' marriages *as if* they were legal marriages, is increasingly to be found in judicial practice – generally under the familiar guise of 'helping women'. For example,

An unmarried woman successfully claimed a quarter share in the house in which she had lived with the father of her two children. He was the owner and she would normally have had no rights in the property unless she had provided part of the purchase money or the house was held jointly. Lord Denning said that strictly Mr Eves owed Ms Eves no obligations but she was entitled to a beneficial interest in the property because of the way he had acted — viz saying that the house was to be for their children and a home for them when they were married. She had improved and maintained the home and this, Lord Denning said, was a valid contribution. (*The Times,* 28 April 1975, quoted in *Women's Report* 3 (4) 1975)

Quite what is going on in this and other similar judgements is not clear. It may be that it is being argued that a quasi-contract existed and so the woman has some equitable rights. (This is very different from the view which would have been held around the turn of the century when she would have been seen as a 'volunteer'/concubine and hence as having no rights to compensation.) Or it may be that the good judge was supporting 'the little woman' and seeking to help (if also to mystify) her by treating her 'as if' she had been married — for only in marriage is domestic work, child-care and painting and decorating some one else's house expected to be done 'for love'. It is of dubious help to women generally to say that the work was gratuitous because done in 'marriage', but because done 'in marriage' it should be recompensed.

Conclusion

In the late nineteenth century Toennies claimed that:

> two diametrically opposed systems of law [exist] : one in which human beings are related to each other as natural members of a whole and another where they come into relations with each other as independent individuals merely by virtue of their own rational wills. In empirical jurisprudence especially of the Roman-modern school, which is a science of binding statute law within and for the Gesellschaft, the Gemeinschaft type of law persists under the name of family law, but the relationships regulated thereby are lacking in legal exactness. (Toennies, 1940, p. 206)

This divide is now less marked. There are 'Gesellschaft' contracts which are quite strongly regulated by the state — e.g. contracts of employment or those between landlord and tenant; and 'Gemeinschaft' family law is, by fits and starts, becoming more like other contracts: less the merging of two complementary units (male and female) into one flesh for life, more the coming together of two individuals in a trust (a situation long established in our laws of marital property, unlike the communal marital property regulations of most European countries.)

But although men and women are now treated more equally in the letter of family law, we have yet to see how the new laws will be applied. Judges vary, and their interpretations of statutes establish precedents. And if the law no longer discriminates between husband and wife, it still certainly supports marriage. It is noteworthy that the most recent edition of the standard work on *Family Law* continues to state baldly that '[marriage] is, *of course*, quite unlike any commercial contract' (Bromley, 1976, p. 14, my emphasis).

The present situation is thus still such that women are persuaded to enter marriage in the belief that it offers protection and a meal-ticket for life, making them accept lower wages and lack of advancement in the labour market without a fight, and encouraging them to give up an independent income altogether to care for their husband and children or relatives. What has changed is the ease of movement between marriages (though contrast the number of women who change husbands to get a better deal with the number of workers who change their boss each year) and a decline in the importance of formal marriage. On the other hand, new statutes and official behaviour presume 'marital relations' even when a man and woman are not married[24] — which continues to ensure that most women are 'married' (i.e. providing unpaid domestic services for a man) most of their lives, and that any man who wants one can have a wife.

Attempts to strengthen 'the family' which support the division of labour in 'marriage', or presume women are provided with subsistence by men, or prolong the dependence of children, or encourage 'community' (home) care of the sick and old, further the exploitation of women, and the domestic hierarchy continues to be justified (as it was under seventeenth century patriarchy, see Schochet, 1975) by the 'inherent' weakness and defencelessness of the subordinates (women need protection because they have to care for children etc., and they cannot earn as much as men anyway) and because they consent to it (marriage is what women 'want' and 'choose').

Notes

*I should like to thank Barbara Cook and Margherita Rendel for help in the production of this paper.

1.   In 1964 90.4 per cent of men and 90.5 per cent of women aged 45-9 had
      married at least once (Registrar General for 1964, Vol. 3, p. 31). In 1971
      72.6 per cent of men and 84.2 per cent of women aged 25-9 and 86.2 per
      cent of men and 88.8 per cent of women aged 30-44 were married (*Social
      Trends* 1972, Population, Table 6).

2.   This interpretation does not preclude other 'functions' that regular, stabilised
      marriage, family and households may have for, e.g., capitalism. Dezalay
      (1976) suggests that marriage involves two overlapping systems of oppression
      – of woman in marriage and (via attributing them women and children as
      dependants) a relatively docile male work force. (At the same time, one could
      add, it also produces an even more docile, flexible *female* labour force.) Gar-
      diner (1976) argues that the family is an effective and cheap means of child-
      care and domestic servicing of adult workers (i.e. means of reproduction of
      labour for capital). Galbraith (1974) sees the multiplicity of household units
      as stimulating consumption, etc. I maintain, however, that support for the
      labour relationship between man and woman is the main reason for state
      support of marriage in the past and today.

3.   Cf., however, Land 1976a, 1976b, 1976c; Dezalay, 1976; McGregor and
      Finer, 1974.

4.   Anthropologists, on the other hand, have long been concerned with the
      principles and practice of statutory and customary laws and the activities
      of religious and legal agents in defining and policing the framework for
      interpersonal, kinship and affinal relations.

5.   Weitzman in a seminal paper (1974) on US marriage law argues that
      marriage as currently legally regulated there contains the following 'ana-
      chronistic assumptions' embedded in the contract:

      1. it assumes a lifelong commitment;
      2. it assumes a first marriage, of young people;
      3. it assumes sexuality (and procreation) are essential elements in the
         relationship;
      4. it assumes a strict division of labour in the family;
      5. it assumes a white, middle class family; and
      6. it assumes Judaeo-Christian ideals of monogamy and heterosexuality.

      There is nothing comparable on English law, though useful material is included
      in Eekelaar, 1971 and Finer and McGregor, 1974, Vol. 2. Appendix 5.

6.   Or after the Reformation a clerk in Holy Orders, or during the Common-
      wealth a Justice of the Peace.

7.   The concern of the upper classes (and their lawyers) with heiresses' property
      was certainly the factor which precipitated the change in the marriage law,
      but in their denunication of 'Fleet' marriages they were joined by the middle
      classes, who objected to the sordid procedures of such marriages and the re-
      duction of the solemnisation of matrimony to a monetary trade, and by those
      who were worried by the forced marriages of destitute pregnant women by
      Poor Law Officers to prevent them becoming a charge on the Parish.

8.   E.g. couples could marry in churches which were the usual place of worship
      of one of them even if it was not the church of the parish in which he or she
      resided; permission to marry without the consent of parents could be ob-
      tained from the county court or from a magistrates court and not just from
      the High Court; there were less ferocious punishments for offenders; and a
      marriage was not automatically void if any of the prescriptions of the 1753
      Act was not complied with, but only if the couple knowingly and wilfully
      married in a place other than the church where the banns ought to have
      been published or before a person not in Holy Orders.

9. There were, however, certain areas in the late nineteenth and early twentieth century where civil marriages comprised nearly two-thirds of all weddings. These were areas where there was an 'absence of the custom of ecclesiastical marriage', either because of the survival of very old traditions and habits, or because of the 'adoption of new ways of behaving under the shock of industrial transformation' (Anderson, 1975, p. 86).

10. Provided (a) that these Authorised Places of Worship were registered for conducting marriages, (b) that advance notice of the wedding was given to the Superintendent Registrar of the district and his certificate obtained in lieu of banns, (c) that at some stage in the ceremony the couple took each other as husband and wife *per verba de praesenti*, and (d) that a registrar was present to record the marriage. A later Act (1898) allowed the governing body of a registered building to authorise a person (often the priest or minister) to register the wedding so that the presence of the civil registrar was no longer needed. Some groups however, such as Humanists and Scientologists, continue to be precluded from conducting their own ceremonies because their meeting places are not technically places of 'worship'.

11. One of the most famous of such cases was the nullity action of Cameron Corbett (the 50-year-old-son and heir of Lord Rowallan, formerly the Chief Scout) against his 35-year-old wife. April Ashley, a model. The couple married in Gibraltar in 1963 and six years later the husband applied to the Divorce Court for a declaration of nullity 'because she was not in fact a woman but was then and at all material times a man'. She replied that she was a woman and cross-petitioned on the grounds of his incapacity or wilful refusal to consummate. His suit was granted, hers dismissed. She got no contribution to her costs and no alimony from him (*The Times,* October 1969: *Guardian,* May 1970).

12. Goody has recently sought to relate polygamy/monogamy to changes in forms of agriculture, pressure on land, production of surplus and patterns of inheritance as between Africa and Eurasia. See Goody, 1976.

13. 'a law which seems to obtain for the whole pre-industrial (Western) world [is] that once a man reached the marriage age he would tend to go on getting married whenever he found himself without a wife . . . The law holds for women too, but is weaker in their case'. (Laslett, 1965, p. 99).

14. In many countries a man has to be 2-3 years older than a woman before he can marry. The minimum age for marriage in the Western world varies from 12-18 (see Latey Report, 1967, Appendix 7).

15. *The Criminal Law Amendment Act 1885,* consolidated by the *Sexual Offences Act 1956* s.5 made it a crime to have intercourse with a girl under marriageable age. To have intercourse with a girl aged 13-16 carries a maximum sentence of 2 years, but with a girl under 13 carries life imprisonment. The older the boy/man, the more seriously the act will be treated: under 14 probably no action will be taken, under 24 some action, over 24 serious action. See also *Criminal Law Act 1967,* section 2.

    There are no criminal sanctions in English law against heterosexual fornication, adultery or illegitimacy as such (cf. many States in the US where fornication is a criminal offence — though how often these laws are enforced or what their influence on behaviour may be is uncertain. Likewise some State laws punish the parents of illegitimate, or a certain number of illegitimate, children). There is, however, restriction on the heterosexual activity of young people in that those thought to be 'in need of care and control' or 'exposed to moral danger' can be brought to court (by the local authority or police *et al.*) and either sent to approved accommodation or supervised while at home. This applies particularly to girls, who are also likely when arrested for other offences to have their crime 'sexualised' – cf. Smith (1975). Once a youth or girl reaches 17, however, *or* when they marry, concern for their 'moral welfare' ends (provided the youth only has heterosexual intercourse).

In all cases the law assumes the sexually (more) active agent to be the man and he is assumed to be attracted to a woman younger than himself (e.g. intercourse between grandmother and grandson is not included among those relationships listed as incestuous – *Sexual Offences Act 1965* – but grandfather-granddaughter intercourse is).

16. These rulings also imply, of course, that a woman can marry her dead sister's husband etc., but reference is always made from the standpoint of a male Ego.

17. We are now witnessing the – not edifying – phenomenon of immigration officers from the Home Office joining DHHS 'snoopers' in a concern with whether couples are or are not cohabiting and having intercourse since these define marriage. Let us wait to see 'how many times' and 'for how long' they are going to decide is necessary to distinguish a 'valid' marriage and a 'real' relationship from one of 'convenience' (see Wilson, 1976).

18. The difficulty of interpreting what on earth this means were outlined by Mr Justice Omrod in *Bennett* v. *Bennett* (1969). He suggested that it could mean no more than 'is this person capable of living in a married state and carrying out the ordinary duties and obligations of marriage'. He confessed himself 'quite unable to suggest any meaning that could be given to the phrase "unfitted for the procreation of children", unless it meant unfit to bring up children, which is not what it says' (Hall Supplement). The Law Commission recommended redrafting of the passage and amalgamation with 'lack of consent' as one ground for voidability.

19. The Law Commission recommended that the bar on approbation after discovery should go so that, if possible, the couple can try to affect a conciliation (as in the new rulings on divorce) (Law Commission 1970).

20. E.g. monogamous and polygamous marriages in Africa (Mair, 1953), marriage and concubinage in Singapore (Freedman, 1957), the variety of forms of marriage among the Nuer (Evans-Pritchard, 1951), and the types of Roman marriage mentioned earlier.

21. E.g. while Spencer in his earlier work advocated a strict Individualism which gave rights and identities not only to women but also to children, he tacitly retreated from this position and in most of his work the concept of an individual refers to a male householder with dependent wife, children and servants (see Barker, 1976, pp. 4-5).

22. See Barker, 1977, Ch. 5 and Appendix 5: 1 for details of changes in Anglican liturgy.

23. However, the man can claim no tax allowance for the woman; she cannot get a pension or maternity grant on his insurance; and if she works she has to pay the single woman's rate of insurance. Neither has a claim on the other's property on death unless so willed. Such regulations provide financial incentives to marry, especially for the poor who are most affected by welfare benefits, and for those of middle income who are affected by fiscal arrangements (see Land, 1976a, 1976b and 1976c).

24. Interestingly, Weitzman reports that in California couples are resorting to law to have it established that they are *not* intending to establish various, automatically imputed, invariable legal obligations to one another when they form emotional, sexual and/or domestic attachments (Weitzman, 1974).

References

Anderson, O., 'The Incidence of Civil Marriage in Victorian England and Wales', *Past and Present,* No. 69 (November 1975).

Barber, D., *Unmarried Fathers* (Hutchinson, 1975).

Barker, R.S. 'Democracy, Citizenship and Political Participation: Perceptions of Women in Politics in England before 1918', paper for European Consortium for Political Research, mimeo, 1976.

Baron R. and G. Norris, 'Sexual Divisions and the Dual Labour Market', in D.M. Leonard Barker and S. Allen (eds.), *Dependence and Exploitation in Work and Marriage* (Longmans, 1976).

Benston, M., 'The Political Economy of Women's Liberation', *Monthly Review,* Vol. 21, No. 4 (September 1969).

Berger, P. and H. Kellner, 'Marriage and the Construction of Reality', *Diogenes,* No. 46 (Summer 1964).

Bernard, J., *The Future of Marriage: His and Hers* (Souvenir Press, 1972).

Bromley, P.M. *Family Law* (Butterworths, 5th ed., 1976).

Brown, R.L., *Clandestine Marriage in London, especially within the Fleet Prison, and their Effects on Hardwicke's Act, 1753,* MA thesis, University of London, 1973).

Busfield, J., 'Ideologies and Reproduction', in M. Richards (ed.), *The Integration of the Child into the Social World* (CUP, 1974).

Comer, L., *Wedlocked Women* (Feminist Books, 1974).

Coote, A. and T. Gill, *Women's Rights. A Practical Guide* (Penguin, 1974).

Davidoff, L., 'Above and Below Stairs', *New Society* (1973).

Delphy, C., 'L'ennemi principal', *Partisans,* No. 54-55 (1970).

—— 'Proto-feminisme et anti-feminisme', *Les Temps Modernes* 345 (Mai 1975). (These two articles are in *The Main Enemy: A Materialist Analysis of the Oppression of Women,* Women's Research and Resources Centre pamphlet, 1977).

—— 'Continuities and Discontinuities in Marriage and Divorce', in D.M. Leonard Barker and S. Allen (eds.), *Sexual Divisions and Society* (Tavistock, 1976).

Dezalay, Y., 'French Judicial Ideology and Working Class Divorce', in D.M. Leonard Barker and S. Allen (eds.), *Sexual Division and Society* (Tavistock, 1976).

Eekelaar, J., *Family Security and Family Breakdown* (Penguin, 1971, with an Introduction by O. Kahn-Freund and K.W. Wedderburn).

Evans-Pritchard, E.E. *Kinship and Marriage among the Nuer* (OUP, 1951).

Farber, B., 'Marriage Law, Kinship Paradigms and Family Stability', in C. Presvelou and P. de Bie (eds.), *Images and Counter-Images of the Young Family* (ICOFA, Louvain, 1970).

Fletcher, R., *The Family and Marriage in Britain* (Penguin, 1966).

Freedman, M., *Chinese Family and Marriage in Singapore* (Althlone Press, 1957).

Galbraith, J.K., *Economics and the Public Purpose* (Deutsch, 1974).

Gardiner, J., 'Domestic Labour in Capitalist Society', in D.M. Leonard Barker and S. Allen (eds.) *Dependence and Exploitation in Work and Marriage* (Longmans, 1976).

Goody, J., *Production and Reproduction* (CUP, 1976).

Graveson R.H. and F.R. Crane, *A Century of Family Law, 1857-1957* (Sweet and Maxwell, 1957).

Hajnal, J., 'European Marriage Patterns in Perspective', in D.V. Glass and D.E.C. Eversley (eds.), *Population in History* (Arnold, 1965).

Hall, J.C., *Sources of Family Law* (CUP 1966).

—— *Supplement* to the above.

Hanmer, J., 'Violence and the Social Control of Women' (this volume pp. 218-39).

Helmholz, R.H., *Marriage Litigation in Medieval England* (CUP 1975).

James, T.E., 'The English Law of Marriage', in Graveson and Crane (eds.).

Land, H., 'Women: Supporters or Supported', in D.M. Leonard Barker and

S. Allen (eds.), *Sexual Division and Society* (Tavistock, 1976).

—— 'Social Security and the Division of Unpaid Work in the Home and Paid Employment in the Labour Market', mimeo, 1976b

——'Social Security and Income Tax Systems', mimeo, 1976c

S. Allen (eds.), *Sexual Division and Society* (Tavistock, 1976).

—— 'Social Security and the Division of Unpaid Work in the Home and Paid Employment in the Labour Market', mimeo, 1976b

—— 1976c 'Social Security and Income Tax Systems; mimeo.

Laslett, P., *The World We Have Lost* (1965).

Latey Report, *Report of the Committee on the Age of Majority* (HMSO, 1967, cmnd. 3342).

Law Commission, *Report on Nullity of Marriage* (HMSO, 1970).

Law Commission, *Report on Solemnisation of Marriage in England and Wales* (HMSO, 1973).

Lister R. and L. Wilson, *The Unequal Breadwinner* (NCCL pamphlet, 1976).

McGregor, O.R., *Divorce in England* (Heinemann, 1957).

McGregor O.R., L. Blom-Cooper and C. Gibson,*Separated Spouses: a Study of the Matrimonial Jurisdiction of Magistrates Courts* (1970).

McGregor, O.R. and M. Finer 'The Evolution of the Obligation to Maintain', in *The Finer Report,* Vol. 2, Appx. 5 (1975).

Maine, H., *Ancient Law* (Dent Everyman, 1965).

Mair, L.P., 'African Marriage and Social Change', in A. Phillips (eds.), *Survey of African Marriage and Family Life* (OUP, 1953).

Mathieu, N.-C., 'Homme-Culture et Femme-Nature?', *L'Homme,* XIII(3) (1973) (to be published shortly in a WRRC pamphlet – *Forms of Knowledge and Perceptions of Women*).

Mathieu, N.-C., 'Masculinity/Femininity', in WRRC pamphlet, No. 2 (1977).

Musgrove, F., *Youth and the Social Order* (Routledge and Kegan Paul, 1964).

National Consumer Council, *For Richer, For Poorer* (pamphlet HMSO, 1975).

O'Neill, P.T., *An Analysis of the Development of the Legal Relationship of Husband and Wife* (PhD thesis, University of London 1974).

Oren, L., 'The Welfare of Women in Laboring Families', *Feminist Studies* 1974.

Pizzey, E., *Scream Quietly or the Neighbours Will Hear* (Penguin, 1974).

Pahl, R. and J. Pahl, *Managers and their Wives* (Allen Lane, 1971).

Puxon, M., *The Family and the Law* (McGibbon and Kee, 1967).

Rapoport R. and Rh. Rapoport, *Dual Career Families* (Penguin, 1971).

Registrar General's Statistical Review of England and Wales for 1964.

Rowntree, G., 'The Finances of Founding a Family', *Scottish Journal of Political Economy,* Vol. 1, No. 3 (1954).

Royal Commission, *Report on Marriage and Divorce* (Morton Commission), (HMSO, 1956).

Schochet, G.J., *Patriarchalism in Political Thought: The Authoritarian Family and Political Speculation and Attitudes especially in Seventeenth Century England* (1975 OUP).

Simon, J., 'The Biblical Background to Marriage and Divorce', *The Law Society's Gazette* (February 1965).

Smith, L. Shacklady, 'Female Delinquency and Social Reaction', unpublished paper presented at University of Essex Women and Deviancy Conference (1975).

Social Trends, 1972 (HMSO).

Toennies, F., *Fundamental Concepts of Sociology,* trans. C.P. Loomis (1940).

Weitzman, L.J., 'Legal Regulation of Marriage: Tradition and Change', *California Law Review,* Vol. 62, No. 4, July-Sept., pp. 1169-1288 (1974).

Wilson, A., Note on 'Immigration' in *New Society,* 11 March, 1976.

Young, M., 'The Distribution of Income within the Family', *BJS* (1952).

Young, M., and P. Willmott, *The Symmetrical Family* (Routledge and Kegan Paul, 1973).

10 SOCIOLOGISTS NOT AT WORK – INSTITUTIONALISED INABILITY: A CASE OF RESEARCH FUNDING

Robert Moore

Introduction

There is nothing new in drawing attention to problems arising from the relations between sociologists and agencies funding social research. Nonetheless, the case of Aberdeen and the SSRC is instructive if only because of the clarity of the issues. The social situation is self-evidently problematic: profound social changes appear to be taking place in the North of Scotland and these changes have an identifiable cause, the exploitation of off-shore oil resources. The sociologists were eager to conduct research from 1972/3 onwards, but in 1977 no major sociological projects were under way. Yet there was a public and wide demand for such research and three major proposals had come from Aberdeen, all to be turned down by the SSRC which avowed great interest in such research.

This paper describes events from 1971 onwards and then attempts an explanation of the failure of sociologists to mount the research that everyone agreed was needed.

Bias and Detachment

Before starting this analysis the question of 'interest' should be raised. The writer has been a disappointed applicant for funds; is he the best person to comment on the events? The answer is that he may not be the best person for many reasons – but disappointment is not one of them. The fact that one may be angry or partisan does not mean that one is disqualified from passing judgements. If persons most affected by events are to be disbarred from comment then only the less informed may make judgements. More importantly, the rejection of an argument solely on the grounds that it derives from someone who has dealt unsuccessfully with an organisation means that only those who have dealt successfully or not at all with an organisation are entitled to comment on its activities. This would be a curious development.

Any defence of what is to follow highlights a problem faced by sociologists in Aberdeen throughout; namely that of being persistent advocates of our own case, who often found ourselves pleading the

267

'special' nature of our research problems. This problem arose because we were *on site* watching social change at close quarters. If we did not plead our case, who would? The nearest department of sociology to Aberdeen is 125 miles away in Edinburgh — remote from the more drastic and visible changes that are taking place.

One final preliminary matter must be dealt with. Perhaps the research applications failed because they were poor or because the applicants were not competent. What constitutes a good or bad application is part of the analysis. But for the sake of the argument we will assume throughout that the applications were bad, unless — that is — there is independent evidence to the contrary. The sociologists directly involved were: Professor Michael Carter, Head of the Department of Sociology in Aberdeen and Robert Moore, then Reader in the same Department. Seniority does not guarantee competence but both have reasonable records in research and publication. Furthermore, their work (or proposed work) on North Sea oil received tributes from the same Committees that turned down the proposals, in general terms: 'I can only stress that the Committee recognises the importance of this research' (Sociology Committee of SSRC to Carter, 24 June 1974). And specifically: 'The panel is impressed both by the extent of your involvement . . . and with the clear vision you are applying to it' (Panel on North Sea Oil to Moore, 22 January 1976).

Oil was 'news' from about 1970 but only in terms of the 'national economy'. There was very little 'sociology of Scotland' available in 1970-75 and even less on the North of Scotland and none at all of oil in the North. Without being on the spot it would be difficult to see how socially profound and sociologically important the changes were that were taking place in the lives of a small and geographically remote proportion of the United Kingdom population. Social scientists working in Scotland frequently report 'nationalistic adrenalin' running in their otherwise tranquil, universalistic and affectively-neutral blood after encounters with colleagues in England. This paper is not written in such a spirit although the analysis offered here includes a discussion of the effect of remoteness upon committees and applicants and the different interests and outlooks of the centre and periphery. This consideration is, however, only the first of three.

1. It is argued that applicants for research funds tend to see courses of activity and local research strategy in the round whereas the 'remote' funding agency sees only separate applications without background

knowledge or intellectual context. This creates mutual unintellig-
ibility. The central funding agency (the subject committee, Research
Initiative Board or Research Council) may also think in terms of the
appropriate or equitable distribution of limited resources in the
periphery in a way that bears little or no relation to the motivations and
demands of sociologists in the periphery.

2. We also examine the organisation of the Sociology Committee and
find that it has a programme and agenda that make it impossible to
react speedily to social change. In addition we observe some of the
dysfunctions of bureaucracy whereby permanent officials define their
tasks in terms of servicing the organisation rather than furthering its
goals. Finally we show the creation of organisational confusion in
response to outside pressure.

3. We also attribute our problems to the state of the discipline of
sociology. It seems that sociology's self-consciousness has led to a
theory-and-concepts fetishism which puts abstraction above social research. This self-consciousness leads to a demand for technical rigour
that takes little account of actual research situations.

These latter two factors combine powerfully because the rigorous
disciplinary demands fit well with the bureaucrats' tidy dislike of loose
ends. Unfortunately, the research situation is often technically messy,
theoretically ambiguous or unclear — and hence stimulating and challenging. A lot more is going on in a research location than can be
written into an application, furthermore. One solution to this problem
of conflicting demands is to make a dishonest but tidy application for
funds, another is to have close contacts with key officials or committee
members so that problems can be talked out informally before the submission of an application. Let us now see what happens when neither
solution is adopted.*

The facts of the case are as follows: Work on the social impact of
industry on sparsely populated areas had been undertaken in Aberdeen,
notably the study of the aluminium smelter at Invergordon.[1] From
1971 onwards it became clear that off-shore oil was going to have a
considerable influence on the social, economic and political structure of
the North of Scotland. The Department of Sociology was aware of this
but unable to take much action: the Department was being reorganised

*A third strategy is to seek funds for work already completed and to use this for
one's next project. Thus keeping one ahead of the Research Council seems to be a
response to the frequent complaint 'If I could answer the Committee's questions I
wouldn't need to do the research'.

and there were many new staff. Carter, and to a lesser extent Moore, were engaged in setting up the Scottish Mobility Study to complement the English study based at Nuffield College. Moore was also writing up previous research.[2] A start was made nonetheless; a newspaper cuttings file was commenced and informal discussion took place within the Department and with the Department of Political Economy who already had a large programme of regional research underway. The Department was ideally situated geographically to observe and analyse social changes of a far-reaching kind, there were almost limitless research opportunities.

Developing a Research Policy: The First Attempt

At the beginning of July 1973 before we were at the stage of being able to formulate detailed proposals Carter wrote to the Scottish Office stating the Department's interest in research on the social impact of North Sea oil. He suggested that the Scottish Mobility Study might provide a data base for such research. In mid-October the Scottish Office replied that 'we have not yet made any judgements about the merits of different proposals . . . I shall keep you in touch'. The proposals were not specified and, in fact, Aberdeen kept the Scottish Office in touch with developments.

Starting Research: The First Attempt

At the end of 1973 the University established an Institute for the Study of Sparsely Populated Areas under the directorship of an economist, Professor Peter Sadler. The Institute had been jointly promoted by the social science departments and was strongly supported by Sociology. It seemed an auspicious moment to approach the SSRC for a grant so that the Institute and Department could collaborate in a project that would set the tone for future collaboration. Accordingly on 11 April 1974 Carter and Sadler applied to the SSRC for £49,855 for a project entitled 'The Social Impact of Oil on Communities in the North of Scotland'.

A copy of the application was sent to the Scottish Office from where an official replied on 9 May, 'My personal view is that your proposal comes closer than many of the others ['the others' have never been specified] to making a contribution to the policy'. In June the Sociology Committee of the SSRC rejected the proposal. The Committee argued that 'the longitudinal nature of this research would be more appropriate to a programme application and that you should be encouraged to think along these lines'. According to the SSRC,

A programme is conceived as being wider in scope than a project, and consisting of several interrelated projects which may be undertaken consecutively or simultaneously. Though centred on a specific theme, a programme allows the investigator greater flexibility than does a project in shifting emphasis within the theme. (SSRC research grant scheme 1975-6)

The main reason for rejection was that 'the proposals were overambitious and inadequately prepared for research in a complex and significant problem'. This phrase was the first recognition of the importance of the oil question and it was to be repeated with every subsequent rejection. Given this recognition it is not easy to explain why the committee secretary said 'I think it would be unrealistic to submit a programme application for the next closing date . . . ' (SSRC to applicants 24 June 1974). The closing date was two months ahead, in August; had we missed this date no research programme could have started before October 1976.

Carter replied that he too preferred a programme to a project but 'Our problem is the need to get social research started as soon as possible in a rapidly changing situation . . . ' A project application can be processed by the SSRC more quickly than a programme, and the research started sooner after processing. Carter did not accept the notion that Aberdeen should delay the application; by October 1976 ' . . . much base-line data and many sociological insights will have been missed, thereby prejudicing the quality of the research which could be done' (Carter to SSRC 10 July 1974).

Already it was felt that the formal SSRC procedures did not lend themselves readily to coping with the local situation either in terms of speed of decision-taking or technical demands upon the applicant:

. . . research grant applicants cannot expect *carte blanche* from the SSRC . . . but I do think that the situation here in Northern Scotland does justify rather more discretion to the researcher on the spot than is usually accepted at the application stage. I hesitate, also, to use a 'special case' argument, because such an argument is doubtless overdone. Nevertheless, there are special features of the situation here consequent upon the introduction of offshore oil, and it seems to me that they call for special procedures in reference to ensuring that research is done — in terms of the importance of such research both for social policy and planning and for the unique opportunities for the furtherance of sociological thought which the situation provides.

(Carter to Sociology Committee, 10 July)

The Project: Some Comments

Carter was referring to the very rapid development of the oil industry; real or assumed local developments of a temporary or permanent nature were taking place or planned in widely dispersed communities situated in an area comprising more than one fifth of the land area of the United Kingdom. It was difficult to write proposals in terms of precise locations, problems and research techniques. Nonetheless, it seemed a matter of some urgency to get full-time research workers on the ground. One very important aspect of employing full-time researchers was that unlike members of academic staff they would be mobile throughout the large area.

The simple bureaucratic demands of running the SSRC committees do not create an organisation capable of coping with immediate needs. For example it would not be possible to obtain SSRC funds to study community responses to a pit disaster, or the organisational problems encountered in coping with a major air crash. Furthermore disasters do not occur in carefully chosen locations neither do large-scale economic developments. The choice of the North of Scotland as a research location is not equivalent to the choice of Bethnal Green or Luton. These latter were chosen to exemplify, amongst other things, a previously worked out set of theoretical interests and problems. Accordingly, the relevant theory would be fully articulated in such a case and its 'operationalisation' in relation to the research location would be detailed and clear in an application for funds. Events in the North of Scotland, by contrast, have an existential integrity which is prior to the problems of existing theory. There has been a sudden and massive intrusion of industrial activity, much of it on the frontiers of technology, and of capital. These events affect not a town but an entire region in an immediate way.

The events taking place cannot fail to be significant for theories of development, for theories of working-class organisation, for ideas on the links between relations of production and social organisation and culture, for the political economy of labour migration. These events are happening now. It seems reasonable, then, to put forward a research strategy which is flexible as to precise location and method and which aims to compare the usefulness of varous theoretical approaches for understanding what is happening rather than to impose a set of narrowly pre-defined theoretical questions.

This is certainly not to deny that existing theory will be useful; on

the contrary we emphasised that events in the North of Scotland could
not be studied in isolation. They spread both over time (as the setting in
which they occur is the product of a continuing social and economic
process) and spatially (as oil-related developments are the product of
international movements of capital in a global context of alternatives).
The point is to do justice both to what is unique and to what is shared
with other places and other times. But it is to assert that if existing
theoretical outlooks and questions were unhelpful in understanding
what is happening (though in fact they are helpful) then the fault
would lie with the theory not with the choice of location or subject.

Developing a Research Policy: The Second Attempt

In order to clarify the whole problem of research, Carter suggested on
10 July 1974 in reply to the Committee's rejection, that he convene a
conference of persons and institutions in Scotland interested in
'effecting a fit between the interests of researchers and the interests of
government and research-granting (sic) bodies'. An additional purpose
of such a conference would have been to inform the SSRC and others at
first hand of the problems of research and to show that Aberdeen's
'special pleading' was dictated by circumstances. No response was ever
received to this suggestion.

In the same month Carter took a further step; he wrote to the MP
for Aberdeen North, who was also Under Secretary of State for Health
and Education, expressing concern at the lack of urgency in drawing up
a research strategy in the Scottish Office and elsewhere. In September
a friendly reply was received, 'I share your concern that due priority
should be given to research in this field . . . the government is very
much alive to the need for research'. There then followed a statement
the full import of which was not to be clear for some time; the SSRC
and Scottish Departments 'are currently working out an arrangement
for a joint exercise for the development of programmes for further
research'.

Starting Research: The Second Attempt

Meanwhile, the Aberdeen sociologists moved quickly to submit a programme application that would enable them to start research in
October 1975. It was clear that migrant labour was going to be a public
issue and that its social impact had already begun. So although the
programme was to include a study of the effects of migrant labour I put
in a separate application for a pilot project to start in January 1975,
with a view to it feeding into the programme, or — if necessary —

standing in its own right as a pilot for a later project. This application was submitted in the middle of August. At the end of the month Carter, Sadler and Moore submitted a programme proposal for £159,595 to study 'The Social Impact of Oil Developments in the North of Scotland'. The short abstract of the research proposal reads as follows:

> Major social consequences following from the development of North Sea oil are already apparent in Northern Scotland. The introduction of large scale industry to hitherto sparsely populated areas affords a unique opportunity to combine in one project a study of (a) changes in orientations to work in traditional communities which are subject to the in-migration of large labour forces composed of workers who are characterised by the values of urban-industrial labour markets, (b) the modes whereby conflicts between residents and in-migrants find expression and accommodations are made, (c) the consequent implications for social policy (especially the provision of housing and other social services) and (d) the nature and incidence of social problems (delinquency, alcoholism, domestic breakdowns etc.) to which social changes of this sort give rise.

In October Carter and Ardern (of the Highlands and Islands Development Board) published their *North of Scotland Register of Research in the Social Sciences,* an essential step in the development of a research strategy.

Late in October the Sociology Committee arranged 18 December as the day for their site visit. Whilst the purpose of the visit might have been to meet the applicants and see their departmental facilities, the fact remained that 'the site' was as long as the distance from London to Aberdeen and one of the main locations proposed for research (the Cromarty Firth) was at its extremity 150 miles away from Aberdeen. A two-day visit was suggested by Aberdeen.

In November my pilot project was accepted in principle. The letter carrying this news also gave the first intimation of the setting up of a joint SSRC/Scottish Office advisory group under W.G. Runciman. We can not know the facts of the case but it is not unreasonable to infer that this committee was the 'joint exercise' referred to by the Under Secretary of State. It seems as if the Under Secretary made enquiries about research and these enquiries precipitated action within the administrations of social science research and the Scottish Office. But the response was administrative action, executed without reference to research workers currently engaged in relevant research.

On the first day of the committee's visit the visitors were taken on a tour of oil related developments in the Cromarty Firth. Our guide was the Social Development Officer for the County, who had conducted the enquiry into the social impact of the Invergordon smelter when he was employed by the Department of Sociology. This tour thus not only acquainted the committee with the scale and dispersal of developments but gave them an opportunity to meet one member of the informal network of specialist contacts who had promised Aberdeen their full support·in the research programme. It provided them with an opportunity to see research as a collective enterprise rather than an abstract exercise. During the tour I was approached by a member of the committee and asked if I would be willing to act as Director of the programme — a full time appointment. I declined because my commitment to research was complementary to and not an alternative to teaching. This looked a good sign, however, because the committee were clearly satisfied with at least one of the sociologists, and the other was already a major SSRC grant holder.

Unfortunately no notes survive from the formal meeting of the following day. No notes seemed necessary at the time; professional colleagues were to discuss matters of mutual interest. The meeting proved frustrating for the applicants and it began on an embarrassing note: a few days before the meeting W.G. Runciman had been named publicly as the Chairman of the SSRC/Scottish Office advisory group; at the meeting members of the visiting committee deferred to him in that role. The applicants thought this deference was because Runciman was chairing the meeting, an impression that the real chairman did little to dispel, by initially remaining silent.

The applicants spoke briefly to their application and were then cross-examined by the committee. The meeting took an increasingly inquisitorial nature and it seemed to the applicants that each time they answered a question the ground of enquiry was shifted. At the time it was hard to understand exactly what was happening and in retrospect it is only a little more clear. Were we really so incompetent that we were unable to cope with the meeting? In advance of the meeting we had no clues as to what would make satisfactory answers to the committee's questions. We also lacked information about the key personnel in the committee — who would be influential in making the final decision, whose views would be deferred to, etc. This is similar to a job interview where one meets an interviewing board 'blind' and has to make quick assessments of the people around the table. In this respect the confusion over the chairmanship was especially disabling.

We formed the opinion during the meeting that one could not assume it to be a meeting in which professional colleagues shared a common theoretical universe and technical vocabulary. The committee wanted every detail spelt out and at one stage I felt obliged to give a short lecture on elementary development theory and its application to the North of Scotland. The committee also wished to know the exact locations in which we intended to do research and the research instruments to be used. The answers to such questions would have been almost entirely contingent upon planning decisions taken by the Secretary of State, commercial decisions by companies and technical developments in the oil industry (the use of steel or concrete platforms, for example). To have answered the committee's questions in a specific way would have been to misrepresent the situation that was to be studied.

There is always a problem of *level* in discussing work with people whom one does not meet day to day. One's daily departmental discourse may be unfamiliar to the stranger or part of his stock-in-trade. One of the committee underlined the difficulty when he said that our application and its defence was obviously based on a theoretical discourse too little of which had been transmitted to the committee. But here we were facing a special problem. The committee was ignorant of Scotland as a whole, so much of our effort comprised setting out basic information about the region. Professional colleagues however demand theory, but without the basic data it is only possible to talk about theory in a general or elementary way. The theoretical discussion becomes complex and interesting at the point where it engages with the specifics of local history and current developments. We were then pursuing incompatible aims in trying *both* to inform the committee *and* demonstrating our theoretical sophistication. This goes some way to explaining the apparent shifting of ground and the lack of a common theoretical language.

Of course, there is an alternative explanation which is not entirely plausible in the present case, but needs to be mentioned. The committee might have been cooling us out – in which case there was no adequate performance possible. How would we have known if this had been the case? The committee would have proceeded in the same way and we would have experienced the same disarticulation and loss of confidence.

The applicants had one special question for the visiting committee: How did the advisory group relate to subject committees; was it an extra hurdle in the application process, would it be consulted on applications to subject committees or would it operate quite independently?

No one could answer the question when it was asked — for the first time it would seem — by an interested party. It should have been anticipated and the answer worked out in setting up the advisory group. The failure to cope with the question shows administrative failure on the part of those responsible within the SSRC. The applicants had to be content with two flatly contradictory answers to this question in January 1975.

Six days after the visit the applicants received a letter asking them to revise the application. Three of the crucial comments were:

1. . . . the design of the research was not sufficiently explicit and it is, therefore, suggested that you should reformulate the conceptual framework and clarify the following points which began to emerge from the discussion; the ways in which the industrial effects upon the area are conceptualised (for example in terms of the involution theory, the disruption/reinforcement of existing power hierarchy; take-off/new stable state; temporary/permanent changes).

ii. The ways in which aspects of the structure of communities are conceptualised (for example how the modes of social control and power 'mediate' the effects considered in (i)).

iii. The expected relationships between variables set out in (i) and (ii) above.

iv. In terms of (iii) the rationale for the choice of sites and the choice of problem areas . . . in the original application.

2. . . . when you redraft your application you should include *rather more* detail on the different survey instruments to be used . . . it was suggested that you should outline the interviewing timetable . . . ' (emphasis added)

Staffing; the sub-committee appeared to think that Aberdeen should have had a Director ready to take on the programme they, therefore, suggested

3. That you should attempt to include a named Director in the resubmission . . .

The 'site visit committee were impressed by your enthusiasm to undertake this research' however.

The Programme: Some Comments

We see the expectations of the applicants and site committee are incompatible.

The applicants wanted to get workers into the field, to start monitoring and recording events. Parallel with this the theoretical side would be developed. The explanation of theoretical problems was work that the applicants wanted to do; if they had had an entirely systematic conceptual and theoretical framework the research would have been largely unnecessary and even more simply descriptive than was intended, and much less interesting. They expected a committee of their peers to recognise the practical difficulties of research and to recognise the applicants' ability to develop the difficult theoretical issues.

The committee, for their part, lacking local knowledge or involvement could only insist on certain professional criteria being met. This could have meant satisfying themselves on the question of the competence of the applicants. But there was also a large sum of public money involved and criteria of professional competence are not easily arrived at. The solution they adopted was to insist on the application being couched in highly abstract terms and the techniques of research closely tied into these. This at least promised a hard, 'professional' way of judging the application.

The committee could have insisted on the criterion of the research making 'some new and significant contribution to factual information'; this objective is clearly permissible according to 'Guidelines to applicants for research grants in Sociology and Social Administration'. That this was possible was hinted at by a member who having read George Rosie's *Cromarty: The Scramble for Oil* asked why the applicants did not try to do something like this? The comment was irrelevant in the intellectual context because Rosie's book is a highly informative but nonetheless non-theoretical book. The comment was also irritatingly at odds with our own intention to make a uniquely sociological contribution to the analysis of events.

Sociology is a highly self-conscious discipline and this self-consciousness affects all the profession. Therefore, the applicants had felt especially constrained to include specific references to theoretical knowledge in their application. The reality of what they wanted to do — which in the first instance was to collect information — had to be bullied into abstractions before it could be presented for consideration. We were in a double bind. To have used conventional theories of development would have undermined our claim that events were uniquely worth studying. But to stress the uniqueness of the North would have drawn us into areas that could only have been speculative at the theoretical level. We were thus vulnerable to a line of criticism to which there was little reply and to criticisms of a kind to which it is not possible to know what would constitute a satisfactory answer. A 'satisfactory answer' is defined by the inquisitor, who, in the event, expects greater and greater abstraction.

These professional demands made upon applicants can be contrasted with the committee's attitude to administrative matters like the appointment of a Director. In the case of the research hard 'professional', objective (if undefinable) criteria are applied: in the case of the Director the committee wanted someone on whose 'quality, capability and initiative' the research would depend. In our opinion the way to find such a person was by open competition, and the applicants were especially anxious to avoid any procedure that looked like patronage, although we had four names in mind. The committee, in fact, expected patronage to be exercised. It would seem that with £152,000 involved they wanted to be sure that a suitable person was available to be responsible for the project rather than having an abstract job description put to the test of the job market. In order to do this they would accept someone by virtue of his *reputation,* something they were not prepared to weigh as heavily (as we hoped they would) in considering the applicants' actual proposals.

Starting Research: The Second Attempt Renewed

The applicants spent some weeks considering the committee's points and they replied at the end of January 1975. The reply reasserted that social change would come to Northern Scotland and that the researchers would have to consider a range of possible outcomes. The actual changes were not dependent on sociological laws but human decision. 'The evidence so far to hand does not enable us to posit any one of these social changes as the crucial basis for sociological research'. The applicants reminded the committee that 'members of the site committee commented [on] the fact that at the moment there is insufficient data to allow of more than informed speculation in sociological terms'. So 'It is for this reason that we place the highest priority on starting the resesarch as soon as possible, on getting research workers into the field and on collating such data as is already available'. The reply then outlined four theoretical formulations concerning the possible outcomes of developments in the region that seemed worth testing, amongst others, against the data: conventional development theory, enclave development, involuted development, and the achievement of a new stable but non-industrialised state.

From experience the applicants were able to say that the kinds of changes taking place might vary from location to location and that it was hard to adopt any single theoretical stance towards Northern Scotland as a whole. Already, however, the research was moving towards general questions that would lead to a consideration of aspects of dependency theory (although the applicants were not absolutely clear about this at the time). Questions of the mediating structures between government and local communities and the oil-related companies and the political brokers and opinion leaders were in the forefront of consideration and this was stated in the reply to the letter from the committee. The salience of these questions had been heightened by research which was just beginning in Aberdeen city on the city business elite.

On the question of the Director the applicants compromised by presenting (with their permission) the curriculum vitae of four people who were known to be interested in the job.

At the end of April 1975, eight months after the original application the programme was turned down. The key issue was 'the lack of a theoretical and conceptual framework'. The letter of clarification in January had failed 'to convince the committee and the Board that the programme would yield more than a collection of miscellaneous descriptive data about the different effects of oil development in different places'. This was a harsh and insulting judgement on the capacities of Carter, Moore, Sadler and four potential Directors. But it was more than harsh. Had not the sounding out of one applicant as a potential director been a 'vote of confidence' in that applicant and an indication that the committee were well satisfied with his ability to carry out this research?

The committee recognised the proposal 'as a topic of potential importance for sociological research' and hoped that 'you will not be discouraged from pursuing your interest in this area'.

The Second Attempt: Some Comments

The genuine ambiguities and perhaps the genuine risk in committing so much money was met by rejecting the proposal because of the lack of 'a worked-out model of oil-related social change for yielding a set of explanatory hypotheses which would effectively be tested within an authentically comparative research design'. Of course, the applicants could not turn the tables on the committee and (a) submit this statement to conceptual and theoretical analysis (b) ask them to explain how it related to actual research and (c) whether they had ever done research this way themselves. The asymmetry of the situation is worthy of remark: a tutor would expect a ready come-back from an under-graduate who found such a comment on his essay — and would have to explain and defend the comment. The professional may not reply to his peers in this case. If the committee had said 'the proposal, like the situation, is messy, the theory is untidy and the methods too dependent upon contingent factors — we do not finance such research' (or 'we do not trust you to do the research') the situation would have been clear. The use of what can be little more than a Euclidean incantation mystifies the situation and generates a sense of injustice and frustration precisely because we all seek conceptual clarity and theoretical rigour. It is humiliating to be told one has not achieved what everyone aspires to. But the use of incantations puts the user on firmly 'professional' grounds and beyond rational criticism, even though he (or they) has not achieved what he demands.

The revision of the application and the expansion of the theoretical discussion had been irrelevant it seems. The site committee had conceded that only 'informed speculation' was possible; they put us through the hoop and we speculated on the basis of our information and were rejected *en bloc* for it. No alternatives were suggested.

Considerations of this kind lead one to reconsider the separate and later issue of the proposal to set up a separate Social Administration Committee, at the beginning of 1976. The interests of social administration whilst by no means lacking theoretical content are bound to be more pragmatic. Furthermore, social administration in attempting to bridge a number of fields must encounter difficulties of theoretical integration that would disqualify them from funds according to the rigorous theoretical demands of the Sociology Committee. To what extent did this contribute to the demand for a separate committee?

In retrospect can we discern what was happening at this stage? Let us assume that we had made all the wrong assumptions about Scotland and oil and that the application combined intellectual poverty with pro-fessional ambition that put it beyond reasonable consideration for funding. What happened, then, was a process of 'cooling out' the applicants. This entailed the cost of flying a committee from London to Inverness and back from Aberdeen. It included writing lengthy letters and playing the applicants along for over eight months, or over a year including the revision of the original project.

We believed that the application was not entirely without merit. From this point of view the expensive and time consuming activity of the committee is more explicable. What can not be explained is the dismissal of the proposal without any suggestions about a more limited study of alternative research strategy. The practical result was the loss of many man-hours which, on our side, could have been devoted to research, on however limited a scale. More importantly events had not stood still for us; while we had been engaged in the futile exchange over theoretical niceties developments in the North continued apace and opportunities for research in the early stages of some particular developments were lost.

There was an ironic twist to the fate of the programme and one that is important for the analysis. A member of the new advisory group (the Runciman Committee) acted as a consultant to the group and visited all oil development locations to assess research needs. This resulted in an 'interim Proposal' which arrived for comment by Carter, Sadler and Moore three days after the receipt of the rejection of the programme. Much of the report was taken up with the advocacy of a programme of research very close to Aberdeen's proposals. The consultant had long discussions with Carter and Moore and was plainly convinced by what he heard and saw. In discussing the Aberdeen programme the consultant noted that the proposal covered topics he thought needed study 'but at a greater depth . . . and with a wider coverage'. In considering all the work under way in Aberdeen, *including* the programme — which he seemed to assume would be funded — he made the most positive and favourable comment possible in saying, 'It may be asked in fact whether a further project would not be superfluous' (para. 13).

    Generous praise in one committee, rejection in another. No apparent communication between them. Why was this so?

1. The consultant to the advisory group was not judging research applications but collecting information. He quite simply discussed problems with research workers, as between peers. He was chosen to act as consultant *because* he was a man with special expertise in the field, the person most likely to make informed and critical judgements on work in progress or proposed. By virtue of his role he had to gain an overall view of research on oil-related developments in Scotland. He had to familiarise himself with local situations; he could not afford to remain relatively ignorant of the nature and scale of changes taking place in various locations in the Scottish periphery. He also had to talk to those researching the developments and those administrators interested in the findings. He was thus able to understand research as a social, collective

activity and to see how projects, persons and ideas related to one another. The Aberdeen programme proposal was seen in relation to research in other departments and institutions. The way in which different projects were dependent on or complementary to one another was clear. Thus any project would (unless it was *entirely* without merit) make more sociological sense to him than one application considered alone. Finally, he was not involved in allocating scarce resources or justifying their allocation, thus his analysis did not have to be couched in unimpeachable professional terms. He merely wrote of needs and ways of meeting them. In addition he was interested in the relation of research to policy and could, therefore, take a more pragmatic stance with less regard to abstract considerations. His judgement might have been accorded special weight, but it seems it was not.

2. We can explain the lack of communication between the two committees in organisational terms. We have suggested that the advisory group was set up *ad hoc* as a response to Minsterial enquiries about research efforts. The timing of events is all we have to go on but it does make sense of our supposition:

25 July	Carter to Under Secretary
3 Sept	Under Secretary to Carter; SSRC and Scottish Office 'currently working out' something
26 Nov	SSRC Sociology Committee to Moore; intimation of setting up advisory group
mid-Dec	Advisory group named

When enquiries were made in July/August the SSRC was doing nothing about oil; the quickest and easiest response was to set up a committee. It was set up without reference to the subject committees or people in the field. It was, therefore, essentially an administrator's response, a reflex action, which took no account of its organisational consequences. The existence of one more committee affected very few but the relation of this committee to other committees was to prove vital to those with a direct interest. 'Oil' being a topical public issue the advisory group was seen by members of some other committees as a threat to their work because oil research might capture substantial funds from the limited resources available. This suspicion of oil related initiatives within the SSRC has continued with the Panel established to succeed the advisory group. Suspicion certainly has not facilitated communication between the committees.

It would appear then that Carter's initiative of July 1974 had been counter-productive in that Minsterial enquiries provoked administrative responses that created confusion for sociologists and others planning research.

In April 1975 the SSRC and the Institute for Development Studies jointly organised a seminar on the social impact of oil at which the consultant to the advisory group was to read a paper on the lessons for Scotland. We were not invited to this seminar and our enquiries showed that this was not the result of administrative confusion; the SSRC had decided that they could not afford our fares to Sussex. The IDS said we were welcome to attend. Our rejection seemed complete.

The advisory group reported in July 1975 and the SSRC agreed to publish their report. At the end of August all the Research Councils were scheduled to make a public presentation of their work at the annual meeting of the British Association for the Advancement of Science. The SSRC was on the programme to discuss its initiative on the North Sea oil. We anticipated that this would coincide with the publication of the report from the group, entitled 'The social impact of North Sea oil development in Scotland'. This was the intention, but in the event publication was delayed by a defect in the SSRC's printing equipment. The presentation was to go ahead nonetheless.

In Aberdeen we were both amused and annoyed that the SSRC should use the word 'initiative' in connection with its efforts on North Sea oil. In our experience the SSRC had inhibited initiatives (and not ours only) in the field of sociology and had come to the oil scene only lately and probably partly as a result of our efforts. We had an advance copy of the report which generously acknowledged the help received from Aberdeen. This was appropriate as the report relied heavily on information received from us and on Carter and Ardern's *Register of Research*. The report contained nothing that we did not know at the time of making our programme application in August 1974.

It seemed to us that it was heaping insult upon injury to use this document to enhance the standing of the SSRC. A table in the report listed 40 research projects only two of which were financed by the SSRC; the North Sea Policy Study at the University of Surrey and an anthropological study of Whalsay. As the person due to reply to the address from the SSRC at the meeting I was disturbed to find that Professor Martin of Glasgow was the speaker to whom I would have to reply. It seemed unlikely that he would know the full history of the SSRC's role in North Sea oil and that he would be surprised and embarrassed by my rejoinder. For my part I would need to work with him in the future, as he was to be Chairman of the new Panel.

In our opinion the SSRC was attempting a public relations *coup* at the British Association. Social science does not enjoy a good press and the British Association meeting provided a chance to meet their critics by showing that they were on top of current issues, dealing with matters of public concern. In the normal course of events the rejoinder might have contained minor criticisms but someone who knew the whole history could really question the presentation in a thorough-going way. In attempting to do this I captured most of the press coverage of the exchange. The SSRC's PR effort misfired to this extent therefore.

The report of the advisory group probably had internal implications for the SSRC also. It is generally known that there had been some debate over the internal reorganisation of the research council, including the setting up of the Research Initiatives Board, in January 1975. The report exemplified what could be achieved by a RIB which was intended 'to help the Council formulate its own policies and to allocate expenditure under the research . . . budget'. But such internal struggles for legitimacy and prestige are not revealed to outsiders.

The report recommended setting up a Panel on North Sea oil with Professor Martin as Chairman and a budget of £90,000 for two years and a further £60,000 (if it was considered necessary) for a further two years. This was £10,000 less than our programme proposal, to be spent over four years as against the five of our proposal. From October 1975 the Panel was to develop 'an SSRC Programme of Research into the Social Impact of North Sea Oil Developments in Scotland' (*Report*, p. 3). Such a programme could have developed from the proposal made by Carter in July 1974 but not followed up by the SSRC.

At the British Association meeting a member of the SSRC Sociology Committee told me that the committee had blundered in not giving us money for the programme proposal.

Starting Research: The Third Attempt

In mid-November 1975 I discussed research problems with an official of the SSRC, especially the unanswered question of the relation between the Panel and subject committees. In the course of this informal conversation, I was advised to make early application to both, even if I felt it to be intellectually premature, because of the coming economic difficulties. My plan was to extend the pilot study of migrant labour into a full project. The question of premature application was discussed with the Chairman of the Panel who was entirely sympathetic to the problem but asked me to go ahead nonetheless.

On 7 December the Chairman asked for a proposal for a Panel meeting on 14 January. This made a deadline of 5 January in Aberdeen if the paper was to be circulated to and read by the Panel members in advance of the meeting.

Research on migrant workers ceased for the writing of a paper. The form of the submission raised problems; it was assumed that the Panel (which had only met twice) was as yet relatively uninformed on oil-related events and research into them – at least most of them would lack detailed knowledge of at least one of these topics. So it was decided to write a very full paper giving the maximum amount of information before making specific research proposals. A paper of some 25,000 words (plus Appendices) entitled 'Migrant Labour in the North and North East of Scotland' was sent to the Panel on 6 January 1976 and circulated to Panel members by the secretariate on the twelfth or thirteenth. We met the Panel on the fourteenth.

In writing the paper my colleague Dan Shapiro and I discovered that the application was not premature. Our theoretical grasp of developments was growing with our empirical knowledge. One effect of the programme having being rejected was that no background work was being done to complement the migrant workers study; our study, therefore, had to extend itself to cover wider 'background' issues (both empirical and theoretical). At the practical level, students and others had come to Aberdeen (mainly from overseas) to work on the social impact of oil. We were also joined by a graduate student who was working offshore in the oil industry and collecting data for his own thesis. All this fed into the migrant workers' project. The research had taken on a life of its own.

On 22 January the Panel replied that the project was beyond its funds. No guidance had been offered to us on levels of financing in the first instance. They suggested a further meeting to work out an acceptable alternative proposal. They were 'impressed both by the extent of your involvement . . . and with the clear vision you are applying to it'. These were encouraging signs for the proposal, the future of which now lay entirely with the Sociology Committee, which was to meet in March.

In early February there seemed to be some recognition by the Panel that their existence caused problems for applicants: perhaps the Sociology Committee would delay making a decision until the Panel's offer was answered, whilst the nature of the answer to the Panel depended on the committee's? The Chairman of the Panel acted to ensure that the Sociology Committee treated the application as the Committee's priority.

Starting Research: The Fourth Attempt

On 6 January I had enquired about the application to the Sociology
Committee. The Panel document 'Migrant Labour in the North and
North East of Scotland' was plainly a fairly comprehensive statement,
gave a lot of information and in terms of a research application in my
opinion met the criticisms made of the 1974 programme. The Secretary
insisted that not more than 2,500 words would be acceptable. Members
of the committee cannot be expected to read long documents she said.
This seems an onerous demand on researchers making an application
after nine months of fruitful research. What interpretation can be
offered?

A subject committee has a heavily laden agenda and its work must be
minimised. Set against this is the reasonable demand that it does an adequate job. Oil research had fared badly before, there was still public
demand for such research and the SSRC's stated aim to promote it.
Given the special difficulties in the history of such research the committee might have been expected to give it extra consideration. But instead
of defining the question in terms of the importance of oil research the
Secretary treated it as an administrative question of servicing a committee. This looks like the pursuit of the objectives of an organisation
being replaced by the sustaining of the organisation's routines. This interpretation was to be reinforced by our experience with the Progress
Report, discussed below.

Work thus started on reducing the 25,000 words to the essential
2,500. Such an operation can be simple if priorities are known. But in
this case I had to (a) meet the criticism made of the 1974 programme
and ensure that the theoretical and conceptual framework was adequate
(b) give details of precise research techniques to be used by the staff
requested *and* (c) inform the committee, most of whom had changed
since the original applications in 1974, of the background to the
research and the work already done. Knowledge does not accumulate in
a committee, so for a virtually new committee we had to start again.

The drafting was done with some misgivings and the application was
submitted with 'Migrant Workers . . . ' as a supporting document. It
was not intended to circulate this latter document widely, but it was
intended to be used to clear up queries arising from the application and
to amplify issues that particularly puzzled or interested referees or
committee members.

At the end of 1976 another SSRC subject committee asked me to write a confidential report on a research application. Excluding appendices the application was 17,000 words long.

Administrative Interlude

A few days after the meeting with the Panel I was reminded that the Sociology Committee required a Progress Report on the research on migrant workers. I called attention to the 61 pages of 'Migrant Workers . . .' and was told that this was too long. 'Then xerox pages 2 to 6 and use that' I suggested. 'But your document is foolscap and our xerox machine only takes A4' was the reply. I can not remember my exact words after this but the line of conversation was brought to a close by the observation that my proposal would be prejudiced by a failure to produce a Progress Report. On the day the Progress Report was started (as a consequence of this conversation) a member of the Sociology Committee told me 'it would not be far from the truth to say that — as far as I know', the 1974 programme fell because I refused to be . Director. On 17 February the Progress Report was submitted. Two months research was thus lost in preparing papers for the Panel and Sociology Committee. Although 'Migrant Workers . . . ' helped clarify many issues for us it took time that could be ill-afforded. Over a month was spent solely writing additional material to meet the administrative requirements of the Sociology Committee. This took time from research.

A request for a Report or a revision of a proposal can be an onerous demand on a sociologist who may be working in a department which has a long queue for secretarial services. Six pages of typing may be a major obstacle to progress in a department where any typing for staff raises problems. Demands may also be inopportunely timed; our three documents, for example, were prepared over Christmas and New Year. They could not have been prepared unless we had been able (a) to hire a foreign secretary with no commitment to Christmas and Hogmanay festivities and (b) to pay her from existing research funds.

Starting Research: The Fourth Attempt (Cont'd)

The Sociology Committee was not as impressed as the Panel by the clarity of our vision. The Secretary's letter said that

> the Committees [the application had been seen by the Management Committee also] were disappointed with the main proposal for a number of reasons:
> (a)   The relative lack of attention to the conceptual and theoretical

framework. There was no discussion in the application of the conceptual framework within which particular areas (for example, the growth of trade unions; class conflict and community conflict) were to be studied nor how this would relate to the overall perspective.

(b) The Committees were not convinced that participant observation was an appropriate technique for studying such global matters as migration and the growth of unionism in parts of Scotland and the development of a satellite economy, all of which have significant historical components.

(c) The application lacked a clear focus. For example there was no precise definition of the geographical area to be covered, no statement as to whether offshore as well as onshore aspects were to be incorporated and no clear indication of the particular firms to be used. It was not clear what overall model of society or social relations was being used or how data derived from participant observation was to be linked to the statistical data.

(d) A third [sic] anxiety related to the time scale of the project and the number of personnel proposed. It was doubted whether such a large area could be covered by 3 full-time researchers using the methods proposed to collect data on all four topics.

(e) Finally, the Committees were concerned that little attention was given to the data analysis aspects, and the purposes the analysis would serve.

The Committee had three documents available: (i) the project application, (ii) the Progress Report on the pilot study and (iii) the paper submitted to the Panel, 'Migrant Workers in the North and North East of Scotland'. This last paper was not fully circulated but available for reference and this fact was noted in (i) and (ii)

In discussing these points there is really no alternative but to discuss the texts in detail, a method we have avoided so far. Let us examine comments (a) to (d) above in this detailed manner. Paragraph (e) can not be commented upon as we do not understand it at all.

(a) The application dealt with the theoretical and conceptual framework in a fairly brief way. It comprised one out of four pages of 'Proposed Investigation'. Following a general treatment of the changes we thought likely in the political economy of the North we asked the following sets of questions:

1. *Migrants and Division of Labour*

This encompasses the following questions for which we are beginning to piece together the answers: Why are migrants employed? What, if any, is the co-relation between migration (legal) status and occupation in terms of: skill levels, rewards, dirt and danger, training and promotion?

2. *The Growth of Trade Unionism*

We have discovered that unionisation has occurred on a massive scale between 1972 and 1975. How was this initiated and organised — and what roles did migrants and locals play in this? Why was it possible for unionisation to take place so quickly and universally when trade union organisation was previously fragmented and localistic? How far does this represent new kinds of conflicts in the region or just a consolidation and extension of existing but perhaps latent conflicts?

3. *Class Conflict and Community Conflict*

Do work-based conflicts extend to the wider community and does unionisation at work entail a change of attitude to authority in the community? In what circumstances are work- and community-based conflicts mutually reinforcing or cancelling? How extensive are overt migrant/local conflicts over resources such as housing, or are conflicts in fact concerned with ethnic or regional antipathies, the clash of urban and rural or 'modern and traditional' values? (Varwell, 1975, p. 103). Especially comparison should be made between the Highlands, the north east, Orkney and Shetland, given their different social and economic histories.

4. *Segregation – Integration*

In what circumstances do locals and migrants form common (for example, class based) solidarities? In what ways do they interact at the personal level and share political, religious and recreational facilities? To what extent if at all is intermarriage taking place? What effects does the physical separation of the work-camp have?

These are all questions related directly to the sociology of migrant labour (although taking us into industrial and community sociology). 2 and 3 are especially relevant to the changes in social structure that accompany dependent development. 3 and 4 are orientated to local community and perhaps to policy issues. The way in which these questions will be approached will be elaborated in the discussion of methods.

In the Progress Report we argued these questions in more detail and presented some of our findings (paras. 7-17, pp. 9-13). In 'Migrant Workers . . . ' we discussed the relevance of dependency theory (pp. 17-22) and then explored the questions of Migration, Industry and Class, Work and Community in a more tentative but nonetheless detailed manner (pp. 22-9). Reference to either of these documents or any of the nineteen separate pages would have shown the relation of specific topics to 'the overall theoretical perspective'. We have here a recurrence of a problem that occurs throughout this account: the application has to be written in 2,500 words and needs both sufficient detail to explain the circumstances to a committee which is not familiar with the region or events and the explicit and systematic development of theory.

(b) The historical components in the development of the Northern economy were not covered in the application but were dealt with at length in the Progress Report (pp. 7-9). The sub-regions of the North were actually *defined* in terms of the historical differences in their economies and cultures. A debt to scholars working on historical research was acknowledged. The discussion of the Grampian agricultural areas drew attention specifically to the possible historical component in trade unionism and attitudes to authority, and their relation to the research proposed (p. 8).

Participant observation was only *one* method of study proposed — but it was an important one nonetheless because we hoped to be able to observe the birth of trade unions on particular sites and the early days of trade union activity in particular localities. All three documents before the Committees indicated that documentary sources and others' research findings were to be used. The interviewing of 'key' personnel was not mentioned in the Methods section because it was mentioned elsewhere and too obvious to need further comment.

(c) The geographical area was discussed briefly in the application; at length in the Progress Report (pp. 7-9) and at great length in 'Migrant Workers . . . ' (pp. 30-51, the longest single section). Offshore oil was not mentioned in the application and so there was no need for the committees to raise the question. Para.14 of the Progress Report and pp. 47-51 in 'Migrant Workers . . . ' indicated that work was in progress offshore and that the problem of access to offshore installations have been solved. We had no need of money for this and so did not waste any of our 2,500 words with discussion of it.

Particular firms: reference is made to firms X, Y and Z in the application, plainly these are the concealed identities of three specific firms. Many of the geographical locations referred to elsewhere in the application are one-company sites and so these would be the firms to be studied. Locations and firms are often used synonomously by researchers and perhaps this had not been made clear enough to the committees.

The uses to which statistical data would be put were described and discussed in the Progress Report (pp. 4-7) and described in 'Migrant Workers . . . ' (pp. 11-16). The connection between this and participant observation could have been spelt out in more detail had the applicants known that this would have been of special interest to the committees.

In this paragraph the secretary refers to an 'overall model of society or social relations'. It is not clear what this means in the context. A dependency model was being developed and it was shown how it applied to historically and culturally diverse areas within the region. The research would have contributed to the refinement of such analysis, and ideally, challenged and extended it.

(d) We agreed with this comment. Our original plan was to ask for about £50,000 over three years for our research. But we felt it politically unwise to ask for so much money. This may have been bad judgement, but we were ready to be persuaded to extend our proposal.

The rejection is made in very non-specific terms in fact. The objection to participant observation is not couched in terms of the specific research problems of a theoretical area and geographical location, nor is an alternative even hinted at. (a) to (c) are statements made *ex cathedra* in impeccable professional language, but the words are devoid of concrete meaning for the researcher on the ground. 'Conceptual and theoretical framework' has, for us, a ritualistic ring about it. Very importantly none of these comments (like all other such comments) allowed us to learn. By reading the comments we would not know how to improve a future application because of the lack of specificity in the committee's observations. Even the praise given to the work invites questions: ' . . . there was no doubt that considerable progress has been made by Mr Shapiro and yourself during the short period of the pilot study . . . ', 'Both Committees stressed that they recognised the importance of this area of study . . . ' *How much* progress is needed to win a grant to continue research; if the area of study is important, why is none financed?

We will probably never know why our proposal was turned down. Words mystify the situation, they conceal more than they reveal. It could be that the application was in every respect poor; but it could not help being an advance upon the programme application – and that may only have been turned down for lack of a Director thought suitable. If it *was* a blunder to turn that application down (as one member of the Committee believed) could the situation not have been redressed by accepting this one? No one seems to have been responsible for communicating the Panel's view to the Committee, or, at least, to bringing the view forward at the Committee meeting.

Late in 1976 I was told that all the referees had recommended rejecting the application, on intellectual grounds. I would accept this if I was sure that their rejection was based on a reading of the relevant papers. As the referees were not fools then comments (a) – (e) above (pp. 23-37) suggest either that they did not have the full documentation (but only the bare application) or that their views were misunderptood by the secretary and therefore inadequately expressed in the letter rejecting the proposal.

Few of the committee considering the application had first hand knowledge of the research and its problems. None could be expected to see its relation to other projects currently under way (unless they read 'Migrant Workers . . . ') and maybe it all seemed incomprehensible to them. Only one of the sociologists considering the application was working north of Watford. The comment on research techniques suggests a certain unfamiliarity with the research; for example, participant observation was not the *only* technique proposed, but leaving this point aside; surveys with questionnaires can only be conducted on the relatively unsatisfactory basis of quota sampling where there is no sampling frame, as in the rapidly changing populations of boom towns or camp sites. No committee can be expected to know all this; but the hapless applicant is not protected from this ignorance, and there is no opportunity to discuss the research or answer criticisms. The turnover of committee personnel is important in this context also: of ten sociologists on the Sociology Committee in mid-1974 five had left the committee to be replaced by two new names, at the beginning of 1976. Thus the committee as a whole would have little idea of the *development* of our work on oil from the first application in April 1974 to the latest proposal in February 1976.

In this last stage it was clear that correct paperwork took precedence over the promotion of good research and that in this situation the applicants' bargaining power with the administration was nil because the ultimate sanction is the rejection of the proposal. Indeed, so heavy is the load on the committee that they do not all consider applications, one member only looks at each application and becomes spokesman for the application, his report is accepted by the committee. The choice of spokesman, over which the applicant (rightly) had no control is thus crucial — but, on what criteria are spokespersons chosen? It may also be significant that the committee which was not able to give finance (the Panel) shows enthusiasm for the research whilst the funding committee dismisses it.

One especially frustrating aspect of this tale is that the Aberdeen sociologists who were working alongside sociologists in other institutions and in close collaboration with economists and others found themselves less able to contribute to the collective research effort. The department was providing one focus for international scholarship and had attracted students from abroad. Locally their research fitted into a wider pattern of enquiry, an expansion of knowledge that could not be explained in one research grant application without detracting from the formal presentation of immediate problems, theories and methods. Research can not easily be made the part-time activity of an academic; the periphery is sparsely populated and large. On the day after the grant was turned down the onshore oil industry in the North of Scotland experienced four simultaneous and unconnected strikes; a visit to each entailed 500 miles of driving on bad roads. Carter observed in July 1974 that if research started in October 1976 ' . . . much base-line data and many sociological insights will have been missed, thereby prejudicing the quality of the research which could be done'. A little research has been done but Carter did not foresee that there might be no research after October 1976.

The SSRC Sociology Committee agreed that the social impact of oil was an important topic for research and they have reiterated this in their dealings with Aberdeen. One official also said, however, that they preferred no research to bad research. If our early proposals were wholly bad what alternatives did the SSRC have to offer? There was no major initiative by the new Research Initiatives Board presumably because of its lack of funds. The Panel's funds suggest a 'pump-priming' operation as an alternative for large-scale research funding.

Their own comments indicate that the Sociology Committee did not regard the various Aberdeen applications as wholly bad. If they were borderline, what could the Committee have built upon? In April 1975 there were sociologists situated in the main centre of oil impact, eager to start research; they had accumulated many preliminary data, established a network of relevant contacts, were promised collaboration by authorities and individuals in positions to offer help. In addition their department and Faculty was becoming an international focus for scholars interested in the topic. Their theoretical and conceptual basis was not, however, perfect. At very small cost the SSRC could have provided help and advice on both theoretical and technical research matters, such help would have been welcomed and with it a major SSRC research programme could have been running in October 1975.

The course of events forces us to raise questions about matters other than the quality of the applications. Firstly, may not the SSRC as a central funding agency have ideas about managing the distribution of resources? For example; Aberdeen, the geographically most marginal of the British Universities already had the Scottish Mobility Study. To have established a further major project on North Sea oil would have given this one university the lion's share of all research funds allocated in Scotland. Additionally, it would have been tantamount to giving the Aberdeen department a virtual monopoly on 'the sociology of Scotland'. If it was thought impolitic to make such an allocation two questions arise: (i) We were not told of such allocative considerations, so were we investing time and effort in foredoomed proposals? (ii) *Who* was going to do the research, because no other department had made claims for funds or shown an interest?

This point relates to what a colleague has called the 'oil in the Clyde' question. The Glasgow conurbation is the major population centre of Scotland the area of highest deprivation, unemployment etc. Oil, the resource to 'save' Scotland, is on the other side of the country. It would have been more convenient if oil had been struck in the Clyde. This misalignment is widely felt and creates some political contention, perhaps one repercussion of this is that it is thought unwise further to favour the North East with most of the research funds.

Secondly by late 1975 is it possible that the personnel in Aberdeen seemed unsuitable to the Sociology Committee? Certainly both were 'troublemakers' for the SSRC. Carter had refused to accede to strong pressures from the then Chairman and other officers of the SSRC to pay research funds to a defaulting market research company. This payment would have jeopardised the Scottish Mobility Study, also Carter considered that it would have been wrong in principle — a position which was belatedly endorsed as correct by the SSRC. Also he had written to an MP causing awkward questions to be asked in the SSRC. I had upset the SSRC's presentation at the British Association.

There is a third possibility and it is highly subversive to the argument of this paper: was it a case not of the SSRC being 'remote' from oil, but too close for comfort — having found the topic to be one of extreme political sensitivity? In our theoretical discussion (especially in our paper to the Panel) Shapiro and I had dwelt on questions of underdevelopment, dependency and the multi-nationals — we would have been hard-pressed to write without mentioning the oil companies. An official of the SSRC had said to a colleague, however, that impact studies must deal 'with the bruise, not the fist'. This comment was doubly interesting because it not only suggested that the oil companies should not be studied but that Scotland would be 'bruised'. But if the companies were not to be studied then part of the 'problem' had been defined away and only a thoroughgoing non-theoretical approach would be possible, or at best an approach in terms of 'the logic of development'. If this was the case — and the advisory group agreed that there should be no studies of the oil industry — then plainly Shapiro and I were not the men for the job.

These questions need to be raised although they will probably never be answered. They raise other questions, notably an objection, 'what is the connection between the opinions of officials and the decision of the professional committees they serve?' It is to this question that the final section is, in part, devoted.

At the beginning of 1977 I began a one year project on migrant labour in the oil industry. This was financed by the Oil Panel which also provided money to bridge the interval from the end of the pilot project. Thus I will have received a total of three years' research funding from the SSRC. This paper is not, therefore, an account of my own failure to obtain funds — I have done very much better in this respect than many other applicants. This brief history is part of an attempt to understand why seven years after oil became a publicly important social and economic issue and four years after sociologists took the first initiative to start research, the SSRC has not been able either to finance one major programme of research nor develop a research strategy. Furthermore the eager sociologists have been delayed in their work. We should add, perhaps, that this outcome is not in the SSRC's own interest; the social sciences would have received a good press had the SSRC been clearly involved with oil in, say, 1970.

No research is better than bad research. If all our applications were bad the SSRC faced a major problem. It would have been incumbent upon them to encourage good research and this they hoped to do through the North Sea Oil Panel. But the Panel could only turn for advice on sociological research, and could only encourage research itself amongst, those interested in the topic. This meant they had to turn to the authors of the bad proposals. It would, therefore, have difficulty in spending its money.

There were, however, other problems involved in using Panel money to encourage research. The SSRC, its subject committees and the Oil Panel not only take into consideration the merits of proposals but overall questions of resource allocation; for example, a proposal which entailed spending the whole of the Council's research budget on one applicant's project would be unlikely to succeed. How such considerations relate to questions of intellectual merit and professional priorities is never made explicit. If these relationships are only implicit in committee deliberations then the applicant is doubly removed from knowledge of the rules by which he is judged.

The Oil Panel made a decision explicitly (although it was not transmitted to applicants). It was decided to put a ceiling on funds for any one project. This was probably done because two proposals from the University of Aberdeen were in the pipeline (my proposal and one from Political Economy) which together bid for all the Panel's limited funds.

Two decisions had been taken; 'no research is better than bad research' and 'spread the money around'. If our proposal of 1976 had been perfect, therefore, we still would not have had it financed by the Oil Panel. The first decision is self-evidently right. The second may be a good one; it means that in the long run more social scientists will be given opportunities to do research and a diversity of theoretical viewpoints will be brought to bear on the problem raised by offshore oil developments. In the short run, however, it delays the start of essential research and perhaps encourages hasty proposals. Most importantly it precludes the development of a programme of research. In the final reckoning this too may be an advantage; as long as the SSRC is unable to develop programmes and strategies, questions of research strategy remain in the hands of the small but growing number of academics and post-graduate students engaged in research in a wide range of disciplines. The Oil Panel will probably not survive beyond 1979. We will.

This final section attempts to a more general analysis of our experiences in a way that underlines their significance for others. In order to understand what was happening in 1972-6 it is not enough to have our one-sided account alone. More information is needed. But it is in the very nature of the problems that this information was not, and will not be available. In which areas will we need to ask questions? What follow are really a set of inter-related questions; they are presented as an attempt at analysis. Embedded in this analysis are a series of hypotheses which need to be tested.

We begin by observing that committees' comments make an appeal to the prevailing professional ethos, none of us would gainsay the possibility of improving our concepts and theories. But such comments do not necessarily engage with actual problems of research. For the committee the research is an abstract operation to be considered according to the canons of ideal research practice (derived largely, it seems, from the natural sciences). For the applicant there are real events taking place before his eyes and upon which he wants to bring his skills to bear. But even when committees and applicants meet face to face the situation remains the same; so lack of detailed local knowledge by a committee is not the whole answer to this question.

If we can not answer the question at least we can set out its major parameters:

1. The sociologists are entirely dependent on the committee. Power is asymmetrically distributed; the applicant may not question the committee or reply to decisions, he does not know beforehand what will satisfy the committee and the committee's decision is final. The SSRC furthermore is the main funding body for sociological research, there are few practicable alternatives.

2. Relations with the committee are *mediated* by a committee secretary who has no formal power over applicants but whose mediating or brokerage role gives him considerable informal power. The Committee secretary is under an obligation to abide by the rules of civil service procedure[3] and to follow the instructions laid down for the processing of letters, applications etc. There are less formal constraints also, especially those arising from the nature of the relationship with the Committee Chairman. Plainly a Chairman's personality and 'style' will affect the performance of the secretary's role. If the secretary defines his role solely in terms of servicing an over-loaded committee the applicant is put at a disadvantage in having to present his work in a truncated, if not mutilated form. The secretary thus controls the form of access to the committee. But the role of the secretary may not conform entirely to this passive definition.

(i) Committee secretaries are able to manipulate the flow of information. They choose, for example, how to edit referees' comments or present committee views in seeking revisions to an application. Referees' comments are not communicated in full and committee members do not have access to the correspondence with applicants. Individual committee members report either inability to understand committee business or the need for lengthy service in order to understand it. The most striking example of withholding information concerned the action of senior SSRC officials against the interests of the Scottish Mobility Study. The sociology committee were not informed of this and only learnt of it through the press.

(ii) Secretaries also know the informal rules of the SSRC and may choose whether or not to make these known to applicants. For example (a) we were not told that we needed a programme director in advance of the grant to make our application more acceptable.

(b) The Panel had made a decision on the general scale of research they would be able to fund; but we were not informed. If we did not know the rules how could we have hoped to succeed?

(iii) Secretaries may however unwittingly, try to influence the theoretical basis of research as evidenced by the comment that we should study 'the bruise and not the fist' in researching the social impact of oil.

The committee secretary thus has a very important role; he or she is, in effect, the gatekeeper to the funds. He is able to mystify or facilitate communication between applicants and the committee. With the present organisation of research funding the secretary is, subject to the constraints above, the sole gatekeeper for the whole profession. How the constraints operate is plainly of prime importance.

3. The power relation between applicant and committee is *mystified* in terms of professional language of abstraction and theory-building. Thus applicants feel obliged to dilate upon matters which are, in practice, the daily stock-in-trade of sociologists or become involved in knotty theoretical questions which the research is intended to clarify. In either case they expose themselves to easy criticism and the committee can respond that more abstraction is needed or that the theory is inadequate. It is a 'heads I win, tails you lose' relationship. As most sociologists agree that our theoretical formulations are inadequate the applicant's position is further weakened — and perhaps his self-confidence undermined. The problem will not be solved by researching the structure of the SSRC — it is a problem in the sociology of sociology.

4. Sociologists were in a *peripheral* relationship to the SSRC in two senses. They were geographically remote: this means that colleagues on

relevant committees are not familiar with the local situation; do not participate in regular discussion with the sociologists in the periphery and participate thereby in the development of sociological thought relevant to the periphery's problems; there is little informal contact through which the ideas contained in research proposals can be promoted, explained, advocated and clarified. The effects of this remoteness were most acute in 1972. It is unlikely that our problems are not to some degree understood today. There is a double disability in Aberdeen which is remote within Scotland. Thus even when the Panel was set up to promote oil research it was based in Glasgow, well away from the main centres of oil-related activity. Such a siting may make sense in the case of the Offshore Supplies Office which brings work to a populous area of high unemployment, but little sense for a research committee.

5. The issues are intellectually *marginal.* Sociology has been concerned either with 'mainstream' issues of advanced industrialised societies (work, stratification, deviance, etc.) or with development in overseas countries. At present the study of developments in the domestic fringe has not been of central intellectual concern and there seem to be some difficulty in sociologists thinking about Scotland other than as a simple extension of England. Scotland has not been much studied: only in a very limited sense is it an extension of 'advanced industrial society' (i.e. England and Wales) but even insofar as it is, it would be unsafe to assume that the social structures are the same. This problem is general to Scotland, even for scholars dealing with 'mainstream' questions. Thus one proposal to study Scottish capital institutions was turned down by an SSRC Subject Committee because it had already been done in England. For anyone working on topics not previously studied, or new developments not previously available for study, the problems are compounded.

The mystification mentioned above has important functions: (i) it conceals the relative ignorance of the committee (a crucial function for applicants working in geographically and hitherto intellectually peripheral areas), (ii) it prevents a specific reply to criticism contained in comments on applications and (iii) protects the committee from having to make open statements about the professional competence of the applicants. In other words; whatever the real grounds for rejecting an application the rejection can always be put into the form of reservations about theory and methods. It provides little satisfaction to realise that the SSRC alone amongst research councils gives *any* reasons for rejecting proposals.

Presumably some applications that are accepted are weak on theory and methods at the time of application but the committee trusts the applicants to carry research to a theoretically successful conclusion. Other applications may be text-book models of how to do research but are turned down because the committee does not think the applicant is competent. He or she will be turned down ostensibly because of inadequate concepts or theories. Paradoxically the more competent the sociologist the more readily he will accept this criticism as valid. We all conspire in this situation by consciously stressing theory at the expense of *information* when framing our applications — we strain at the gnat to show how theoretically important our work will be even when its importance is a hunch, or dimly seen. We disregard the possibility of useful social research being done using the limited theoretical resources available and without making major contribution to theory (how much research *does* make a major theoretical contribution?).One result may be that sociologists neglect the study of society in order to study sociology. This, it seems to me, is the most important single conclusion of this paper, and it is a conclusion not about the SSRC but the state of the discipline.

It was emphasised at the beginning of this paper that the Sociology Committee praised our work throughout. In addition they negotiated with us for over a year. These may have been the usual politenesses that accompany rejection and an elaborate cooling out process respectively. This interpretation must be premised on the assumption that our applications were bad. The first may not have been very good; our subsequent applications were good and offered two opportunities at least for the SSRC to underwrite programmes of systematic research on matters of public concern. If the Sociology Committee were pursuing perfection we believe that the (hypothetical) perfect research project has driven out some good proposals. Crucially we had to work without any clear idea of what constitutes even a 'good' application for the committee.

I have said that our applications were good because I believed we were on the right lines. But this is not all; both for the programme and the migrant labour study we had *independent* testimony from the consultant and the Panel respectively both of whom, *in the SSRC's opinion*, were expert in the field and therefore better able to judge than the sociology committee. Their opinions flatly contradict the committee and support our judgement. There is also the rather exiguous evidence of the committee members who suggested that our programme was turned down for administrative reasons or that the refusal was a blunder. So far as I know this is the only case in which, in effect, Sociology Committee decisions on research applications have been subjected to independent and open scrutiny. The outcome speaks for itself.

The treatment of research applications by the SSRC in fact creates a situation that is unique: no committee member or referee has to defend his judgments. A paper, a book review, a lecture or a comment on an essay are public and open to criticism and must be defended. Only judgments relating to the allocation of jobs and resources − the means of intellectual production− are protected from scrutiny.

Notes

1. Varvell, A., *The Social Impact of Large Scale Industry*, unpublished report, SSF 1975.
2. *Pitman, Preachers and Politics,* C.U.P., 1974.
3. The rules preclude officials making public comments of a kind that would, for example, illuminate some of the questions raised by this paper. This confers an unfair advantage on the writer, but more importantly, prevents the kind of open discussion needed from taking place.

NOTES ON CONTRIBUTORS

Diana Leonard Barker studied Natural Science and Archaeology and
Anthropology at Cambridge. Trained as a teacher and taught science
for several years. PhD at University College Swansea on *Sex and
Generation: a study of the process and ritual of courtship and
marriage in South Wales*. Various temporary jobs at the University of
Essex and elsewhere, and now Lecturer in the Sociology of Education at the University of London Institute of Education. Editor,
with Sheila Allen, of the two volumes of papers from the 1974 BSA
conference (*Sexual Divisions and Society: Process and Change* and
Dependence and Exploitation in Work and Marriage). Currently
working with Christine Delphy of the CNRS, Paris, on the political
economy of the family, and active in the Women's Liberation Movement.

Miriam E. David is Lecturer in Social Administration at the University
of Bristol and teaches on Extra-Mural courses in Women's Studies.
Author of *School Rule in the USA* (Cambridge, Mass., Ballinger, 1975);
*Reform, Reaction and Resources: the three Rs of Educational
Planning* (National Foundation for Educational Research, 1977);
joint author of *Gambling, Work and Leisure* (Routledge and Kegan
Paul, 1976) and articles and reviews in *Journal of Social Policy,
Universities Quarterly, Education* and *New Society*. Currently
writing a book on the family and education to be published by
Routledge and Kegan Paul in 1978.

Jalna Hanmer is Lecturer in Applied Social Studies at the University of
Bradford. Current interests include the sociology of sexual divisions
and of community action.

Barry Hindess is Senior Lecturer in Sociology at the University of
Liverpool. He has served on the editorial boards of *Economy and
Society* and *Theoretical Practice* and is the author of *The Decline of
Working Class Politics, The Use of Official Statistics in Sociology,
Philosophy and Methodology in the Social Sciences* and co-author
(with Paul Hirst) of *Pre-Capitalist Modes of Production* and *Mode of
Production and Social Formation,* and (with Anthony Cutler, Paul

Hirst and Arthur Hussain) of *Marx's Capital and Capitalism Today.*

Bob Jessop studied at Exeter University (BA) and the University of
Cambridge (MA and PhD). He was a Research Fellow at Downing
College, Cambridge from 1970-75 and since 1975, has been a lecturer in government at Essex University. He is the author of *Social
Order, Reform and Revolution* (1972) and *Conservatism, Tradition-
alism, and British Political Culture* (1974); as well as various articles
and reviews. He is currently working on the theory of the state and
the political economy of Britain.

Gary Littlejohn lectures in Sociology at the University of Bradford and
is the convenor of the BSA Political Sociology Study Group. His
current research is on 'Class Structure and Production Relations in
the USSR'. Publications include several articles in *Economy and
Society,* articles on education and a paper on 'Peasant Economy and
Society' in B. Hindess (ed.) *Sociological Theories of the Economy*
(Macmillan, 1977).

Jane Marceau studied at the London School of Business Studies (BA)
and Cambridge University (PhD). She was Lecturer in Sociology at
the University of Essex from 1967-72 and Senior Research Fellow
there from 1973-5. From 1973-7 she has also been *Chargé de Cours*
at the *Universite de Paris X.* Currently, she is part-time Lecturer in
Sociology at the University of Manchester, Manchester Business
School. She is engaged in a study on European Business elites and is
author of *Class and Status in France,* 1977.

Doreen J. McBarnet graduated in 1969 from the University of Glasgow
with an MA (hons.) in History and Sociology. From 1969-76 she was
Lecturer in Sociology, Glasgow University and is now Research
fellow in Sociology at the Centre for Socio-legal Studies, Wolfson
College, Oxford.

Robert Moore is Professor of Sociology at the University of Aberdeen
and is currently working on the social impact of North Sea Oil in the
north of Scotland. He is the author of *Race, Community and Conflict*
(with John Rex); *Pitmen,Preachers and Politics; Slamming the Door*
(with Tina Wallace) and *Racism and Black Resistance in Britain.*

Philip Schlesinger studied at Oxford University (BA in PPE, 1970) and the London School of Economics (PhD in Sociology, 1975) and since 1974 has been lecturer in Sociology at Thames Polytechnic. He is author of *Putting 'reality' together: BBC News* (1978) and various academic and journalistic articles. Currently working on studies of counter-insurgency and the state, Cold War ideologies, and 'Euro-Communism'.

Barry Smart is Lecturer in Sociology at the University of Sheffield where he teaches courses on Social Theory and the Sociology of Culture. He is a member of the Executive Committee of the BSA. Current research includes empirical work on popular culture and the mass media. He is the author of *Sociology, Phenomenology and Marxian Analysis* (Routledge and Kegan Paul, 1976) and editor, with Carol Smart of *Women, Sexuality and Social Control* (Routledge and Kegan Paul, 1978.

Alan B. Thomas, BA (Liverpool),PhD (Open) worked at Leeds University, Department of Social Studies and has spent five years at the Open University's Institute of Educational Technology. He is currently Research Fellow at Manchester Business School working on the project directed by Richard Whitley entitled 'The Background and Development of a Business Elite'.

John Wakeford is Senior Lecturer in Sociology at the University of Lancaster and a member of the Executive Committee of the BSA. He is the author of *The Strategy of Social Enquiry* (1968), *The Cloistered Elite* (1969),joint editor of *Power in Britain* (1973) and editor of *New Perspectives in Sociology.*

Richard Whitley has degrees from the Universities of Leeds and Pennsylvania. He has worked at Manchester Business School since 1968 as Research Fellow, Lecturer and Senior Lecturer in Sociology. He is currently directing the SSRC funded project on The Background and Development of a Business Elite and is also the Managing Editor of the *Sociology of the Sciences Yearbook.*

Nira Yuval-Davis is a lecturer in Sociology at Thames Polytechnic in London. Author of *Matzpen: The Israeli Socialist Organization* (Hebrew) (Hebrew University, 1977) and a co-editor of *Israel and The Palestinians* (Ithaca Press, London, 1975) she has also published and presented papers on Arab education in Israel, radical Jewish and women's liberation in the US and the questions of the co-optation of radical political movements. Currently working on the theoretical and political problems raised in the examination of the historical attempts to incorporate Jewish nationalism and socialism.

Sami Zubaida is Senior Lecturer in Sociology at Birkbeck College, London and a joint editor of *Economy and Society*.

INDEX

Aberdeen University 267-303 *passim*
academics, subversion and 110-12
accumulation 40-7 *passim;* barriers to 17-18; democracy and 36-40; forms of capitalist state and 20-2, 47
Ackroyd, Carol 98, 105, 106
Administrative Staff College 149n
Agee, Philip 108, 114
agriculture, capitalist 24-5
Ahmad, Eqbal 99
Algeria 102, 103
Althusser, L. 76-82, 94, 157, 159-64, 170, 173, 174, 176, 192
Amado-Fishgrund, G. 139
Ambler, John S. 103
Amin, Samir 66
Anderson, O. 246
Anderson, Perry 27, 28, 69
armed forces 36; counter-insurgency and 105-6
Armstrong, G. 206
arrest 196-216; bail and 204; breach of the peace and 204, 205-7; challenging 204; corroboration and 207; evidence for 210-11, 214n; grounds for 214n; helping the police with their inquiries 201; holding charges and 207-10; illegal 201-3; Judges' rules and 201, 209, 211; judicial sanctions on 206-7; law on 201-12; on suspicion 198, 205-6; protection against 196; reasons for making 199, 206; resisting 201-2; safeguards and 198; solicitors and 195; 210; specific offences and 205; unlawful 210; warrants for 203
Asad, Talal 100
Auld report 178, 179, 184, 190

BBC 114
Bachrach, P. 225
Balibar, E. 28, 80, 81
Baratz, M. 225
Barber, D. 240, 259
bargaining, industrial 42
Barker, D. 230

Barnett, Richard J. 99
Baron, R. 173, 241
Beechey, V. 173
Beldon, J. 239n
Belgium 22
Benston, M. 239
Benton, T. 165-6, 169, 176
Berg, Leila 173
Bernstein, B. 169-70, 171, 186, 188, 192
Bettignies, H.C. De 139
Bill of Rights 36, 37
Bismarckism 24-5
Blackstone, T. 171-2
Boer war 99-100
X Bonapartism 24-5
Bottomley, A.K. 204
Bottoms, A.E. 204
boundaries, national 52, 53
Bourdieu, P. 128, 137, 170-1, 186
bourgeois democracy 27; capitalism and 13;
bourgeoisie: crises and 38; family influences of 17; petit 46, 47, 62, 63; political domination of 19, 28, 38, 39-40, 48; upper classes and 24
Box, S. 204
British Society for Social Responsibility in Science 120
Brittan, Sam 37
Bromley, P.M. 261
Brown, R.L. 245
Buijenhuijs, Robert 101
Bunyan, T. 35, 98, 106
bureaucracy: corporation and 42; representation and 34-5
Burton, Anthony 108, 112, 115
Busfield, J. 240
business elites 127-57, 148n; careers of 140; education of 139-44, 154n; professionalisation of 150-1n; qualities required for 155; recruitment to 129, 137-40, 148; social origins of 139-44, 153n, 154n

CIA 107, 114
Cain, M. 197, 206

capital: concessions from 33; restructuring of 42; small and medium 42, 45; strike of 18; *see also* accumulation

capitalism: competitive 22; defined 10; democracy and 10-51; epistemology of 11-14; expansion of 17; in developing countries 59-60; reproduction of 159; variations in form of 11; *see also* free market

capitalist state: dual movement hypothesis of 22-3; forms of 19-22

Carter, Michael 268-95 *passim*

Centre for Policy Studies 16

Centre for Research in Social Systems 102

chartism 33

Chibnall, Steve 113, 114

child rearing 159, 217, 262n

China, women in 238n

citizenship 13-14, 32, 48

Clark, Lawrence 15

class consciousness 75-7, 85; history and 86, 88-9

Class struggle 10-11, 24-6; corporatism and 44; economic 29; education and 160, 164, 168, 177, 187, 189-93; electoral politics and 32; forms of state and 23; ideological 29; modes of production and 73; political 29; purpose of 162-3; social structure and 77-82; state intervention in 31; state's influence on 12

classes 62-3; as intersubjective unities 82-5; class *in-itself* and *for itself* 83, 85; conceptualisation of 73, 80-1, 84, 94-6; history and 85-90; Marxist theory of 72; political power of 12, Poulantzas' theory of 91-4; social structure and 77-82; unity of 75-7, 83-4

Clutterbuck, Richard 107, 109, 110-12

cold war 109

colonialism: nationalism and 57, 60-1, 65-8   6

Comer, L. 239

commodity fetishism 27, 28, 32

communal action 84-5

communism: counter-insurgency and 102, 104, 109, 125n

conditions of existence 95

conflict: between labour and capital 17

Conservative Party 46-7

control: of means of production 10, 32; political 14 *see also* ideology *and* state, the

Cooper, Lord Justice General 210

Coote, A. 259

Copans, Jean 98, 122

corporatism 39, 40-7, 48-9; defined 41; labour and employer organisations under 46

corruption 35

counter-insurgency 98-127; cold war and 102-4; conspiracy theory and 116; critiques of 121-4; ethics and 121-3; fallacies of 122-4; imperialism and 99-102; technology of 105-6

counter-insurgency thinkers 98-127; British 104-16; French 102-4; function of 98

Coventry, W.F. 152

Cox, B. 197

crises 37-40, 49; counter-insurgency and 105-6; representational 38-9

Crozier, Brian 106-7, 109, 111, 112-14, 115, 116

cultural capital 137, 138, 141, 147, 148

cultural transmission 169-70

culture 72, 94; autonomy of 76, 90

current situations, analysis of 82

Das Kapital 23

David, M.E. 175

Davidoff, L. 250

Deas, Lord 204

decision making 43

Delefortrie-Soubeyroux, N. 139

Dell, S. 204

Delmar, Rosiland 232

Delphy, C. 238, 241, 239, 242

democracy 47-8; capitalism and 10-51; epistemology of 11-14; occurrence of 20-2; plebiscitary 34; *see also* bourgeois democracy

democratic theories: liberal 13; radical 13

De Pao, Liam 119

dependency, female 222-8, 223-29

development, sociology of 55-63 *passim*

Dezalay, Y. 253, 263n

dialectical method 87
dictatorship 18; military 33, 39
divorce 247, 254-5, 256, 258;
    grounds for 258; maintenance
    after 239, 257; Matrimonial
    Causes Act *1973* 256
Dobash, R. and R. 220
Dollard, J. 230, 237n
domination *see* ideology *and* political
    domination
Downing, John 120
Due process (of law) 196-7, 199, 212

Eckstein, Harry 104, 116
Ecole des Hautes Etudes Commer-
    ciales 134-5
economic capital 137, 141, 148
economic planning 15
economic policy 42
economic power: diffusion of 17;
    political power and 17; econom-
    ism 96-7;
economy, the: classes and 76; educa-
    tion and 165-6
education: as a panacea 131, compul-
    sory 163, 164, 172, 173; crisis in
    165; division of labour and 168;
    economy and 166-7; feminist
    study of 171-3; feminist view
    of 159; in developing countries 58;
    inequality and 128; parents and
    174, 176; pre-school 173; respon-
    sibility for 17; skills and 162;
    theories of 160-73;
Eekelaar, J. 241, 246, 255-6
electoral politics 30-1, 43; effect of,
    on the economy 36-40 *passim*
electoral reform 37, 44
Elliott, Phillip 113
Ellis, T. 178, 180
Emanuel, Arrighi 66
embourgeoisement 35-6
Engels, F. 23, 27, 64, 231-2
England 22
equality: legal 211; political 19
Erben, M. 161
essentialism 26, 81, 97; defined 72
ethnic groups: nationality and 52-3,
    54
European Foundation for Manage-
    ment Education 149
Evershed, Lord 257
exploitation 18-19; of women by
    men 230-2, 239; the state and 30

extra-parliamentary organisation 38

factory legislation 33
Fairbairn, Geoffrey 99, 108, 113, 116,
    125n
family, the 240; education and 161-
    74; law 255-61; nuclear 256-7;
    strengthening 261; *see also*
    marriage
family-education couple 158-95
fascism 33, 38-9, 45, 65
Fernbach, D. 30
Fidler, J. 146
Finer, M. 259
Finer, Sam 36, 37
Finer Committee Report (1974) 228
Foundation for Management Educa-
    tion 133
France 24, 25, 67; counter-insurgency
    and 102-4; *see also* management
    education
franchise: extension of 21, 31
Franks Report (1963) 133-4, 148
free market: political freedom and 15
freedom; political 14
Friedman, Milton 14-17

Gamble, Andrew 30-1, 32, 39
Gardiner, J. 162
Gayford, J. 236n
Gelles, R. 222
Gellner, Ernest 69, 56, 61, 67, 69
General Powers Act 1960 206, 208
Germany 67
Gill, T. 259
Gintis, H. 129, 167-9, 176, 186,
    192, 195
Gleeson, D. 162
Goode, W. 223
government *see* state, the
Gramsci, A. 38, 48, 160, 162, 163
Gretton, J. 178-91 *passim*
Griffith, J.A.G. 189
Gunder Frank, A. 59, 66

Hailsham, Lord 36, 37
Hajnal, J. 249
Hall, D. 139
Halsey, A.H. 176
Hanmer, J. 240
Hansard Society Commission on
    Electoral Reform *Report* 37
Harries-Jenkins, Gwyn 112
Harris, O. 218

hegemony 162; crisis of 38-9
Heller, R. 149, 153-4n
Helmholz, R.H. 243, 250-1
Heydon, J.D. 210
Hirst, P.Q. 35, 80-1, 95, 161
history: conceptions of 85-90; of
    nations 54
Hobsbawm, E. 118
Hogart, Commandant 104
Holland 22
Holloway, J. 20-21, 27, 34
Hongronje, C. Snouk 101
Horowitz, Irving L. 101
Huntington, S.P. 39
Hussain, A. 168, 191

INSEAD 139, 136-7, 140-2, 144-6,
    149n, 153n
ideas 88-9
ideological state apparatuses 163,
    173-4, 184-5, 190
ideology: autonomy of 75, 93, 94, 97;
    classes and 73; class and sex relations
    and 159; counter-revolution-
    ary 123; education and 160, 164,
    177, 187-91; juridico-political 28;
    law and 212-13; nationalist 52-5;
    patriarchal 160; questioning of
    38; violence and 222-3;
imperialism 99-102; anthropologists and
    and 100; see also colonialism
India, counter-insurgency in 99
industrial action 42; repression of
    106; as subversion 111-12
industrial power 29
industrial reorganisation 44, 130-1
industrialisation 56, 57, 58-9
information, state control of 35,
    106, 112-14
infrastructure 17; superstructure and
    87-8
Institute for the Study of Conflict
    106-7, 108
institutions 11-12; democratic 13, 14;
    economic and political 29; private'
    12, 29
intelligentsia 57-8; definitions of 63
internationalism, protelarian 64, 65
Ireland 64; counter-insurgency in 100,
    105, 112; terrorism in 118, 119,
    120
Italy 67
Iviansky, Ze'ev 98

Jacklin, C. 236n
Jackson, M. 178-92 passim
Japan 67
Jay, Peter 36, 37
Johnson, J. 235n
Jones, B. 234n
Joseph, Sir Keith 15

Kedourie, Elie 54, 70n
Kelly, George 103
Kelly, Phil 106
Kenya 101
Keynsian economic policies 46
Kitson, Frank 107-8, 109, 110, 111,
    113, 114-16, 125
Kline, R. 36
Kogan, M. 176
Kohl, John 125
Kuper, Adam 100

Lacheroy, Col. 104
Laclau, E. 38, 59
Lafave, W.R. 204
Lambert, P. 176
landed upper classes 24
language and nationality 52-3
Laqueur, Walter 98
late capitalism 21-2; corporatism and
    41-2
Latin America 59, 102, 125
law and legal framework 17, 18-19,
    95; bourgeois 27; counter-
    insurgency and 115; politics of
    200; state and 200
law of value 49n
Leacock, E. 235n
Leakey, Louis 101
Left, the, subversion and 110-11
legality 196-201; dominant ideology
    and 212-13
Legett, John C. 98, 102
legitimacy: liberal democracy and
    21; management education and
    135, 138, 146-7
Lenin, V.I. 25, 163; Agrarian Pro-
    gramme of Social Democracy in
    the First Russian Revolution
    74-5; essays on the 'National
    Question' 65, 70; The State and
    Revolution 27, 35
Levi Strauss, C. 225
liberal democracies 49; business con-
    dence and 18; counter-insurgency

and 110-15 *passim*, 119-21, 124
liberal institutions 32
liberal states, capitalism and 21
liberation movements 70
liberty, political 19
Lightfoot, S.L. 167, 172
literacy, in developing countries 58
Litt, J. 125
Local Education Authorities 175,
    183; acting 'in loco parentis' 178,
    180, 187
local government 45
London Business School 141-5, 142-
    7, 148n, 149n, 153, 154n
love 223; as ideology 241
Lowy, Michael 64
Lukacs, G. 72, 85-90, 93
Lupton, T. 150
Luxemburg, Rosa 20, 22, 64, 65

McBarnet, D.J. 199
McClean J.D. 205
Maccoby, E. 236n
McGivering, I.C. 149n, 150n, 153n
McGregor, O.R. 240, 257, 259
McGuffin, John 120
Mack, J.A. 198, 207, 214
McLennan, G. 161
MacNally, Roger 115
MacPherson, C.B. 15, 18
Maine, H. 256
Mair, L.P. 253
Malaya 102
management education 128-57;
    American 131, 150n; attitude of
    business to 132-4, 151n; British
    129, 131-4; careers after 144-6;
    development of 129-31; French
    129, 134-7; legitimacy conferred
    by 138; legitimation of 135; types
    of course 134, 147-8,
    152n
Manchester Business School 141-6,
    142-6, 148n, 153, 154n
Mandel, Ernest 21
Mark, Sir Robert 198
market regulation 28
Marks, P. 171-2
marriage 238-65; Act of *1836* 245-6;
    Act of *1949* 246; Age of Marriage
    Act *1929* 250; as a form of
    control 230-2; capacities needed
    to contract 248-52, 264n; cere-
    mony 243-7; church control of

243-4, 262n; civil weddings 246,
    262-3n; clandestine 244-5;
    common law 258-59, 259-60;
    consummation of 252-3; contract
    245-6, 247; difference for men
    and women 241; effect on rights
    and duties 255; Established
    Church and 246; financial incen-
    tives to 264n; heterosexuality and
    248; homosexuality and 248-49;
    indissolubility of 244; Law Com-
    mission report on (1973) 246;
    Lord Hardwicke's Act 245, 247;
    morals and 244, 263n; poly-
    gynous 249-50, 263n; relatives
    and 250-2; rights and duties and
    242; sex discrimination and 258;
    social desirability of 240; sound-
    ness of mind and 251-2; state
    control of 239; state regulation of
    243-53; state support of 265;
    unwillingness to interfere in 257;
    voidable 252-3, 259, 263n;
    women's dependency on 227-8;
    241
Martin, Professor 283, 284
Marx, E. 243-4
Marx, Karl 23, 24, 64, 76-8, 82;
    Communist Manifesto 82-3;
    *Contribution to the Critique of
    Political Economy* 77; criticism of
    bourgeois democracy 13;
    *Eighteenth Brumaire of Louis
    Bonaparte* 73, 82-3, 87-8
Marxism: classes and politics in 72-97;
    nationalism and 64-70
mass communication 58
Mathieu, N. 238n
means of production *see under*
    production
media, propaganda and 112-14
mercantilism 22
middle classes 46; education 169,
    178-91 *passim*; in developing
    countries 58
Midwinter, E. 175
migrant labour, research into 271-2
Minerup, Gunther 106
Mitchell, J. 238n
mode of production: family and
    161-2; levels of 72-3; relations and
    forces in 73; transition from one
    to another 73, 79-80
modernisation 56-8

modes of control 218
monetarist economic policy 46
monopoly capitalism 21, 35, 42,
    44-5; education and 147
Moore jun., Barrington 24
Moore, Robert 267, 269, 279
Moss, Robert 107, 109, 111, 114, 115
Mosson, T.M. 149n
mothers see parents
Murphy, S.D. 39
Musgrove, F. 172, 174

NEDC 133
Nairn, Tom 66-70
nation state: concept of 54; European
    model of 60
National Association for Freedom
    107
National Council for Civil Liberties
    198
national liberation movements 104
national loyalty 57
national self determination 65
National Women's Aid Federation
    238n
nationalism 52-71; definitions of 52;
    Marxist theory of 64-70; social
    composition of 61; sociological
    theories of 55-63
nationalist movements 61-3, 69-70
natural governing party 34; social
    democrats as 45, 46
Nazism 38-9, 65
Nichols, T. 149
non-historic nations 64-5
Norris, G. 173, 241
North Sea oil research 267, 269, dis-
    cussions of with SSRC 274-6; first
    proposal 269, 271-2; fourth
    proposal 287-93; migrant
    workers study 286-97 passim; oil
    companies, research into 294;
    project director 285; second pro-
    posal 271-83, 273-87; theoretical
    aspects of 278-80; third proposal
    285-7
Nun, J. 39-40

Offe, C. 29-30
offences: criminal 205-7; sexual 220
Ollman, B. 27
Omrod, Mr. Justice 264n
Ottoman Empire 54

Packer, H.L. 197, 212-13
Pahl, R. 45
parents: class position of 191; educa-
    tion and 173-90 passim
Paris Dauphine University 136
parliamentarism 28, 49; bourgeoisie
    and 31-3; corporatism and 40-1,
    44; liberal states and 21
parliaments 31; corporatism and 44;
    limiting power of 36
Pashukanis, Eugen 18-19, 27
Passeron, J.C. 128
peasantry 24, 62-3; Marxist view of
    83
people, the 14
Picciotto, S. 20-1, 27, 34
Pizzey, E. 257
Poggi, Dominique 219-20
Poland 64
police 36, 196-216; behaviour 197,
    199, 200, 212; decisions 199,
    influences on 197
political domination 12, 243; by the
    bourgeoisie 19, 28, 38-40, 48
political fetishism 27, 28-9
political forces 72, 81-2, 94-5; auto-
    nomy of 75-6, 90, 93, 94, 97;
    classes and 73-7
political parties, class struggle and 32
political power 26; accumulation and
    30; centralisation of 35; economic
    power and 17; of the state 11
Poulantzas, N. 28, 31-3, 38, 76, 77,
    91-4, 160, 166
power: of labour 42; separation of
    29-30, 35
power see political power
production: means of 10, 32, 162;
    relations of 92, 161, 192; see
    also mode of production
Project Camelot 101, 123
proletariat, the 62, 82-3; class struggle
    and 86-90 passim; peasantry and
    25
propaganda 98, 104, 112-14
property, forms of 88
Prussia 24-5
Puxon, M. 251-2
Pye, Lucian 122-3

quasi-non governmental organisations
    36, 46

rape 228-29, 234
Rechtstaat 27-8
Rees, Alwyn 219
reformism 34
Reiss, A.J. 197
Renton, R.W. 203, 204, 209
representation, political 11-12,
    26-36, 39, 49; administration and
    34; class and 96-7; corporatism
    and 40, 41-7 *passim*
repression 36, 40; education and 160,
    168, 169, 177, 189, 190-3; tech-
    nology of 105, 120; terrorism and
    119-21
resource theory 223
revolution, class struggle and 32;
    see also terrorism
revolutionary socialists 46
Richardson, E. 172
rights, civil and political 109
Robbins Report (1963) 133
Ronge, V. 29-30
Rose, H.R. 150
Rosie, George 279
Rostow, W.W. 71
ruling class 163
Runciman, W.G. 274, 275
Russia 25, 64

Sadler, Peter 270, 280
Salmon, Lord Justice 208
Savoy Group 133
Schlesinger, Philip 113
schools: attendance 174-5; choice of
    174; *see also* William Tyndale's
    School
science and technology 59
scientific investigation 85-6
Scottish office 270, 273, 274
Secombe, W. 162
Select Committee on Violence in
    Marriage, 221, 227, 235n, 236n
sensory deprivation 120
sexual division of labour 159-77
    passim, 181-93 *passim,* 217, 225,
    241
sexual relationships 250
sexuality 223, 263-4n
Simon, B. 174
Simonds, Lord 209
Skolnick, J. 197, 198, 204
Smith, Anthony 61, 63
Sobel, Lester, A. 118
social capital 137, 148

social cohesion 33
social democracy 45
social formation *see* social structure
social market economy 15, 16
social relations: ideological 29; of
    production 161-4, 191, 192-3;
    structure and 91-4
Social Science Research Council 267-
    302; and Scottish Office Advisory
    Group 270-76, 282-3; inade-
    quacies of 272; Panel on North
    Sea Oil 285, 286, 296-7; report on
    North Sea oil research 284-5;
    Research Initiatives Board 285,
    294; visit to Aberdeen 273-5;
    workings of 298-302
social structure: classes and 72-7, 94;
    levels of 78, nationalism and 56;
    social relations and 91-4; violence
    220-2
social welfare provision 260
social work 237n
socialisation 221-3
sociologists 267-302; bias and
    detachment of 267-70; pro-
    fessional competence of 278; the
    state and 9
South Africa 26, 59
Soviet Union, counter-insurgency
    and 108-9
Sowle, C.R. 199
Stalin, J. 64, 65, 71n; *Dialectical and
    Historical Materialism* 78, 94
state, the: as a subject 13; autonomy
    of 31, 163; bourgeois character of
    12; business and 128, 129, 130,
    135; constraints on 30-1; depen-
    dence of on tax revenue 30;
    economic intervention by 15-16,
    19, 20-2, 29, 35; education and
    160-73 *passim;* exploitation and
    18, 30; forms of 47; institutional
    boundaries of 12; instrumentalist
    theory of 30; instrumentalist view
    of 12; intervention by 34; male
    power and 226-29; nature of 11-
    13; necessity of for capital 17;
    neutral 32, 128, political power of
    11; power of 12-13, 44, 48, 81,
    125; repressive character of 23;
    terrorism and 99; violence and
    223-6; *see also* governments
state power: use of 29
Stone, Lawrence 249-50

strategic social science 101, 120,
    121-3
strikes *see* industrial action
students, subversion and 110-12
subversion 110; responses to 114-16
surplus labour 32-3
surplus value 161
structural causality 79-82
superstructure 87-8, 93
surplus value 10

Taber, Robert 122, 123-4
Taylor, I. 213
teachers 178, 189; in the class struc-
    ture 166; responsibilities 176,
    181-2, 185, 186
teaching methods 178-79, 180
tendency of the rate of profit to fall
    19, 21, 42, 49-50n
territorial disputes 52
terrorism 116-21; definition of 117-
    18
Thompson, Sir Robert 107, 109, 115,
    116
Thompson Report 197, 202-4
Titmuss, R. 237n
Toennies, F. 260
totalitarian states: economic power
    and 17; freedom in 15
trade union movement 35
traditional society 56-8
Trinquier, Col. 104
tripartite institutions 43

United States 22; counter-insurgency
    programmes 101-2
universities 129; business and 132-4;
    Oxbridge 144 *see also* manage-
    ment education
Urwick, Col. 152n

Van Doorn, J. 112
violence, male 217-38; causes of 222-
    6; 231, 236n; challenging use of
    233-4; class and 230-2; defined
    219-20; effect on behaviour 219,
    229; extent of 220-1; family and
    non-family 221; female subordin-
    ation and 217-19; ideology and
    222-3; joking as 219-20; official
    statistics of 220; purpose of 232-
    3; re-education of men and 234;
    sub-cultures of 222; the state and
    222-29

Wages for Housework Campaign 230
Walker, D. 178
Wallerstein, I. 69
Walter, E.V. 118, 119
Weber, Max 34, 75-6, 84
Wengraf, Tom 23
Wertheim, W.F. 100-1, 123
Western Germany, terrorism in 106
Weston, R. 152-3n
Wheatcroft, M. 132-3, 151n
Wheatley, Lord 210-11
Whitehead, Anne 218
Whitley, R.D. 139
Wilkinson, Paul 98, 108, 116-22
William Tyndale's school 173-91; cost
    of enquiry into 178; headmaster's
    appointment 179; ILEA and 183-
    4, 191; managers 180-1, 182, 188
Wilson, M. 207
Winkler, J. 45
Wolpe, A.M. 171-2
Wolpe, Harold 59
women: lesbian 233-4; protection for
    229; role of 192-3, 217, 233;
    schools and 169-91 *passim*; safety
    of 228-29
Women's Liberation Movement 223
working class movement: corporatism
    and 42, 45; political influence of
    21; representation and 33-4; 38
Worsley, Peter 61
Wright, E.O. 35

Young, J. 235n
Young, K. 248